HAMILTON, ADAMS, JEFFERSON

HAMILTON, ADAMS, JEFFERSON

The Politics of Enlightenment and the American Founding

DARREN STALOFF

Hill and Wang

A division of Farrar, Straus and Giroux

NEW YORK

Hill and Wang

A division of Farrar, Straus and Giroux

19 Union Square West, New York 10003

Distributed in Canada by Douglas & McIntyre Ltd.

Printed in the United States of America

First edition, 2005

Library of Congress Cataloging-in-Publication Data

Staloff, Darren, 1961–

 Hamilton, Adams, Jefferson : the politics of enlightenment and the American founding / Darren Staloff.— 1st ed.

 p. cm.

 Includes bibliographical references and index.

 ISBN-13: 978-0-8090-7784-7

 ISBN-10: 0-8090-7784-1 (hardcover : alk. paper)

 1. Hamilton, Alexander, 1757–1804—Political and social views. 2. Adams, John, 1735–1826—Political and social views. 3. Jefferson, Thomas, 1743–1826—Political and social views. 4. Enlightenment—United States. 5. United States—Politics and government—1775–1783. 6. United States—Politics and government—1783–1789. 7. United States—Politics and government—1789–1815. 8. United States—Intellectual life—18th century. I. Title.

E302.6.H2S78 2005

973.4—dc22

2005040433

Designed by Robert C. Olsson

www.fsgbooks.com

1   3   5   7   9   10   8   6   4   2

FOR TATIANA,

for whom there are always too many words

CONTENTS

Contents

CHAPTER THREE. THOMAS JEFFERSON:
ROMANTIC AMERICA

HAMILTON, ADAMS, JEFFERSON

INTRODUCTION

THE UNITED STATES OF AMERICA was forged in the crucible of the Enlightenment; no other nation bears its imprint as deeply. Our ideals of liberty and equality, the ringing "self-evident truths" of the Declaration of Independence, and the measured tones of the Constitution and *The Federalist* all echo the language of the Enlightenment and express its most profound convictions about the political life and natural rights of mankind. The contributions of men like Alexander Hamilton, John Adams, and Thomas Jefferson to the founding and development of America and its ideals are inconceivable outside of an Enlightenment context. If we wish to understand the relevance and legacy of these founding fathers, we must come to terms with the intellectual and cultural milieu from which they arose. We must understand the Enlightenment and its politics.

Complex and diverse, the Enlightenment defies simple categorization. What makes such categorization even more problematic is the fact that the Enlightenment is contested. Whatever else they disagree about, historians of the Enlightenment recognize it as the source of our modern, secular worldview, from our ideals of religious toleration, individual liberty, and free speech to our practices of representative government and unfettered commercial development. Wherever this worldview has taken root, it has transformed society, sweeping aside traditional values and institutions in its wake. How historians feel about this legacy unavoidably influences the way they choose to define the Enlightenment.

Even as it occurred, the Enlightenment was a contested notion. The famed Prussian philosopher Immanuel Kant summed up the Enlightenment in the phrase "dare to know!," bringing to mind an image of heroic humanism. The enlightened individual, despite the hostile forces of authority, tradition, and popular prejudice, searches for the truth in a spirit of open rationality free from dogma and superstition and thereby secures the progressive improvement of the human condition. On the other hand, Kant's great nemesis, the Scottish philosopher David Hume, defined the Enlightenment as the "League betwixt the learned and conversable Worlds" or, more plainly, the social and cultural interaction of intellectuals with the polite and propertied "high society" of the day. In stark contrast to Kant's heroic individual searching for the truth, Hume's definition brings to mind refined conversations in a fashionable salon, political disputations over a newspaper in a coffeehouse, or even irreverent and inebriated raillery among members of the local "club" in a neighborhood tavern. Which is the true image of the Enlightenment?[1]

Two hundred years of hindsight have not made the problem any easier. Historians still disagree about the fundamental nature and precise definition of the Enlightenment, and they assess its impact in wildly divergent ways. Fortunately, what we need is not a full-blown definition but a mere *characterization*, one that suggests the range of cases in which it is appropriate to use the term. The Enlightenment was not a simple event or process; it was a full-scale cultural movement that animated an important minority of European society for over a century. The key to understanding the distinctive *features*, *sources*, and *forms* of a cultural movement is to place the movement in the historical *context* from which it emerged. Only then can we appreciate some of its distinctive features and the forms through which it was expressed. And in turn, only after having thus characterized the Enlightenment can we move on to the real issue: delimiting its politics.[2]

THE BACKGROUND OF THE ENLIGHTENMENT

The Historical Context

The Enlightenment was a reaction to more than a century of intense religious ferment across central and western Europe. The Protestant Reformation and Catholic Counter-Reformation of the sixteenth century ushered in an age of religious controversy, persecution, and war. Beginning with the Spanish Inquisition and the carnage surrounding the German peasant wars of the early Reformation, and continuing all the way through the persecution of English Protestant "heretics" by Queen Mary (and of Catholic recusants by her successors), to the infamous St. Bartholomew's day massacre of the Huguenot minority in France, the public bonfires of Europe were stoked with a steady stream of often quite willing heretical martyrs and others (including a surprisingly large number of witches) charged with being in league with Satan. Rarely has the quickening of the spirit of religion been so immersed in human blood and cruelty.

What made this religious ferment so explosive was the fact that it transformed the very nature of Christian piety and belief. Medieval Christianity had been a largely liturgical affair, with the church binding the local community through the shared rhythms of its rituals. Salvation hinged on obedience to the authority of the church—the great dispenser of grace that held the keys to the kingdom of heaven—and performance of the duties it enjoined. Beginning with the Reformation, ritual gave way to revelation and customary obedience was displaced by the introspective search for saving truths. No longer a community affair, salvation now lay in belief in—and therefore *understanding* of—the promises of redemption found in the newly printed vernacular Bibles and systematically declaimed in sermons, theological treatises, and cheap printed works of devotion and didacticism.

In this atmosphere, the fervency of one's beliefs was as often a sign as a result of a conscientious Christian's search for the wholesome truths of the Lord. Nor were these truths exclusively concerned with the state of the individual soul. More than a source of saving knowledge, the Bible revealed God's plan for His creation, including His prescribed pattern for government of church, state, and society. Led by earnest clergymen, congregations of Christian true believers combined the fervency of their shared convictions with an unflagging zeal to impose those sacred and salutary truths on the world at large. It was this combination of dogmatic, unswerving true belief with the zealous urge to proselytize and impose it that made pious Christians eager perpetrators and victims of savage religious persecution.

The partisans of the Enlightenment had a name for this combination of religious fervor and zeal. They called it "enthusiasm." In its most precise sense, enthusiasm referred to the belief in personal divine revelation or inspiration. More generally, however, enthusiasm was dogmatic certainty in the infallibility of one's religious beliefs coupled with the implacable and unrelenting effort to impose those beliefs on all persons and institutions. The struggle against enthusiasm was the central project of the Enlightenment.

The Sources of the Enlightenment

The Enlightenment was not, in fact, the first intellectual effort to contain the contagion of religious ferment that was infecting the European body politic. By the middle decades of the seventeenth century, a distinctly modern philosophical movement known as Rationalism struggled against the spirit of enthusiasm and dogmatic intolerance. Constituting a sort of proto-Enlightenment, the Rationalists shared many core intellectual concerns with the men and women of the Enlightenment, and their work had immense influence on the *philosophes* of the following century.

Beginning with René Descartes, Rationalists rejected traditional appeals to religious dogma and scholarly authority. They insisted instead that the only reliable source of truth was the sort of careful and explicit reasoning from self-evident truths associated with mathematics, especially geometry. In contrast to the credulity and "superstition" of his age, Descartes subjected all beliefs to systematic doubt, accepting only those truths that were inherently "clear and distinct" as premises for further inference. For Descartes, the existence of God was a matter of rigorous analysis and mathematical demonstration rather than pious belief based on scriptural assurances.

Thomas Hobbes demonstrated the utter irrelevance of the revealed word of God for government in both church and state. The origins of government lay in natural law rather than in scriptural edict, and these natural laws arose from rational self-interest. Without government, society would quickly revert to a savage "state of nature" where life would be "nasty, brutal and short." Given that inevitable outcome, it was in the individual's best interest to enter into a "social contract" whereby each person pledged to submit to the constituted authorities in exchange for protection from one another and from enemies abroad. Since religion was capable of producing dissent, its forms must be entirely subject to the Erastian control of the sovereign.

Baruch Spinoza shared Hobbes's belief in the political irrelevance of Scripture and theological creed. In fact, Spinoza shared many political views with Hobbes, including social contractarianism, the importance of rational self-interest, the anarchic character of the "state of nature," and the duty to submit to constituted authorities. But Spinoza went much further, arguing that the Bible was a historical rather than a theological document. Indeed, Spinoza's application of the Cartesian rationalist method of systematic doubt and geometrical demonstration resulted in his wholesale rejection of the personal transcendental deity of Judeo-Christianity. There were no angels or devils, or even saints or sinners, in Spinoza's universe, just a single purely rational order of being or "substance" that could be called either nature, God, or both.

The problem with Rationalism was that it simply went too far. Descartes had indeed undermined the tenability of religious dogma, but only by displacing it with the equally infallible power of reason. Hobbes's critique of the political activism of religious zealots and radical republicans offended all sides of the political divide. On the one hand, his unequivocal embrace of absolute monarchy horrified the English upper and middle classes. On the other hand, monarchs could hardly be pleased that Hobbes predicated their authority on the consent implicit in a social contract rather than on divine right. As for Spinoza, he had thrown the Judeo-Christian baby out with the bathwater. A truly rational inquiry into the nature of things—one based on the consistent application of the Cartesian method—revealed a universe in which there was no transcendent creator presiding over and sustaining it, no overarching purpose or goal, and no meaningful human free will. Banished to the realm of irrational superstition was any belief in and pious devotion to the personal God of Christianity. In its place was at best a diffuse and mystical pantheism if not, as most of his critics suspected, outright atheism.

The works of the Rationalists were not the only cultural resources upon which the men and women of the Enlightenment drew. The Renaissance humanists also had an immense impact on the citizens of the eighteenth century "republic of letters." The philosophes' taste in painting, architecture, sculpture, and literature; their faith in the mathematical method of reasoning from observation in astronomy and physics; and their code of personal refinement and civility were all deeply informed by Renaissance precedents and practices. Perhaps the most profound impact of the Renaissance was in the political thought of the Enlightenment. The new "scientific" realism of the Florentine Renaissance associated with Niccolò Machiavelli and his glittering circle of republican illuminati transformed European political thinking. Machiavelli's political and historical writing had a particularly powerful impact on mid-seventeenth-century English republicans such as James Harrington and Algernon Sidney. Their works, in turn, were widely read throughout the following century. In the background of any discussion of republican government or political science during the Enlightenment lurked the imposing presence of western Europe's extended "Machiavellian moment."

The Enlightenment also drew directly on the very sources of the Renaissance itself: the works of classical Greece and Rome. The poetry, philosophy, and drama of Greece, and the oratory, political theory, and statecraft of Rome represented the pinnacle of human achievement for eighteenth-century "moderns." Its very centrality to the eighteenth-century realm of letters served a subtle didactic purpose. The classical Greeks and Romans were, after all, pagans. Despite the absence of the word of God (or perhaps because of it), the ancients had produced unrivaled works of politics, ethics, philosophy, and art. Their achievements, both in culture and in virtuous civic life, demonstrated more vividly than any Rationalist geometric proof the fundamental irrelevance of religious revelation to the great issues of public life.

THE FEATURES OF THE ENLIGHTENMENT

The Enlightenment was a remarkably diverse and even diffuse movement. Its supporters embraced a variety of positions on matters religious, political, and social, many of which were in conflict. Fortunately, despite their differences, the men and women of the Enlightenment did share quite a bit beyond their sources. The three features listed below, perhaps best thought of as attitudes or cultural dispositions, attempt to give the broadest possible outline of the distinctive qualities and assumptions that lay behind this vast cultural movement. The first addresses the epistemology of the Enlightenment, its unique posture toward the nature of knowledge, belief, and human inquiry. The second focuses on the metaphysics of the Enlightenment. It describes the peculiar worldview, its account of the nature of reality, the universe, and the human condition and role of man, that distinguished the beliefs of the eighteenth-century republic of letters. The final feature is a bit harder to characterize than the first two. It deals not with a doctrinal orientation like epistemology or metaphysics but rather with a cultural quality, tone, or posture.

The Epistemological Turn: From Scientism to Empiricism

The epistemology of the Enlightenment was distinctive in two respects. The first concerns the uniquely central role that the theory of knowledge played in eighteenth-century philosophy as a whole. Where the Rationalists had tried to displace the delusions of enthusiasm with metaphysical truths, the Enlightenment attacked such delusions epistemologically by showing that such "knowledge" of things divine was impossible. The second respect in which the epistemology of the Enlightenment was distinctive was its model of rational inquiry and knowledge. Science, not reason, was the preferred cure for religious fanaticism and superstition because science restrained religion without destroying it or replacing it with alternative truths. Drawing on the work of the seventeenth-century English philosopher Francis Bacon, the Enlightenment conceived of science as a Promethean project that sought to control and manipulate the forces of nature through careful observation and experimentation rather than to elucidate the "essences" of things through scholastic disputation.

The Enlightenment cult of science was hardly fortuitous. The Enlightenment was hitching its wagon to a rising star. The seventeenth century had witnessed a series of remarkable breakthroughs in the development of modern science. The work of Tycho Brahe, Johann Kepler, and Galileo Galilei had led to striking advances in both astronomy and mechanics. Robert Boyle's work on thermodynamics laid the foundation for the development of modern chemistry, and physician William Harvey put anatomy on a scientific footing by establishing that the heart was a mechanical pump that circulated blood throughout the body rather than the seat of human emotions. By the seventeenth century, science had already commenced the process of revolutionizing traditional beliefs and techniques that it has continued ever since. Its prestige was unmatched, its status unimpeachable.

Of all the glittering stars of the enlightened firmament of science, one shone brighter than all the rest. Sir Isaac Newton was, for the Enlightenment, the scientist par excellence, the definitive cultural hero of the age. Perhaps the current view of Newton was best captured in Alexander Pope's heroic couplet:

> *Nature and Nature's laws lay hid in night;*
> *God said, Let Newton be, and all was light.*

Whatever philosophers as diverse as Kant and Hume, Francis Hutcheson and Bernard Mandeville, or Voltaire and Jean-Jacques Rousseau might disagree about, they all shared in the universal esteem for and adulation of the great Isaac Newton.[3]

Newton's scientific accomplishments are, of course, legendary. His optics, theory of "fluxions" (differential calculus), three laws of motion, and theory of gravitation are all justly famous contributions that dominated the practice of physics for centuries. But there was more than his scientific accomplishments to the cult of Newton. Newton claimed to have arrived at his simple and universal laws of motion through induction from observation and experiment rather than through derivation from metaphysical hypotheses. By his own account then, his mechanical laws were no more than "very nearly true" and should be embraced in a merely probabilistic spirit "till such time as other phenomena occur by which they may either be made more accurate or liable to exceptions." The diffidence with which Newton himself believed in his laws was the very antitype of dogmatic certainty. Nor did his laws of motion undermine the veracity of Scripture, despite the fact that their account of the universe and its laws directly contradicted that found in the Bible. This contradiction was only apparent, for according to Newton, the word of God "described realities in a language artificially adapted to the sense of the vulgar." And while Newton's orthodoxy might be questioned, his Christian piety, however loosely conceived, could not be doubted. Even his private life was considered a model of propriety. His combination of religious devotion, scientific acuity, moral probity, and open-mindedness made Newton the exemplar of the enlightened individual.[4]

The scientism of the Enlightenment was more than the cult of Newton, however. Equally important was the way the Enlightenment interpreted Newtonian science and applied its methods to other issues. Here the critical figure was John Locke, the father of modern empiricism. Drawing on Newton's focus on the observation of "phenomena," Locke argued in his immensely influential *Essay Concerning Human Understanding* that all our knowledge of the world (not just science) was the result of such "empirical" experience. Rejecting the Cartesian doctrine of innate ideas, Locke argued that the mind of an infant was a tabula rasa or blank slate. Those ideas it would eventually come to hold were the result of the impressions the external world made on its five senses. Whatever could not be reduced to its empirical origins in sense (like divinely inspired enthusiasm) could safely be dismissed as irrational and untrue.

The empiricism of Locke had several virtues that made it particularly congenial to the disciples of the Enlightenment. Its account of scientific knowledge was remarkably thorough and consistent; Voltaire compared Locke's exposition of human understanding to the mechanical dissection of "an excellent anatomist." Lockean empiricism also had the virtue of restraining enthusiastic excess while preserving the tenability of Christianity and its scriptures. The greatest virtue of empiricism, however, was its inherent skepticism. Empirical or sensory knowledge was by its very nature uncertain and liable to alteration (we all learn new lessons from new experiences), and thus diffidence of belief, rather than dogmatic confidence, became the mark of reasonableness. Locke "dares to doubt," Voltaire rejoiced, and "instead of defining at one fell swoop what we don't know, he examines by degrees what we want to know." Diffidence of belief was the Enlightenment's preferred antidote to enthusiasm and fanaticism.[5]

It was this skeptical tendency within empiricism that the Scottish philosopher David Hume brought out and pushed to its logical culmination in his infamous *Treatise of Human Nature* and *Enquiry Concerning Human Understanding*. Where Lockean empiricism had exposed the irrationality of immediate revelations, Hume went further and extended this empirical critique to all alleged miracles, even those found in the Scriptures. Indeed, Hume's posthumous *Dialogues Concerning Natural Religion* confirmed what most of his critics had suspected all along: that his religious skepticism went as far as outright atheism. Even more troubling, Hume argued that the very principles upon which all empirical reasoning was grounded—resemblance, spatial-temporal contiguity, and (most critically) cause and effect—were themselves neither self-evident truths nor directly derived from experience. In a sense, then, they were irrational, the results of habit and instinct rather than reflection and inference. Indeed, even the most basic assumption behind all our thinking about the world, namely that the future will resemble the past, was shown at bottom to be an instinctual belief, without foundation in either experience or reason. Such corrosive skepticism was considered extreme, if not downright suspect. But the moral Hume drew from this "whimsical" state of affairs was the basic lesson shared by all eighteenth-century empiricists, and might be taken as the very credo of the epistemology of the Enlightenment: "In general, there is a degree of doubt, and caution, and modesty, which, in all kinds of scrutiny and decision, ought for ever to accompany a just reasoner."[6]

Metaphysical Disenchantment

The philosophers of the Enlightenment held a wide array of metaphysical beliefs. Anglican bishop George Berkeley proffered a strict idealism; the only real entities were individual minds whose ideas came from a universal and providential God. The French philosophes Julian Offray de La Mettrie and Paul Heinrich Dietrich (Baron d'Holbach) took the opposite, materialist position. Their universe was made up of physical, corporeal bodies; the mind and its ideas were at bottom reducible to the activity of the brain. The German philosopher and inventor of the integral calculus, G. W. Leibniz, argued for a plurality of indivisible "monads" whose autonomous internal development unfolded in a divinely inspired preestablished harmony. Most men and women of the Enlightenment avoided such extremes, either adopting some tepid variant of Descartes's mind-body dualism or professing a noncommittal agnosticism. All of these views, however, shared one fundamental feature: they all strictly precluded any appeal to the supernatural or divine revelation. Each of these metaphysical theories was based on reason and observation, and each assumed a world whose elements obeyed the laws of Newtonian science. In short, the distinguishing feature of the Enlightenment's worldview was its very worldliness.

Historians describe the impact of this worldliness as a process of *disenchantment*. The word has the peculiar virtue of reminding us just how *enchanted* the worldview of the preceding centuries had been. Comets, earthquakes, volcanoes, and even severe storms were not natural phenomena but portents of divine wrath and judgment. Ghosts walked the earth, and demons possessed the bodies of human victims. Satan was not a symbol of evil but a real, active presence—Martin Luther once reportedly threw an inkwell at him. Miraculous and supernatural cures for a variety of ailments were an accepted part of conventional belief. Kings still "touched" their affected subjects to cure them of scrofula (the "King's Evil"), and hermetic and alchemical doctrines were widely respected among the learned. The central goal of the Enlightenment's metaphysical disenchantment was to subject such time-worn and traditional beliefs to ridicule as childish superstitions.

The Enlightenment achieved this disenchantment through *naturalizing* the world. The universe was not "the creation" but "nature," and nature was a system of interacting entities, not an overarching unity. This deanimated universe was made up of discrete bodies whose interactions were purely mechanical (like billiard balls striking one another) and whose actions were reducible to mathematical laws. Such a worldview clearly precluded the possibility of sympathetic magic and miraculous portents that violated the observed laws of nature. But its disenchantment went much further than merely proscribing the supernatural. It rendered senseless the effort to seek the purpose or "why" of natural phenomena. The only legitimate explanation of such events came from addressing the "what" and "how" of "secondary" mechanical causality. The universe of the Enlightenment was a purely mechanistic realm whose entities blindly followed the ineluctable, if rational, laws that described its order.

The Enlightenment's disenchantment of the world was not limited to the "external" realm of objects. Man himself was no longer conceived as occupying an intermediary position in the great chain of being between the realm of pure spirit (angels) above and the dumb brute creation of animals below. Instead, he was an animal, no more and no less. What distinguished him from the rest of the animal kingdom was not his eternal soul—made in the image of God—but his unique capacity for reasoned speech. For the Enlightenment, however, man was, like all animals, subject to emotions and passions that disturbed and dominated the mind and its operations. Such passions were not subject to the human will. They were (like gravity) blind and ineluctable forces that followed strict causal laws. Nor were they necessarily deleterious. For most Enlightenment thinkers, the passions were conceived as instincts that served human interest and survival. Guidance and government they might require, but the very notion of eliminating them was as absurd and harmful as ignoring the signs of hunger or illness. Hume might have been extreme in his famous dictum that "reason is, and ought be, the slave of the passions," yet as is so often the case with the great Scottish thinker, his extremism came from his propensity to push enlightened beliefs to their logical conclusions.[7]

The Enlightenment's disenchantment of the world may have discredited the supernatural, but it did not necessarily entail atheism. The most common proof of the existence of God was the one that Newton himself embraced. Given the remarkable intricacy of the universe and the mathematical regularity of its laws, it was only natural to infer that a divine workman had designed and executed that order in accordance with His own rational plan. A great cosmic "watchmaker" had designed the clockwork of the universe, set it in motion, and then let it run according to its own infallible mechanical principles and laws.

Naturalizing religion may have made belief rational, but it did not make it recognizably Christian. Without the divinity of Christ, the miracle of his atonement and resurrection, and belief in the Scriptures, natural religion was more a refined modern paganism (albeit monotheistic) than anything even remotely Judeo-Christian. The real problem with natural religion, however, was that it failed to satisfy either spiritual needs or the intellectual conscience. Its tepid compromises and moderate doctrines proved weak tea for lost souls. And natural religion failed to satisfy the intellectual conscience because, at bottom, its doctrines were based on wish fulfillment. As Hume demonstrated in his posthumous *Dialogues Concerning Natural Religion*, the argument from design will simply not bear inspection. We cannot infer a pattern from a single case (the universe), and even if we could, we would have to infer that the creator of the world was a sloppy and capricious workman who left no small number of errors and "evils" in his creation that might easily have been rectified. The danger of metaphysical disenchantment, then, was that it always threatened to go beyond the bounds of "propriety" and at least marginal orthodoxy in religion.

The Posture of Urbanity

If there is a common thread to the epistemology and metaphysics of the Enlightenment, it is their worldliness. Worldliness also characterizes the third distinctive feature of the Enlightenment, its posture of urbanity. Unlike the previous features, this "posture" is not easily defined or characterized. It is the distinctive quality or style of the Enlightenment, what historians once called the "spirit" of the times. It is much more a matter of tone of voice than content of communication. Put another way, the men and women of the Enlightenment were not distinguishable simply by their beliefs; they also represented a new social type, with its own intellectual mores, habits, and values.

In its most literal sense, urbanity meant urban residence. The Enlightenment was, if nothing else, a remarkably urban phenomenon, finding its center in the great metropolises of the age: London, Paris, and Amsterdam. Its major peripheries were lesser cities such as Edinburgh, Berlin, Philadelphia, and Naples. Its tendrils, however, could be found in almost any urban center whose commerce opened it to the larger world, from lowly Charleston, South Carolina, to tiny Königsberg, Prussia. This urban character is all the more striking when we remember that the vast bulk of Europeans were still tied to the rural life of agriculture. Urban residents were a small minority of the overall population, but it was from that minority that the partisans of the Enlightenment were recruited.

There were, of course, many reasons why the Enlightenment was an urban affair, and most of them were tied to the dynamic expansion of cities in early modern Europe, itself the result of burgeoning commerce. By the early eighteenth century, the major metropolises of northwestern Europe had displaced the older royal courts as centers of political administration, arts patronage, and, via the advent of newspapers and journals, information. The cities also contained the learned associations and societies of the age from which the new scientific learning would emanate. Despite their tiny share of the overall population, eighteenth-century cities were becoming increasingly central to the cultural and political order of Europe and its colonial peripheries.

This new centrality of the eighteenth-century city entailed a reassessment of the very nature of urban life. Even into the late seventeenth century, urban denizens had traditionally been seen as essentially parasitic men and women who, practicing guile and deceit under the cover of anonymity, lived off the labors of their more virtuous rural countrymen. The Enlightenment posture of urbanity reversed this scale of values. Country folk were now simple bumpkins; city folk were industrious and rational, far less susceptible to bigotry and superstition. The posture of urbanity stressed the civilizing nature of the city, its potential to produce a new type of learned gentleman whose leisure was devoted to cultivation and whose sociability was based on a new appreciation of pleasure and utility.[8]

The Enlightenment's posture of urbanity was, however, more than a mere matter of residence. An urbane gentleman was distinguished by his strict adherence to the new code of manners known as *politeness*, a code that governed a range of behaviors from modes of discourse to table manners, personal deportment, and hygiene. Arising out of and in counterdistinction to earlier codes of behavior, eighteenth-century urban politeness was oriented toward dispensing pleasure to others and "refining" the human passions by rubbing off their rough edges through patterned forms of interaction and thus smoothing social relations. In part with this in mind, the urban gentleman of the eighteenth century frequently sought the friendship of cultivated women. To accommodate the more refined sensibility of the "fair sex," urbane gentlefolk embraced "delicacy," the equivalent in conversations between the sexes of complaisance between classes.

Politeness was only part of the posture of urbanity; equally important was *cultivation*. A cultivated person was a cultural connoisseur,
someone who could "converse with a picture, and find an agreeable
companion in a statue." A cultivated person also struggled against received prejudices, national or otherwise. Voltaire and Montesquieu
celebrated the glories of England (their national rival) while Hume returned the gesture in his profuse praise of Paris.[9]

The Enlightenment's posture of learned urbanity was the very
antithesis of the older seventeenth-century image of the academic intellectual. In place of the narrow professionalism of the scholastic, the
modern intellectual cultivated the widest possible range of cultural interests and tastes. Perhaps the starkest contrast, however, is in the central
role of humor in enlightened urbanity. Seventeenth-century high culture had been a remarkably earnest and humorless affair; the stakes were
incredibly high, and intellectual disputes were often accompanied with
personal vitriol and vituperation. By contrast, the urbane citizens of the
Enlightenment commonwealth of learning were distinguished by their
devotion to wit and humor. Wit became a sign of cultural refinement,
but it could also be pointed in its application. Jonathan Swift's ironic
Modest Proposal exposed the cruelty and brutality of English attitudes
toward the Irish for all to see. Voltaire's sardonic *Candide* subjected
many of the "superstitious" and "scholastic" absurdities of the day—
from philosophical optimism to religious persecution and torture—to
ridicule by means of farce.

THE FORMS OF THE ENLIGHTENMENT

The features of the Enlightenment—scientism, disenchantment, and
urbanity—characterize the beliefs of the philosophes. Equally important for understanding the Enlightenment are the forms by which it was
propagated. Obviously, a movement as diffuse as the Enlightenment
found expression in many and varied contexts, from outings to the pleasure gardens at Vauxhall to voyages of scientific discovery. Nonetheless,
there were three principal forms by which the Enlightenment was mobi-

lized and spread: printed texts, learned societies, and sociable associations. Individually, these forms were merely media through which Enlightened doctrines were transmitted. Collectively, however, they transformed the consumers of Enlightened discourse from discrete high cultural connoisseurs into a unified and cohesive "public" whose judgment and opinion was, for the first time in European history, a major factor in politics. As such, these forms created the very conditions that have allowed the emergence of a modern practice of politics based on the representation of secular public opinion.

Printed Texts

Printed texts were the single most important form the Enlightenment took. Although the print revolution of the early modern period was not *the* cause of the Enlightenment, it was a critical and essential precondition. The introduction of printing into European society had been accompanied by state censorship, but commencing in the years immediately preceding the Enlightenment, a gradual but ineluctable loosening of restraints was readily apparent. For much of the seventeenth century, the Dutch had turned a blind eye to the clandestine publication of all but the most scandalous works, thus rendering Amsterdam the vital center of publication for new "modern" works of philosophy. England followed suit in 1696 when Parliament declined to renew the Licensing Act, and even in absolutist France, where censorship was retained until the fall of the old regime, a growing "liberality" was extended to enlightened authors by sympathetic (and often like-minded) censors and regional parlements. Nor was such censorship particularly effective at suppressing a flourishing underground book trade in "prohibited" works, whose content ranged from religious heterodoxy to radical political expression and outright pornography.

Enlightened texts also had the distinct virtue of fostering an abstract and rational cognitive style in their readers. Where the veracity of oral communication can rest on the "credit" of recognized persons and respected authorities, the truth of written prose can be ascertained only by carefully judging the text for consistency, coherence, and factual accuracy. Written arguments are usually far more systematically elaborate, formal, and general than oral ones. And given the possibility of rereading critical passages, authors can link long and complex chains of inference that far outstrip the mnemonic limits of conversation. All of these factors forced enlightened readers to adopt a critical and attentive posture toward their texts. The abstract, formal, and decontextual nature of reading created a cognitive style that thus lies at the very core of modern notions of objectivity and rationality. For the Enlightenment, then, the very medium of printed texts was, in part at least, the message itself.

Finally, the printed texts of the Enlightenment had the additional advantage of coming in a wide variety of forms, from multivolume works supported by advance subscription, to periodicals, newspapers, and even newly remodeled almanacs. Because these publications came in a wide variety of prices, they were able to fill different enlightened market niches. The period also saw an explosion of new literary genres, like epistolary novels, critical reviews, and polite essays. Just as different forms of publication filled different cost markets, so different genres appealed to varying tastes and educational backgrounds.

At the apex of enlightened publication was the philosophical *treatise* or *inquiry*, addressing topics from politics and economics to metaphysics and aesthetics. Authored by luminaries such as John Locke, Francis Hutcheson, Immanuel Kant, Adam Smith, and Jean-Jacques Rousseau, such full-length treatments were of enormous influence, but they were not in themselves fully capable of transmitting the new learning. Even though they were written in the vernacular, not every literate person could pick up a philosophical inquiry and read it. And because of their limited audience, they were often quite expensive. Hume's philosophically motivated *History of England* took up six volumes; a complete set published in 1770 cost a whopping £7.7s (at least a month's wages for all but the most skilled professionals). Edward Gibbon's magisterial *History of the Decline and Fall of the Roman Empire* also filled six volumes, while Diderot and D'Alembert's *Encyclopédie* ran to thirty-five! Obviously, such works were well out of the financial reach of all but the wealthiest members of society.

Although the direct influence of such scholarly works was somewhat limited, their indirect influence was massive. Scholarly arguments were summarized in a rapidly growing number of newspapers, journals, and cheap and brief pamphlets. Debates and developments within the republic of letters were chronicled in critical reviews and evaluated in periodical essays. Nor was the exposition of Enlightenment beliefs limited to the realm of nonfiction: poems and novels also served the didactic purpose of spreading enlightenment to a mass audience. Daniel Defoe's wildly popular *Robinson Crusoe* gave narrative form to Locke's belief that the rational pursuit of individual self-interest could impose moral and social order on a chaotic state of nature. Voltaire pilloried the residues of superstition, intolerance, and irrationality in European society and politics in *Candide*, as well as the blithe metaphysical optimism of Leibniz in the comic bombast of Dr. Pangloss. Even almanacs, the traditional staples of every solid farming family's annual printed purchases, could serve as vehicles for disseminating enlightened maxims, as Benjamin Franklin demonstrated in the sayings of Poor Richard.

Of all the new literary genres, however, it was the *polite essay*, expressing modern convictions on a plentitude of topics, that served as the ideal venue for spreading Enlightenment. Polished and witty, the brief length of polite essays—rarely longer than ten pages—forced authors to clarify and simplify their presentation while keeping the prose lively. The form found its apogee in the celebrated *Spectator* and *Tatler* essays of Joseph Addison and Richard Steele. The influence of these short pieces was enormous. It was precisely because they were so brief and easily read that Addison believed essays could bring "Philosophy out of closets and libraries" and into "clubs and assemblies" as well as to "tea-tables and coffee-houses." David Hume saw his role as an essayist as that of an "Ambassador from the Dominions of Learning to those of Conversation," purveying enlightened knowledge in brief pieces "with which I endeavor to entertain the public." Its combination of enlightened didacticism and witty entertainment made the polite essay the ideal genre for spreading the new learning to a broad readership.[10]

Learned Societies

Learned societies, the second principal form of the Enlightenment, were critical to the formulation of Enlightenment doctrines, as they facilitated research and inquiry, offering pensions, stipends, scholarships, and prizes, and served as clearinghouses for new work in different fields. More important, however, learned societies transformed a collection of fractious (if like-minded) intellectuals into a cohesive republic of letters.

Among learned societies, universities were perhaps the most obvious source of commonality. It was from the universities, after all, that the educated absorbed Latin classicism, their cultural lingua franca. Initially quite reluctant to incorporate the "new learning" into their curricula, slowly they began to change. In the latter half of the seventeenth century, the Dutch universities led the way by incorporating experimental "natural philosophy" as well as such modern teachings as Hugo Grotius's works on natural law and Pierre Bayle's fideistic critique of scholastic reasoning in matters of religion. In the following century, the Dutch were eclipsed by the Scots, whose universities of Aberdeen, Edinburgh, and Glasgow were at the forefront of modern education. Their preeminence was not only the result of their incorporation of Newtonian science; the Scottish universities filled many of their chairs in philosophy with such decidedly enlightened thinkers as Francis Hutcheson, Adam Smith, Thomas Reid, and James Beattie, all of whom spread the empiricist gospel of experimental reason rather than the older cant of dogmatic argument from self-evident first principles.

By the middle of the century, the imprint of the new learning of the Enlightenment could be found in universities on both sides of the Atlantic. Beginning in 1738, Harvard required all students to study mathematics and science with the newly appointed Hollis Professor of Natural Philosophy John Winthrop, the most distinguished mathematical astronomer in North America and a member of London's famed Royal Society. In 1753 Samuel Johnson, a disciple of George Berkeley's empirically derived immaterialism, whose exposure and conversion to the new learning some three decades earlier led him to renounce his Congregational ministry and his position on the faculty of Yale, assumed the presidency of the newly established King's (later Columbia) College. In Manhattan's first college he established a fully modern course of study, drawing on a wealth of enlightened works. The doctrines of the Scottish Enlightenment were inculcated by such émigrés from that land as William Smith, provost of the infant College of Philadelphia (University of Pennsylvania) in the early 1750s, and John Witherspoon, who succeeded "New Light" Calvinist Samuel Finley as president of the College of New Jersey (Princeton) in 1766. Even tiny William and Mary's curriculum was brought up to date when William Small joined the faculty in the early 1760s, just in time to serve as Thomas Jefferson's tutor and personal guide to the new learning of his native Scotland.

Yet there were distinct limits to the "enlightenment" of universities, almost all of which remained affiliated with particular Christian churches or denominations and were expected to focus their energies on the training of orthodox clergymen. Far more important than the universities in promulgating the Enlightenment were learned academies, explicitly committed to fostering new high cultural work. The two most prestigious learned academies, the Royal Society of London for the Promotion of Knowledge and the Paris Académie des Sciences, were scientific societies that had been chartered in the second half of the seventeenth century, but by 1780 there were at least seventy such officially incorporated scientific societies in Europe, with one in practically every major urban center.

Science was not, of course, the only focus of learned academies. The study of literature was incorporated in a number of chartered societies, as were music, painting, and all the other arts. Such academies were not exclusively focused on the practice of the artistic crafts in question. Quite the contrary, they were often far more interested in criticism, connoisseurship, and aesthetic theory—precisely the issues that could engage an enlightened and educated public hungry for high cultural entertainment and edification.

Even more impressive than these great chartered academies was the proliferation of local and provincial societies devoted to a dizzying array of interests in the second half of the eighteenth century. Some of these became quite celebrated in their own right, like Birmingham's Lunar Society, Philadelphia's American Philosophical Society, and Boston's American Academy of Arts and Sciences. Most, however, were simply bodies where educated cognoscenti could congregate to exchange ideas and enjoy one another's company. The learned and curious often belonged to more than one society, and multiple membership further fomented cohesion within the ranks of the learned, and fostered intellectual exchange across disciplinary boundaries, just as provincial boundaries were transgressed by "corresponding" membership in societies in distant cities. It is no exaggeration to say that, without learned societies, the philosophes of the eighteenth century could never have constituted themselves as a unified republic of letters, much less a party of humanity.

Sociable Associations

The third principal form of the Enlightenment, sociable associations, shared properties with both learned societies and printed texts. Like learned societies, they promoted cohesion and commonality among their members by situating informed discussion in a rule-bound setting designed to promote mutual pleasure. Like printed texts, they broadcast the message of enlightenment to a broader audience than those capable of reading and comprehending abstruse tomes. Sociable associations made edifying discussions about shared interests in the new learning available to those who lacked the means, time, or skills to acquire such knowledge on their own. Most important, however, as in the case of printed texts, much of the message of sociable associations for the Enlightenment was in the medium itself.

Sociable associations were the first modern and secular voluntary organizations of individuals. Prior to the Enlightenment, the only extra-political organized bodies in Western society were religious. These bodies were generally hierarchical, committed to salvific goals, and often sanctioned by existing authorities. By contrast, sociable associations were communities of pleasure rather than conscience, and self-governing rather than subject to external authority. Moreover, within such voluntary bodies, social rank conferred few privileges. Modes of interaction were governed by explicit rules meant to promote the mutual pleasure of association through "complaisance," the conscious attempt to ignore social inequalities by behaving with a uniform politeness to all fellow associators. Most important, zeal was replaced with good-humored fellowship.

It cannot be stressed too much what a remarkably liberating and transformative effect such sociable associations could have. "When men are thus knit together by a love of society, not a spirit of faction, and do not meet to censure those that are absent, but to enjoy one another," noted Addison, "there may be something very useful in these little establishments." Specifically, when people gathered in self-governing societies devoted to mutual pleasure and interest, where precedence was determined by the will of the majority, and agendas were set by amicable discourse and consent, they enacted the very ideals associated with the enlightened republic of letters. Sociable associations thus afforded their members—and society as a whole—an empirical model of a well-ordered community organized in pursuit of individual and collective pleasures.[11]

The most common and influential form of sociable association over the course of the eighteenth century was the club. Coming in myriad guises, clubs shared certain common features. Membership was private and often shrouded in strict secrecy. Members met at fixed times, generally over dinner and drinks, and clubs were governed by mutually accepted and explicit rules designed to eliminate factionalism and promote a spirit of polite fellowship and complaisance. Despite their privacy, clubs were often devoted to both mutual edification and civic improvement. Benjamin Franklin's Junto club—probably early America's most celebrated club—exemplified all of these features. And while Franklin may have immodestly exaggerated when he claimed that his club was "the best School of Philosophy, Morals and Politics" in Pennsylvania, nonetheless the accomplishments of the Junto were quite substantial.

The American Philosophical Society, Philadelphia's first subscription library ("the Mother of all the North American subscription libraries"), and the emission of the colony's first paper currency all began as secret Junto projects. By 1736 at least five sub-Juntos had been organized on identical lines by members of the original club, and by mid-century Junto-like clubs could be found in the taverns of every major seaport in British North America. Such clubs gave merchants, tradesmen, skilled artisans, and educated elites an opportunity to exchange ideas and form friendships and alliances that transcended religious, ethnic, and traditional social boundaries.[12]

In contrast to the club, with its private nature, the coffeehouse was a distinctly public venue of enlightened sociable association. Beginning in the second half of the seventeenth century, coffeehouses exploded onto the urban European scene, and no major city on either side of the Atlantic was without their presence. Dispensing far more than caffeinated beverages, coffeehouses made available issues of the latest newspapers, journals, and gazettes for the perusal of their paying customers. They were places where one could go to engage in conversation, conviviality, and intellectual exchange. And coffeehouse sociability was governed by the rule of complaisance, which ignored social hierarchies. The 1674 poetical "Rules and Orders of the Coffee House" stated quite explicitly that

> *Pre-eminence of place, none here should mind,*
> *But take the next fit seat that he can find:*
> *Nor need any, if Finer persons come,*
> *Rise up to assigne them his room.*

Like the club, the coffeehouse sought to eliminate zealous and dogmatic disputation in favor of more polite and amicable conversation.[13]

For the nominal price of a cup of coffee, then, any man could enter a site of sociable association, where he could participate in a civil and egalitarian public discussion of the latest developments in the worlds of business, politics, literature, and enlightened learning. Indeed, the only limit to such associations were their all-male nature, a lacuna filled by the parallel development of female tea-table assemblies. The most famous and accomplished of these was London's Bluestockings of the 1760s, whose gatherings included such female literary luminaries as Hannah Moore and Fanny Burney, and which attracted celebrated male visitors like Samuel Johnson, Edmund Burke, and the famed Shakespearean actor David Garrick.

The only enlightened sociable association that truly challenged the gender divide, however, was the *salon*. Presided over by a female hostess or *salonnière*, the salon was a private gathering that commingled political, social, and business notables with men of letters for polite conversation over a refined repast. Although salons could be found in every major urban center in the second half of the eighteenth century – Elizabeth Graeme and Anne Willing Bingham ran early America's most prestigious salon in Philadelphia—the acknowledged center of salon culture was undeniably Paris. At the height of the institution's influence in the years 1765 to 1776, an enlightened philosophe could attend a different salon every night of the week, each one devoted to a different intellectual pursuit or school of thought. More than that, they were settings where men of letters could vet their latest intellectual productions; in their heyday, few philosophes would dare to publish a work that had not first been aired in salon conversation and received the commendation of some *salonnière*.

Salonnières were not simply gracious hostesses; their subtle yet firm governance of polite conversation obviated the need for specific rules to ensure complaisance and inhibit dogmatic intellectual pugnacity. Largely self-educated, *salonnières* were accomplished citizens of the republic of letters in their own right, whose judgment in matters of learning and letters was highly valued and sought out by the philosophes. Speaking of the leading ladies of Parisian salon society, David Hume forthrightly acknowledged that they were the true "Sovereigns of the *learned* World, as well as of the *conversible*."[14]

These three principal forms of the Enlightenment—printed texts, learned societies, and sociable associations—did more than merely propagate the tenets of the philosophes. They inculcated in literate, critical, and informed persons a shared set of values, attitudes, tastes, and cultural presuppositions that crossed social, gender, religious, and national boundaries. Historians refer to this development as the growth of a "public sphere," an arcane phrase that might more easily be styled "the emergence of public opinion." Heralded at the time, the new public opinion of the eighteenth century was pervasive and influential. Even absolute monarchs had to take the opinion of this new public into account; its judgment could literally make or break government initiatives and even ministries.

It was through their ability to mold public opinion that the philosophes were able to influence the policies and politics of their day. Their cause of "humanity" would have a transformative, even revolutionary, impact on the political landscape of the Atlantic world, ultimately toppling the ancien régime and ushering in a new epoch of modernity. It was thus the emergence of a new literate, critical, and cohesive public opinion that gave power and force to the politics of Enlightenment.

THE POLITICS OF ENLIGHTENMENT

Any discussion of the politics of Enlightenment must come to terms with several complicating factors, not least of which were the wide variety of political positions adopted by enlightened authors. These positions ranged from an open embrace of the "enlightened despotism" of absolute kings and queens, to an avowal of mixed and constitutional monarchy, to a call for outright popular republican government, occasionally of a decidedly democratic character. Although much of this variety can be attributed to the differing national political constructs confronting various thinkers, even within such national contexts philosophes disagreed in their political prescriptions.

Further complicating the politics of Enlightenment was the curiously bifurcated nature of the philosophes' writings on the subject. Such works tended to be either extremely abstract and general treatments of the nature of sovereignty, government, or natural law on the one hand, or remarkably specific exposés of particular and narrow problems, issues, or scandals on the other. Lacking, with a few notable exceptions, were analyses of the nuts and bolts of political reality, such as constitutional design, party and partisan balance, and concrete military and economic policy. Indeed, it was not until the American revolutionary and constitutional epochs that this lacuna was finally filled and a distinctly enlightened practical "political science" was ultimately formulated.

Finally, and perhaps most complicating of all, is the problem of discerning the actual intentions of the philosophes, intentions that were as often obscured as revealed in their texts. Although the eighteenth century saw a gradual decline in the practice of state censorship, authors still had to be careful not to run afoul of the constituted authorities in their public political pronouncements. Voltaire fixed his residence near the French border so that he could escape capture and imprisonment if any of his works proved too offensive to the French government. Most philosophes, however, sought to elude the constraints of censorship and public respectability either by publishing anonymously or, more commonly, through the practice of esotericism. Enlightened esotericism entailed explicitly stating "acceptable" positions that were then undermined by adducing arguments that surreptitiously implied variant, often contrary, conclusions. As a result, any attempt to limn the politics of Enlightenment encounters difficulties precisely because the line between sincerity and obfuscation was, by intention, difficult to mark.

Despite these complicating factors, there was a fundamental coherence to the politics of Enlightenment. This coherence was not doctrinal, much less ideological. Rather, what unified the political thought of the philosophes was a shared commitment to a common set of core concerns and projects. These concerns animated the political ruminations of enlightened thinkers, and it was around these projects that the politics of Enlightenment was constructed. First and foremost was the struggle against enthusiasm in all its guises. It was this struggle that had first given rise to the Enlightenment, and as long as the movement persisted, it devoted much of its energy to wiping out the scourge of religious zealotry and political fanaticism. A second major focus of the politics of

Enlightenment was to promote a reevaluation of the social, cultural, moral, and political value of commerce and market activity. These two enlightened projects are the most obvious starting points for any discussion of the politics of Enlightenment and have understandably been at the center of most scholarly treatments of the topic. Somewhat less examined, but equally critical, was the construction of a new public and political role for the enlightened philosophe himself. Though less heralded in historical accounts, this role was at the very center of the politics of Enlightenment. Nor should it be particularly surprising that the quest for a rational political order would entail the political empowerment of the rational.

The Struggle Against Enthusiasm

No issue was more central to the politics of Enlightenment than the struggle against enthusiasm. Enthusiasm and its largely Catholic counterpart, superstition, were held responsible for the confessional struggles and religious persecutions of the sixteenth and seventeenth centuries that had first inspired the philosophes to take up their pens. Superstition, born of ignorance and fear of the supernatural, led people to timidly submit to priestly ordained tyranny; enthusiasm emboldened its purveyors to impose their views on those around them. Self-evidently, the problem of enthusiasm had a decidedly political dimension. The dogmatic certitude and self-righteous pride of the enthusiast combined to produce a spirit of political zealotry.

This conviction that religious zeal resulted in fanatical factions and divisive parties was central to the enlightened struggle against enthusiasm. Voltaire pointedly reminded his readers that it was not reputedly radical philosophes like Locke, Bayle, or Spinoza "who have carried the torch of discord into their countries." Rather, it was "theologians who, having begun by aiming at being heads of a sect, soon aimed at being heads of a party." Unfortunately, once unleashed, the spirit and practice of political zealotry was difficult to contain. Combining the zealous fanaticism of the enthusiast with dogmatic first principles produced what Hume called "speculative parties" that were utterly incapable of seeing any sense or even virtue in their political opponents. Such bitter and uncompromising divisions of "principle" were a constant threat to the regular and orderly processes of government, and might, in extreme circumstances, give rise to popular tumults that could rend the entire political fabric.[15]

If enthusiastic zealotry was the disease affecting the body politic, then the philosophes saw themselves as the physicians and their culture of Enlightenment as the prescribed cure. Drama and belles lettres could "easily dissipate" the melancholic and "gloomy humour" of enthusiasm if, as Adam Smith insisted, the state would ensure perfect "freedom of arts and entertainment." Even more salutary was the impact of enlightened empirical science. "Science is the great antidote to the poison of enthusiasm," Smith claimed, "and where all the superior ranks of people were secured from it, the inferior ranks could not be much exposed to it." It was only through moderation and the promulgation of "moderate opinions" that political zeal could be contained, if not vanquished. Such moderation restrained the excesses of partisan zealots by showing "each that its antagonist may possibly be sometimes in the right." This was, in fact, precisely the course that Hume pursued in trying to bridge the gap between the two "principled" partisan rifts in contemporary England. Enlightened "scientific" criticism promoted moderation by uncovering or "unmasking" the political zealots' flawed reasoning as well as the more mundane, sordid, and petty motives that lay behind their affected posture of principle.[16]

Assessing the overall political character of enlightened moderation is a decidedly complicated task. There is no denying that the campaign against enthusiasm and zealotry could serve conservative interests and even assume a conservative tone. As Adam Smith noted approvingly, enlightened criticism armed the public to see "through the interested complaints of faction and sedition." This in turn made the public far more politically quiescent and far "less apt to be misled into any wanton or unnecessary opposition to the measures of government." Moderation, then, could serve as a support of the status quo, with the philosophe a heroic bulwark of the standing order. Diderot considered conscientious philosophes "the best defenders of the sovereign" and in a compelling analogy compared them to "those buckets of water hanging up in the corridors of our police commissioners, ready to be thrown over the flames of fanaticism."[17]

Nonetheless, it would be a mistake to conclude that the Enlightenment struggle against enthusiasm was essentially conservative. The philosophes opposed what they called popular "tumult" and "confusion," but they were not simply spokesmen for the status quo. Rather, they were reformers who sought to bring their own political projects to fruition by gradual and consensual changes in law, politics, and society. These projects were unquestionably modern and progressive, but the means of fulfilling them were decidedly moderate. The philosophes sought to expand both personal liberty and political participation to their widest practical extent, but they sought to do so without destabilizing the steady and regular administration of government and tearing the social fabric with violent eruptions. They sought a republican order, but one that evolved from monarchical origins without wholesale carnage and ideological division. For evidence that such a moderate, stable, yet essentially republican order was possible, even advisable, the philosophes referred to the illustrative case of England. Indeed, so frequent and fervent was this reference that in the first half of the eighteenth century there emerged something like a philosophic cult of English liberties and institutions, a cult known in France as *Anglomanie* or Anglomania.

Anglomania took root in all the enlightened pockets of Europe, but it found its fullest expression in France, where it could be used as a critical counterpoint to the failures of French policies and politics. All Anglomaniacs, however, shared the conviction that the British constitution was the very apex of human liberty and ingenuity. Only in England, Montesquieu insisted, was "political liberty" the "direct end of the constitution." The political liberty that resulted from this constitution made England, in Diderot's phrase, "the country of great political phenomena." The most striking of these phenomena was the fact that only England among the great powers of the world afforded its people an integral part in the government of the nation through its vaunted House of

Commons. Only in England was the "nation" represented in the "state," Voltaire alleged. Moreover, the legion personal liberties of Englishmen—property rights, freedom of speech and print, jury trials, government by law, and freedom of conscience—were in essence a "restoration to all men of all those natural rights" that the monarchs of other European states had ravaged.[18]

What allowed for such broad liberty without threatening stability was, at least according to the philosophes, the mixed nature of the English constitution. Rather than adopting one of the traditional "pure" forms of government like democracy, aristocracy, or monarchy, the English combined all three forms into one political frame. Since each salient interest was, in theory at least, represented in a mixed government, each could serve as a check or balance on the others by defending its own interests. It was this system of checking and balancing interests that played a critical moderating role in English politics, giving the government its basic stability. The spirit of moderation even infected England's foreign policy. Rather than pursue "the brilliant folly of making conquests," England sought merely (and prudently) to "prevent its neighbors" from becoming too powerful through conquests of their own.[19]

British liberty was, of course, the fruit of struggles by the English people against their monarchs. Yet even these struggles taught a lesson of moderation and Enlightenment. England had witnessed not one but two major revolutions in the seventeenth century. The first, the so-called Puritan revolution of the 1640s and 1650s, was animated by religious enthusiasm and, in Montesquieu's words, "the spirit of faction." This violent struggle against the Stuart monarch Charles I had cost the king his head and witnessed several abortive efforts to "create a commonwealth." As Voltaire acknowledged, the fanatical opposition of the House of Commons had led to "the most frightful abuses that have ever made human nature shudder," abuses that ultimately terminated in the military dictatorship of Oliver Cromwell.[20]

In stark contrast to the violent turbulence of the first English revolution and its ensuing civil wars, England's second "Glorious" Revolution of 1688–89 and the revolution settlement of the following years were a model of moderate success. The transfer of the crown by Parliament from hated, draconian, and Catholic James II to his nephew and son-in-law William of Orange was achieved without shedding a drop of blood. No doubt part of this miracle was due to James's cowardly flight to France in the face of William's imminent arrival with an army. Yet part was also due to the moderate course adopted by the revolutionaries. Unlike their Puritan predecessors, the Glorious Revolutionaries avoided factional conflicts. The revolution and its ensuing acts of settlement—acts that ensured regular parliamentary government and the full panoply of rights celebrated by the Anglomaniacs—had been a largely consensual affair that united both Whigs and Tories. Naturally, such consensus had required much compromise and even some studied ambiguity at times, but the result of this moderation was a sturdy fabric of laws, liberties, and institutions. The resulting constitution may not have been perfect, Diderot acknowledged, but it was "perhaps the only one, since man lived in society, in which the laws have ensured him his dignity, personal liberty, and freedom of thought."[21]

What had induced the English people to eschew the tumult of mid-century and steer a more moderate course at century's end was, of course, the spread of Enlightenment itself. It was only "as they became more enlightened," Voltaire insisted, that the English "love of freedom" became "their dominant characteristic." The moderating influence of late-seventeenth-century England's republic of letters had taught that nation to pursue its liberty in a spirit of rational self-interest rather than fanatical enthusiasm. As Voltaire succinctly put it, it was in the English Glorious Revolution that "philosophy" had successfully "destroyed the fanaticism that shakes the most solid of states." The result had been the world's first great example of ordered liberty.[22]

The Case for Commerce

The philosophes' case for commerce was central to the politics of Enlightenment. It was also, in many ways, their greatest theoretical achievement. From the enlightened defense of commerce, and the capitalist social and market relations it produced, would issue the modern disciplines of economics, political economy, and sociology. Its explanatory breadth was matched by the radically modern nature of its arguments. Born of enlightened modernism, urbanity, and cosmopolitanism, the enlightened case for commerce was far more than a novel account of economic activity and the wealth of nations. It entailed a new way of thinking about politics and the state, one based on the unabashed embrace of the transformative impact of trade and capitalist production. Even more radically, it proposed a thorough reassessment of ethical theories and moral values. Enlightened political economy was, at bottom, a fundamental critique of contemporary social relations and a call for a modern and secular moral and ethical order. Just how radical this critique was can best be seen in contrast to the traditional views of commerce that the philosophes opposed.

Beginning in the late medieval period and accelerating through the age of exploration and discovery, the rise of commerce had spread Europe's trade to the far reaches of the world and market relations to every corner of western Europe. This sparked a demographic explosion and price rise that dramatically increased the wealth of European societies and afforded sufficient revenues for the establishment of powerful and integrated national monarchies and commercial republics. By the early eighteenth century, commerce had not only financed and prompted the projection of European power on a global scale, it had also, in the case of Europe's most commercially advanced nation, England, contributed to the birth of the Industrial Revolution. Nonetheless, most Europeans and early Americans were still rural agriculturalists who held traditional and decidedly hostile views about commercial activity. Animated by their rural fear of the city, they saw commerce—and its symbolic representative, the merchant—as essentially parasitic. While the people of the countryside worked to fill the basic and natural needs of the society, urban merchants were motivated solely by greed and self-interest, an unnatural and base motivation exemplified in the practice of usury.

Born of cupidity, commerce had a morally debilitating effect on society. It was also a source of political corruption. Unlike virtuous landed proprietors, whose possession of "real" estates gave them an "independent" and permanent stake in their society, the trade of wealthy merchants depended on the protection of the state, and they thus used their wealth to "influence" and corrupt the government to serve their selfish commercial interests. In short, the commercial capitalism of the growing cities was a sinkhole of vice and luxury that threatened, if unchecked, to destroy the natural moral order of the countryside and its selfless virtue and patriotism. Without such rural virtue, the government would become hopelessly corrupt and despotic.

The enlightened case for commerce rejected this traditional view in its entirety. Far from being economically parasitic, the human "propensity to truck, barter, and exchange" was, according to Adam Smith, the basic wellspring of economic prosperity. Long before Smith penned his *Wealth of Nations*, however, Bernard Mandeville had made the enlightened case for commerce. Commerce might well draw on and nurture greed and vanity, but such private vices produced economically "public benefits." Locke and Samuel von Pufendorf had shown that the true source of property and wealth was labor, for it was through laboring that we acquire the right to possession and produce the various goods we consume and exchange. Commerce promoted the national wealth, Mandeville argued, by increasing the amount of labor in a society; the demand for luxury goods, sparked by vanity and fed by greed, provided employment for a vast throng of urban mechanics, manufacturers, and professionals who would otherwise be unsustainable. It also made labor more productive. As Adam Smith argued, the spread of commercial markets gave rise to an increasing division of labor, the specialization of which promoted greater efficiency and technological development, especially in the form of labor-saving machinery. Even agricultural labor became more productive as a result of commerce. The desire to acquire the new commodities "which men's luxury now makes them covet," Hume remarked, spurred rural folk to "study agriculture as a science, and redouble their industry and attention."[23]

Commerce produced national power and greatness in addition to wealth. By promoting the manufacture of consumer goods, commerce created employment for a growing population. It also facilitated ship-building and the naval power that allowed European states to project their power overseas. That such wealth and power ultimately issued from the greed of merchants and the vanity of consumers only proved, to Mandeville, the foolish nature of calls for a return to a more virtuous social order:

> *Then leave Complaints: Fools only strive*
> *To make a Great an Honest Hive*
> *T'enjoy the World's Conveniencies,*
> *Be fam'd in War, yet live in Ease,*
> *Without great Vices, is a vain*
> *Eutopia seated in the Brain.*

Rustic simplicity might assuage moral anxieties, but it resulted in national poverty, insignificance, and impotence. Without commerce, national greatness was a chimera.[24]

Commerce was not only connected to national wealth and power; it was also deeply enmeshed in the very fabric of public freedom. On the one hand, commerce depended on the security of private possession that could only emerge in free governments. On the other hand, commerce promoted liberty. In the third book of his *Wealth of Nations*, Adam Smith argued that it was commerce that had destroyed the despotism of the great feudal barons. As commerce made exotic luxuries available, the overly great lords chose to sack their idle retainers and military henchmen in order to devote all of their resources to conspicuous and selfish consumption. This consumption ultimately led to the transfer of much of their wealth to hands that were more diligent and industrious. It also meant that the growing wealth of urban merchants and artisans began to serve as a counterweight in the hands of monarchs against the licentious power of the aristocratic warlords. In exchange, these monarchs rewarded these urban tradesmen with self-government, political power, and a newfound social dignity. Thus commerce, Smith concluded, had given birth to urban freedom and undermined the feudal despotism of the countryside.

Hume agreed. Only when "luxury nourishes commerce and industry" could the otherwise servile rural peasant "become rich and independent." Only commerce allowed the urban "tradesmen and merchants" to "acquire a share of the property." And of course, only commerce drew "authority and consideration to that middling rank of men, who are the best and firmest basis of public liberty." Commerce thus had a "natural tendency to preserve, if not produce a free government," a development that could be most clearly seen in England. The English were more free than other Europeans because, according to Montesquieu, "other nations have made the interests of commerce yield to those of politics" while the English "have ever made their political interests give way to those of commerce."[25]

Liberty, power, and wealth were not the only fruits of commerce. Equally important was its support of the Enlightenment itself. Part of this support was a consequence of commerce's tendency to promote public liberty. Commerce had produced so many wealthy and worldly citizens that even "absolute" monarchs did not dare give vent to their "full tyranny" for fear their subjects might "new-mould their constitution, having so many prospects of liberty within their view."[26]

But commerce did more to advance the Enlightenment than promote "free government" and personal liberty. It also provided the wealth that assured the learned of what Addison called "a competency of all the conveniences of life." This "competency" freed the minds of the learned from concern for the "necessaries" of life and allowed them to focus their thoughts on loftier and weightier concerns. Commerce also led to the development and "refinement" of the mechanical arts, which Hume claimed further promoted Enlightenment. The development of industry and the mechanical arts kept their practitioners "in perpetual occupation" and focused their attention on the solution of technical problems of production. This sharpened their minds and fostered a "mechanical" or instrumental rationality that matched means to ends in a disciplined fashion. As this intellectual vigor and rationality spread through the populace, and as wealth and luxury grew, men became more sociable and urbane. For the philosophes, commerce and modern civilization went hand in glove.[27]

Perhaps the most radical aspect of the Enlightenment case for commerce, however, came in the field of ethical inquiry. When Mandeville first made his case for commerce in the early eighteenth century, he claimed that it led to a moral paradox. Commerce indeed produced national wealth, power, liberty, and learning, but it was ultimately based on the vices of greed and vanity. By contrast, the virtues of honesty, integrity, and independence resulted only in poverty and insignificance. In solving this paradox in the ensuing decades, the enlightened case for commerce instituted a revolution in ethical theory. This first part of this revolution entailed changing the locus of moral reasoning. Rather than judge an act by the intention of the actor, philosophes from Hutcheson and Hume to D'Holbach and Voltaire focused on the consequences of the act itself. If these consequences were useful to the individual and the society at large, then the act was "benevolent" and morally worthy. The rational pursuit of self-interest was not in itself vicious unless it resulted in injury to others. When it actually promoted public wealth or other desirable ends, it was enlightened and praiseworthy.

The second part of this revolution comprised a reevaluation of the very nature of virtue. The older classical virtues associated with personal honor—courage, self-control, and unflagging independence and integrity—were undoubtedly admirable but were, as Hume noted, too "violent" and "unnatural" for a modern and "refined" age. In his *Theory of Moral Sentiments*, Adam Smith contrasted these older virtues to the "softer" and more "amiable" modern virtues of "candid condescension and indulgent humanity."[28]

When Benjamin Franklin listed the thirteen principal virtues in his *Autobiography*, conspicuously absent were both the classical ideals of courage, self-sacrifice, and generosity, and the Christian norms of piety and faith. Instead, Franklin's virtues were thoroughly modern and "bourgeois." In the place of magnanimity, Franklin celebrated "frugality," "industry," and "temperance." Such pedestrian virtues as "order," "cleanliness," and "moderation" took the place of devotion and penitence. The older classical and Christian virtues were austere and impressive, but the modern ones were more tender-hearted and far more conducive to human happiness, plenty, and power. And here lay the truly revolutionary impact of enlightened "consequential" moral reasoning. Morality was a matter of adapting means to ends, where the truly desirable end was human happiness rather than a virtuous character or a great soul. That the commerce that produced such happiness gave rise to private vices simply demonstrated that no means was without its drawbacks. Despite such "enormous abuses," ages of commerce and industry were, according to Hume, "both the happiest and most virtuous." Subject to the softer and more amiable modern virtues, commercial epochs produced a more humanitarian ethos that looked with a benevolent eye on all of humanity. "Thus *industry*, *knowledge*, and *humanity*, are linked together by an indissoluble chain," he concluded, "and are found from experience as well as reason, to be peculiar to the more polished, and what are commonly denominated the more luxurious ages."[29]

For the philosophes, then, commerce was a source of national wealth and power. It was also the font of personal and public liberty as well as enlightenment and the flowering of the arts and sciences. More than that, however, commerce was an essentially humanistic and humanitarian activity. As a "great lover of mankind," Addison could not "forbear expressing my joy with tears" when he visited the Royal Exchange in London. There he found assembled from the far corners of the earth "a body of men thriving in their own private fortunes" while "promoting the public stock." These men achieved these publicly useful ends by importing into their societies "whatever is wanting" and exporting "whatever is superfluous." Merchants were thus the most "useful" and beneficial members of a commonwealth, for they "knit mankind together in a mutual intercourse of good offices, distribute the gifts of nature, find work for the poor," and supply "wealth to the rich and magnificence to the great." For the politics of Enlightenment, the continued vitality and development of commerce was essential to human progress.[30]

The Empowerment of the Philosophes

The politics of Enlightenment did more than celebrate commerce and criticize zealotry. The philosophes also sought and gained political power. Indeed, implicit in the politics of Enlightenment was the empowerment of the enlightened. An intellectual elite whose status rested on high cultural achievement, the philosophes considered themselves a "natural aristocracy" of talent and merit. They were, in their own minds at least, ideally suited to guiding politics and policy in an enlightened and progressive direction. Who better, after all, than political scientists to put public policy on a scientific basis? As Plato had urged more than two thousand years before, a rational political order entailed the political rule of the most rational. Like most intellectuals, the philosophes' will to power took the form of a "Platonic complex," the belief that their superior high cultural expertise entitled them to a privileged political role.

How the philosophes sought to acquire and use this power varied enormously over time and place. The hostility or openness of the political authorities, the relative freedom of expression and publication, and the size and impact of the literary market all impinged on the strategies and tactics that enlightened intellectuals deployed in their quest for public recognition and power. Despite these constraining factors, the philosophes organized their quest for power around three new public roles. First and foremost, they constituted themselves as the spokesmen for the public. They legitimated this claim through their labors as both champions and censors of public opinion. This was certainly their most central and prominent political role, especially in Europe. A secondary role was that of political counselor or government official. This role was occupied by a fortunate fraction, but those who enjoyed this access, as clients, advisers, and friends of statesmen, were often able to guide policy more directly than their less privileged colleagues were as spokesmen for the public. The most exalted enlightened political role, however, was that of "the legislator." By "legislators," the philosophes meant what we might call constitutional statesmen, those figures who not only administer and preside over government and policy but actually design the institutions of government and distribute powers throughout those institutions. This truly Platonic role represented the culmination of the politics of the Enlightenment, its greatest and most fantastic goal.

While several prominent European philosophes presented their theoretical credentials for this role, it would only actually be achieved in America. Only there would the politics of Enlightenment come to its true fruition. Only in America would the enlightened philosophes recapture the power and historic influence of the great legislators of antiquity. Only in America could enlightened statesmen create a new nation and government out of whole cloth.

John Adams was thrilled to "have been sent into life at a time when the greatest lawgivers of antiquity would have wished to have lived." The American Revolution rendered the colonies a virtual tabula rasa on which men like Hamilton, Adams, and Jefferson could seek to "form and establish the wisest and happiest government that human wisdom can contrive." And contrive they did. As their European counterparts could only dream, America's enlightened statesmen applied their knowledge of politics, society, and history to inaugurate a host of modern innovations in constitutional government. Where Locke had conjured the social contract as an implicit, theoretical explanation of the origins of government, men like Hamilton, Adams, and Jefferson rendered it a reality by, for the first time in modern history, actually drafting constitutional frames of government and then submitting them to the people at large for ratification. Whereas philosophes like Voltaire, Montesquieu, and Hume had celebrated the checks and balances in European governments that had emerged by unintentional evolution over long centuries, America's philosophes explicitly designed them into the structures of the state. The independence of the judiciary was not a goal to be achieved through reform or the slow weight of precedent; it was a reality forthrightly declared and imposed. The abolition of monarchy and hereditary aristocracy, the establishment of freedom of the press and of assembly, and the separation of church and state were all built into the very fabric of American nationhood. American constitutional government would emerge fully formed from the pens and voices of American philosophical statesmen, much as Athena burst fully clad from the head of Zeus. From its outset it would bear the unmistakable imprint of the politics of Enlightenment. It continues to bear that imprint to this very day.[31]

❦

CHAPTER ONE

ALEXANDER HAMILTON: THE ENLIGHTENMENT FULFILLED

THE ENIGMA OF HAMILTON

A T A SLENDER five feet seven inches, Alexander Hamilton cast an immense shadow over his times. The famed French diplomat the Marquis de Talleyrand-Périgord considered "Napoleon, Pitt, and Hamilton" the three greatest political figures of the age. If forced "to choose among the three," the legendary master of *réal politique* "would without hesitation give the first place to Hamilton." This was no empty compliment. Talleyrand was the resident French expert on American affairs and had met most of the leading statesmen of the United States during a two-year stay.[1]

Hamilton's varied public accomplishments are the stuff of legend. As a revolutionary soldier, he saw action in most of the major engagements of the war, acquitting himself with a gallantry that occasionally bordered on the suicidal. At the ripe old age of twenty, he joined George Washington's staff, where he quickly emerged as the commander in chief's most indispensable aide and most trusted adviser on military and political matters. As a lawyer, Hamilton was the leading member of the New York bar and the nation's foremost theorist of judicial supremacy and review; Supreme Court chief justice John Marshall considered himself a "mere schoolchild" in jurisprudence in comparison. As a legislator, Hamilton was a leading member of the New York Assembly and the Continental Congress. As a delegate to the Annapolis convention of 1786 from New York, Hamilton authored the call for the Philadelphia Constitutional Convention of the following year. In all posts, he was one of the most outspoken advocates of a strong national government. He was the single most important figure in securing the adoption of the Constitution in New York State and, with Washington and Madison, was one of the most critical figures in the national campaign for the new federal frame of government.

As secretary of the Treasury in Washington's administration, Hamilton not only headed the most important and largest cabinet office in the executive branch, he also formulated most of the administration's foreign and domestic policies. By Washington's second term he had become the president's de facto prime minister. Hamilton published well over 150 works and essays, including two-thirds of *The Federalist Papers*, drafted many of the most important state documents of his time (most famously his three *Reports on Public Credit* and Washington's Farewell Address), and founded the *New York Post*, the longest-running newspaper in the United States. In a more private capacity, Hamilton was one of the founders of the Bank of New York, the Society for Promoting Useful Manufactures, and the Society for Promoting the Manumission of Slaves, New York's premier abolitionist organization. An impressive résumé for any founding father, much less a poor, orphaned bastard from the West Indies.

More than any other figure of the American founding, Alexander Hamilton evoked extreme passions. Friends and supporters admired him with a reverence bordering on hero worship. Adversaries loathed him with a hatred that was truly visceral. Thomas Jefferson saw him as a contagion of corruption, whose public career was "a tissue of machinations against the liberty of the country." John Adams dismissed him as "an insolent coxcomb" and the "bastard brat of a Scotch pedlar." Yet even his enemies acknowledged his greatness. "Hamilton is really a colossus," Jefferson confessed, "without numbers, he is an host within himself." Somewhat more begrudging, even Adams noted his remarkable "effervescence." More tellingly, he sought Hamilton's supervision of his son's legal training.[2]

Animus was no doubt fueled by jealousy, for Hamilton's meteoric success was exacerbated by his remarkable youth. A mere thirty-two years of age when he joined Washington's cabinet, Hamilton nonetheless dominated the administration. But it was more than jealousy that made him such a polarizing figure. His character, both public and private, sparked wildly divergent responses. Moreover, the political forces he represented and the vision of the new nation he pursued were both powerfully alluring and deeply troubling to his fellow Americans. They remain so to this day.

"A Singular Character"—The Contradictions of Hamilton

The character of Alexander Hamilton was a jumble of contradictions. Witty and earnest, affable and distant, and alternately animated by a tender-hearted concern for the sufferings of the disadvantaged and an aristocratic contempt for the common herd, Hamilton has always been a bit of an enigma. Arguably the most impressive of the founding fathers, Hamilton was also, in the words of one of his biographers, "by far the most psychologically troubled." This is not to say that Hamilton was a villain. Quite the contrary, he was a deeply principled and essentially decent man, one blessed with remarkable talents. Yet even his greatest virtues and most remarkable abilities were complicated by contradictory flaws.[3]

On the one hand, Hamilton's intellectual abilities were indisputable. The most brilliant political figure of his age, he was endowed with a mind that was quick, agile, and perceptive. Throughout his life Hamilton dazzled those around him with truly prodigious feats of acuity. To cite just one example, without any formal education except a brief stint in a Hebrew school, he crammed several years' worth of college preparation in Greek and Latin into about six months of intensive study, gaining him admission to King's (now Columbia) College in the fall of 1773. Allowed to study at his own accelerated pace, roughly two years later he had, to his own satisfaction at least, completed his higher education. On the other hand, he was capable of incredibly bad judgment. As a member of the Continental Congress in early 1783, he sought to extract nationalist concessions from his colleagues through the threat of a military coup by the unpaid and disgruntled Continental Army camped at Newburgh, New York. It took an angry and pointed letter from George Washington to remind him that "the Army . . . is a dangerous instrument to play with." Most famously, when James Thompson Callender, the most notoriously scurrilous journalistic "hack" of his day, charged the former secretary of the Treasury with financial malfeasance with one James Reynolds during his tenure in office, Hamilton published the complete correspondence with Reynolds in a pamphlet. In so doing, he cleared himself of a totally unsubstantiated charge and convicted himself of having an adulterous relationship with Reynolds's wife. Hamilton's friends were mortified; his foes cackled with glee.[4]

Just as poor judgment marred his brilliance, his remarkable diligence was shadowed by his frailty. Hamilton was undeniably capable of astounding, almost Herculean feats of industry. In the little more than six months between mid-October 1787 and May 1788, he penned fifty-one of those *Federalist* papers whose attribution is exclusive and fixed, averaging roughly two essays per week. The comparable number for Madison was fourteen, and a mere five for Jay. Indeed, on more than one occasion Hamilton's feats of industry foiled his political foes. In early 1793 Republican partisans in the House and Senate passed resolutions questioning his management of the Treasury Department. The resolutions were introduced just over a month before Congress was to adjourn, and since the House had previously acknowledged that the thorough accounting necessary to clear Hamilton would entail at least nine months of work, the plan was clearly to have Congress adjourn with an unanswered charge of malfeasance hanging over his head. Much to their amazement and chagrin, Hamilton submitted seven separate reports to Congress in the following three weeks detailing every financial transaction the government had made over the previous two years. The resolutions were resoundingly defeated. Hamilton was vindicated.[5]

Yet for all his industry, Hamilton was remarkably frail. In an age when men tended to be rather portly, he was strikingly slender, almost gaunt in appearance, with long, spindly legs. Beginning in his youth, he suffered from bouts of rheumatic fever that left him bedridden for weeks at a time. In the autumn of 1777 Washington sent Hamilton on an arduous and delicate mission to extract soldiers from General Horatio Gates, the recently victorious hero of the battle of Saratoga. Gates was part of a cabal within the army and Congress that sought to replace Washington as commander in chief with himself. As such, he was none too eager to send any of his own troops to relieve his rival. Hamilton's dogged persistence ultimately bore fruit—but left the twenty-year-old lieutenant colonel physically spent. In mid-November he collapsed, writing to Washington of his incapacity from "a fever and rheumatic pains throughout my body." This was to be a pattern in Hamilton's career, great exertions followed by physical collapse. Eventual recuperation would then give way to fresh efforts, beginning the cycle anew.[6]

Hamilton was acutely aware of his own frailty, an awareness his foes took as hypochondria. Jefferson was filled with contempt for Hamilton's "excessive alarm" for his health during an outbreak of yellow fever in Philadelphia in the summer of 1793. A man so "timid in sickness," Jefferson remarked sarcastically, "would be a phenomenon if the courage of which he has the reputation in military occasions were genuine." Jefferson may have been uncharitable in his doubts about Hamilton's "manly" fortitude, but he was not alone.[7]

Hamilton's emotional makeup was similarly split between light and dark. Friends and acquaintances were struck by his charm, wit, and affability. The Duc de La Rochefoucauld-Liancourt pronounced him one of those rare figures who combine "breadth of mind" with "cheerfulness, excellence of character, and much affability," an assessment that even Jefferson shared. With his good looks and easy charm, Hamilton invites comparison with the hero of Henry Fielding's contemporary sentimental novel, *Tom Jones*. Yet Hamilton had another, darker side to his personality. As his friend Gouverneur Morris confessed in his diary, for all his charm Hamilton could be "indiscreet, vain, and opinionated." More than that, when frustrated by forces opposing him personally or politically, he was susceptible to fits of depression that are more reminiscent of the morose broodings of Hamlet than the sunny disposition of the bastard Jones. Perceived favoritism toward foreign officers left him "contemptible in my own eyes." It was in the midst of one of these self-pitying fits of despair, brought on by resistance to his nationalizing program in the Continental Congress, that Hamilton dabbled with the threat of a military coup. When Washington called him to account and back to his senses, Hamilton confessed that "I often feel a mortification, which it would be impolitic to express, that sets my passions at variance with my reason." With John Laurens, perhaps his closest friend, Hamilton was far less "politic": "I hate Congress—I hate the army—I hate the world—I hate myself."[8]

Perhaps the greatest contrast in Hamilton's character, however, was in the realm of the public and political rather than the private and personal. Hamilton's program was the most modern and progressive of the founding era. Ever the champion of commercial interests, he promoted rapid industrialization and urban growth fostered by a strong central government capable of projecting its interests and power in the world at large. In place of the classical "republican" quest for virtue, austerity, and personal independence, Hamilton sought the modern goals of commercial prosperity, economic growth, and social mobility. While many Americans piously envisioned politics as a struggle over principles and convictions, the worldly Hamilton saw it as a clash of rival socioeconomic interests. And where others saw those very interests as the source of political corruption, Hamilton saw such corruption as the necessary lubricant for the wheels of government.

At one dinner party John Adams claimed that the British frame of government could be "the most perfect constitution ever devised" if purged of its corruption and its legislature reformed along more representative lines. Hamilton wryly responded that such "reforms" would only render it "an *impractical* government: as it stands at present, with all its supposed defects, it is the most perfect government which ever existed." Like the archmodern Bernard Mandeville, Hamilton sought to turn private vices into public benefits rather than vainly attempt to banish them from the world of politics. It was for good reason that

Hamilton's opponents considered him an American Robert Walpole, the notorious "corrupting" prime minister of midcentury Great Britain and master of patronage, whose thoroughly modern credo was "no saint, no Spartan, no reformer."[9]

Yet while Hamilton's political principles were thoroughly modern, his public behavior was decidedly classical. Most of Hamilton's political writings were pseudonymously attributed to virtuous classical heroes of antiquity; more than that, Hamilton often assumed a rhetorical air of strict, almost austere classical honesty in his writings, refusing to flatter the people or to pander to their desires. As one scholar has recently noted, Hamilton's public mien was reminiscent of the Roman patrician Coriolanus of the early Republic, who Shakespeare depicts as filled with aristocratic hauteur when responding to the grumblings of the poor plebeians: "hang 'em!" Indeed, Hamilton's truths were not popular, but they were salutary. As he pointedly reminded his readers (again drawing on Hume), "*Caesar*, who *overturned* the republic was the WHIG, *Cato*, who *died* for it, the TORY of Rome." Despite believing that class and self-interest were the glue of politics, Hamilton personally conducted himself with Spartan purity. He publicly eschewed any compensation for his military services so that he could argue for pensions for the officer corps without any appearance of personal advantage. Similarly, when Henry Lee wrote to the newly appointed secretary of the Treasury for inside information on the likelihood of future payment of the national debt, Hamilton refused to provide it. "You remember the saying with regard to Caesar's wife," Hamilton replied. (Caesar's wife had to be spotless in reputation, not merely fact.) "I think the spirit of it applicable to every man concerned in the administration of the finances of a Country." And in fact, despite numerous charges against him, every investigation into his official conduct by his congressional opponents revealed that he had discharged his duties with the utmost honesty and integrity, leaving office with the nation's finances in order and his own in shambles.[10]

Hamilton was one of those misanthropic hypocrites who, judging mankind incapable of benevolence or selflessness in public life, then hold themselves to the most virtuous standards of conduct. Perhaps no one grasped this contradiction in Hamilton's public character better than Jefferson. Although "under thorough conviction that corruption was essential to the government of a nation," Hamilton was nonetheless "of astute understanding, disinterested, honest, and honorable." Jefferson aptly concluded that "Hamilton was, indeed, a singular character."[11]

A Portrait of the Statesman as a Young Man

Much of the turmoil in Hamilton's character can be attributed to his childhood. Most of the leading statesmen of the founding era hailed from prominent families within the social elite. Some, such as Thomas Jefferson, William Livingston, and Hamilton's father-in-law, Philip Schuyler, were truly to the manor born. Only a small handful were drawn from the common sort. Benjamin Franklin, John Adams, and Thomas Paine may have been critical figures in the politics of early America, but their plebeian backgrounds were decidedly exceptional. None, however, came from origins as obscure or difficult as Alexander Hamilton's.

Hamilton's mother, Rachel Faucett, was born in 1729 on the tiny island of Nevis in the Lesser Antilles. Her early years were spent in an unhappy and broken family; her mother, Mary, separated from her father in 1740, taking the eleven-year-old Rachel with her to the nearby island of St. Kitts (St. Christopher). Five years later, at the age of sixteen, Rachel married John Michael Lavien, a small-time Danish merchant and erstwhile planter who was at least twelve years older than she. Together, the following year, they moved to the Danish-controlled island of St. Croix. Despite the birth of a son, Peter, Rachel's marriage was no happier than her mother's. In 1749 John Lavien had his wife imprisoned in the fort of Christiansted for adultery. Whether Rachel was guilty of the charge is unknown, but in any case Lavien's action was unremittingly draconian. In the tiny white community that sat atop the large slave societies of the West Indies, Rachel's imprisonment among drunken sailors, common criminals, and unruly slaves entailed her complete social ostracism. Unable to show her face in respectable society, no sooner was Rachel released than she fled the island, abandoning her husband and young son. She would never see either again.[12]

Presumably Rachel ran to her mother in St. Kitts, but there is no clear evidence establishing this. What is known is that in the following few years she hooked up with James Hamilton on the island of Nevis, another man at least ten years her senior. No mere "Scotch pedlar," Hamilton was the son of a Scottish lord; Alexander would later name his small country home in what is now Harlem after the ancestral family estate in Ayrshire. As the fourth son, however, James was propertyless and had come to the West Indies to make his fortune. At this task he was utterly unsuccessful. Rachel bore him two sons out of wedlock, James Jr. in 1755 and Alexander—named after his grandfather, the "laird of the Grange"—on January 11, 1757. In later years Alexander remembered his father fondly. Presumably it was from him that he learned to view the "money grubbing" ways of merchants with aristocratic disdain, despite the fact that, in stark contrast to his ne'er-do-well father, young Alexander was to prove quite adept at them. Together the family eked out a modest existence at the fringes of white island society.[13]

Ultimately, Rachel's relationship with James Hamilton was to prove no happier and not much more enduring than her previous marriage. In 1765 she returned to St. Croix, where James was commissioned to recover a debt. Having discharged his duty, he returned to St. Kitts, leaving Rachel and their two sons behind. Alexander, then eight or nine, would never see his father again, though in later years he would send him whatever sums he could spare. Rachel opened a small store in their home that Alexander helped tend, perhaps also clerking at the nearby firm of Nicholas Cruger, a merchant from New York who headed the West Indian branch of the family trade. Rachel's relative poverty and scandalous reputation precluded any hope of formal education for her sons. It was a hard lot that only got harder.[14]

On February 19, 1768, Rachel died. As illegitimate children, James Jr. and Alexander could not inherit what few assets she had; John

Michael Lavien promptly claimed her small estate for his son Peter. The authorities placed the Hamilton boys in service, where they could learn a trade to support themselves. James Jr. was apprenticed to a carpenter, and Alexander became a clerk for Nicholas Cruger. Hamilton was just one month past his eleventh birthday.[15]

Despite his poverty and the obscurity of his birth, Hamilton's first extant letter, written to his friend Edward "Ned" Stevens just two months before his thirteenth birthday, testifies to his dreams of glory: "to confess my weakness, Ned, my ambition is so prevalent, so that I contemn the groveling condition of a clerk or the like, to which my fortune, etc., condemns me, and would willingly risk my life, though not my character to exalt my station." Fame and glory for Hamilton were the necessary salve for the wounds of his childhood. An exalted "station" would atone for his abandonment by his parents and finally answer the taunts of "whore child" that he had endured as a boy on the streets of Christiansted. Only extraordinary achievement could vindicate Hamilton. Ominously he ended his letter: "I wish there was a war."[16]

Hamilton's burning ambition spurred him to great accomplishments, much to the benefit of his adopted country. Hamilton's remarkable efforts in the revolutionary and early national epochs were critical to the founding of American freedom, prosperity, and national greatness. Indeed, by the time he retired from public life, Hamilton had achieved everything a man of his age could dream of, much less hope for. He had married into one of the wealthiest and most illustrious families in North America, with a handsome wife who adored him and a brood of devoted children. He was the leading member of the New York bar whose services were eagerly sought by all who needed legal representation. His political career was an unqualified success. Short of the presidency, he had been honored with every high office and title, both military and civilian, that his country could bestow. Revered by his followers, admired by his colleagues, and respected by his foes, Hamilton in his lifetime climbed the summits of acclaim that are usually reserved for those long deceased. Yet he remained unsatisfied. Success never brought the relief he pined for. "Mine is an odd destiny," he wrote to his friend and fellow

Federalist Gouverneur Morris in 1802. "Perhaps no man in the United States has sacrificed or done more for the present Constitution than myself . . . Yet I have the murmurs of its friends no less than the curses of its foes for my reward." This was the tragedy of Alexander Hamilton: no worldly success could remove the scars of his childhood wounds.[17]

A Native New Yorker

There was, of course, more to Hamilton than a wounded inner child. He was molded by, and reflected, the environment in which he came of age. Throughout his life in America Hamilton knew only one place as home: New York City. It was in New York that he attended college. It was in New York that he began his military career, organizing a patriot militia in the winter of 1774. It was in New York that he entered the Continental service, receiving a commission as a captain in the New York artillery in the spring of 1776. At war's end he represented New York in the state legislature and the Continental Congress. As a lawyer, he fixed his practice in New York City, where he resided with his family at 57 Wall Street. And at the end of his political career, it was in northern Manhattan that Hamilton built his country house, the Grange, which still sits nestled among the buildings surrounding the City College of New York in Harlem. Finally, it was in New York that he was buried after his famous duel with Aaron Burr, finding his final resting place in the Trinity churchyard in lower Manhattan.[18]

The New York of Hamilton's day was a relatively small city of some twenty thousand souls. Yet it was already growing at an astounding rate and undeniably was a unique place in early America, even among the handful of urban seaports that dominated the trade of the country. Boston had been part of the Puritan plan to build a godly "City upon a Hill" in the new world, and Philadelphia was envisioned as a Quaker city of brotherly love. New York, by contrast, from its very inception had been committed exclusively to commercial advantage. A remarkably diverse place, host to Dutch Calvinists, English Puritans, German Baptists, French Huguenots, and a smattering of creolized Angolans and

Sephardic Jews, by the mid-seventeenth century New York's politics were characterized by religious and ethnic factionalism. So intense was the partisanship in New York that some historians have seen in it the origins of our own modern party politics.

By Hamilton's time, New Yorkers had already been noted for many of the distinctive characteristics with which they are associated to this very day. New Yorkers walked and talked faster, worked and played harder, and pursued wealth with a greater avidity (if not cupidity) than their fellow Americans. It was Hamilton's natural home.

Like so many true New Yorkers, Hamilton was an immigrant who was attracted by its scintillating energy and enamored of its bustling tempo. Just as Jefferson represented the Virginia gentry in the public imagination, Hamilton was the embodiment of the New York City slicker, so much so that his contemporaries came to call the town "Hamiltonopolis." No doubt it was the identification with New York that, in part at least, made Hamilton such a polarizing figure. Then and now Americans have felt a strange ambivalence toward Gotham, proud of its colossal wealth and power yet uncomfortable with its moral excesses and worldly pursuit of gain.[19]

Ultimately, however, it was not merely his embodiment of New York City that made Hamilton such a divisive figure. Hamilton represented the politics of Enlightenment in the early republic. Indeed, he embodied them. His own dramatic social mobility exemplified the Enlightenment's meritocratic ideal of the career open to talents rather than birth or wealth. By dint of diligence and learning, Hamilton pulled himself out of obscurity to the heights of fame and fortune. A bastard by birth, Hamilton was one of those "natural aristocrats" whom the philosophes celebrated and whom Thomas Jefferson hoped could be "raked from the rubbish" by means of public education. His political vision, drawn from his reading and his experience as a New Yorker, represented the Enlightenment's program of commercial and urban development put into practice.[20]

In a country that was still overwhelmingly agrarian, this enlightened program could not help but spark controversy. Coupled with the worldliness and disenchanted *réal politique* that Hamilton drew from the eighteenth-century philosophes, it is not hard to understand why he was and remains a troubling figure in the American founding. His career was the Enlightenment put into operation, and his political program represented its projection in the newly created United States of America. Hamilton was the Enlightenment fulfilled. It had not always been so.

THE TURNING

When Hamilton matriculated at King's College in the fall of 1773, a lull had fallen over the imperial crisis between Great Britain and her North American colonies. Of the Townshend Acts of 1767—a series of duties that Parliament had imposed on American imports—all but the tax on tea had been repealed. As a consequence, the colonial protest movement's efforts to retaliate through a boycott of British imports had largely collapsed. For most Americans, the conflict with England seemed to have been resolved. That all changed on December 16 when the Sons of Liberty cast 340 chests of tea belonging to the British East India Company into Boston Harbor. In short order Parliament responded with the draconian Intolerable Acts, which closed the port of Boston, revoked the Massachusetts charter, and remodeled its government under the military control of General Thomas Gage. According to the recollection of his friend Robert Troup, Hamilton had previously sided with the British in the imperial controversy. But after the famous Tea Party he began to reconsider his position, traveling to Boston to assess the situation for himself. Once there, he was galvanized by the radical rhetoric and patriotic posture of the beleaguered Bostonians. Thenceforth Hamilton would be among the most committed patriots in the American cause.[21]

"Inviolably Attached to the Essential Rights of Mankind"— Hamilton the Radical Republican

Unlike solidly patriotic New England, the mid-Atlantic colonies of New York, Pennsylvania, New Jersey, and Delaware were deeply divided between loyalists to the British crown and partisans of colonial resistance. Tory publicists like the Anglican clergyman Samuel Seabury (writing under the pseudonym "A Westchester Farmer") filled the presses with pamphlets defending king and country and castigating the rebellious counsels of the Continental Congress. In the winter of 1774–75, Hamilton entered the lists on behalf of the patriots, publishing two essays—"A Full Vindication of the Measures of the Continental Congress" and "The Farmer Refuted"—in reply to Seabury. These were followed up in the ensuing summer with two additional pieces, entitled "Remarks on the Quebec Bill," that further elaborated the case for colonial resistance. In these writings, Hamilton took a decidedly radical position.

The colonies, Hamilton insisted, were in no way subject to the authority of Parliament; their sole tie to the empire was through their shared monarch. This was a view held by only a handful of the more committed revolutionaries at the time, such as James Wilson, Thomas Jefferson, and John Adams. These polemical pieces by the still-teenaged collegian galvanized the forces of resistance in New York and the mid-Atlantic region at large. They also cemented Hamilton's reputation as a spokesman for the colonial cause. What is most striking about these essays, however, and about Hamilton's correspondence over the following years, is what they betray about his political thought at the time. The young propagandist was not merely an American partisan. In stark contrast to his later views, the revolutionary Alexander Hamilton was a committed republican. "I am inviolably attached to the essential rights of mankind," he insisted, "and the true interests of society."[22]

To be a republican in the eighteenth century meant far more than merely favoring representative or even popular government. As historians have demonstrated over the last fifty years, republicanism was a peculiar worldview that inspired the American revolutionaries. Its origins lay in the Florentine Renaissance, whose famous political theorists such as Machiavelli and Gucciardini sought to rekindle the civic humanism of classical Greece and Rome. Popularized in succeeding generations by authors like James Harrington and Algernon Sidney, republicans championed the ideal of active political engagement. For republicans, man was, in Aristotle's phrase, "by nature a political animal" whose public existence was "defined by no other thing so much as by sharing in decision and office." Such active citizenship required the practice of virtue, the essential principle of republican government according to the famed Baron de Montesquieu. Political virtue meant the voluntary sacrifice of one's personal interests on behalf of the public good, a sacrifice exemplified in the willingness to fight and die for one's country.[23]

There were, of course, problems in adapting the civic humanism of the classical republicans to the politics of early modern Europe. Sparta, Athens, and Rome had been self-contained city-states, not territorially extended dominions. Moreover, with the exception of Switzerland and the Protestant Netherlands, most northern European polities were not republics at all but monarchies, and some, like France, were of the "absolute" variety. In this context, republican civic virtue took the form of an abiding suspicion that kings and their ministers were constantly conspiring to increase their power at the expense of the liberties of the people (the latter being the propertied and landed classes). Additionally, the ancient republics had been pagan rather than Christian. Thus post-Renaissance republicans supplemented classical political teachings with the "natural law" theories of late medieval Christianity. Nor had the classical republics been rent by confessional and sectarian controversies. In the case of English-speaking republicans in particular, their civic humanism was strongly colored by their pious Protestant hatred of Roman Catholicism. By the seventeenth century, English republicans were convinced that "Popery" was not merely heretical and anti-Christian but the religious source of tyranny and arbitrary government.

Each of these elements of the republican worldview found ample expression in Hamilton's revolutionary writings. Political self-government was not a privilege but a fundamental right. Without this right to civic participation, the colonists were no better than slaves. "The only distinction between freedom and slavery," Hamilton insisted, "consists in this: in the former state, a man is governed by the laws to which he has given his consent" while "in the latter, he is governed by the will of another." This right to active political participation flowed from the fact of human equality. "All men have one common original," he reasoned, "and consequently have one common right." Given this equality, there was no justification "why one man should exercise any power, or pre-eminence over his fellow creatures," unless they had explicitly and "voluntarily vested him with it." This the colonists had pointedly refused to do. American self-legislation in defiance of British parliamentary pretensions was thus "an inherent right," one "founded upon the right of all men to freedom and happiness." Without that right "civil liberty cannot possibly have any existence," and the colonials, denied their birthright as freeborn Britons, would be reduced to thralldom.[24]

Parliament's assault on the rights of America was not fortuitous. It was "the offspring of mature deliberation," part of the never-ending quest of the king's ministers to expand their powers at the expense of popular liberty. What lay behind this plot was a growing apprehension of the rise of American glory, "a jealousy of our dawning splendour." This fear of American potential greatness was "one of the principal incitements to the present rigorous and unconstitutional proceedings against us." American resistance to these parliamentary violations was, therefore, not the result of "peevish and petulant humours" but the principled determination of colonials "to shew them, that we know the value of freedom."[25]

Proof that the British were conspiring against American liberty could be found in the Quebec Act, which established the Catholic religion and the French legal system in Canada. Clearly this was an unwarranted abrogation of power, for Parliament "had no more right" to "establish popery" in Quebec than in "New York and the other colonies." More than that, though, the absence of representative institutions and the English jury system in that province "invests the king with absolute power over a little world." This absolute power was a threat to the liberty of Protestant America. While Tory partisans of the crown dismissed such fears as "the dismal sounds of New-England's republicanism, bigotry, and intolerance," Hamilton insisted to the contrary that there could be no clearer evidence of "the corruption of the British Parliament" than "its act" in establishing the principles of arbitrary government in French Canada.[26]

Even with right on their side, how could the colonials hope to prevail against the most powerful empire in the history of the world? The answer for Hamilton lay in the appeal of republican virtue to the hearts and minds of the American people. "There is a certain enthusiasm in liberty, that makes human nature rise above itself in acts of bravery and heroism," intoned the young idealist. "It cannot be expected that America would yield, without a magnanimous, persevering, and bloody struggle." The British would certainly have advantages on their side. Equipped with a powerful navy, professional soldiers, experienced officers, and ample military supplies, the British enjoyed what Hamilton frankly acknowledged was a "vast superiority." Yet they were hardly "invincible." American patriotic virtue would supply "superior numbers" that, "joined to natural intrepidity and that animation which is inspired by a desire of freedom and a love of one's country," Hamilton argued, "may very well overbalance" the more traditional assets the British enjoyed. Moreover, a prolonged military struggle would devastate British commerce, an intolerable development for a nation of shopkeepers already burdened with a crippling debt.[27]

Hamilton's republican rhetoric may have been rousing, but it was hardly unique. Appeals to patriotic virtue against ministerial conspiracies were the stock in trade of American revolutionary polemic. Even antipopery was a fairly common element of the accepted arguments for colonial resistance. Indeed, republicanism has long been recognized as the ideological basis of the American revolutionary movement. What was distinctive about Hamilton's position was not its republicanism per se but the extremes to which he took it. His republicanism was remarkably radical, even among partisans of the American cause.

For all their talk of popular liberty and the rule of the people, most American revolutionary leaders were republicans, not democrats. They acknowledged the legitimate voice of the people in government but hardly accorded it full sovereignty. Instead, they favored what was known at the time as "mixed government." The ideal of mixed government was drawn from the classical republican theories of Aristotle and Polybius, who taught that combining elements of democratic, aristocratic, and monarchical government in one constitutional frame eliminated the potential dangers of the "pure" forms by allowing each to check the excesses of the others. In legislative terms, a mixed government balanced the participation of the people with an equal representation of the elite.[28]

The British Parliament was just such a mixed government. The people had their representatives in the House of Commons, but that body was offset by the aristocratic House of Lords. Both in turn were checked by the king. Most colonial legislatures had incorporated this mixed ideal, with popularly elected assemblies balanced by small appointed councils made up of the social and political elite. Both branches of the legislature were in turn checked by an independent governor, generally appointed by the crown. Thus when the colonies broke with the empire, their new state constitutions replicated this mixed, bicameral mode of legislative organization. Popularly elected lower houses were matched with elite upper houses or "senates" whose members generally served longer terms. Only Pennsylvania and Vermont adopted the more radical and democratic unicameral legislature, where the people's representatives were the only source of law and policy.

Most revolutionaries were, like John Adams, appalled by the democratic nature of such unicameral legislatures. Thomas Jefferson preferred an appointed senate whose members enjoyed life tenures "rather than a mere creation by and dependence on the people." Hamilton was, in fact, one of those few radicals who favored democracy over mixed government.[29]

"That instability is inherent in the nature of popular governments," Hamilton acknowledged, was a common conviction among political leaders. But such charges were the result of elitist prejudices, he insisted, not a "strict examination of the matter." On the contrary, a careful perusal of the historical facts demonstrated that such instability in "governments in which the popular principle has borne a considerable sway" was the result of its mixture "with other principles." Combining popular sovereignty with elite checks and balances forced democracy to "operate in an improper channel." Unfortunately, this was precisely what revolutionary New York had done in its own constitution by balancing the popularly elected assembly with an upper house. The newly created New York Senate, both by its "very name" as well as "the mere circumstance of its being a separate member of the legislature," was likely to destabilize the state government and "degenerate into a body purely aristocratical." Such aristocracy was both unwarranted and unnecessary because there was little "danger of an abuse of power" in a unicameral assembly "where the equality and fullness of popular representation is so wisely provided for." A far cry from his later sentiment, the revolutionary Hamilton was a proud democrat.[30]

Hamilton did more than champion the principles of popular democracy. He also sought to extend republican liberties beyond the political nation of white male property owners. Hamilton dismissed racist arguments that blacks lacked the intellectual and moral capacity for the virtuous defense of American liberty, going so far as to propose a plan to enlist South Carolina slaves in the army and thus "give them their freedom with their muskets." "The contempt we have been taught to entertain of the blacks," he averred, is "founded neither in reason nor experience." Indeed, he was convinced that "the negroes will make excellent soldiers" if only they were enlisted with emancipation as an inducement and placed under "proper management." But his scheme would do more than aid the war effort. It would also promote the cause of a general emancipation, an advantage that had "no small weight" for the young abolitionist. Hamilton's plan to enlist slaves as soldiers issued from the depths of his republican convictions. In refuting Seabury two years earlier, he had argued that "the whole human race is intitled" to the blessings of civil liberty and human dignity, and "it can be wrested from no part of them," African or European, "without the blackest and most aggravated guilt." Abolition was an essential element of Hamilton's revolutionary credo.[31]

In the years that followed the outbreak of the Revolutionary War, Hamilton's political thinking would undergo a sea change. Disillusionment would replace republican enthusiasm, and youthful idealism would give way to worldly realism. Hamilton never lost his hatred of slavery and his commitment to abolition, but his commitment to pure democracy and his faith in public virtue would dissipate. The young Hamilton was a republican dreamer whose political vision drew on classical sources. The mature Hamilton was a modern who considered appeals to republican virtue futile and childish. Government, the older Hamilton concluded, was founded on interest and opinion, not on abstract rights. The Hamilton that emerged from the maelstrom of revolutionary struggle was a decided realist whose thought was imbued with the worldly teachings and philosophies of the Enlightenment. As one biographer has noted, the young Hamilton "often sounded like his opponents in maturity."[32]

"These Things Wound My Feelings as a Republican"— The Sources of Disillusionment

Hamilton's break with republicanism was a direct result of his experience as an officer in the Continental Army. The Revolutionary War for independence forced him to reexamine his political beliefs and come to terms with realities that ran counter to his idealistic aspirations. Part of this reexamination included a reassessment of the role of the nation's fledgling political institutions. Additionally, Hamilton was led to confront the nature of American society and the character of its citizens. His youthful belief in the power of republican virtue and self-sacrifice was challenged by the course of events and the selfishness of his adopted countrymen. Idealism gave way to realism, and worldliness replaced heroic optimism in his thought. Hamilton ceased to be a republican stalwart and became the nation's most outspoken champion of the politics of Enlightenment.

By the time Hamilton joined General George Washington's staff in the spring of 1777, he had seen extensive military action in numerous engagements. Most of these battles had been disheartening and disastrous defeats. In early spring 1776 General William Howe evacuated Boston and moved the locus of British military operations to the mid-Atlantic colonies. In early July he established a military base on Staten Island. Toward the end of the following month he landed a force of fifteen thousand troops on Long Island. On August 27 he routed the Continental Army at Brooklyn Heights. Washington was fortunate to be able to evacuate his surviving force of 9,500 men to Manhattan under cover of night two days later. In mid-September the British landed at Kip's Bay (presently East Thirtieth Street), facing little opposition from American militia, which fled as quickly as possible. Only Howe's failure to press his advantage and march directly across the island allowed Hamilton and the rest of the American army in New York City to escape complete encirclement by streaming up the western edge of Manhattan and holding off the British advance at Harlem Heights the following day, September 16. The British now occupied Hamilton's beloved New York City, as they would for the following seven years, using it as their primary base of operations.[33]

By mid-October, Washington realized that his position in New York was utterly untenable. Most of the thirteen thousand militia under his command had deserted, and his force of ten thousand Continentals had been repeatedly routed. On October 16 he moved the bulk of his army to higher ground north of Manhattan, leaving a large force of roughly three thousand to hold Fort Washington (in what is now Washington Heights). At the end of the month he was again defeated in White Plains and beat a hasty retreat across the Hudson and down through New Jersey. When he arrived at Hackensack in mid-November, he had a mere three thousand men. On November 16 Fort Washington surrendered unconditionally in the face of a British siege, with the loss of most of its force and a large cache of vital supplies. Three days later Fort Lee, just across the Hudson in New Jersey, fell with an additional loss of men and supplies—almost 150 cannons, 2,800 muskets, 400,000 cartridges, 12,000 rounds of cannon shot, and the bulk of the army's blankets, tents, and tools. Washington's diminished and dispirited forces continued their brisk flight across New Jersey with Howe's regulars close at their heels. By the end of the month they reached New Brunswick, where Hamilton's artillery, stationed at what is now Rutgers College, laid a protective covering barrage that held off the British and allowed Washington to safely cross the Raritan River. There Washington's forces were further depleted by the loss of two thousand militia from New Jersey and other states whose term of enlistment ended on December 1. Washington reached Trenton two days later and crossed the Delaware to Pennsylvania less than a week after that with little more than half of his original force of Continentals.[34]

Dispirited and repeatedly defeated, Washington confided to his brother in a letter that "I think the game is pretty near up." Only his daring Christmas raid at Trenton and his successful assault on Princeton the following week kept the American forces intact and revived at least some hope for eventual victory.[35]

Unfortunately, Washington's victories at Trenton and Princeton were to be his last for four years, until the final success at Yorktown in 1781. In 1777 Howe dispatched his forces by fleet for an assault on Philadelphia. Washington's efforts to defend the nation's capital were thwarted in the second week of September when he was handed a thorough drubbing at Brandywine Creek, forcing the Continental Congress to flee Philadelphia. The following week the British occupied Philadelphia without opposition. The very next week they dealt Washington another humiliating defeat at Germantown. To make matters even more galling for the commander in chief, while Washington went from crushing defeat to defeat, his great rival Horatio Gates scored the most stunning American victory of the Revolutionary War at Saratoga in late September and early October 1777. The British general John Burgoyne was forced to surrender with a force of nearly six thousand men. Gates's success, aided by the brilliant field leadership of the future traitor Benedict Arnold, was instrumental in gaining diplomatic recognition from France and, with it, much-needed military and financial support. Not surprisingly, many congressmen seriously considered replacing Washington with Gates as 1777 came to a close.[36]

Although Washington ultimately retained his command, the course of the war did not improve for the American cause in the following years. In the spring of 1778 General Henry Clinton replaced Howe as British commander and shortly evacuated Philadelphia to shift the war to the southern colonies. By the end of the year Georgia had been conquered. Mid-May 1780 brought the capitulation of Charleston, South Carolina, and with it the surrender of 5,500 American soldiers. Clinton then returned to New York and left Lord Charles Cornwallis to pacify the rest of the South. By the end of June he had gained control of most of the Carolinas, an area of some fifteen thousand square miles. At the battle of Camden on August 16 he destroyed the remnants of the American army in the South, sending its commander Horatio Gates (the hero of Saratoga) into panicked flight. Charlotte, North Carolina, fell by the end of September, at which point the British controlled most of the American South. In the interim, the best Washington had to show for himself was a minor tactical victory at Monmouth Court House in New Jersey, where his soldiers actually held their ground in a full pitched battle on June 28, 1778. As the year 1780 drew to a close, the American Revolution was on the verge of collapse.[37]

The American cause finally prevailed the following year, but only after the British had dislodged the Virginia legislature from its capital in Charlottesville on June 4, almost capturing Governor Thomas Jefferson at his Monticello estate. And when victory did come at Yorktown that fall, it was more the result of French land and naval forces—and stormy weather that scattered the British fleet—than American military effort. American independence had been achieved despite, not because of, the military activity of the Continental Army. It was a bitter pill for American soldiers and their officers to swallow. For none did it go down harder than for Alexander Hamilton. The experience, and the lessons he drew from it, permanently changed his political and intellectual orientation.

The failures of the Continental Army can be attributed to a variety of factors. Although far superior to their brethren in the militias, Continental soldiers lacked discipline and training. Not until the arrival of "Baron" von Steuben—in fact, a common mercenary and drill instructor from the Prussian army—at Valley Forge in the winter of 1777–78 did the American forces have even the basic rudiments of close order drill, the essential requirement for both proficiency in the field and unit cohesion in modern land armies. Recruitment was another problem. Congress called for enlistments for the duration of the war in 1776, but there were very few takers. The following year Congress resorted to a state quota system that persisted throughout the war. When enlistments proved inadequate to fill these quotas by the middle of the year, soldiers were drafted for service ending that December, and the lacuna was filled with ineffective militia. Once trained, these recruits would be discharged by the end of the year, and so the whole process would begin again the following January. Naturally, this left the army in a state of perpetual flux. This flux was exacerbated by desertion. Until the final year of the war, roughly 20 to 25 percent of the Continental Army fled from its posts. During the harsh winter months at Valley Forge in 1777–78, that number ballooned to almost ten desertions per day.[38]

The Continental Army was also hampered by a lack of able leadership. Untrained and inexperienced, American officers were forced to learn on the job. At Monmouth Court House, General Charles Lee inexplicably lost his nerve (a failure that resulted in his court-martial), almost snatching defeat from the jaws of victory. Only the timely arrival of Hamilton and Washington to rally his panicked troops prevented another dispiriting rout. At Camden, South Carolina, the aged Horatio Gates vastly underestimated the strength of his foe and then turned to headlong flight, leaving his soldiers to fend for themselves. Even Washington dithered aimlessly in New York in 1776, failing to evacuate Forts Lee and Washington when their positions were hopeless.

Discouraged and disunited, officers fell into infighting and intrigue. After his victory at Saratoga, Gates jockeyed to replace Washington. In November 1777 Gates was appointed president of the Board of War, and his minion Brigadier General Thomas Conway was made inspector general, reporting directly to Gates and the Board rather than through Washington. Further eroding Washington's authority and sapping the morale of his officers was Congress's penchant for commissioning foreign, especially French, officers and promoting them above those Americans who had been serving in the field. More than simply galling, Hamilton complained that "these things wound my feelings as a republican more than I can express." Military experience had begun to erode Hamilton's faith in his political creed.[39]

The greatest single cause of the failures of the Continental Army, however, was the lack of vital supplies. The army simply lacked the food, clothing, and military matériel to take the field, much less mount an offensive. As early as 1776, one officer reported that the march to Trenton of Washington's army on Christmas Day was "tinged here and there with blood from the feet of men who wore broken shoes." For most of the war, Washington's soldiers were unpaid, poorly fed, and clad in rags or half-naked. Almost one-quarter of his force died at the winter encampment at Valley Forge from cold, disease, and outright starvation. By all accounts the encampment at Morristown the following winter—one of the coldest in New Jersey history—was even harsher. On January 1 the Massachusetts line mutinied, followed by the Connecticut line in late May and the New York line the following month.[40]

A beleaguered George Washington warned the president of the Continental Congress, Joseph Reed, that, unless the problem of supply was addressed shortly, "our affairs must soon become desperate beyond the possibility of recovery." "Indeed," he added, "I have almost ceased to hope."[41]

What made the suffering of the army especially exasperating was that it occurred in the midst of economic prosperity. The struggle for independence had brought with it a remarkable war boom that stretched from 1778 to 1780, precisely those years when Hamilton and his fellow Continentals experienced their greatest privations. Thus, for example, the starvation at Valley Forge followed a bumper crop. Unfortunately, Congress had tried to economize by setting compensation for wagons and draft animals at roughly a third of current market rates. Not surprisingly, teamsters refused to transport supplies to the army when they could make far more money contracting with private parties. The problem of supply, then, was the result not of a dearth of resources but of a failure of policies for procuring those supplies and the lack of political will to see that procurement through.[42]

By 1780 many officers in the Continental Army believed that the failures of supply and support for the army had reached the point of a genuine national crisis. In October of that year Hamilton wrote to Isaac

Sears (one of the leaders of New York's Sons of Liberty) that "it is impossible the Contest can be much longer Supported on the present footing." What followed was a series of demands that would form the core of Hamilton's program for the rest of his life. Foreign loans were needed to finance the war, and a national bank was required to administer those finances. Congressional boards must be replaced with executive bodies headed by individuals with the authority to enforce their orders. In the interim, a "tax in kind" should be imposed on the farmers of America to see that the army was fed. Simply put, Hamilton insisted that "we must have a Government with more power."[43]

Much of the blame for the crises of the army and the nation could be laid at the feet of the Continental Congress. Lacking a source of revenue, the Congress had adopted the expedient of printing money. As the money depreciated in value, Congress responded by simply printing more of it. At the beginning of 1779 it took $8 to purchase the same goods that had sold for one a mere two years earlier. By March 1780 the currency had become so worthless that Congress was forced to devalue its own money by a factor of forty to one. Congress thus practically declared bankruptcy and reduced its debt by fiat from $200 million to $5 million. Even that extraordinary measure failed to arrest the depreciation of the currency. In April 1781 it took $167 to purchase what had cost only one dollar at the outset of the war. Having failed to supply the army, in 1780 Congress simply abdicated its responsibility. Henceforth the states would be charged with provisioning the troops, an arrangement that proved no more satisfactory the following winter at Morristown.[44]

When Hamilton first took up his pen in the American cause, he did so as a champion of the Continental Congress. By 1778 he had become disillusioned with that body. At first he attributed its failures to the removal of leading statesmen to military, state, and diplomatic offices. But Congress not only lacked quality representation, it also suffered from an absence of moral scruple. In the winter of 1777–78 Hamilton became involved in a congressionally authorized cartel to exchange prisoners with the British. He was shocked to learn that Congress sought merely to string the British along with impossible preconditions in order to blame the failure of exchanges on their foe and thus score a propaganda coup. "Such a cruel policy of exposing those men who are foremost in defense of their country to the misery of hopeless captivity" was scandalous, Hamilton thundered, particularly when it was foisted on "a republican army."[45]

Congressional immorality was compounded by sheer cupidity. When Congressman Samuel Chase of Maryland learned that a French fleet was shortly to arrive in American waters, he cornered the flour market for provisioning that fleet, doubling the price Congress had to pay for that commodity and reaping a handsome profit. Disgusted by Chase's venality, Hamilton attacked him in the press. Writing under the pseudonym "Publius"—the same name he would adopt in *The Federalist*—Hamilton charged the congressman with stooping "to the dishonest artifices of a mercantile projector" and sacrificing "his conscience and his trust to pecuniary motives." Such a "degenerate character" who had abused "the knowledge of secrets, to which his office gave him access" was worthy of "the utmost rigor of public resentment" and ought to "be detested as a traitor of the worst and most dangerous kind." For Hamilton, Congress had lost its luster as the embodiment of American republican virtue.[46]

Hamilton's disillusionment was not limited to the Congress. The states had also been remiss in fulfilling their obligations. Had the states retired the Continental currency through taxation, as Congress had enjoined, much of its devaluation might have been avoided. Yet to curry favor with their constituents, state legislators consistently refused to do this. Nor were they any more willing to shoulder their burdens under the system of state supply adopted by the Congress in 1780. When state price controls did not thwart the task of supply, those states not under attack by the British found more pressing needs for the tax revenues. Ultimately, the army was reduced to impressing the goods it desperately needed, leaving the victims of such seizures with increasingly worthless promissory certificates. By war's end, more than $93 million of such certificates had been foisted on unwilling farmers and tradesmen, and that was excluding those issued in Georgia and the Carolinas. The "conduct of the states," according to Hamilton, was so "pitiful" that "if we are saved France and Spain must save us."[47]

Having failed to discharge their duties, the states would henceforth be a perennial object of Hamilton's political enmity. He devoted much of the rest of his public career to weakening their pernicious stranglehold on political power in the new republic.

Hamilton's greatest disillusionment, however, was with the American people. Prior to his military service, Hamilton had waxed rhapsodic about the great republican virtue of the American people and the "enthusiasm in liberty, that makes human nature rise above itself." Years of suffering and privation in the field had taught him otherwise. Although the ineffectual policies of Congress and the states exacerbated the army's critical lack of supplies, overshadowing these failures was, in the words of one historian, "the speculative practices of countless farmers." They hoarded their crops, sold them at inflated prices to merchants rather than to army quartermasters, and as a last resort distilled their grains into alcohol for more profitable sale to half-starved soldiers. Civilian theft of army supplies was rampant both in camp and throughout the countryside.[48]

Magistrates and residents routinely found ways to avoid meeting their quotas of supplies and conscripts. Indeed, the failure of the states to supply the Continental Army was itself the result of their citizens' utter unwillingness to pay higher taxes to support the war effort, a lesson not lost on Hamilton and his fellow soldiers. This was particularly evident after France entered the war on the American side. As Hamilton correctly noted, Americans expected the French to secure their independence without having to sacrifice themselves. "Our countrymen have all the folly of the ass," wrote a disgusted Hamilton in 1780, "and all the passiveness of the sheep."[49]

Perhaps most discouraging of all, just as the southern colonies faced British conquest, South Carolina rejected John Laurens's plan to raise several regiments of black soldiers, a scheme that had the backing of the Continental Congress. Laurens's plan would have immeasurably aided the American war effort. Additionally, it would have at least made a dent in one of the gravest injustices that all Americans recognized as a blight on the nation's moral and republican character. Even before the legislature had rejected Laurens's proposal, Hamilton confessed that, although it was "the best resource the situation of your country will admit," his hopes were "very feeble." "Prejudice and private interest," he predicted, "will be antagonists too powerful for public spirit and the public good." The plan went down to defeat in South Carolina. Several years later Hamilton confessed to George Washington that "I have an indifferent opinion of the honesty of this country." To his friend Laurens he was far more direct: "there is no virtue in America."[50]

Adding to Hamilton's disillusionment was his frustration with the dead end his military career had taken. When he joined Washington's staff, he had received a double promotion from captain to lieutenant colonel. As the years passed, however, he remained fixed at that rank while others with field command were promoted ahead of him. As a child, Hamilton had hoped for a war to free him from the "groveling" clerical work he was assigned. Ironically, war had returned him to precisely that work. Worse yet, his very competence in that work made him indispensable to Washington. When he sought the command of a battalion under Lafayette for an expedition against Staten Island in November 1780, Washington flatly refused. His close friend John Laurens urged Congress to appoint Hamilton secretary to the American ministry in France. On December 11, 1780, Congress chose Laurens instead. Four days later Hamilton was nominated for the post of minister to Russia. Again he was passed over, this time for Francis Dana. Lafayette and Nathanael Greene then urged Washington to appoint Hamilton to the vacant post of adjutant general. Once again Hamilton was denied.[51]

Angry and disheartened, Hamilton reached an emotional low. In February 1781, after an angry outburst from Washington (his volcanic temper was well known by those who had access to him in private), Hamilton resigned from the general's staff and rejected all of the commander in chief's attempts at reconciliation. Still, Hamilton's frustrations grew. In early 1781 he was proposed for the post of financier, but

Congress instead opted for the far more experienced merchant Robert Morris of Philadelphia. Shortly thereafter he was nominated and rejected as secretary of foreign affairs. Only an angry letter of resignation from the army finally secured him the command he desired from Washington for the final assault at Yorktown.[52]

The war Hamilton had wished for as a boy had brought only frustration, bitterness, and disillusionment. His youthful idealism was gone. Henceforth the great revolutionary republican and soldier would assume an entirely different public posture.

The Bitter Lessons of Experience

Despite his frustration and disillusionment, Hamilton had learned valuable lessons from his wartime experience. These lessons would inform his subsequent political career and mold his statesmanship as both a founding father and a leading light of Washington's Federalist administration. Two themes unified these lessons. The first was the need for sober realism in political discourse. If the fledgling experiment in American national self-government was to succeed, it would require a painstakingly honest, frank assessment of the challenges it faced and the resources it could draw on. The second theme was responsibility. Political leaders must be accountable for their actions. They must resist the temptation to pander to the popular prejudices and passions of the electorate. They must not promise more than they can deliver. And they must ensure that government has the power to deliver what they have promised.

The most obvious lesson Hamilton drew from his military travails was the inadequacy of his own republican convictions. The republicanism of the revolutionary movement had been an opposition creed, one well suited to resist the "usurpations of tyranny." Understandably, public opinion was animated by "an extreme spirit of jealousy" of centralized power. Unfortunately, although this jealousy or "zeal of liberty" was natural, it had become "predominant and excessive." "An extreme jealousy of power is the attendant on all popular revolutions," Hamilton averred, yet it "has seldom been without its evils." Republican fears of central authority had led to the great defect that had crippled the war effort and "endangered the common cause," namely "A WANT OF POWER IN CONGRESS." The republican vision may have been adequate for arousing the public's attention to the dangers of British imperial policy, but it was not suited "to the government of an INDEPENDENT NATION." Popular liberty was not the only goal of statecraft; just as important was "strength and stability in the organization of our government, and vigor in its operation." This, alas, "our enthusiasm rendered us little capable of regarding." Such strength and vigor would have to be cultivated if the new nation was to reap the fruits of its independence.[53]

An equally important lesson of Hamilton's wartime experience, learned as early as 1781, was that the power of the states posed a danger to the union. It was true that in unified nations the people had just cause to fear the power of centralized authority. But in federal schemes of the American variety, the real danger was that the states "will be an overmatch for the common head," and as a consequence, the central organs of government "will not have sufficient authority to secure the obedience of the several parts of the confederacy." At the federal Constitutional Convention, Hamilton observed that "the states have constantly shewn a disposition rather to regain the powers delegated by them than to part with more, or to give effect to what they had parted with." The emasculation of the union not only resulted in national impotence, it also opened the prospect of potential civil wars between the states. Given the profound sectional differences in the United States at the time, this was a very real danger, as events demonstrated tragically some fourscore years later.[54]

Nor was civil conflict the only danger the power of the states posed to the body politic. Demagoguery was itself a threat to republican liberty. "History will teach us," Hamilton warned, that "those men who have overturned the liberties of republics" generally rose to power "by paying an obsequious court to the people, commencing Demagogues and ending Tyrants." The classic examples from Roman history were the *populares* Lucius Sergius Catiline and Julius Caesar; Hamilton insisted that such men were "to be found in every republic." By "leading the dance to the tune of liberty without law," popular demagogues delude the people and "render them the easier victims of their rapacious ambition." The real threat to the "republican system of the Country," Hamilton told Washington, was from popular state demagogues who produced political "confusion" and "civil commotion" by "flattering the prejudices of the people, and exciting their jealousies and apprehensions" of the national government.[55]

If political realism entailed an honest assessment of the dangers of state power, then political responsibility demanded the avowal of the ethical truism that *ought* implies *can*. If a government is to be charged with certain tasks and duties, it must be armed with the requisite authority and resources to discharge those duties. Means must be matched to ends, and not the other way around. For Hamilton, this was one of those "primary truths or first principles upon which all subsequent reasonings must depend." Just as geometry was based on self-evident axioms, political science depended on fundamental "maxims," like "there cannot be an effect without a cause" and "the means ought to be proportioned to the end." These maxims in turn entailed that "every power ought to be commensurate with its object" and that "there ought to be no limitation of a power destined to effect a purpose," especially when that purpose, like the security and general welfare of a nation, "is itself incapable of limitation." Here lay the real problem with the Articles of Confederation created during the struggle for independence: it had placed "the great interests of the nation" in "hands incapable of managing them."[56]

Congress had been given the authority to contract debts without the means of discharging them. It was entrusted with securing treaties without the authority to execute them. Most disturbing of all, it was charged with the "common defense" but lacked the power to "raise troops— have a fleet—raise money" or deploy any of the other means necessary to secure "the public peace." "These great interests must be well managed," Hamilton insisted at the Constitutional Convention, "or the public prosperity must be the victim." This same message that *ought* implies *can* applied to the convention itself. "The states sent us here to provide for the exigencies of the Union," he reminded his fellow delegates. To embrace a plan of government that fell short of those exigencies "merely because it was not clearly within our powers" to address them more fully "would be to sacrifice the means to the end."[57]

Perhaps the most important lesson Hamilton learned from his revolutionary experience was the true basis of government. Hamilton had entered the war a wide-eyed idealist whose democratic convictions entailed the belief that political authority rested exclusively on the will of the majority. The struggle for independence disabused him of this belief. "The people are turbulent and changing," he insisted, and "seldom judge or determine right." Instead, Hamilton came to see that government depended on three critical factors.[58]

The first foundations of government were finance and revenue. These were the sinews of state power. In the spring of 1781 he wrote to Robert Morris that independence would not be secured "by gaining battles" but by "introducing order into our finances." Hamilton hammered this point home in *The Federalist*. The modern "science of finance" had "produced an intire revolution in the system of war." It had replaced the armed camps of citizen-soldiers of the classical age with "disciplined armies, distinct from the body of the citizens." More than merely the means of modern warfare, however, finance was "the vital principle of the body politic," the resource that "sustains its life and motion, and enables it to perform its most essential functions." The power to procure revenue in an orderly and efficient fashion was therefore "an indispensable ingredient in every constitution." Money made the state go 'round.[59]

The second foundation of government was interest. As a young revolutionary, Hamilton had joined in calls for republican disinterestedness in the public sphere. Now he found such injunctions visionary. "We may preach till we are tired" of the "necessity of disinterestedness in republics," he wrote in "The Continentalist," "without making a single proselyte." Such calls to virtue will never convince any public official to "be content with a double mess of porridge, instead of a reasonable stipend for his services." The interest, indeed the self-interest, of officeholders, bureaucrats, and financiers was one of "the great and essential principles necessary for the support of Government." It was the need for this vital support that had prompted Hamilton while in the Continental Congress to urge that national revenues should only be collected by "officers under the appointment of Congress." Such an arrangement would strengthen the central government because those officeholders would know what side their bread was buttered on. Interest made the personal political.[60]

Finally, the third critical support of government was public opinion. Here, as in so many other points, Hamilton drew on the inspiration of that archetypal enlightenment thinker, David Hume. Hume had argued that opinion was one of the "first principles of government." In even the most despotic state, the resources of the rulers were never a match for those of the ruled. "As force is always on the side of the governed," Hume concluded that "the governors have nothing to support them but opinion." Hence his maxim that it is "on opinion only that government is founded." When public opinion did not believe that a regime had the right to rule, that regime was robbed of legitimacy and rested on a precarious foundation.[61]

This was precisely the point Hamilton made at the Constitutional Convention in Philadelphia. The public opinion of the "necessity and utility" of an administration and constitutional scheme was one of the basic "principles of civil obedience" and one of the essential "supports of government." Hamilton reiterated this claim one year later at New York's ratifying convention for the new federal Constitution. "All governments, even the most despotic," he insisted, "depend, in a great degree, on opinion." This was particularly true of republics. "In these, the will of the people makes the essential principle of the government," he argued, "and the laws which control the community, receive their tone and spirit from the public wishes." Yet public opinion was not a fixed datum. It was moved by changing circumstances and could be informed by public debate. Hamilton would devote much of his subsequent efforts as a public polemicist to molding and marshaling the opinion of the young republic along lines that were both realistic and responsible.[62]

THE HAMILTONIAN VISION:
THE ENLIGHTENMENT FULFILLED

Hamilton's vision for America was the most modern and progressive in the new republic. He saw the prospect of a nation both powerful and prosperous, whose resources were deployed by an enlightened government to promote domestic tranquillity and the general welfare. Hamilton's projected America was a place much like his beloved New York City, bursting with economic activity, a nation whose future power rested on urban and industrial development. He envisioned a worldly and wealthy nation that faced modernity foursquare and embraced it unflinchingly. Hamilton's vision was the fulfillment of the politics of Enlightenment.

The sources of Hamilton's vision were broad and diverse. He read widely into eighteenth-century history, sociology, political theory, and economics. He pored over Malachy Postlethwayt's *Universal Dictionary of Trade and Commerce* to learn the intricacies of international trade. He studied the history of banking from Renaissance Venice and seventeenth-century Holland to the Bank of England and the French schemes of financiers like John Law, Anne-Robert Turgot, and Jacques Necker. The evolution of modern society was culled from authors as varied as Adam Ferguson, Thomas Hobbes, John Locke, William Robertson, and Adam Smith. But one figure loomed larger than all the others: David Hume exercised an influence on Hamilton's vision greater than that of any other author. It was from Hume that he learned of the central role that commercial capitalism played in the evolution of modern society. And it was Hume who taught him to appreciate the necessity of worldly realism in political thought. Hume showed him that what republican ideologues castigated as corruption was an ineradicable, indeed essential, component of modern politics. Commercial capitalism and self-interested "corruption" would form two of the three critical components of the Hamiltonian vision.

Hamilton also drew on his own personal experience. It was the failure of the states and the Continental Congress to honestly address the realities of self-interested political behavior that had crippled the war effort, starving the Continental Army and jeopardizing the struggle for independence. Similarly, it was commercial capitalism that gave energy and force to the life of Manhattan. And it was commercial capitalism, after all, that afforded poor men like Hamilton the opportunity to move up in the world. What had really set Hamilton's career on a meteoric path, however, was not merely commercial activity but the high cultural expertise that came from education. King's College had exposed him to the philosophical and political tracts that gave him the theoretical insights he put to use as a military aide, lawyer, congressman, and state legislator. Education made Hamilton both a gentleman and a leading statesman of the new republic. This awareness of the importance of high cultural expertise informed the third component of Hamilton's vision of American politics, namely the role of the enlightened intellectual as statesman in a republican government. It was the role of the philosophe, combined with the importance of commerce and corruption, that defined Hamilton's contribution to the politics of Enlightenment in the American strand.

The Virtues of Commercial Activity

"The prosperity of commerce," Hamilton announced in *Federalist* number 12, was one of the most important goals of modern statecraft. Despite the fact that this was "now perceived and acknowledged by all enlightened statesmen," Hamilton knew it was a hard sell to make to the overwhelmingly agricultural citizenry of the United States. Urban entrepôts like Charleston, Baltimore, Philadelphia, Manhattan, and Boston may have been vital to the economic life of the nation, but they represented a tiny fraction of the population. Country folk often viewed the sharp trading practices of urban tradesmen and merchants with suspicion. It was vital for Hamilton to allay these suspicions, for commerce lay at the heart of his vision for America.[63]

Trade did more than circulate goods and capital throughout society. It was the primary object of taxation and thus the essential resource of government. Without a regular and predictable supply of revenue, government must either resort to plundering the property of the people or "sink into a fatal apathy, and in a short course of time perish." No calls for public-spirited sacrifice could ever replace the need for the revenues government drew from commercial activity.[64]

The rise of commerce and the revenues it generated for government had enabled modern nations to fund professional armies and navies. Without such military forces, no nation could hope to defend itself from foreign predation. The genius of commercial capitalism had given rise to "the science of finance" and banking, and national banking both reinforced commercial development and promoted the power of modern nation-states. Nowhere was this more apparent than in England, the most commercially advanced and powerful state in Europe. Without its remarkable commercial activity and nationally chartered bank, "England would never have found sufficient funds to carry on her wars," Hamilton remarked, "but with the help of this she has done, and is doing wonders." Commercial development could work the same wonders for America.[65]

Commerce did more than contribute to the strength of the nation: it also ensured its liberties. Confident of a steady stream of revenues from taxes on trade, government had no need to plunder the property of its citizens, and the security of private property was an essential buttress of personal independence and freedom. Indeed, one of the central themes of Scottish social theory from Adam Smith and Adam Ferguson to David Hume and William Robertson had been the role of commerce in producing modern liberty. It was the rise of commerce that had destroyed the baronial despotism of the feudal epoch, redistributing property from the landed aristocracy to the urban tradesman and the people at large, a point Hamilton made at the New York ratifying convention for the federal Constitution. "As commerce enlarged," he informed his fellow delegates, "wealth and civilization encreased," slowly illuminating the darkness that had prevailed during the medieval era. In time "the people began to feel their own weight and consequence" as a result of their newfound commercial wealth. "They grew tired of their oppressions" and, joining forces with their monarchs, "threw off the yoke of aristocracy." Freedom and commerce went hand in glove.[66]

Adam Smith had taught that commerce was the prime cause of the wealth of nations. Trade promoted markets and demand. These in turn promoted the division of labor, the principal cause of the growth of human productivity. Hume had made a similar claim in his defense of the "refinement in the arts" in commercial society. When commerce enlivened the mechanical arts, "men are kept in perpetual occupation" to secure "the fruits of their labour" in purchasable commodities. The availability of those trade goods, whether luxuries or necessities, was thus a spur to industry. Hamilton made that same argument in *The Federalist*. "By multiplying the means of gratification," commerce helped "vivify and invigorate channels of industry," making them "flow with greater activity and copiousness." Such activity would clearly benefit urban tradesmen and merchants. Just as important, however, it would spur "the active mechanic and industrious manufacturer." Even farmers were prompted to greater exertions when commerce made desirable goods available for purchase, just as they benefited from "a more certain and steady demand for the surplus produce of the soil." This spur to industry was no small benefit for American society. With the growth of commercial activity, "all orders of men look forward with eager expectation" to the "pleasing rewards of their toils." The rising tide of trade lifted all ships, silencing the age-old rivalry between merchants and farmers.[67]

The virtues of commerce were not merely pragmatic, however. Enlightened philosophes had long held that commerce was a humanistic force for social uplift and enlightenment. As commerce spread, it gave rise to an increasing division of labor, as Smith had stressed, leading to both increased efficiency in production and a greater range of potential forms of employment. Hume further argued that, immersed in the diverse activities of a commercial society, "the mind acquires new vigour" and thus "enlarges its powers and faculties." This was one of the principal virtues of commerce, as Hamilton stressed in his *Report on Manufactures*. Commerce, and the manufactures it supported, not only resulted in "a more ample and various field for enterprise," it also enriched the opportunities of laborers by "furnishing greater scope for the diversity of talents and dispositions which discriminate men from each other." Nor was it merely incidental that commercial activity itself inculcated rational habits of thought. Means had to be matched to ends, risks calculated and balanced against rewards, and consequences foreseen before actions were taken. Such instrumental rationality, even in the pursuit of narrow self-interest, was a vital part of the general process of Enlightenment. Not surprisingly, Hamilton often referred to those most deeply entrenched in the web of commerce—urban tradesmen in general and merchants in particular—as "that enlightened class of citizens." The font of power, liberty, wealth, and Enlightenment, commerce lay at the center of the Hamiltonian vision.[68]

The Case for "Corruption"

Thomas Jefferson grossly exaggerated when he claimed that Hamilton was "under thorough conviction that corruption was essential to the government of a nation." Hamilton deeply deplored the abuse of office for pecuniary gain, as his wartime denunciation of Samuel Chase demonstrated. Bribery, profiteering, and graft by public officials were anathema to him. Yet Jefferson was not entirely wide of the mark. The cry of corruption was the great shibboleth of republican ideologues. The charge included far more than malfeasance in office. Corruption also encompassed ambitious political behavior, factional partisanship, and even the pursuit of local and self-interest. In short, any public action that was not purely and selflessly motivated by the imagined public good was proscribed as corrupt. Although bribery and abuse of office were beyond the pale for Hamilton, he did believe that corruption in the broader sense was indeed "essential to the government of a nation." Hamilton's case for corruption marked him as the most enlightened and modern statesman of the new republic.[69]

Hamilton's case for corruption was based on the psychological tenets of enlightened philosophy that were characterized by a worldly reevaluation of the role of the passions. Traditional Christian doctrine held that the passions—such as pride, lust, ambition, and desire—were the source of humanity's sinful dispositions, and thus required resistance from the pious conscience fortified by divine grace. Seventeenth-century Rationalists decried the passions as the cause of error and superstition that needed to be reined in by the ruling power of reason. In stark contrast, the philosophes of the Enlightenment saw the role of the passions in a far more positive light. On the one hand, they denied the Rationalist notion that reason had the power to suppress or govern the passions. Reason was instrumental and calculative. It could match means to ends but was incapable of arriving at ends on its own. On the other hand, they rejected the Christian view of the passions as inherently sinful. Passion and desire were natural and were the essential and generally salutary seat of human motivation and action. Hume summed up this enlightened view in his famous dictum that "reason is, and ought only to be the slave of the passions, and can never pretend to any other office than to serve and obey them."[70]

Hamilton stressed the importance of this enlightened and realistic view of human psychology at the Constitutional Convention. "Take mankind as they are, and what are they governed by?" The answer was obvious: "their passions." It was a "great error," he warned, to "suppose mankind more honest than they are." This was particularly true in the political realm, where the "prevailing passions are ambition and interest." Hume had made this point at the outset of his essay "Of the Independency of Parliament." Although it was not true in all cases, political prudence demanded that "every man ought to be supposed a *knave*, and to have no other end, in all his actions, than private interest." Through taking such interests into account, the individual could be made to serve the public good, "notwithstanding his insatiable avarice and ambition." Specifically citing this passage from Hume, Hamilton drove the argument home to his fellow delegates: "It will ever be the duty of a wise government to avail itself" of the passions of ambition and interest. The real challenge was to "make them subservient to the public good."[71]

To avail itself of these passions, government needed to acknowledge the importance of "influence." Far from considering influence corrupt,

Hamilton believed it was one of the essential "supports of government." Indeed, the new federal government must have sufficient influence to overcome the power of the states. As things stood, the great passions of "avarice, ambition, interest," passions that "govern most individuals, and all public bodies," all "fall into the current of the States." Only the states had lucrative offices to confer and revenues to attract creditors. If the federal government was to survive, it needed influence of its own.[72]

Hamilton had seen this as early as 1780, when he argued that a congressional award to army officers of a pension of half pay for life "would be a great stroke of policy, and would give Congress a stronger tie upon them, than any thing else they can do." Seven years of increasing state encroachment on the power of the national government had only confirmed Hamilton in his view. The federal government must have enough influence "to interest all the *passions* of individuals."[73]

Using "all the passions of individuals" to support the new federal government required an honest assessment of the various interests that divided the body politic. "Society naturally divides itself into two political divisions," Hamilton informed his fellow delegates, "the *few* and the *many*." The few were, of course, "the rich and well born," while the many were "the mass of the people." Neither had a monopoly of virtue, and either would "tyrannize" the other if allowed to dominate the government. The obvious solution was to place political power "in the hands of both." This power ought to be separated into different bodies of the government, and "this separation must be permanent." The few, rather than the states, should be represented in the Senate. Only then could it serve as a "principle in government capable of resisting the popular current." The many would be represented in the House. To resist the tyranny of the few, the House "should be on a broad foundation" and as democratic as possible. In fact, Hamilton feared that the representation outlined in the Constitution for the House was not sufficiently democratic.[74]

In any event, both the few and the many must have a separate and permanent voice in the government where they could be assured that their interests would be considered. Each of these voices required a "mutual check" in the executive—ideally a monarch, as in Great Britain. Hamilton sang the praises of the British Constitution, "not as a thing attainable by us, but as a model which we ought to approach as near as possible." Hamilton was fully aware that the American people would never tolerate either monarchy or hereditary aristocracy. Nonetheless his defense of the British Constitution at Philadelphia forced his fellow delegates to broaden their debate beyond the competing Virginia and New Jersey Plans, the former of which would have benefited the large states while the latter favored the smaller ones. Hamilton's arguments may have shocked and scandalized many at the convention, but few failed to see his point. Although such a scheme was impractical for the new nation, it forced the founders to recognize that no pure ideal could be realized. Instead, as Hamilton insisted, calculating interests required a spirit of compromise and realistic accommodation in constitutional design.[75]

Calculating different interests was also essential for formulating government policy. Although Hamilton insisted that the presumed rivalry between commerce and agriculture was illusory, he was not so naïve as to assume that fiscal and tax policy would not have different impacts on different segments of the nation. No policy, "however salutary to the whole and to every part" of society, can fail to be more to the "benefit of some parts, than of others." The key to prudent policy was to balance interests and overcome sectional and class jealousies.[76]

On no issue was this key more vital than that of putting the financial credit of the nation on a sure footing. The establishment of public credit was "the great *desideratum*," Hamilton informed Washington, and was the only means to "supply the future wants of government." Yet building public credit required the cooperation and support of those with surplus capital and cash. Appealing to their patriotism was hopeless. As early as 1780, Hamilton concluded that "the only certain manner" of establishing the credit of the nation was "to engage the monied interest immediately in it." The only way to "engage" the "monied," and induce them to supply credit to the government, was to make it in their own selfish interest by "giving them the whole or part of the profits." Establishing public credit was vital to the nation and its future economic prosperity, but it would require further enriching the wealthiest Americans. This, in fact, proved an extremely delicate and politically difficult task. Although Hamilton's financial projects as secretary of the Treasury did establish the credit of the nation and led to dramatic commercial expansion, they also lined the pockets of financiers and speculators, a class of individuals most morally suspect to a nation of farmers.[77]

Hamilton and Hamiltonians ever since have been accused of being the servants of the wealthy. That Hamilton's policies benefited the financial capitalists of the new nation is certainly true. But that he was their servant is far more dubious. Hamilton enriched the nation's creditors, but he also used them to pursue his own vision of America's future. That can be seen most clearly by examining the role of intellectuals in his politics of Enlightenment.

The Role of the Philosophes

At the Constitutional Convention, Hamilton had divided the political community into the wealthy few and the common many. In *Federalist* number 35, however, he offered a far more nuanced analysis of American political society. On the one hand, there was the urban commercial interest of artisans, manufacturers, shopkeepers, and merchants. On the other hand, there was the rural-agricultural interest. This interest would be represented by large-scale landlords and planters. Urban commerce and rural agriculture did not, however, exhaust the principal divisions within the body politic. Hamilton noted the presence of a third, vital element within the body politic: the learned professions.[78]

Lawyers, doctors, and other educated intellectuals who derived their income from their high cultural expertise formed a distinct stratum within the political community. Unlike the landed and commercial interests, however, enlightened intellectuals lacked a distinct interest of their own. Indeed, they were distinguished by their very disinterestedness, making them the natural arbiters of the public good. Disinterested and informed by enlightened views, the learned intellectuals were the critical arbiters of the national interest, balancing the wishes of commerce and agriculture on behalf of the general welfare. The philosophes were thus the critical political check and balance to both the monied and the landed, the "Platonic guardians" of the American republic.[79]

Hamilton envisioned a distinct place for the learned in all three branches of the federal government. Within the legislature, they would find their voice as an important component of the Senate. Unlike the popular representatives of the people in the House, senators required "greater knowledge and more extensive information," a requirement that could be fulfilled only by high cultural expertise. Lacking a distinct interest of their own, the educated elite "will be less apt to be tainted by the spirit of faction." Moreover, they would be insulated from "those occasional ill humors or temporary prejudices" that "contaminate the public councils" and thus "beget injustice and oppression of a part of the community." This was a vital role for the learned in the legislature, for although such "prejudices" often "gratify a momentary inclination or desire," they invariably result in "general distress, dissatisfaction and disgust." Only the presence of enlightened intellectuals in the Senate could curtail this threat.[80]

For Hamilton, whereas the learned would make up just one element of the legislature, they were to fill the entire judiciary. Republican government demanded an extensive and "voluminous code of laws." In addition, it required that the federal judiciary be "bound down by strict rules and precedents" in order to "avoid an arbitrary discretion in the courts." Such laws and precedents would quickly "swell to a very considerable bulk" and would therefore "demand long and laborious study to acquire a competent knowledge of them." Only the most learned and distinguished jurisprudential scholars in the nation would "have sufficient skill in the laws to qualify them for the stations of judges" in the federal courts. To attract such legal expertise to the federal branch, Hamilton insisted that they be offered tenure for life. Already at the apex of the legal profession, anything less "would naturally discourage such characters from quitting a lucrative line of practice."[81]

Moreover, the review of the federal judiciary over the laws of the land must be final and decisive. To allow for legislative or popular review of the laws would be to subject "the decisions of men selected for their knowledge of the laws," knowledge "acquired by long and laborious study," Hamilton insisted, "to the revision and control of men, who for want of the same advantage cannot but be deficient in that knowledge." Only an independent and learned judiciary could ensure the practice of justice and equity and check the partisan passions of the people. Like the censors of Republican Rome, the legal scholars of the new republic would speak law and justice to the nation at large.[82]

Higher education and learning were also vital requirements for several offices within the executive branch. Obviously, the attorney general required the same level of legal expertise as that found in the federal judiciary. The secretary of state also demanded high cultural expertise. The management of foreign affairs entailed extensive knowledge of political affairs abroad as well as diplomatic and treaty history. More than that, it also necessitated a thorough immersion in the abstract philosophical literature dealing with the law of nations. But Hamilton singled out one executive office in particular as requiring ample high cultural training. That was, of course, the very office he himself assumed, the secretary of the Treasury. There was, he insisted, "no part of the administration of government" that required such "extensive information." The management of the Treasury entailed a complete mastery of finance, commerce, and taxation. The revenues of the government hinged on such mastery as well as the commercial prosperity of the nation. As such, a Treasury secretary must have "a thorough knowledge of the principles of political economy" as well as a practical grasp of "the business of taxation." Knowledge was power, and only with knowledge and learning could the new federal frame of government fulfill its promise.[83]

Understanding the role of the learned in Hamilton's enlightened vision of America sheds new light on his policies within Washington's Federalist administration. Hamilton's opponents accused him of simply serving the interests of speculators and financiers, the nascent financial bourgeoisie of the young republic. Many historians have seconded this charge.

Hamilton was certainly solicitous of "the men of property in America": they were "enlightened about their own interest," he explained to Robert

Morris, "and would easily be brought to see the advantages of a good plan." Yet Hamilton used the financiers every bit as much as he served their interests. Indeed, he served their interests precisely because he knew that that was the only way to secure their financial resources for the benefit of the government. Hamilton sought to use the nation's small financial community not only to secure public credit but to promote commercial and industrial expansion as well. He was fully aware that market forces on their own were insufficient to achieve these goals. Their fulfillment required the strong hand of an activist government.[84]

Unlike subsequent boosters of American business, Hamilton was no fan of laissez-faire. Commercial expansion and rapid industrialization were vital American goals, and Hamilton sought to achieve them through a powerful, activist federal government. Hamilton practiced the American variant of what the scholar Barrington Moore referred to as "the Prussian road to modernity." Commercial and industrial development would be imposed from above by a strong centralized state. Two features distinguished the Hamiltonian vision from that of the conservative leaders of Prussia and Germany. First, its Constitution was committed to a popular and pluralist republican form of government rather than an absolutist monarchy. Second, the republic would be led, in part at least, by enlightened philosophes rather than hereditary monarchs and landed Junker aristocrats. Whatever similarities exist between Hamilton's and Bismarck's statism and practice of worldly *réal politique*, a fundamental distinction remains. Hamilton was a child of the Enlightenment, not of European reaction. His vision of America represented the achievement of its central goals.[85]

THE PRACTICE OF HAMILTONIANISM

For all its theoretical brilliance, Hamilton knew that his enlightened vision for America was useless if it could not be translated into political practice. Encapsulating his goals into functioning policies and legislative acts was the great challenge of his career once the federal Constitution had been adopted. His response to that challenge was informed both by the worldly realism of his enlightened politics and by the lessons of responsibility he culled from his military experiences.

As President George Washington's secretary of the Treasury, Hamilton's primary responsibility was to repair the shattered credit of the nation and put the new government on a sound financial footing. This proved a Herculean task. The nation was deeply in debt, and a slumping economy offered the prospect of relatively modest revenues. Moreover, financial policy on a national scale was an alarmingly novel phenomenon in America at the time, and one that understandably provoked differing and partisan responses from the diverse social and economic interests that made up the young republic.

Hamilton's influence extended well beyond the realms of finance and revenue. Hamilton had a decisive role in formulating foreign policy. This too was a task fraught with difficulties. At every turn he found himself at loggerheads with Secretary of State Thomas Jefferson, who enjoyed both Washington's confidence and respect. The eruption of the French Revolution just as the new federal government was being organized at the close of the 1780s further complicated matters. Partisan splits began to coalesce over attitudes toward the revolutionary movement across the Atlantic. Federalists condemned its excesses and increasingly saw Great Britain as a bulwark of order in an alarmingly anarchic international order. In stark contrast, Jeffersonian Republicans celebrated the cause and victories of revolutionary France and vilified Britain's hostility to the new order as evidence of hopeless corruption and reactionary monarchical principles.

Perhaps most pervasively, Hamilton was pivotal in the process we have now come to know as nation building. More than any other member of Washington's cabinet, he transformed the federal government from an abstract constitutional frame into a concrete political reality. His policies projected the power of the nation both at home and abroad, giving it, in a few short years, a psychological reality and weight that was truly impressive. His broad construction of the Constitution ensured the ascendancy of the national government over the states. It also delineated a powerful role for the judiciary within that government. Both of these developments were deeply controversial in their day and have remained so in our own time. Arguably, neither would have happened but for the efforts of the young secretary of the Treasury.

Financial Solutions

As Treasury secretary, Alexander Hamilton submitted several reports to Congress, three of which have had a profound impact on the practice of American government. The first addressed the problem of the national debt and the means to establish the public credit. The second detailed a plan for a national bank closely modeled on the Bank of England. The third encapsulated Hamilton's proposals for a national industrial policy to promote manufacturing. Although submitted separately, the three reports were interrelated parts of Hamilton's fiscal and economic policy for the young republic. Immensely detailed, closely reasoned, and filled with statistical tables, the reports were nonetheless far more than simple statements of economic data and fact. They were argumentative, almost pugnaciously so. They thoroughly challenged the conventional wisdom of the day. The most important and influential state papers of their time, they remain among the most brilliant government reports in American history.[86]

Their genius lay in the way they built upon one another, each succeeding report drawing upon the conclusions of the previous ones. Two scholarly collaborators have characterized this technique as "projection," "an ordering of facts and circumstances into patterns which present conditions have not as yet made actual but which future ones will." Hamilton's projection outlined much of the nation's fiscal policy for his time and its economic destiny for the centuries that followed.[87]

Funding and Assumption

Hamilton's first report, submitted in mid-January 1790, focused on the problem of securing the credit of the nation. The new federal government had inherited a staggering burden of debt. The Continental

Congress had borrowed roughly $10 million from foreign public and private sources to help pay for the war effort, none of which had been repaid. Indeed, arrears in scheduled interest and principal payments had ballooned the total foreign debt to almost $13 million. Hamilton calculated the cost of servicing the foreign debt at roughly $1 million per year, a sum that virtually exhausted projected revenues from tariffs and excise taxes on spirituous liquors and luxury goods. An additional $40 million was due to domestic creditors through a combination of loan office certificates, army certificates, various securities, and accruing arrears of unpaid interest. Financing the domestic debt was further complicated by two factors. First, the lack of an independent source of revenue had forced the Continental Congress to borrow at the then-high rate of six percent interest. Second, the federal government would have to compete with the states for tax revenues to retire the debt since the states themselves had borrowed about $25 million to pay for the war. These debts were also contracted at six percent interest. Combined, the annual interest due on foreign, national, and state debts was a whopping $4.5 million dollars—three times the projected revenue of the federal government. Hamilton had his work cut out for him.[88]

Hamilton's solution was bold and innovative. The federal government would not only fund the inherited national debt, it would also assume the burdens incurred by the states. The new nation would then commence with a staggering debt of over $76 million. The funding of the debt would be made manageable by renegotiating the rate of interest from six to four percent. Creditors were offered a variety of terms of settlement, from strict payment at the original rates to reissued securities at the lower rate of interest that could serve as annuities. Since "probabilities are always a rational ground of contract," Hamilton reasoned that if sufficient taxes were imposed to cover the lower rate of interest, most investors would opt for the safe annuities. The rest of the debt could be purchased by the federal government with funds borrowed from European investors at the lower rate of four percent interest. Once the large Dutch and English banking houses saw that America was committed to honoring its debts and had imposed sufficient taxes to meet its commitments, Hamilton assumed that the nation's public credit would be restored and foreign capital would be obtainable on favorable terms, an assumption that was fully borne out within one year of the passage of his scheme.[89]

Hamilton's financial plan was not quite a Ponzi scheme, though it looked that way to its critics. It was, however, a precarious project that rested on the most slender of supports, namely the public opinion of speculative investors that could create a favorable climate for investment in government securities. To secure this public opinion, Hamilton proposed sufficiently high taxes to assure regular payments of interest. He also called for the creation of a sinking fund. Sinking funds were a well-established part of British national finance whereby specific tax revenues were earmarked for the purchase of particular contracted debts. This assured investors that they would be repaid, which in turn ensured that they would continue to lend to the government. Hamilton's sinking fund would draw on revenues generated from the post office to purchase outstanding debt. Its purpose, however, was not to actually retire the debt but to ensure that government securities continued to trade at par, thus reinforcing the impression in capital markets that the American government was an excellent investment. This in turn would mean that the government could borrow at low interest rates, which in itself enhanced the perceived creditworthiness of the nation.[90]

The brilliance of Hamilton's plan was that it turned an immense liability—the public debt—into an equally large boon. It did so because, if properly funded and transformed into "an object of established confidence," the public debt could serve as capital, the one element the resource-rich nation sorely lacked. Once public credit had been established by creating investor confidence, government securities would be treated as legal tender and thus "transfers of stock of public debt" would become "equivalent to payments in specie." And once government debt was sufficiently creditworthy that it "passes current as specie," the nation would enjoy a dramatic increase in its money supply.[91]

Increasing the money supply would have manifold economic benefits. Commerce would boom "because there is a larger capital to carry it on." This in turn meant that merchants making more frequent trans-actions could "afford to trade for smaller profits," thus cutting prices for consumers. Indeed, stock in government debt was even better than specie for the merchant, for "when unemployed" it did not sit idly but continued to accrue "an interest from the government." The increased money supply would also help both agriculture and manufacturing since "more capital can be commanded to be employed in both." Agriculture would also benefit from a boost in land values. Hamilton calculated that southern land values had fallen by 20 to 25 percent, even more in some parts of South Carolina and Georgia. Since most of this decline was "at-tributed to the scarcity of money," increasing the money supply by funding the debt "must have a proportionate effect in raising that value." Not only would more money be available, but the cost of bor-rowing it would be reduced, "for this is always in a ratio, to the quantity of money, and the quickness of circulation." This spur to commercial and agricultural prosperity would in turn make the taxes necessary to manage the debt less burdensome. In its simplest terms, Hamilton's pro-jection was that, given time and the right circumstances, America could grow its way out of debt.[92]

For all its brilliance, Hamilton's plan was deeply controversial. At the time Hamilton took office, government securities were trading at 20 to 25 percent of their face value. Funding them at par, even at a reduced rate of interest, would thus represent an immense windfall profit for those who held those securities. Much of that debt had been issued to Continental soldiers in lieu of pay and to farmers as compensation for goods taken to provision the army. In the intervening years, however, al-most three-quarters of those securities had been purchased by largely northern speculators, derisively called "stockjobbers" or bloodsuckers. Indeed, shortly after ratification of the federal Constitution, northern stockjobbers dispatched boatloads of agents to the southern and western states to purchase outstanding securities at a deep discount, betting that the government would fund them at par.[93]

Many congressmen, particularly those from southern and western states, favored what became known as discrimination. Discrimination meant repaying stockjobbers only what they had paid for the securities they held and returning the bulk of the profits to their original holders. Many southern congressmen also objected to the assumption of state debts on the grounds that their states (especially Virginia) had already retired most of their debts. Assumption and funding, they claimed, would effectively transfer wealth from the southern and western states to the commercial centers of the north and east. Behind such rhetoric lay more tangible, if sordid, interests. With independence, the states had acquired title to vast domains previously held by the crown. Many wealthy southerners and westerners speculated heavily in these lands, using continental and state securities as collateral. The state governments accepted these securities at par although they were purchased at a fraction of their nominal value. Although funding and assumption would increase the value of the lands, it would also mean that the purchase price that such land speculators had contracted for would be substantially increased. As Hamilton wryly observed some years later, "many of the noisy Patriots" who denounced stockjobbing were in fact "land-jobbers, and have a becoming tenderness for this species of extravagance."[94]

Hamilton objected to discrimination on the grounds that it was both unjust and impolitic. It was unjust because it constituted a clear "breach of contract." Hamilton explained that the government had issued securities on the stipulation that it would "pay the sum expressed" to either "the first holder, or its assignee." That some original holders had been forced by hardship to sell their securities at a great discount was undeniable, but it was the failure of the government to secure the public credit that had caused that hardship, not the greed of the purchaser. Discrimination was impolitic both because it destroyed the debt's capacity to serve as capital and "it introduces a breach of faith" with the current holders of the debt. In so doing it "renders property in the funds less valuable," which in turn would force "lenders to demand a higher premium for what they lend." The ultimate result would be all the "inconvenience of a bad state of public credit," one of the principal weaknesses of the previous confederation that had prompted the federalist movement in the first place.[95]

An ultimately unworkable plan, discrimination was easily defeated, and Hamilton's funding scheme found fairly smooth passage through Congress. The assumption of state debts was another matter. Hamilton noted that assuming the state debts would not cost any more than leaving them to the states, since they had to be paid in any event. The real question was whether such expenditure could be "more conveniently and effectually made, by one general plan" from the federal government or by a variety of "different plans" formulated by the various states. The latter course, Hamilton objected, would lead to a struggle over tax revenues between the states and the central government. Far more serious was the effect that failure to assume the state debts would have on public creditors. If the public creditors were divided between the federal and state governments, they would have distinct interests, some favoring the central and others the state establishments. Instead of "that union and concert of views, among the creditors"—one that "in every government is of great importance to their security, and to that of public credit"—there would be "mutual jealousy and opposition." The likely consequence would be that the fiscal and tax policies of the federal government "will be in danger of being counteracted" by the states and their wealthy creditors. Funding the national debt without assumption was a recipe for fiscal disaster.[96]

Despite the cogency of his arguments, Hamilton was unable to ensure passage of assumption. Ultimately he was reduced to political horse-trading with Secretary of State Thomas Jefferson and Speaker of the House James Madison at an infamous dinner held in the summer of 1790. The two Virginians extracted two very large concessions. The first was that Hamilton must help them secure removal of the federal government from Manhattan to Philadelphia for a ten-year interim, and then to its permanent and present site, a swampy morass not far from the falls of the Potomac where Madison had substantial real estate investments. Their second condition was that Hamilton ensure a readjustment of the state debts that would net Virginia over $13 million. It was a high price to pay, but with the passage of funding and assumption Hamilton had set his financial plan into operation. At long last the nation's credit would be secure. The Hamiltonian vision was becoming a reality.[97]

The Bank of the United States and the Report on Manufactures

Hamilton's first report had argued that a funded debt could be turned into capital. How that was to be achieved, however, was only intimated at the end of the report. Because Hamilton issued federal securities in notes for their full value—their denominations were far too large to circulate as cash—some further means was necessary to monetize the debt. Thus Hamilton suggested that the "application of this money" generated through funding and assumption should be performed "through the medium of a national bank." He submitted his plan to Congress on December 14, 1790, just one day after he submitted his schedule of taxes. Hamilton's proposed bank would monetize the debt by accepting securities in payment for bank stock and then issuing bank notes, backed by the collateral of those securities and some gold and silver, in denominations that could serve as ready money. Through the medium of the bank, the nation would enjoy a dramatically expanded money supply.[98]

Hamilton's proposed bank was bold in its proportions. Capitalized at $10 million (far more than all the available specie in the nation), it easily dwarfed all contemporary American banks. The government would purchase $2 million of bank stock with funds borrowed from the bank itself. The bank would enjoy an exclusive twenty-year charter. Like the Bank of England, whose charter Hamilton relied on heavily in drafting his report, the bank would serve both as the depository of government funds and as a source of emergency loans. The bank would also aid in the collection of federal revenues by short-term loans to taxpayers and more generally by "encreasing the quantity of circulating medium and the quickening of that circulation." Yet unlike the Bank of England, the Bank of the United States was not a purely public institution that served the financial needs of the government. Like our own Federal Reserve Bank system, it was a private lending body. In fact, the Bank of the United States was envisioned as only a short-term lender to the federal government and, after its capitalization, was prohibited from buying government bonds. Its primary public function was to monetize the debt and thus expand the money supply.[99]

Although Hamilton secured enactment for his bank fairly easily, it was still controversial. Most farmers viewed banks, and large national banks in particular, with a suspicion born of provincial incomprehension. Their more educated rural brethren were often equally hostile. Like their English counterparts, American landed gentry viewed national banking—and the larger financial revolution of which it was a part—as a source of political and moral corruption. Jefferson considered Hamilton's entire financial plan "a machine for the corruption of the legislature" whose most insidious "engine" was the Bank of the United States. Jefferson also attacked the legality of the bank. Following Madison's lead, he claimed that a strict reading of the Constitution demonstrated that Congress lacked the authority to charter such an institution. Underlying Jefferson and Madison's constitutional scruples lay deeper worries. What was the ultimate purpose of Hamilton's bank and its expansion of the money supply? Was it simply to secure the nation's credit? If so, why was the bank so large, and why was it a largely private, though nationally chartered, institution? Hamilton's funding and assumption scheme had made the Bank of the United States necessary. What would the bank lead to? What was the final term of Hamilton's projection?[100]

Hamilton's answer to these questions, the *Report on Manufactures*, was not submitted for another twelve months. The linchpin of his entire financial plan, the *Report on Manufactures* was Hamilton's blueprint for a national policy of rapid industrialization. The enactment of its provisions would fulfill his vision for America, turning a backward rural nation into an urban and industrial powerhouse. In so doing, it would require and create an active and powerful federal government that could serve as a unifying counterweight to the centrifugal force of the states. It represented the fruition of one of the central threads of the politics of Enlightenment, namely the celebration and promotion of capitalist commercial and industrial society.

Hamilton knew his final report would spark controversy. The vast bulk of Americans were agriculturalists who had grave misgivings about the workings of commercial and industrial society. Their more educated representatives adhered to the belief that, in Hamilton's words, "agriculture is, not only, the most productive, but the only productive species of industry." Land was the sole source of value as realized through farming. Commerce and manufactures simply transformed part of the value of the harvest into another form, adding no additional value at all. Moreover, industry promoted cities, which Jefferson considered sinkholes of vice and corruption. Indeed, for Republicans like Jefferson and Madison, urban and industrial development was a curse to be postponed, if not avoided, by focusing the nation's resources on the more salutary goal of westward expansion. Even those favorably disposed toward industrialization doubted that the United States as yet had the vital resources of capital, labor, and internal market demand to achieve any notable results. Even if Hamilton's monetized debt and national bank had alleviated the capital shortage, the perennial American shortage of labor—and therefore high wages—and limited market infrastructure meant that the newly created capital would seek more profitable and secure investment outlets in land and trade.[101]

Against these reservations, Hamilton came out swinging. In answer to his agrarian critics, he argued that manufacturing was both productive in its own right and beneficial to American agriculture. Physiocracy was a speculative castle of sand, far more "subtil and paradoxical, than solid or convincing." Following Locke, Hume, and Smith, Hamilton insisted that labor rather than land was the ultimate source of value. As such, it was highly dubious that farmers were more productive than "artificers." The former could scratch out a comfortable subsistence "with a considerable degree of carelessness in the mode of cultivation," while the latter could survive only by "exerting himself pretty equally" with all his competitors. Indeed, it was likely that artisans were more productive, if only because their labor was "at once more constant, more uniform, and more ingenious." Moreover, industrialization would be a boon to agriculture. True, in the short run it might mean higher prices for manufactured goods. In the long run, however, prices would drop. As an industry matures and becomes competitive, Hamilton argued, its product "seldom or never fails to be sold cheaper, in process of time, than was the foreign [imported] Article for which it is a substitute." Manufacturing also created urban markets for agricultural products. It was the strength of these markets, after all, that determined whether "the exertions of the husbandman will be steady or fluctuating, vigorous or feeble."[102]

Having answered his agrarian critics, Hamilton turned to the objections of sympathetic skeptics. Industrialists had three means immediately at hand to ameliorate the labor shortage. The overall need for labor could be curtailed by the extensive use of steam-powered machinery, "which substituting the Agency of fire and water, has prodigiously lessened the necessity for manual labor." In addition they could draw on a pool of "underemployed" agriculturalists. But Hamilton saw the major source of potential factory workers—quite accurately as it turned out— among women and children. Indeed, as had been proven in the English cotton mills, by being put to work in factories, they would be "rendered more useful" than if left to their normal regimen of farm chores. Even with these resources at hand, wages would still remain a bit high, but that in turn would induce the immigration of European workmen, who would enjoy high wages and "a moral certainty of employment."[103]

Capital would be drawn to industry by a variety of measures. Hamilton knew that American investors were chary of risky schemes and that therefore "it is of importance that the confidence of cautious sagacious capitalists, both citizens and foreigners, should be excited." High tariffs, pecuniary bounties for new manufactures and raw materials, and the ban of export of raw materials would ensure the profitability of infant ventures. Exclusive patent privileges would reward investment in labor-saving technology. The domestic market would be cultivated by an extensive system of internal improvements in roads and canals. Entry into the foreign market would be assured by high quality control, itself secured by "judicious regulations for the inspection of manufactured commodities." The whole industrial development program would be overseen by a federal board "for promoting Arts, Agriculture, Manufacture, and Commerce." The board would pay for the passage of skilled European workers and would seek to "induce the prosecution and introduction of useful discoveries, inventions, and improvements, by proportionate rewards judiciously held out and applied."[104]

Rapid industrial development was not only feasible, it was essential to the welfare and security of the nation. In addition to its benefits to all sectors of the economy, manufactures would promote a "favorable balance of Trade" in the Atlantic economy and therefore a greater amount of "pecuniary wealth, or money," than would otherwise be the case. In fact, as the relation of Europe and her colonies demonstrated, "the importations of manufactured supplies seem invariably to drain the merely Agricultural people of their wealth." Even more important was the support industry lent to national security. The revolution had been fraught with "extreme embarrassments" because of the states' "incapacity to supply themselves" with the means of defense, means that had to be manufactured. If not rectified shortly, future conflicts would expose the same weakness with similarly disastrous results.[105]

Hamilton believed that industrialization would also help ameliorate the growing sectional tensions between North and South. Industrial development would tie the commercial and manufacturing North to the agrarian South through "mutual wants," surely "one of the strongest links of political connection." Specifically, northern manufactures would create a "demand" for southern "Timber, flax, Hemp, Cotton, Wool, raw silk, Indigo," and other raw materials. Further, "the critical moment for entering with Zeal upon the important business" was at hand. The eruption of war on the Continent due to the French Revolution was disrupting the European economy, and American manufactures would be an attractive source of investment for European financiers. Foreign workers would also be "more easily acquired than at another time." Hamilton did not revel in the agonies of Europe, but he believed in seizing an opportunity when it was presented.[106]

Despite his cogent arguments and passionate appeals, the provisions of Hamilton's *Report on Manufactures* were not adopted. Hamilton's vision was simply too bold and aggressive for the rural nation. America's early industrial development would occur at a more leisurely pace, one prompted by the growth of domestic demand rather than federal policy. Too far ahead of their time, Hamilton's pleadings fell on the deaf ears of his incredulous countrymen. But while the *Report* was defeated, it did not die. Its provisions cropped up whenever war reminded statesmen like John Calhoun and even James Madison of the necessity of industry for national defense. It was revived when nationalist politicians like Henry Clay sought an "American System" of industrialization to unite the fractious sections. And it was finally embraced in the aftermath of secession when the Republican Party fulfilled Hamilton's vision, creating a strong and active federal government that promoted industrial prosperity and power. In the meantime, Hamilton had at least secured the credit of the nation, set the conditions for commercial expansion, and laid out the path to industrial progress.

Freedom from Foreign Entanglements— National Interest and Policy

In his Farewell Address, outgoing president George Washington urged his countrymen to avoid "antipathies against particular nations and passionate attachments for others." Americans should "cultivate just and amicable feelings towards all" while having as "little *political* connection with them as possible," especially avoiding any "permanent alliance." For Hamilton, who had penned that address, these were the guiding principles of his foreign policy. Despite his own marked Anglophilia, Hamilton insisted that "the true path" for America was "the Neutral and Pacific Policy." Embroilment in European affairs might lead to war, which would place an immense burden on the nation's already precarious finances. Even more ominous, Hamilton recognized that war would further polarize the sectional and partisan divisions within the country. Only freedom from foreign entanglements could assure the United States the time it required to put its house in order and establish its new federal republic.[107]

Hamilton's pursuit of peace and neutrality was complicated by several factors. In spite of its vast domains, America was a relatively weak nation, one whose weight counted for little in European councils and that was therefore liable to depredations by the great continental rivals, England and France. Moreover, many Americans still harbored resentment against Great Britain from the revolution as well as for her failure to relinquish several northwestern military posts in violation of the peace treaties of 1783. Equally powerful was the feeling of gratitude toward France for her role in aiding the struggle for independence. Such an American was Secretary of State Thomas Jefferson. Hamilton was no doubt uncharitable when he accused Jefferson of *"a womanish attachment to France and a womanish resentment against Great Britain,"* but he was not entirely wrong. The revolutionary struggle had left Jefferson with an implacable hatred of all things English, and his experience as a diplomat in Paris had filled him with an equally ardent love of France, an affection that was only intensified by the outbreak of the French Revolution.[108]

At every turn, Jefferson and Hamilton were at loggerheads on matters of foreign policy. Jefferson deeply resented Hamilton's incursions into his own province, particularly his semisecret meetings with various English diplomats. Hamilton justified his own private diplomacy on the accurate grounds that Jefferson had proven himself unwilling to enter into any serious negotiations with his British counterparts. Hamilton feared that if Jefferson were left to his own devices, "there would be in less than six months *an open War between the U*[nited] *States & Great Britain.*" Maintaining peace and neutrality required Hamilton's meddling in foreign policy. That Washington shared this view is demonstrated by the fact that he both was apprized of and approved Hamilton's secret negotiations.[109]

The greatest obstacle to Hamilton's pursuit of peace and neutrality, however, was the eruption of the French Revolution. The passions evoked by that struggle were inordinately intense. Many Americans saw in the French struggle the European fulfillment of their own republican convictions. Others came to see the French Revolution, especially after the execution of Louis XVI, as an anarchic assault on all forms of civilization and order. More than that, the French Revolution inaugurated a new epoch in political history characterized by a hyperideological orientation that threatened to unleash a new wave of secular "enthusiasm" and fanaticism. This new style of political thought and action gave a new edge to struggles within and between countries, especially as the revolution began to proselytize. As the stakes of the contest between France and her enemies grew ever greater, both sides resorted to tactics that threatened to draw the United States into the fray. In Washington's administration the first threat of involvement came principally from France and the second from Great Britain. In both cases, it was Hamilton more than any other figure who kept America out of war.

France, Neutrality, and the Genet Affair

Unlike most Americans, Hamilton greeted the eruption of the French Revolution with "a mixture of Pleasure and apprehension." Writing in the autumn of 1789, he congratulated his friend Lafayette on his nation's efforts to secure republican liberty and the rights of mankind. Yet he could not suppress his fears "for the final success" of these efforts. Internal disagreements, the selfishness of the aristocracy, and the "vehement character of your people" all filled Hamilton with dread lest the revolution exceed the limits of reason and self-interest and lead to "innovations greater than will consist with the real felicity of your nation." Particularly troubling were "the reveries of your Philosophic politicians" who, lacking practical experience, "may aim at more refinement than suits either with human nature or the composition of your Nation."[110]

Hamilton's fears were well founded. Beginning in the mid-1760s, the French Enlightenment had become destabilized by a militant wing of proto-Romantics, symbolized by the Physiocratic "sect," the growing cult of Rousseau, and what French historian Daniel Roche has called "the crisis of sensibility." Few of his countrymen shared Hamilton's fears. Most saw in France the extension of their own revolutionary principles, and they could not help hoping that the revolution in France represented a new dawn of liberty in the old world that would sweep away the regime of kings and nobles and usher in a new age of human dignity. While uncommon, Hamilton's apprehension unfortunately proved all too accurate.[111]

Despite its vehemence, American support of the French Revolution was a matter of sentimental attachment without political or policy ramifications. That all changed on February 1, 1793, when France declared war on Holland and Great Britain. That same month, Washington's cabinet met to discuss a request from outgoing French minister Jean-Baptiste Ternant for "three millions of livres to be furnished on account of our debt to France." A large advance on the outstanding debt, the money was to be spent in the United States on provisions that would be shipped to France. Secretary of State Thomas Jefferson, Secretary of War Henry Knox, and Attorney General Edmund Randolph all urged the president to comply with this request. Only Hamilton dissented. Providing that sum would put an undue strain on the nation's finances. Even more important, Great Britain would take such generosity to an adversary as a hostile act, threatening relations with a crucial trading partner. Hamilton instead proposed that Ternant be furnished with $318,000, a sum equivalent to "the arrearages equitably due to France at the end of 1792." Washington sided with Hamilton, but the problem of Franco-American relations had only just begun.[112]

In 1778 the United States had entered into a military alliance with France, and many Americans felt their nation should honor that treaty by entering the war on the side of their sister republic. Hamilton strenuously rejected this position. That alliance had been defensive in nature, but in the current war France was clearly the aggressor. Moreover, that treaty had been made with Louis XVI, "a prince who has been dethroned and decapitated." Given the unsettled state of French politics, Hamilton urged that the treaty be considered "temporarily and provisionally suspended." Washington instead sought a middle course, issuing a proclamation of American neutrality on April 22, 1793.[113]

Washington's proclamation was met with howls of protest. "Democratic-Republican" political clubs were organized across the country to express their solidarity with the French struggle and their disillusionment at the president's temporizing neutrality. Such feeling was exacerbated by the arrival of the new French minister, citizen Edmond Genet. A member of France's then-ascendant Girondin party, Genet had been commissioned to negotiate a more thorough treaty of alliance with the United States. He was also instructed to facilitate uprisings among the peoples of Louisiana, Florida, and Canada against their British and Spanish colonial masters. This was to be achieved by spreading revolutionary doctrine and, more ominously, by organizing military incursions from Kentucky and other western frontier settlements in the United States. To harass British shipping, he was armed with letters of marque to commission privateers that would operate from American ports with American sailors. Obviously, such hostile acts threatened to draw the United States into the armed struggle against England and her allies.[114]

Genet arrived in Charleston, South Carolina, to a hero's welcome on April 8, 1793. Ten days later, after addressing the legislature of that state and commissioning a number of privateering vessels, he set out for Philadelphia. Along the way he was feted by the newly created Democratic-Republican clubs and addressed large crowds of enthusiastic supporters. In mid-May he finally arrived in Philadelphia, where he was cordially received by the president. In the interim his privateers had taken a number of British prizes, one having been seized at anchor in Delaware Bay. Throughout he had been in close contact with Jefferson. Apprised of Genet's mission, Jefferson was filled with warmth and encouragement. Although he warned the French diplomat that any Americans caught planning military actions against foreign colonial possessions would be judged guilty of treason and face execution, he nonetheless supplied him with a list of likely contacts in Kentucky. Moreover, he assured him that the president's policy of neutrality did not reflect the sentiment of Congress or the nation at large.[115]

Washington was alarmed to learn that privateers commissioned by

Genet had captured British vessels in American waters and that French consuls were busily presiding over the disposition of those prizes in American seaports. Recognizing that the British would treat such behavior as an act of war, he ordered Genet to immediately cease all such operations on June 5. Genet ignored this order, and on the fifteenth began refitting a captured British ship called the *Little Sarah*—now renamed the *Little Democrat*—in the national capital. Emboldened by Jefferson's assurances that he was backed by public opinion, on July 7 he informed Washington that he would not detain the *Little Democrat* and would go over the president's head and appeal directly to the American people if he continued to thwart his goals.[116]

Genet had grossly overplayed his hand. An irate Washington decided to demand his recall, an action that the new Jacobin government in France would be only too happy to comply with. Indeed, if the president had not granted the now-deposed minister political asylum, he would undoubtedly have faced the guillotine rather than spending his remaining days in rural isolation in New York. But even more important than Genet's gaffe in stemming the tide of pro-French war sentiment in the United States was Hamilton's remarkable journalistic crusade. Beginning in late June 1793, Hamilton wrote a series of powerful essays on the French Revolution and American diplomacy that dramatically moved public opinion away from war frenzy and toward acceptance and eventual appreciation of Washington's policy of neutrality.

Hamilton built his case methodically. He began by noting that much of the "acrimony and invective" directed against American neutrality was a thinly veiled attack on the president by his partisan Republican opponents. Nor was neutrality a violation of the treaty of alliance with France. That treaty had been defensive in nature, whereas "France first declared and began the War against Austria, Prussia, Savoy, Holland, England and Spain." France had given a "general and just cause of alarm" on November 19, 1792, when she declared her support for "every people who wish to recover their liberty," a proclamation which "was ordered to be printed *in all languages*." Her subsequent annexation of those territories she had conquered was not only a "violation of the rights of Nations" but an act of unmitigated imperialism and "culpable ambition." Such irregular proceedings were certainly "questionable enough to free the U[nited] States from all embarrassment" arising from its treaty of alliance.[117]

Hamilton then turned to the argument advanced by Madison that, despite treaty stipulations, the United States owed France a debt of gratitude that ought to be repaid in her hour of need. While "faith and justice between nations are virtues of a nature sacred and inviolable," Hamilton acknowledged, "the same cannot be said of gratitude." The debt of gratitude was due to disinterested acts of benevolence. Such acts were common between individuals, "but among nations they perhaps never occur." Foreign aids were invariably the result of "the interest or advantage" of the party "which performs them." The true motive behind French support of the American Revolution had not been benevolence at all. Rather, France sought to weaken its British rival and avenge its prior defeat and consequent loss of empire in the Seven Years' War of 1756–63. In fact, such support had not been forthcoming until the British defeat at the battle of Saratoga, "which went a great way towards deciding the issue of the contest" and thus gave France "a confidence in our ability to accomplish our purpose." Interest, not sentiment, was the true motive force of foreign relations.[118]

Having disarmed the critics of neutrality, Hamilton moved on to an assault on French diplomacy. In a series of articles signed "No Jacobin," Hamilton recounted the details of Genet's mission in America. In the first four essays he carefully demonstrated that "the claim of right on the part of France to fit out privateers in the ports of the United States, as derived from treaty, is without foundation." The relevant treaty articles were at best "doubtful or obscure" and were more reasonably interpreted as "merely a prohibition" against allowing "a power at war with the other to fit or arm its privateers in the ports of the party at peace." Moreover, it was a recognized principle of international law that neutral states "cannot lawfully succor, aid, countenance, or support either of the parties at war with each other." Despite these recognized principles,

Genet had fitted out privateers "under French colours and commissions" in Charleston. This high-handed act was taken "without a possibility of sounding or knowing the disposition of our government on the point." Not only might these acts have precipitated British reprisals against American shipping, they betrayed an arrogant lack of respect for the American people and the sovereignty of their government.[119]

Hamilton then turned to the French minister's unwarranted intrusion into American politics. Genet's leisurely journey from Charleston to Philadelphia was no mere goodwill mission. Rather, it represented the execution of a planned "system of electrifying the people" meant to circumvent the normal channels of diplomatic exchange with "popular intrigue." His addresses to political clubs were bad enough, but his "placing himself at the head" of one such society in Philadephia (he had assumed the presidential chair) was an act without precedent in "the history of diplomatic enterprize." Here was a dangerous precedent that "demands the exercise of republican jealousy." But such behavior paled in comparison to Genet's threat to circumvent Washington entirely and take his case directly to the American people. Such a threat betrayed his view of Americans as "light, vain, and precipitate," a people "likely to be governed by impulse more than reason" and capable of being duped into "measures inconsistent with their dignity, their interest, their peace and their safety." The real wonder, according to Hamilton, was that "there are men among us, who call themselves citizens of the United States, degenerate enough to become the apologists of Mr. Genet."[120]

The impact of Hamilton's essays on public opinion was staggering. By early July, after the first pieces had been published, Jefferson was alarmed. He urged his friend and fellow Republican leader James Madison to "take up your pen, select the most striking heresies, and cut him to pieces in the face of the public." Only Madison could hope to counter Hamilton, for "there is nobody else who can and will enter the lists with him." Madison did reply with his "Helvidius" essays, but to no avail. Hamilton swept the field and turned American opinion against Genet and in favor of the very policy of neutrality that had so recently been the source of derision. In mid-August a despondent Jefferson reported that a recent town meeting had voted "9 out of 10" against Genet and "for the Proclamation" of neutrality. He shortly expected all the northern towns to follow suit. Jefferson advised Madison that the Republican opposition now had no choice but to reverse field, "approve unequivocally of a state of neutrality," and "abandon G[enet] entirely."[121]

Hamilton had utterly shifted the tide of political battle, putting Jefferson and his fellow Republicans on the defensive and rallying the nation to the Federalist policies of Washington. More than that, he had rescued the nation from entanglement in a costly foreign struggle and preserved its peace and neutrality, at least for the time being.

Great Britain and the Jay Treaty

Within months of settling the Genet affair, Hamilton was faced with a fresh challenge to American peace and neutrality. This time the threat came from Great Britain. In early November 1793 the British government had issued Orders in Council instructing its naval officers to seize all shipping to or from the French West Indies. The order was kept secret for almost two months, however, by which time American merchants had dispatched their trading fleets to the Caribbean. The result was the capture of hundreds of American ships and their cargoes. When news of these seizures reached the mainland, a wave of anti-British sentiment swept the nation, threatening to plunge the country into war with its old adversary.[122]

Hamilton advised a two-pronged approach. On the one hand, he urged the president to place the nation in "a respectable military posture." Seaports should be fortified, an army of twenty thousand should be raised, and the executive should obtain power "to lay an embargo" on all foreign commerce. On the other hand, when Hamilton learned that the British had revoked the offending Orders in Council and had offered compensation for seized American shipping, he counseled diplomatic engagement. War should be avoided if at all possible. Realistically, the United States was simply too weak to expect any great success against

British military might. Of even greater concern was the likely impact of armed hostility on American politics. The French Revolution had already "unhinged the orderly principles of the people of this country," he noted, and a war fought in alliance with that power "may prove to be the threshold of disorganization and anarchy."[123]

In keeping with Hamilton's counsel, Washington decided to send an envoy to England to negotiate a treaty settling the outstanding issues between the two countries. Although Hamilton was the obvious candidate for this task, he had become so feared and hated by the Republican opposition that he finally urged the president to appoint the Supreme Court chief justice John Jay instead. Jay's instructions, largely written by Hamilton, contained three central goals. Jay must demand compensation for the capture of American vessels the previous winter. The posts in the Northwest that the British held in violation of the peace treaty of 1783 must be surrendered. Finally, he should negotiate a general commercial pact ensuring the American carrying trade in the West Indies. Ideally, he should also get compensation for slaves carried off by the British at the end of the Revolutionary War. If Jay could achieve these objectives, they would represent a long-term settlement of the outstanding differences between the United States and her old colonial master. If not, war would become unavoidable.[124]

The treaty Jay brought back in early 1795 fulfilled most of the goals Hamilton had set. The British agreed to return the frontier posts stipulated in the treaty of 1783 and to establish commissions to settle compensations for the spoliation of American shipping. American vessels would be given complete access to the West Indies, but only if under a fixed weight and if they did not re-export certain enumerated tropical products (restrictions that were eventually deleted from the ratified treaty). For its part, America would establish commissions to facilitate the payment of prerevolutionary debts to British merchants. Jay did fail to extract compensation for slaves liberated by the British—not too surprising, given his abolitionist convictions—but even Jefferson saw this as a minor issue. On the whole, Jay had succeeded in advancing

American commerce, settling most of the outstanding issues with Great Britain, and keeping the United States out of war.

Despite these accomplishments, news of Jay's treaty was met with public rage. The Republican press denounced the treaty as a pusillanimous betrayal of France on behalf of the forces of monarchy and reaction. Rather than manfully asserting American rights, the chief justice had betrayed national honor and interest out of craven fear. In the spring and summer of 1795, Jay was burned in effigy by angry crowds in the principal ports of the eastern seaboard. Frontier settlers in Kentucky and elsewhere threatened to secede from the union if the treaty became law. When Hamilton tried to address an enraged mob, he was pelted by stones. Even after the Federalist-controlled Senate had ratified the treaty, Washington remained undecided whether he should actually sign the document given the intense opposition to it. Naturally, he turned to Hamilton for advice.[125]

Hamilton had in fact retired into private life, having resigned his post in the Treasury Department at the beginning of the year. Nonetheless, in early July 1795 he responded to his old commander's call for counsel with a lengthy letter. Hamilton carefully dissected the provisions of the treaty, meticulously analyzing their strengths and weaknesses. Despite its failings, Hamilton concluded that Jay's handiwork successfully settled the "controverted points between the two Countries." The commercial terms of the treaty would have little impact, but it would secure "an object of primary consequence," namely the recovery of "our Western Posts." Most important of all, however, was the fact that the treaty would keep the nation "from being implicated in the dreadful war which is ruining Europe." Peace would "enable us to make our way sufficiently fast in trade" so that if, after a dozen years, war should become unavoidable, "we may then meet it without much inquietude" and a reasonable prospect of success. And in fact, the peace that followed the Jay Treaty was accompanied by one of the most dramatic commercial and economic booms in American history. Overall, Hamilton judged that "more is gained than given" and thus urged the president to sign the treaty. Though not the only determining factor, Hamilton's advice was an important source of Washington's decision to put the treaty into effect and thus close the prospect of war with Great Britain.[126]

Perhaps even more important than his role in settling Washington's judgment, however, were Hamilton's efforts in transforming public opinion. Writing as "Camillus," Hamilton published a series of essays beginning in late July in defense of the Jay Treaty. As in his previous defense of the neutrality proclamation, Hamilton began by noting the partisan motives of the treaty's critics, namely Jefferson's ambition to succeed Washington. Moreover, those who condemned the treaty and the measures taken to secure it gave the false impression that the United States was "among the first rate powers of the world." This was foolhardy in the extreme. Although "a very powerful state may frequently hazard a high and haughty tone" in foreign affairs, "a weak state can hardly ever do it without imprudence," and truth be told, "the last is yet our character." In brief, the great virtue of the treaty was that it secured peace, while "the too probable result of a refusal to ratify is war" or national humiliation.[127]

The treaty had, Hamilton insisted, secured its primary objectives. Great Britain had agreed to turn over the western posts and compensate "the spoliations of our property" by her navy. True, Jay had failed to secure payment for slaves liberated and removed by the British at the end of the Revolutionary War, an apparent violation of the terms of peace. But these terms were liable to various interpretations, one being that the British should not transport any slaves liberated *after* the close of hostilities. That was the British construction of the article in question, and it was neither as "odious or immoral" as the alternative of returning freedmen to a state of bondage. In any event, "the whole number" of such freedmen did not exceed three thousand, which fairly valued came to a mere $600,000. This sum paled in comparison to what southerners owed their British creditors, especially in Virginia where "her courts in defiance of the Treaty [of 1783] have constantly remained shut to the recovery of British debts."[128]

As usual, Hamilton was meticulous in his analysis of the treaty. The most powerful impact of his essays, however, was his refutation of the central assumptions of its Republican critics and his efforts in revealing their partisan motives. Their most dangerous assumption was evident in their fervid "declamations which describe Great Britain to us as vanquished and humbled," merely requiring stiff defiance to conjure capitulation. Such views were "either the chimeras of over-heated imaginations, or the fabrications of imposture." Hamilton urged his countrymen to shun Republican "sycophants" who "flatter the errors and prejudices of the people." Instead they should hearken to those "honest and independent men" like himself who were willing "to tell unpalatable truths." One of those truths was that America was relatively weak, while Britain remained the preeminent superpower of the day.[129]

The impact of Hamilton's essays was extraordinary. As soon as the first appeared, Washington sent him his hearty congratulations. Jefferson was understandably less sanguine. Indeed, by mid-September he had seen more than enough. "Hamilton is really a colossus to the antirepublican party," he complained; "without numbers, he is an host within himself." Again he urged Madison to respond in print, and again Madison proved no match for Hamilton. The New Yorker's essays turned the tide of public sentiment. By the spring of 1796 public opinion was every bit as adamant in favor of the treaty as it had been vociferous in opposition to it the previous year. Once again Hamilton had rescued the Washington administration and its foreign policy in the public mind. Once again he had preserved the peace and neutrality of the republic.[130]

The Future of an Illusion—
Alexander Hamilton and American Nation Building

Alexander Hamilton had warned his fellow delegates at the Constitutional Convention that he saw "the Union dissolving or already dissolved." Some three years later he was more optimistic. There was, he assured Washington, a "growing conviction" in the public mind "of the Utility and benefits of National Government." This was the key to Hamilton's understanding of nation building. If the public perceived the federal government to be effective and capable, the government's powers and authority would be accepted and approved. Regardless of its constitutional and theoretical strictures, however, if the new government failed to govern effectively, it would go the way of the previous confederation. As the proverb went, the proof of the pudding would be in the eating.[131]

Hamilton's financial system had obviously gone a long way toward registering the utility of the new government. The creditworthiness of the new regime, its ability to handle its finances and assume its debt obligations, had helped create the sense that it was competent and stable in a way that the old confederation had never been. The commercial prosperity that these measures ushered in helped establish the reality and desirability of the government in the public mind. Hamilton's dogged efforts on behalf of American neutrality had also been instrumental in nation building. Keeping the United States free from the wars of the French Revolution allowed Hamilton to obscure from public view the real military and diplomatic weakness of the infant nation. Peace also kept the new government from facing the strains of internal dissent and sectional strife that would surely have surfaced had war been declared, thus creating the illusion of national stability in advance of its achievement.

Hamilton's contributions to American nation building were not limited to financial and foreign policy measures, however. Equally vital were his efforts in the one field in which he had professional expertise, namely, the rule of law. Twice during his tenure as secretary of the Treasury, Hamilton decisively influenced the course of legal and constitutional development, each time with dramatic and far-reaching effect. The first moment occurred shortly after the passage of his proposal for a national bank. Hamilton championed a liberal or "broad" interpretation of the Constitution, one that took an expansive view of federal power and strengthened the nation against emasculation by the states. The second moment came in the aftermath of the so-called "Whiskey Rebellion" in western Pennsylvania. Hamilton's decisive and thoroughgoing resolution of that insurrection during Washington's second term signaled for all Americans the reality of the federal government and its power and willingness to uphold the rule of law in the face of violent civil disobedience.

The Bank of the United States and Broad Construction

Congressional approval of Hamilton's Bank of the United States seemed all but a foregone conclusion in early 1791. Few questioned the desirability of the institution. In little more than a month after Hamilton had submitted his report for its incorporation, a bill codifying his proposals had been drafted and passed by the Senate. The legislation promptly moved through the House of Representatives without a single attempt at amendment. But on February 2, as the House neared its final vote on the measure, James Madison rose in opposition.

The Constitution conferred on the federal government decidedly limited powers, Madison argued, and "it was not possible to discover in it the power to incorporate a bank." Supporters of the bank found that power in Article I, Section 8, which granted Congress authority to "make all laws which shall be necessary and proper" to achieve its enumerated ends, among which were the collection of taxes and the regulation of commerce. The power to incorporate a bank was thus "implied" by those ends rather than strictly specified. But Madison warned that "the doctrine of implication" was fraught with dangers. If given free rein in the interpretation of the "necessary and proper" clause, it would "give an unlimited discretion to Congress" and threatened the very ideal of a government "composed of limited and enumerated powers." Only a strict and literal construction of the Constitution could avoid such dangers. And by a strict construction, Hamilton's bank simply did not pass constitutional muster.[132]

Madison's excursion into constitutional exegesis had little impact on congressional approval of the bank. His Federalist opponents challenged his interpretation of the "necessary and proper" clause with that found in *Federalist* number 44. In that essay, Publius had explicitly defended that clause. In the absence of implied powers, the government would be reduced to the dismal "alternative of betraying the public interest by doing nothing, or violating the Constitution by exercising powers indispensably necessary and proper, but, at the same time, not *expressly* granted." This must have been especially galling to Madison for, unbeknownst to his congressional opponents, he had in fact been the author of that essay. Refuted by his own words, Madison was powerless to stop the passage of the bank bill.[133]

Madison's argument did, however, have a profound impact on the president. Washington had immense respect for Madison and regarded him as the leading light on the Constitution. Troubled by his fellow Virginian's misgivings, he seriously considered vetoing the bank legislation. He turned to his cabinet and requested written opinions from Secretary of State Jefferson, Attorney General Randolph, and Secretary of the Treasury Hamilton. Jefferson and Randolph largely rehashed Madison's argument. Jefferson added the proviso that the entire dispute over constitutional interpretation should be considered in the light of the Tenth Amendment, which "reserved to the States respectively, or to the people," all those powers "not delegated to the United States by the Constitution or prohibited by it to the States." Combined with Madison's call for strict construction, Jefferson had advanced what became the classic case for states' rights and limited federal power.

Hamilton had the advantage of replying last, after he had read the opinions of Randolph and Jefferson. On February 23, 1791, he sent Washington a lengthy brief on behalf of the constitutionality of the bank. Immensely learned and justifiably famous in constitutional lore, Hamilton's brief refuted each of Jefferson's and Randolph's assertions in great detail. The crux of his argument was that "the principles of construction" maintained by the bank's opponents "would be fatal to the just & indisputable authority of the United States." The power to create corporate bodies like the Bank of the United States, even if not explicitly enumerated in the Constitution, "is *inherent* in the very definition of *Government*." Corporations were merely means to pursue specified ends, and "every power vested in a Government is in its nature *sovereign*, and includes by *force* of the *term*, a right to employ all the *means* requisite, and fairly *applicable* to the attainment of the *ends* of such power." This was a recapitulation of Hamilton's maxim of ethical responsibility. Ought implies can; a nation must have the power to fulfill its assigned tasks.[134]

Jefferson's invocation of the Tenth Amendment was beside the point. The power of incorporation may not have been explicitly enumerated, but it was surely implied. Nor could this lead to the slippery slope Madison feared. An implicit power to create corporations did not mean unlimited power in the hands of the federal legislature. Congress could not, for example, incorporate the police department of Philadelphia "because they are not authorized to *regulate*" the government of localities. But Congress was authorized to regulate trade and collect taxes and could thus "employ all the means which relate to its regulation to the *best & greatest advantage*," means that clearly included the incorporation of a national bank. Hamilton similarly rejected Jefferson's restrictive gloss on the word "necessary" in the "necessary and proper" clause. Jefferson read the word as allowing only "those means, without which the grant of the power would be nugatory." This would hamper the government by limiting its "exercise of any implied power" to only a "*case of extreme necessity*." True, taxes might be collected without a bank, but by the same reasoning towns ought not to be incorporated by the states because it was possible for residents to coexist without such formal organization. The case was exactly analogous for, as Hamilton reminded Washington, "there is no *express* power in any State constitution to erect corporations." Somehow they managed to do so anyway, even creating banks of their own.[135]

The proposed principles of strict interpretation not only threatened to limit the potential powers of the federal government; they also ran counter to existing practices. The national legislature had created "light houses, beacons, buoys & public piers" without either *express* constitutional authority or ironclad necessity. Moreover, if the Constitution did not sanction the creation of corporate bodies, by what authority had the federal government created territorial governments? In fact, two such governments had been established, "one northwest of the river Ohio, and the other south-west," and in the latter case "*independent of any antecedent compact*." "Why then," Hamilton asked, "does not the same clause authorize the erection of a corporation in respect of the regulation of any other of the property of the United States?"[136]

Strict interpretation thus ran counter to the established practice of American government. States exercised implied powers routinely, as did other nations. Neither shied from erecting corporations when deemed beneficial, regardless of explicit constitutional authorization. In such circumstances, Hamilton reasoned, "the practice of mankind ought to have great weight against the theories of individuals." National banks were a widely accepted "engine in the administration of national finances." They were "the most effectual instrument of loans" and "one which in this country has been found essential." Contrary to Jefferson's warnings, the incorporation of a national bank in no way intruded on the prerogatives of the states or the people. "Each state may still erect as many banks as it pleases," Hamilton noted, "and every individual may still carry on the banking business to any extent he pleases." The real test of constitutionality was the ends to which means like the Bank of the United States were related. "If the end be clearly comprehended within any of the specified powers" of the Constitution—in this case, the collection of taxes, regulation of trade, and procurement of credit—"it may safely be deemed to come within the compass of national authority."[137]

The impact of Hamilton's opinion was far reaching. To be sure, it had the immediate effect of inducing Washington to sign the bank bill. But Hamilton was interested in far more than national banking. His broad construction of implied constitutional powers was meant to be a bulwark to the national organs of government. He invoked the same principles in his *Report on Manufactures*, arguing that "the terms 'general welfare'" in the preface to the Constitution "were doubtless intended to signify" a host of powers and "a vast variety of particulars, which are susceptible neither of specification nor of definition." These powers were vital, as he later claimed, to defend the ideal of enlightened republicanism.[138]

It was his fundamental goal "to see the *equality* of political rights exclusive of all *hereditary* distinction firmly established by a practical demonstration of its being consistent with the order and happiness of society." That order and happiness, without which equality could not hope to survive, was threatened not by the national government, but by the "too potent and counteracting influence" of the states. The states threatened the sovereignty of the nation, and the nation was the ultimate support of public happiness and ordered liberty. Hamilton's augmentation of centralized powers was meant to offset that threat. "Hence a disposition on my part towards a liberal construction of the powers of the national government" he wrote to Edward Carrington, "and to erect every fence to guard it from depredations, which is, in my opinion, consistent with constitutional propriety." Such liberal construction was a critical component in the process of American nation building.[139]

The Whiskey Rebellion and the Rule of Law

In the spring and summer of 1794 the new federal republic faced the first major challenge to its domestic tranquillity. An insurrection raged in the four westernmost counties of Pennsylvania. Federal officials were tarred and feathered, the federal mail was intercepted, and a wave of violent intimidation was unleashed on wealthy residents. An angry mob of five hundred armed men assaulted the home of excise inspector John Neville in mid-July, forcing the surrender of seventeen federal soldiers and prompting the panicked flight of Neville and federal marshal David Lenox. Shortly thereafter a force of some six thousand gathered to march on Pittsburgh, threatening to burn it. The rebels had already attempted to form an alliance with other disgruntled frontiersmen in Kentucky and the Carolinas and had entered into negotiations with representatives of Great Britain and Spain to secure their independence in the event of their secession from the union. The Whiskey Rebellion was the first great test of federal authority and its ability to uphold the rule of law.[140]

The roots of the uprising lay in Hamilton's excise on distilled liquor. Passed in early March 1791, the excise imposed a modest tax of seven and a half cents per gallon on distilled whiskey and rum. Hamilton proposed the tax to help defray the costs of funding and assumption. He also hoped to curtail "the consumption of ardent spirits" that "on account of their cheapness, is carried to an extreme." Hamilton's moralizing might seem quaint today, but the citizens of the early republic drank truly astounding quantities of alcohol. Hamilton estimated that the average American family consumed roughly sixteen gallons of hard liquor per year, not including wine, beer, and the ubiquitous hard cider (thirty-six proof) that was served at each meal. The most thorough study of the subject suggests that the total consumption of pure or "absolute" alcohol by adults in 1795 was a whopping 6.2 gallons per year, almost three times the current rate and greater than almost any other contemporary European nation. Hamilton was hardly being alarmist when he described American bingeing as a danger "to the health and morals" of the people and a drag on "the oeconomy [*sic*] of the community."[141]

Collection of the excise from the rum distilleries of the eastern seaboard went fairly well. The same could not be said, however, of the whiskey producers of the western frontier. From the outset, opposition was widespread and violent. Westerners complained that distilling their grain into whiskey was the only economical way of transporting their harvests across the mountains to eastern markets. As such, the tax on whiskey would strip them of the little cash they had. The requirement of oaths of compliance from distillers was assailed as an assault on public morality, presumably because it implied their dishonesty absent such pledges. The tax was also an invasion of privacy in the guise of intrusive excise inspectors.[142]

These complaints were largely specious. The tax on whiskey, like all excises, would be passed on to consumers. Westerners would shoulder an undue burden only if they were "greater consumers of Spirits, than those of other parts of the Country." In any event, it would be more than offset by the army's purchase of whiskey rations, which Hamilton directed to be made from complying western distillers. As for the danger to public morality, oaths were required in the execution of all revenue laws and "constantly occur in jury trials." If oaths and inspections were precluded, Hamilton noted, "it is not easy to imagine what security there can be for any species of revenue, which is to be collected from articles of consumption." As it was, westerners contributed almost nothing to the federal Treasury while draining it through costly military actions that were taken to protect frontiersmen from the Amerindians whose land they continually encroached upon. The whiskey tax was the least they could be expected to pay in support of their government.[143]

As secretary of the Treasury, Hamilton was privy to reports of often gruesome assaults on his agents. In the fall of 1791 a young man in western Pennsylvania falsely claimed to be an excise officer. For his pains he was stripped naked, beaten, and tortured with a red-hot iron bar "both behind and before," enduring injuries that were "sufficient to make human nature shudder." The following summer an actual inspector was locked in a distillery for three days without food. He was then assured no harm would come to him, "but he must submit to the mild punishment of having his Nose ground off at the Grindstone." To assault federal officials with such impunity showed an utter disregard for the authority of the nation's government and contempt for its sovereignty. "Such persevering and violent opposition to the Law," Hamilton informed the president in early September 1792, "seems to call for vigorous measure on the part of the Government."[144]

Washington preferred a more conciliatory approach. He issued a proclamation calling for an end to "all unlawful combinations and proceedings" against the excise. For his part, Hamilton adjusted the tax to make it less onerous and costly for home distillers. Although revenue collection improved only marginally at first, the worst violence abated. By early 1794 the vast bulk of distillers in western Pennsylvania were, officially at least, in compliance with the law. Only thirty-seven were still delinquent. When excise inspector Neville and federal marshal Lenox attempted to serve subpoenas on those delinquents, however, all hell broke loose. In the years since the measure had first passed, many residents of western Pennsylvania had been convinced by the Republican press that the excise was part of an insidious Federalist conspiracy to foist a monarchical regime on the nation and deliver its government to a cabal of commercial plutocrats. The newly created Democratic-Republican clubs in the region added fuel to the fire. European governments contacted by the insurgents began speculating how long it would take for the new federal government to collapse in the face of armed insurrection.[145]

On August 2 an angry George Washington convened a cabinet meeting with the principal officials of Pennsylvania. The state officers held their peace until Washington expressed his intention of taking military action against the insurgents. At that point Pennsylvania chief justice Thomas McKean interjected that the state courts were more than capable of handling the problem and "that the employment of a military force, at this period, would be as bad as anything the Rioters had done— equally unconstitutional and illegal." Hamilton fired back that, on the contrary, the moment had come "when it must be determined whether the Government can maintain itself." Pennsylvania secretary Alexander J. Dallas countered that the presiding judge in the western district had assured him that the local courts were adequate to the task, and that military action would merely galvanize opposition throughout the region. Hamilton then pointedly reminded Dallas that "the Judge alluded [to] was among those who had most promoted the opposition in an insidious manner," a fact that Washington was all too aware of. With the exception of Secretary of State Edmund Randolph, the entire cabinet supported Hamilton in his call for the suppression of the Whiskey Rebellion by force if necessary.[146]

Hamilton proposed the assembly of a massive force of twelve thousand militia, half of which should be raised from Pennsylvania itself. Such a large army would eliminate the danger of battle since the rebels could not hope to withstand it. More important, it would signal both to the citizens of the nation and to foreign powers the willingness of the federal government to defend its sovereignty and the authority of its laws. In the interim, the president should issue a proclamation announcing his intention of using force to quell the rebellion and offering a general amnesty to all those who lay down their arms and swore allegiance to the federal government. Washington followed Hamilton's counsel, issuing his proclamation on August 7. The response to his call was enthusiastic. The militia had begun to assemble by early September, and at the end of that month Washington and Hamilton had joined the force of twelve thousand men.[147]

Hamilton had been busy in the intervening weeks. Secretary of War Henry Knox had taken a leave of absence and Hamilton was forced to assume his duties, securing provisions and looking after other logistical details for the gathering army. Far more critically, however, he took up his pen to prepare public opinion for the use of force. Beginning in late August he published a series of essays signed "Tully," the popular name for the legendary Roman republican patriot Cicero. In these essays, Hamilton made the case for the administration's forthcoming measures against the Whiskey Rebels.

The issue at hand was simple enough. "Shall the majority govern or be governed? shall the nation rule or be ruled? shall the general will prevail or the will of a faction?" All these questions could be reduced to one: "shall there be government, or no government?" The American people had ratified a constitution that explicitly authorized excise taxes. They had elected representatives who had duly passed such excises year after year. "But the four western counties of Pennsylvania," Hamilton declared, "undertake to rejudge and reverse your decrees." Those who sought to minimize the danger of the insurgents by "ill timed declamations against excise laws" and questioned the use of force were enemies to the nation. Such a villain "may prate and babble republicanism" but ultimately set "the *will* of a *faction*, against the *will* of a *nation*" and "the violence of a lawless combination against the sacred authority of laws pronounced under your indisputable commission."[148]

Respect for the nation's laws and the constitution under which they were formulated was "the most sacred duty and the greatest source of security in a Republic." The rule of law was the only bulwark against the designs of malevolent elites "against the common liberty." To resist these laws by force of arms was thus "treason against society, against liberty, against every thing that ought to be dear to a free, enlightened, and prudent people." Those who sought to appease such treason were, Hamilton warned, "your worst enemies," foes who "treat you either as fools or cowards, too weak to perceive your interest and your duty, or too dastardly to pursue them." Only cowardice or perfidy could counsel inaction in face of such a dangerous threat to the rule of law in a free and enlightened republic.[149]

The combination of Hamilton's essays and military preparations worked like a charm. The army that he led into western Pennsylvania that fall pacified the region without even a scintilla of resistance. Two thousand of the most hardened rebels fled at the approach of the militia. The rest were cowed into submission. In all, twenty men were dispatched to Philadelphia to face charges of treason. Of these, two were convicted and subsequently pardoned by the president. The Whiskey Rebellion had been thoroughly crushed without firing a shot in anger. At the same time, the public rallied to the administration's measures. Federalists regained control of both houses of Congress in that year's elections. Most important of all, Hamilton had vindicated the rule of law and the authority of the federal government, one of the most critical elements in nation building. It would be almost another fourscore years before the nation was seriously threatened by domestic insurrection.[150]

"MINE IS AN ODD DESTINY"—
THE LEGACY OF ALEXANDER HAMILTON

By almost any measure, Alexander Hamilton was the most important figure in the founding of the American republic. Soldier, statesman, legislator, constitutional theorist, political polemicist, and national administrator, Hamilton combined all the roles that were vital to American nation building. His vision of a strong federal government with an independent judiciary and a vigorous executive has become second nature to most Americans. His goal of state-supported industrial and commercial development and modernization is the unstated desideratum of every successful American political movement in the last century. His understanding of American foreign policy in terms of realistic assessments of national strengths and worldly interests has become, in fact if not theory, the dominant view in American government, regardless of the party in power. Indeed, in terms of political and economic practice, it is fair to say that we are all Hamiltonians, whether Democrats or Republicans, progressives or conservatives, radicals or reactionaries.

No other founding father or leader of the early republic grasped as clearly and embraced as unflinchingly the modern world we have inherited. To that extent at least, as modern Americans in the most powerful country on earth, we are the children of Alexander Hamilton.

Despite his myriad accomplishments and larger-than-life legacy, Hamilton is perhaps the least loved founding father. No national or state holiday celebrates his life. No memorial commemorates his contributions to American life and ideals. His words are rarely quoted by politicians, and his writings are even less frequently cited by pundits. But for the ten-dollar bill, his visage would be utterly unknown to the American people. Unlike Monticello, Mount Vernon, and even Montpelier, his home sits largely unheralded in Harlem just north of City College, begrudgingly preserved and almost never visited. Washington became the father of his nation, and Jefferson its most beloved spokesman. Perhaps fittingly, Hamilton has become its bastard, unrecognized and somehow illegitimate in the public mind.

Why Hamilton should have suffered this fate is itself an interesting subject of speculation. Some of his scholarly defenders have pointed to the propaganda of his Jeffersonian opponents, both in his day and ours. Jefferson and his fellow Republicans heaped calumny upon Hamilton, depicting him as an embryo-Caesar and a tool of plutocratic elites. In this century, politicians of both parties—and writers sympathetic to them—have adopted Jefferson as their guiding light among the founding generation. On both left and right, there have been few willing to oppose the reigning dogma and defend the ambitious New Yorker. The legendary progressive novelist John Dos Passos described him as a crypto-Napoleon who "consolidated property interests" and "inaugurated the authoritarian trend" in American government. Dos Passos's facist counterpart, the expatriate poet Ezra Pound, dismissed Hamilton as "the Prime snot in ALL American history," derisively adding elsewhere that he "was a kike" and "a red headed scotch chew [*sic*]."[151]

These calumnies have been exacerbated by the real flaws in Hamilton's personality. Lacking Jefferson's endearing optimism or Washington's stolidly stoic demeanor, Hamilton was and remains a remote and almost forbidding persona. Arrogant and imperious, disdainful of dissent and utterly unwilling to suffer those he considered fools, Hamilton had little of that warmth or folksiness that Americans have always embraced in their heroes. It is impossible to imagine Hamilton, the ultimate neurotic New Yorker, telling fireside stories and passing a whiskey bottle in a log cabin. By dint of personality and character, he is almost the stereotype of the fast-talking, city-slicking urban "boss" in a Hollywood tale of American politics and history. If Frank Capra or Oliver Stone had made a movie about the American founding, Hamilton would undoubtedly have been cast as the villain, the Gordon Gecko of the early republic.

Ultimately, however, neither bad press nor personal flaws explain the American people's loveless feelings for Hamilton. All of the founders were pilloried in the early American press. Washington was depicted as a senile old fool and Jefferson was denounced as a radical Jacobin atheist. Nor did they lack personality flaws. Washington was known to have a volcanic temper and a deeply avaricious streak, and those intimate with Jefferson were aware of his rather strained relationship with truth-telling. Historians have since remarked Washington's self-centered absorption with his reputation and stunning lack of military skill, while Jefferson has been exposed as a self-deluded ideologue and an outspoken racist crank. Yet both continue to captivate the national imagination. Both still retain their hold on the American heart. Hamilton is different. He is different because the source of his reputation lies neither in the press he has received nor in the traits that defined his character. The problem with Hamilton lies in the self-image of the American people and the way we like to think of ourselves and our past. In the last analysis, we are the problem. We are responsible for Hamilton's historical fate.

At the most elemental level, Americans *do* understand Hamilton. We know that his vision of an enlightened and modern American republic and his practice of the politics of enlightenment are largely responsible for the privileged position, unrivaled power, and unmatched wealth we enjoy. But while we know this, we like to think otherwise. We prefer to see ourselves as uniquely blessed and exceptional, a nation whose might and prosperity are the result of superior virtue, the natural consequence of a unique character, or the blessings of an approving deity. Hamilton forces us to abandon these illusions. His unflinching honesty demands that we recognize that our success is part and parcel of the march of modernity in the western world and our singular embrace of it. We are not exceptional, Hamilton tells us, only more fortunate in our immense resources and lack of traditional cultural and political baggage. Resenting this message, we ignore the messenger lest we feel compelled to preach what we practice.

The people of the United States like to think of American capitalism as a natural system. Our economy is based on the free development and exchange of free individuals, its lineaments set by universal market forces like supply and demand. Hamilton destroys this myth. His legacy reminds us that the American economy never was a "laissez-faire" system determined solely by impersonal market forces. From the outset, the overall trajectory of American economic development has been influenced, if not determined, by initiatives of state, local, and federal government. As much as Americans of all stripes hate to acknowledge this, they know it is true. That is why, with remarkable inconsistency, they demand that all levels of government intercede in their "natural" capitalist economy whenever a recession strikes and unemployment rises.

Even more troubling, Hamilton reminds us that America's great industrial base was not solely the result of technological "Yankee ingenuity" and rags-to-riches tales of enterprising poor boys made good. Rather, it was, in part at least, built on the backs of women and children who filled our first factories and whose descendants could be found there for a full century. Hamilton also reminds us that those women and children who were not in factories worked just as hard and long in the nation's fields and farms as their counterparts in sweatshops. Americans are embarrassed by these truths. We are uncomfortable with the fact that our comforts and wealth are, in part at least, the fruits of such heartless exploitation, an exploitation we currently decry in the third world. We are embarrassed, and so we turn our back on the figure that brings this embarrassment to mind.

Americans like to think of their role in the world as uniquely pacific and idealistic. America is a beacon of freedom and democracy, a light unto the nations. Without doubt, there is some truth in this image. But Hamilton reminds us that this is only part of the picture. Rhetoric aside, American foreign policy has always been based on *réal politique* and cold calculations of national interest. Many of our first hundred years of national history were absorbed with an aggressive and occasionally brutal program of territorial expansion and conquest. Since then our projection of power on a global basis, while often serving the interests of stability and order, has hardly been modest. America is not unique in this regard. Our friends and foes alike operate on the same principles and pursue the same objectives. What is unique about America is our obdurate insistence on cloaking our understandable objectives and policies in idealistic Wilsonian rhetoric. Hamilton removes this rhetorical facade. He reminds us that only a child or a fool could believe that a colonial backwater could emerge as a global hegemon by means of neutrality, high-mindedness, and pacifism. No one becomes a superpower by being nice. Hamilton forces us to acknowledge this obvious truth. And so we turn away from him.

Our greatest problem with Hamilton, however, involves our understanding of the nature of American government itself. We pride ourselves on being a democratic nation, one governed by the will of the people. In a vague way, this is true. Political power is ultimately grounded in popular consent. But in any precise sense of the term, America is not a democracy at all. Ours may be a government for the people, but it has never been a government by or of the people. On the contrary, it is a representative republic whose institutions were explicitly designed to ensure that the popular will would rarely directly drive political policy, and whose representatives have always been drawn from the social and economic elite. Nor does the majority hold sway in all elections, as the presidential ballot of 2000 demonstrated. Indeed, if the popular will were to reign in American elections, most offices would remain vacant, since a clear majority of potential voters consistently refuses to participate in the process. Those who do participate wield influence only if they are organized in a cohesive faction or interest. Whether benign or malevolent, selfish or selfless, these interest groups represent a small minority of the population. They are the elites that govern the nation.

Hamilton knew this, and his experience and legacy remind us of it. More than that, he reminds us why, despite our protestations to the contrary, we want it that way: the people do not always know best. "The people are turbulent and changing," Hamilton claimed; "they seldom judge or determine right." These words offend our sensibilities, in large part because we know they are true. Had the people of Arkansas or even the nation been consulted in 1954 rather than nine un-elected Supreme Court justices, it is highly doubtful that the principle and practice of racial segregation in public education would have been found unconstitutional. Nor is it any more likely that the accused would have been given the safeguards they received in the following decade, or that women in the decade after that would have been given the right to choose whether to have abortions.[152]

Hamilton was the greatest champion of the federal judiciary among the founders precisely because he understood that the least democratic branch of our government was likely to be the strongest bastion of our liberties. Hamilton reminds us that for all our vaunted talk of democracy, it is the rule of law that ensures our freedom and pluralism, and that simple majority rule can all too easily degenerate into mob rule. Hamilton believed this not because he thought the American people were particularly vicious. Rather, it was an unavoidable danger associated with the mass melding of opinion that occurs in any democratic gathering of public sentiment. "In all very numerous assemblies, of whatever characters composed, passion never fails to wrest the scepter from reason," Hamilton tell us in *The Federalist*. "Had every Athenian citizen been a Socrates, every Athenian assembly would still have been a mob." In our most honest, soul-searching moments, we know that Hamilton is telling the truth. For this, he can never be forgiven.[153]

And yet for all his brutal honesty, for all the uncomfortable and unwanted truths he forces upon us, we do honor Hamilton. We honor him implicitly if not explicitly, in practice if not in theory. We honor him when we bask in the glow of our unrivaled power in the world. We honor him when we enjoy our unparalleled wealth and robust prosperity. And we honor him when we embrace the remarkable pluralism and diversity of American life, a pluralism based on individual liberties secured by the rule of law and protected by a strong federal government. When the nation opened its heart to his beloved city of New York in the aftermath of September 11, 2001, it also silently honored him.

Americans have always felt a profound ambivalence about "Hamiltonopolis." New York, and the urban-industrial-commercial order it represents, has often been seen as the source of the nation's corruption, the home of Wall Street financiers who foreclose family farms and are in perennial war against main street U.S.A. But after September 11, Americans remembered that New York, and the other great urban centers like it, are a vital, indeed essential, element in the American dream. The source of our national wealth and power, cities like New York have made America the land of opportunity and the asylum of the world's downtrodden. In grieving for New York and rallying to her defense, America implicitly acknowledged that Hamilton, despite being a bastard and an immigrant, was one of our nation's proudest and greatest sons. His was an odd destiny indeed.

❦

CHAPTER TWO

JOHN ADAMS:
THE ENLIGHTENMENT TRANSCENDED

AN AMERICAN CURMUDGEON

EDMUND BURKE was not one to bandy compliments lightly. None-theless, when told that George Washington was the greatest living man, his answer was remarkably direct. "I thought so too," replied the famed philosopher-statesman, "till I knew John Adams." Almost a quarter century earlier, James Otis had predicted that Adams "would one day be the greatest man in North America." Adams's career as a revolutionary and early American statesman more than vindicated Otis's premonition.[1]

Beginning in 1765 with the Stamp Act crisis—almost a decade before Hamilton, Jefferson, or Franklin joined the cause—Adams had been a diligent and conspicuous champion of the colonial protest movement against Parliament. He published over fifty essays in local newspapers and drafted numerous state and legal papers in defense of colonial rights. As a delegate to the Continental Congress, he quickly emerged as a leading radical and the most outspoken proponent of military resistance and independence. Richard Stockton, a delegate from New Jersey, considered him "the man to whom the country is most indebted for the great measure of independency," calling him "the Atlas of American Independence." His efforts in the Continental Congress, both before and after independence, were truly Herculean. Adams sat on almost one hundred committees and chaired twenty-five of them. He drafted the Declaration of Rights and Grievances, the plan of treaties, and the articles of war. He also oversaw the creation of the fledgling American navy, a lifelong concern.[2]

John Adams was also the foremost constitutional theorist in revolutionary America. Over a decade before the Constitution was drafted, Adams championed a bicameral legislature checked and balanced by a powerful and separate executive and an independent judiciary. At the same time, he was the first to insist that constitutions should be drafted by specially elected conventions and then submitted for popular ratification or rejection. In 1779 he drafted the constitution for his beloved Massachusetts, the only state constitution of that era still in operation.

As a diplomat, Adams served for the better part of a decade in various European courts. At Versailles he fought a bitter and ultimately successful battle for greater French naval and military assistance. At The Hague he single-handedly secured diplomatic recognition of the United States from the Netherlands as well as much-needed financial support. He helped draft the definitive treaty of peace that finally secured American independence and brought the Revolutionary War to a close in 1783. He then served as the first American ambassador to Great Britain while securing diplomatic recognition from Prussia and, with fellow diplomat Thomas Jefferson, negotiating for American shipping rights in the Mediterranean.

Vice President Adams took an active role presiding over the Senate. A loyal supporter of the first president, he cast over thirty tie-breaking votes—more than any other vice president in American history—on behalf of Washington's Federalist administration and its policies. Finally, as Washington's successor in the Oval Office, Adams successfully prosecuted an undeclared naval war with France. Then, with war hysteria gripping the nation—and against the urging of many within his own party and cabinet—he made peace with France, resolving the crisis diplomatically before it could erupt into a dangerously divisive and full-blown armed struggle. No other American founder served his country as long or as effectively as Adams. His credentials as a revolutionary and his résumé as a statesman were the most distinguished in the new nation. Burke knew of what he spoke. By dint of achievement and sacrifice, John Adams was the most important American political leader of his time.

Despite his numerous accomplishments, however, Adams never felt he got the recognition he was due from the American people. He deeply resented the fact that after his dogged struggle for independence in the Continental Congress, it was Thomas Jefferson who secured the laurels for drafting the Declaration of Independence. He chafed at the popular affection for Benjamin Franklin, a relative newcomer to the revolutionary movement, and the downright idolatry of George Washington, a man whom Adams himself had nominated to be commander in chief of the American forces. The history of the revolution, he once complained, would be encapsulated in the following anecdote: "Dr. Franklin's electrical Rod smote the Earth and out sprang General Washington. That Franklin electrified him with his rod—and henceforth these two conducted all the Policy, Negotiations, Legislatures, and War." Adams's sarcasm and self-pity were undoubtedly hyperbolic—he was elected president, after all—but not entirely wide of the mark. Widely respected, he was rarely revered.[3]

Adams attributed his own relative obscurity to his unwillingness to shamelessly puff up his own reputation and accomplishments in the manner he believed his rivals did. Yet the real cause lay elsewhere. Simply put, Adams was a most unlikely hero. His achievements and efforts were splendid and his integrity unquestioned, yet at bottom he was an almost impossible figure for the public to embrace. He may have been the nation's greatest statesman, but was also its most notable curmudgeon.

A Most Unlikely Hero

Adams was not helped by his appearance. Of average height at best, fat, bald, with round, puffy eyes, soft jowls, and mutton-chop whiskers, he looked more a Dickensian merchant than a revolutionary hero. His stiff and awkward manner and penchant for wearing a sword while presiding over the Senate inspired his critics to derisively hail him as "His Rotundity." Adams was acutely aware of how his appearance revealed what he called the "feebleness" and "languor" in his character. Even when animated with rage, his visage was "not like the Lion—there is Extravagance and Distraction in it, that still betrays the same Weakness." Almost a generation older than Hamilton and Madison, and dwarfed in stature by Washington and Jefferson, Adams cut a soft and uninspiring figure.[4]

Adams's flaws were hardly skin deep. His stiff and reserved manner utterly failed to mask a deeply passionate and often emotionally volatile nature. His moods could swing from soaring elation to the blackest despair at an alarmingly rapid pace. Normally warm and affectionate with an earthy sense of humor, when Adams was in a funk he could be testy and downright rude. A mixed delegation of young Bostonians and American naval officers caught Adams in just such a dark mood in 1799. Visiting the president at his summer retreat in Quincy, they were promptly sent packing with an angry diatribe on their effrontery of having dared to pay tribute and honor him without invitation or prior approval.[5]

Like Washington, Adams had an explosive temper; if anything, Adams's fuse was even shorter, and he certainly had less success in restraining his rage. What made his anger all the more unfortunate was that it was combined with a streak of stubbornness that bordered on pigheadedness. Convinced of the righteousness of his own motives and the rectitude of his judgment, Adams was easily goaded into acts of verbal self-destruction. While in diplomatic service in France, the Comte de Vergennes requested that he secure compensation for French merchants and financiers from Congress after that body devalued its currency. Not only did Adams refuse, he sent the French minister of foreign affairs a series of letters demanding greater military and naval resources and questioning the latter's diplomatic strategy. Although polite in tone and largely correct in content, Adams's missives were extremely impolitic. An irate Vergennes broke off the correspondence and sent it to Congress, demanding the blustering Yankee's recall. Franklin's commentary on his colleague's behavior in this episode was acerbic but apt: "he means well for his Country, is always an honest Man, and often a Wise One, but sometimes and in some things, absolutely out of his Senses."[6]

Adams's greatest character flaw, however, was his vanity. It was also the trait with which he was most commonly associated. His diplomatic dispatches were "not remarkable for anything," according to James Madison, "unless it be a display of his vanity." Jefferson reluctantly acknowledged the trait in his friend. Time spent with Adams in Europe had exposed him to overwhelming proof "of a degree of vanity, and blindness to it, of which no germ had appeared in Congress." Jefferson was entirely wrong in one regard, however: no one was more aware of his vanity than Adams himself. "Vanity," he had confided in his diary as a twenty-year-old, "is my cardinal Vice and cardinal Folly." Fully aware that "no accomplishments" or "Virtues are a sufficient Atonement for Vanity" and its inevitable residue, "a haughty and overbearing Temper in Conversation," Adams struggled early and often against his own overweening self-regard. It was a valiant struggle but ultimately futile. Incapable of either containing or concealing his vanity, Adams was as often its victim as its perpetrator.[7]

Adams's flaws were hardly unique. Tiny and frail "Jemmy" Madison was no more physically inspiring than the portly New Englander. George Washington's temper was every bit as volcanic, if more easily governed, and when it came to vanity, Alexander Hamilton took a backseat to no man. What was unique about Adams's foibles, however, was their transparency. It was not that Adams was incapable of concealing them; his diplomatic tenure had taught him the art of masking emotions and presenting a studied appearance to an audience. Rather, he simply refused, indeed disdained, dissimulating his character to his countrymen. This refusal evinces his most distinctive character trait, his dogged honesty. In fact, it was his honesty, far more than his appearance, temper, or vanity, that hurt Adams's reputation with the American public. Adams would no more dissemble his views than mask his flaws. When, beginning in the mid-1780s, those views diverged from the popular wisdom accepted by his countrymen, Adams refused to hold his tongue. On the contrary, he publicized his dissent, lashing out at the received judgment of his time and challenging the cherished verities of his nation. Adams became America's first great political gadfly. Given the inherently unpopular and curmudgeonly nature of that role, it was a marvel that he garnered any public affection at all.

From Common Man to Gentleman

Many of Adams's idiosyncrasies, both foibles and virtues, can be traced to his social and regional background. He lacked the polish, savoir-faire, and gentlemanly manners of a Jefferson, Burr, or Madison for good reason. Those traits were the result of what was known at the time as "good breeding," an immersion in the mores of genteel behavior that was inculcated in the social elite from earliest childhood. Adams was simply not born of that elite. As a result, he was not exposed to those patterns of polite behavior until adulthood. Although his background was hardly as obscure as that of Alexander Hamilton, Adams hailed from distinctly common stock. His father was a common farmer in Braintree, Massachusetts, a provincial rural community on the outskirts of Boston. Although the elder Adams was a respectable figure—he was a deacon in the local church and selectman in the town—he was of the middling stratum at best, supplementing his income as a farmer by making shoes in the winter. In his later years, John fondly recalled a youth spent doing farm chores, tending animals, weeding fields, and carting manure (something he took a lifetime interest and pride in). It was the life to which he was born. But for the imposition of his father, he would willingly have remained in it.

What catapulted Adams out of the ranks of common farmers and into the social and political elite of his province and then his nation was his higher education. As with Alexander Hamilton, college training and high cultural expertise made a gentleman of John Adams. Born in 1735, John was the eldest son of Deacon Adams. Despite young John's own preference for farming, the deacon decided early that his eldest boy was to be educated for a higher, presumably clerical, calling. The only one of his siblings to receive higher education, Adams found his métier in grammar school and later at Harvard. He was an apt and quick student, especially excelling in mathematics and science. Harvard transformed him, opening his eyes to grander vistas and filling him with ambition. College instilled the longing to "start some new Thought" that would "surprize the World" and "raise me at once to fame." Even more than ambition, Harvard left him with a lifelong love of learning. In 1760 he confided to his old college classmate and friend Jonathan Sewall that a life without high cultural pursuits "would be a punishment."[8]

Deacon Adams had intended his son for a ministerial career, and young John seems to have shared his inclination. But his years at Harvard raised troubling doubts. His immersion in the learning of the Enlightenment led him to question several of the central dogmas of the reigning Congregational churches in Massachusetts. After graduation, Adams took a position as a schoolteacher in Worcester while he pondered his future calling. There he fell in with a small circle of deists and radical freethinkers. Although Adams did not share the depths of their alienation and outright hostility to the mainstream of New England Protestantism, his exposure to their views seems to have deepened his own doubts and reservations. The orthodox Calvinist doctrines of predestination and limited atonement struck him as "frigid" and irrational. Even the great mystery of Christ's divinity was no more than "a convenient Cover for absurdity." Given the heterodox nature of his convictions, a clerical career was clearly not in the offing. A little over one year after arriving in Worcester, John Adams reached an agreement with James Putnam, a young attorney, to clerk and study law.[9]

The choice of a legal career proved propitious for the young Adams. The profession was still in its infancy in Massachusetts, and its study encompassed far more than procedures and writs. Sir Edward Coke's *Institutes of the Common Law* was supplemented by Montesquieu's *Spirit of the Laws* and other theoretical works by authors as diverse as Thomas Hobbes and Jean-Jacques Rousseau. "I find myself entering an unlimited Field," he wrote to his friend John Wentworth, one in which "Demosthenes, Cicero, and others of immortal Fame have exulted before me!" In his estimation, the study of the law "incloses the whole Circle of Science and Literature, the History, Wisdom, and Virtue of all ages." Even more than its intellectual content, mastery of the law offered the prospect of earning "the Esteem and perhaps Admiration" of his colleagues who "will spread my Fame thro the Province." Finally, the law represented an excellent venue for Adams's powerful oratorical skills as well as a vent for his undeniably argumentative nature. The law would bring Adams, as one of the most distinguished and celebrated members of the bar, security, wealth, and status. Perhaps most important of all, it would bring him fame and serve as a springboard for his political ambitions. Yet the practice of the law also confirmed him in his stiff and ceremonious manners.[10]

"I was John Yankee and such I shall live and die"

The character of John Adams was influenced by his social background and career trajectory. Equally formative, however, was the regional context from which he came. John Adams was a New England Yankee—in fact, the most prominent Yankee in the early republic. Adams believed that most of his foibles, especially his awkward and formal manner, were typical of his beloved region. The cockpit of colonial protest and resistance, New England—and Massachusetts in particular—was at the vanguard of the revolutionary struggle for independence. Adams not only emerged as his region's most prominent leader in that struggle; he self-consciously represented New England and all it stood for to the nation at large. "I never was however much of John Bull," he confided to his friend James Warren. "I was John Yankee and such I shall live and die."[11]

Aside from mere geography, several features marked New England as a distinct part of early America. Where the southern colonies were riven by a deep racial divide and the mid-Atlantic was peopled by a wide range of national immigrants—English, Germans, Dutch, Scotch-Irish, Welshman, and French Huguenots to name just a few—New England was remarkably ethnically homogenous. Its Puritan past imparted both a unifying and cohesive cultural tradition and a profoundly religious character to its residents. Socially, New England was also homogenous, with a decidedly middle-class character. Outside of cities like Boston, the elite was not as rich or the poor as downtrodden as in other regions in the British colonies. The average New Englander was a middling farmer who, like Deacon Adams, scratched a moderate livelihood from the rocky soil. Families were large, and communities were tightly knit.

The most formative feature of New England was its unique settlement pattern. The vast majority of Yankees lived cheek by jowl in small, nucleated towns. Central to these towns were a set of interlocking institutions that created the intense civic culture and participatory life of its residents. "The Meetinghouse, the Schoolhouse and Training Field," Adams claimed, "are the Scenes where New England men were formed." On the training field the townsmen mustered as militia, democratically electing their officers and forming the nucleus of the most effective fighting force in the colonies. In the meetinghouse the townspeople gathered to hear the Word of God opened, declared, and improved by the locally elected minister. There too they met to choose their representatives to the provincial assembly and elect various town officials. The meetinghouse was also the site where the residents gathered to debate and resolve the issues facing their local community. It was in such meetings that Yankees like John Adams learned to speak their minds, if often in an argumentative, long-winded, and even cantankerous fashion. But perhaps most of all, it was the schoolhouse that made New Englanders such a distinctive folk.[12]

A legacy of the Puritan era, New England in the eighteenth century boasted (with the possible exception of Scotland) the most extensive and effective system of public education in the English-speaking world. An illiterate Yankee was a rare phenomenon, and learning was both broadly distributed and widely recognized as an object of respect and social deference. Indeed, the single strongest correlation to political leadership and power in the Massachusetts Assembly was neither mercantile wealth nor a large landed estate but rather a Harvard education. As Adams would insist at several points throughout his life, the true aristocracy or ruling class of New England was the learned.[13]

The upward trajectory of Adams's life, his ascent from obscurity to wealth and fame by means of higher education, was typically Yankee. In an age when William and Mary, Princeton, and King's College in Manhattan were reserved for the scions of the social elite, the average Harvard student was the son of a respectable middling farmer like Deacon Adams and was the first member of his family to receive a college education. Roughly half of those who graduated entered one of the learned professions—the ministry, medicine, or the law—and, like Adams, succeeded in achieving gentlemanly status. The enlightened ideal of a career open to talent and education was a reality in New England. It was Harvard that set Adams on that path and exposed him to the learning of the Enlightenment that would inform his legal and political career.[14]

Ironically, that very enlightened learning itself led Adams to reject the ministerial career his father had envisioned for him. The rigid doctrines of predestination and limited atonement simply did not square with a modern scientific and secular worldview. Yet for all his philosophical modernism, Adams still bore the imprint of the Puritan legacy that was his Yankee heritage. Original sin and innate human depravity were undeniably absurd theological dogmas, but John Yankee did not entirely reject them. Rather, he secularized them. Man might not be born in a spiritually fallen state, yet Adams remained convinced that human nature was inherently selfish and self-regarding. The doctrine of human perfectibility, so fashionable at the end of the eighteenth century, Adams rejected as an absurd chimera.[15]

While still in his twenties, Adams wrote "An Essay on Man's Lust for Power." Its stated maxim was that "all men would be Tyrants if they could," and its central message was that "the selfish Passions are stronger than the social, and that the former would always prevail over the latter in any Man, left to the natural Emotions of his own Mind." It was this dark reading of human nature—one shared by Machiavelli and even Hume in his political thinking—that informed Adams's fundamental conviction that "no simple Form of Government can possibly secure Men against the Violences of Power." Only a mixed government that combined the voices of the many with those of the few; that contained checks and balances within its various branches; and that clearly separated powers among those branches could ensure the freedom of the public and the liberty of the individual. This conviction was the core of Adams's political message throughout his long political career and his greatest legacy to his nation.[16]

Another Puritan holdover in Adams's Yankee character was his powerful predilection for introspection. Puritans kept journals to monitor their spiritual yearnings and their progress in divine grace and sanctified living. Adams's diary recorded his inner, psychological life and his efforts to reform his behavior. His inward gaze was unflinching and brutally honest. If he was a harsh critic of those around him—and he most assuredly was—it was because he was an even harsher critic of himself. It was this awareness that made it impossible for him ever to complete his own autobiography, despite several attempts. "I look so much like a small boy in my own eyes," he confided to the Philadelphia physician Benjamin Rush, "that with all my vanity I cannot endure the sight of the picture."[17]

Such self-knowledge and critical scrutiny are rare among great and powerful men, and the founding fathers were no exception. Hamilton rarely examined himself; he did not much like what he saw. Jefferson was wise enough to never try. Adams was unique in having the courage to face his own inadequacies.

Adams was acutely aware that his life was filled with "follies, indiscretions, and trifles, enough and too many," but he knew that "crimes, I thank God, I have none to record." He also knew that his maxim that "all men would be Tyrants if they could" applied to himself every bit as much as to others. It was that self-knowledge that animated what historian Joseph Ellis has identified as "the established Adams pattern: to sense where history was headed, make decisions that positioned America to be carried forward on those currents, but to do so in a way that assured his alienation from success." Only then could he be sure that his actions were truly virtuous and that his motives could withstand the scrutiny of his most ruthless critic, namely himself. Such men are rare, and rarer still in political life.[18]

In and of itself, introspection can easily degenerate into wistful navel-gazing or neurotic narcissism. What kept Adams's introspection from degenerating was his secularized Puritan conscience. For Adams this took the form of a fearless self-scrutiny and a fierce sense of duty to the truth. He continuously challenged himself by taking unpopular but principled stands such as his successful legal defense of the British soldiers charged in the Boston Massacre and his dire warnings about the excesses of the French Revolution. Ultimately it was his conscience and duty to the truth that hurt Adams's reputation in his day and that continue to undermine it in our own. For when Adams came to see that the politics of Enlightenment upon which the American republic was founded had taken a turn toward enthusiasm and self-destructive delusion, his conscience forced him to speak out.

Adams became the spokesman for doubt, the great political skeptic warning of the growing irrationalism of the political culture and the failings of his nation. When John Taylor of Virginia preached the popular gospel of innate human equality, Adams was almost shrill in his reply. "That all men are born to equal rights" he readily acknowledged, "but to teach that all men are born with equal powers and faculties, to equal influence in society, to equal property and advantages through life, is as gross as fraud, as glaring an imposition on the credulity of the people as ever was practiced by monks."[19]

Like the sole sober man lecturing his fellows at a bacchanal, Adams's position was not one likely to endear him to his countrymen. He was assailed as an aristocrat, monarchist, Angloman, and Tory and roundly denounced as a hopeless reactionary, incapable of embracing the dawn of the new day heralded by the age of revolutions. Yet Adams also represents an important strain in American thought and culture. Drawing on the tradition of Puritan Jeremiahs, Adams was the first in a long and distinguished line of Yankee critics who raised conscientious doubts about their nation to a public that was not entirely receptive. Such critics and gadflies are never popular figures, and Adams was no exception. Adams's critique of the politics of Enlightenment in the late eighteenth century alienated him from much of the public of his time and assured its view of him as an irascible and pompous curmudgeon. He was a man self-consciously and willfully out of step with his nation. It had not always been so.

THE TURNING

In the years leading up to and through the American Revolution, John Adams was entirely in step with the political currents of his time. Indeed, if anything, he was ahead of them. Adams had been among the first to recognize the dangers of the new imperial policies inaugurated by the Stamp Act crisis of the mid-1760s, and he was one of the first to grasp the necessity of a joint colonial program of resistance. He was at the vanguard of those calling for military measures against the occupying British forces and was the most outspoken champion of independence in the Continental Congress. He was also the first to call for diplomatic engagement in Europe and the new-modeling of state governments along thoroughly republican lines. Most striking of all, however, was the role of enlightened learning in Adams's revolutionary thought. Indeed, such learning was the critical component in his thinking about public liberty during the 1760s and 1770s. Its centrality to his thought bears witness to his complete immersion in the politics of Enlightenment.

Liberty and Learning: The Politics of Enlightenment in John Adams's Revolutionary Thought

For Adams, as for so many philosophes of the eighteenth century, learning was critical. Not only did it promote progress in the arts and sciences, it was also essential for the preservation and growth of public liberty. Adams held that an epoch of modern liberty had emerged as a result of the birth of the new "scientific" learning exemplified by Newton and celebrated by Locke. He shared the confidence in science and scientific rationality that was so characteristic of the Enlightenment, just as he shared its social Epicureanism and its belief in progress. Like most enlightened thinkers, Adams believed that the moderns had indeed surpassed the ancients in knowledge of both natural and political science. For Adams, this new learning both promoted and was buttressed by a rising tide of personal and public liberty. A critical corollary of this belief was his conviction that the learned themselves had a unique role in both fomenting and guiding an enlightened republican politics. Learning and liberty comprised the axis along which Adams constructed his politics of Enlightenment.

In fact, much of Adams's early political writing and thinking emerged from the clubbical practices of enlightened learned associations. In early 1765 Adams joined a small legal club or "sodality" devoted to the "study of Law and oratory." When the group decided to study the feudal law and the orations of Cicero, Adams seized the opportunity to draft an extended piece of political analysis subsequently known as *A Dissertation on the Canon and the Feudal Law*. The *Dissertation* proved a powerful work of colonial protest that earned him election to the English Society for the Bill of Rights. This intercourse between the private realm of learned and voluntary associations and the public world of politics and the press was characteristic of the Enlightenment and one of its most vital means of forming public opinion. Adams saw even such radical political institutions as the Sons of Liberty—the most famous patriot association in the years leading up to independence—through the lens of his own learned, clubbical experiences. His diary entry of a meeting with them "at their own Apartment in Hanover Square" in January 1766 reads like any other eighteenth-century fraternal gathering devoted to sociable gustatory and conversational pleasure: "We had Punch, Wine, Pipes and Tobacco, Bisquit and Cheese." Even more notable was the discourse itself, "nothing but such Conversation as passes at all Clubbs among Gentlemen about the Times."[20]

"Knowledge," Adams claimed, "is among the most essential Foundations of Liberty." In his first major publication he claimed that "whenever a general knowledge and sensibility have prevail'd among the people, arbitrary government, and every kind of oppression, have lessened and disappeared in proportion." Just as virtue gave the people the moral character to resist attempts upon their liberties, learning gave them the requisite "intellectual" means to recognize and respond to such threats. "As long as Knowledge and Virtue are diffused generally among the Body of a Nation," Adams told his fellow residents of Braintree in 1772, "it is impossible they should be enslaved." Conversely, Adams observed in his "Novanglus" essays of 1774, "almost all mankind have lost their liberties through ignorance."[21]

Although such encomiums on learning might be found in the classical and seventeenth-century commonwealth traditions, what marked Adams's thought as enlightened was his insistence that the rise of modern liberty in the post-feudal epoch depended on the rise of a distinctly modern high cultural tradition. For Adams, it was not the Renaissance recovery of classicism that created a new age of public liberty, but rather the development of enlightened scientific learning. This modern revolution in knowledge was sparked by the rise of commerce and printing in the age of the Protestant Reformation and reached its apogee in the works of Newton and Locke.

The advantages of this modern learning over its rivals were obvious. Ancient and scholastic learning had built speculative systems on the basis of dogmatic first principles. Modern, post-Newtonian learning, by contrast, was based on the development of a scientific method of careful empirical research and the discovery of lawlike (and often mechanistic) regularities. While still a student at Harvard, Adams noted that it was modern "natural philosophy" or physics that had resulted in the remarkable material progress in "the state of all the Civilized nations of Europe, compared to many nations."[22]

Just as modern learning in the realm of nature was based on the empirical method exemplified by Newton and celebrated by Locke, so too the "Science of Government" was "best pursued by Observation and Experiment." Indeed, it was in this scientific spirit that Adams read many of the republican writings of the seventeenth century. He compared the relation of property and power in the writings of James Harrington—one of the most famed English republicans of the previous century—to Newton's first law of gravity. That "Power always follows Property," he held, is every bit "as infallible a Maxim in Politicks, as, that Action and Re-action are equal, is in Mechanicks." And just as each modern science had its own unique objects, so too the modern science of politics took as its object "human nature and human life."[23]

For Adams, only the vast sweep of human history could "spread before Us a Map of Man" in all its varying states. Such a "map of man" must examine the human condition in its "different Soils and Climates, in different Nations and Countries, under different Religions and Customs, in Barbarity and Civility, in a State of Ignorance and enlightened with Knowledge, in Slavery and in freedom," as well as "in Infancy and Age." And in fact, the vast bulk of Adams's political "science" consisted of historical exegesis and analysis, not only in such early works as the *Dissertation* and "Novanglus" but in his later *Defense of the Constitutions of the Government of the United States of America* and his *Discourses on Davila* as well. Such a science of government, however, was more than a merely academic object of high cultural curiosity. Only by learning the lessons of history, and by understanding the universal laws of political and social development that its study disclosed, could the people recognize assaults on their liberties and successfully resist them. For Adams, it was hardly an exaggeration to claim that "the divine science of politics is the science of social happiness."[24]

Given the signal importance of learning for liberty, Adams insisted that it was critical that it be diffused as broadly as possible. Obviously this entailed a thoroughgoing commitment to public education. As early as 1760 Adams had responded tartly to the suggestion that Massachusetts's "Free schools are the very bane of society" in that "they make the lowest part of the People infinitely conceited." Adams noted caustically that such sentiments "would come naturally enough from the mouth of a Tyrant or of a K[ing] or Ministry about introducing an Arbitrary Power." Five years later his position had not changed. Although the maintenance of free public schools often required taxing the wealthy for a service they did not use, "the preservation of the means of knowledge, among the lowest ranks, is of more importance to the public, than all the property of all the rich men in the country." On the eve of independence he remained just as adamant. In a proclamation he drafted for the General Court of Massachusetts in early 1776, Adams reminded the newly republicanized political community that "a Government so popular can be Supported only by universal Knowledge." In *Thoughts on Government*, published the same year, he urged his counterparts in other states to undertake a similar program of mass public education, arguing that "to a humane and generous mind, no expense for this purpose would be thought extravagant."[25]

Adams's goal of diffusing learning was not, however, limited to institutions of formal education. The press was equally important. The press kept a vigilant public informed of events abroad as well as developments at home. It had been the wisdom of previous Bay legislators to insist that "the art of printing should be encouraged, and that it should be easy and cheap and safe for any person to communicate his thoughts to the public." Public schools and a free press had produced a society of enlightened people capable of defending their liberties in the face of threats from the most powerful nation in Europe. "All ranks and orders of our People, are intelligent," Adams observed, and a New Englander who "cannot read and write is as rare a Phenomenon as a Comet."[26]

As essential as the broad diffusion of learning was to the preservation of liberty, it was not in itself sufficient. The defense of liberty also required the further advance of learning at the university level. Adams's commitment to higher education was predicated on his belief that an enlightened republican order placed special demands on the learned. In New England, Adams noted, Harvard had not only facilitated scientific research, it had also produced "persons of great eminence" and "initiated them in those arts and sciences which qualified them for public employments, both in church and state." For Adams, these demands on a learned and enlightened elite were both theoretical and practical. That a truly republican political order would require high cultural expertise seemed intuitive to him; only by careful analysis and instruction could statesmen accurately perceive threats to public liberty. Indeed, such habits of reflection and learned discussion were critical in forging a united front against British encroachment.[27]

It was in this light that he first came to view the Continental Congress. In the summer of 1774 he described the upcoming assemblage as "a Conclave, a Sanhedrin, A Divan" fully comparable to the classical "Court of Ariopagus" or "the council of the Amphyctions." Such a learned body was critical, in Adams's judgment, because so few men were truly "fit to govern Such mighty Interests, as are clashing in the present Contest." Adams proposed to solve this shortage by coopting the congress as a political "university" to train statesmen: "I am for making it an annual [event], and for Sending an entire new set every Year, that all the principal Geniuses may go to the University in Rotation." Liberty thus required more than just an educated public—it also needed a central and public role for the learned themselves.[28]

Part of this public role for the learned was theoretical or scholarly. Educated elites should devote their energies to the study of history and political theory with an eye toward educating the people about their rights and obligations. In his 1765 *Dissertation on the Canon and the Feudal Law*, Adams called on his learned brethren to take up this intellectual challenge. "Let every sluice of knowledge be open'd and set a flowing," he urged. Just as the famed "encroachments upon liberty in the reigns of the first James and the first Charles" Stuart had "produced the greatest number of consummate statesmen, which has ever been seen in any age or nation," so the "prospect, now before us, in America, ought in the same manner to engage the attention of every man of learning to matters of power and right." Only through such study could they ensure that "we may be neither led nor driven blindfolded to irretrievable destruction" by the threats to American liberties from Great Britain. And such high cultural efforts on behalf of liberty could in turn benefit learning itself, which could only further redound to the advance of freedom.[29]

What marks Adams's revolutionary thought as so thoroughly enlightened is this conviction that the relation between learning and liberty was progressive. Learning helped promote liberty, which in turn promoted further learning. The result was potentially unlimited progress in the theory and practice of "social happiness," progress grounded in the advancement of high cultural knowledge and expertise among an educated elite. As the famed Scottish philosopher Dugald Stewart put it, "if the multitude must be led, it is of consequence, surely, that it should be led by Enlightened conductors."[30]

When it came to his own scholarly responsibilities, Adams was certainly diligent. His *Dissertation on the Canon and the Feudal Law* exemplified that kind of learned and scholarly defense of liberty that he had demanded from early America's educated elite. Begun in 1765 in response to a proposal from his newly formed club of attornies, the essay was ostensibly an analysis of an arcane and outdated legal code. In fact, however, the *Dissertation* was a heroic narrative of the phoenixlike rise of modern liberty from the ashes of medieval despotism. This rise of modern liberty served as the backdrop for Adams's exegesis of the history of early America and New England in particular. Nor was this tale of purely academic interest. As Adams later recalled, his intention was to educate his fellow citizens about "the means by which human nature had been degraded in Europe" and how "their ancestors had wisely and virtuously endeavored, to Screen them from those means." If nothing else, Adams's history did not lack in relevance.[31]

Central to Adams's tale of the rise of modern liberty was the role of learning. The tyrannical system of absolute monarchy that ensued with the fall of the Roman Empire in western Europe was exemplified by the canon and feudal legal codes that enslaved the minds of Europeans. The canon law promoted superstition and debased the popular mind. The "Romish Clergy" claimed the "power of procuring or withholding rain" and even the "management of earthquakes, pestilence and famine." The fruits of the feudal law were no better. Originally designed "for the necessary defense of a barbarous people against her neighbouring nations," it was a "code of laws, for a vast army, in a perpetual encampment," that placed all power and landed property in the hands of the supreme military chief. The result was that the "common people were held together, in herds and clans, in a state of servile dependence on their lords." But this degradation was not purely political, for the feudal law also produced a society whose members were kept "in a state of total ignorance of everything divine and human, excepting the use of arms and the culture [cultivation] of their lands." The canon and feudal law had combined to usher in a veritable dark age in western Europe.[32]

What finally ended this dark age was the onset of the Protestant Reformation. With its questioning of authority and its diffusion of saving knowledge through the printing press, the Reformation sparked a new spirit of inquiry and liberty. Nowhere was the consequent spread of knowledge more dramatic than in the England of Thomas More, William Shakespeare, and Francis Bacon. As this new learning "increased and spread among the people," they asserted their rights and laid claim to their liberties. The ensuing struggle for liberty reached a violent and critical crescendo during the Stuart dynasty of the seventeenth century, when the English people at long last secured that system of ordered liberty for which they had become so justly famous.[33]

It was this very struggle for liberty and a free constitution that had "peopled America." It was "a love of universal Liberty," Adams insisted, and not simply "religion alone," that had inspired the Great Migration of the founders of New England. The elimination of episcopacy and sacerdotal ordination not only liberated the Puritan ministers from "the civil powers"; it also "imposed an obligation on the whole body of the clergy, to industry, virtue, piety, and learning," an obligation that was heroically met. Prudently, the first settlers had created a system of free public schools. "The education of all ranks of people was made the care and expense of the public in a manner," Adams declared with obvious pride, "that I believe has been unknown to any other people ancient or modern." But the founders did not stop there. The earliest New England legislators had immediately set about creating and publicly supporting institutions of higher learning. They had also sought to encourage "the art of printing," as had subsequent generations of New England legislators. Such a wise and learned policy had produced the most remarkable results: "All Ranks and orders of our People" were both "intelligent" and "accomplished."[34]

Given this achievement, Adams was understandably concerned that such learning be deployed to deflect the threat posed by the Stamp Act, which was nothing less than "a direct and formal design on foot, to enslave all America." Nor was the Stamp Act the only issue illuminated by the past. History also taught the dangers of simple, unmixed, and unbalanced constitutional schemes. In 1772 Adams informed his fellow residents of Braintree that a historical analysis of the classical republics of "Greece, Rome, Carthage," as well as their modern counterparts such as "the English, Dutch and Swiss," demonstrated that "the best Governments of the World have been mixed." History also justified resistance to the newly created and crown-funded civil list in Massachusetts by which colony officials would have been paid directly by the metropolitan authorities rather than by the Bay legislature. The examples of France, Spain, Sweden, Denmark, and Poland all showed that legislative payment of judicial and executive salaries was essential. "If our Governors and Judges and other Officers and Magistrates are to be supported by the Ministry, without the Gifts of the People," Adams reasoned, it would be impossible to "remonstrate against Grievances and demand and obtain Redress of them." Obviously, it was the pedagogical responsibility of the learned to defend public liberty by revealing and diffusing the lessons of history.[35]

In addition to these scholarly duties, the learned also faced imposing practical responsibilities in an enlightened republican order. Not only were the intellectuals to enlighten the public mind; they also had to lead the political community in its struggle for liberty. Statesmen as well as scholars, the educated elite of early America had to be prepared to assume control of the political communities' legislatures and councils. This was a purported role that was hardly unique to the thought of Adams. The presumably beneficial results of the political empowerment of the educated elite was a byword of the politics of Enlightenment, whether it took the form of chosen advisers to "enlightened despots" or an emerging notability among the bureaucratic *noblesse de robe* and its growing association with the learned academies and sophisticated salons. But for Adams in 1776, this role took on an extended dimension.

Educated statesmen were not merely enacting laws, they were "new-modeling" polities. Adams reveled in the opportunity to craft constitutions with a freedom from constraint unknown since the time of Solon and Lycurgus, the famed legendary constitutional statesmen of ancient Greece. "You and I," he informed Richard Henry Lee of Virginia, "have been sent into life at a time when the greatest lawgivers of antiquity would have wished to live."[36]

Adams, Lee, and other learned political leaders comprised a special elite in revolutionary America, one commonly characterized as a *natural aristocracy*. Unlike traditional aristocracies based on heredity, these natural aristocrats were purportedly public-minded, virtuous men distinguished from their more common brethren by their high cultural attainment or merit. It was, in part at least, this notion of natural aristocracy that both displayed the Enlightenment's influence on American republican political culture and evinced the limits of its egalitarianism.

In the years after 1780 Adams wrote extensively—and quite controversially—on natural aristocracy. Well into his retirement from politics in the early nineteenth century, he entered into a lengthy and passionate debate on the subject with Thomas Jefferson. But the phrase simply does not occur in his revolutionary writings. Instead, Adams referred to the political role of the learned as that of "public attorneys." Unlike aristocrats (natural or otherwise), who represent a qualitatively higher order of humanity than the vulgar, public attorneys were mere "agents and trustees for the people." This choice of phrase is deeply revealing. Most obviously, as a prominent lawyer, Adams was clearly thinking of himself and his own role as a political leader and public intellectual. And lawyers did have a central role in Massachusetts politics, one that would expand with the revolution and its aftermath.[37]

What distinguished an attorney from a common pettifogger was his technical expertise and training in a rigorous form of judicial reasoning and disputation. Such expertise enabled attorneys to pursue the interests of their clients. Thus, relative to the proceedings for which they were employed, attorneys were a disinterested lot, at least to the extent that they pursued their clients' interests directly and their own only indirectly. It was this disinterested nature of the attorney relative to his client that made the educated elite, at least in Adams's mind, worthy of public trust as attorneys for the body politic. As a good attorney practices his craft with an understanding of his client's wishes, so in politics the people reserved to themselves "a right to give their attornies instructions how to vote." And just as a client can replace an ineffective or intransigent lawyer with another, so public elections gave the people the ultimate power of "discarding an old attorney, and choosing a wiser and a better" one to speak on behalf of the public interest. Although learned statesmen and legislators would use their high cultural expertise to serve the public according to the dictates of reason and conscience, the people reserved to themselves the "fundamentals of government."[38]

If drafting the law required high cultural expertise, the same training and knowledge were necessary to interpret and administer it. Whether appointed by the executive or elected by the legislature, the judiciary, Adams argued, "ought to be independent" so that "it may be a check upon both." Such independent jurists must "always be men of learning and experience in the laws" as well as exemplary in their character. The goal of a learned judiciary was not unique to Adams, but he was willing to go further than most to secure it. In order to induce legal scholars to serve the public, he thought they should be granted "estates for life in their offices" and rewarded with handsome "salaries ascertained and established by law." Only impeachment by the popular branch of the legislature before the executive could remove the appointed and chief judicial officers in Adams's enlightened ideal order.[39]

For Adams, then, the interdependence of liberty and learning rested on two fundamental requirements. First, learning must be diffused as broadly as possible. This would ensure an enlightened citizenry capable of making informed political decisions and recognizing threats to their public liberties. It would also result in a virtuous citizenry, even if those virtues were decidedly modern and "bourgeois" rather than classically severe or traditionally Christian. But every bit as important as the diffusion of knowledge, the learned themselves must both assume and be entrusted with positions of authority. Only then could advances in political science impact the practice of government. It was this dual role of learning and the learned in the ideal republican order that lay at the heart of Adams's revolutionary politics of Enlightenment.[40]

Given the critical importance of learning to liberty, Adams's rather hyperbolic reaction to the imperial legislation of the 1760s and 1770s becomes more comprehensible. No small part of what made the threat of Parliament's imperial initiatives so frightening to Adams was that they often seemed to attack liberty at its learned root. As Adams saw it, a ministerial conspiracy seemed afoot to undermine the public mind of America. What made this conspiracy so dangerous was that it undermined the power of learning to promote liberty at the most fundamental level. On the one hand, British politicians—and their Tory allies in America—sought to render the people pliant by promoting ignorance. On the other hand, British and Tory policies threatened the disinterested role of the learned as political attorneys of the people by either displacing or corrupting them. It was in part the depth and subtlety of these combined strategies that convinced Adams that a plot had been hatched to destroy the liberties of America.

The British attempt to foster ignorance in the colonies was apparent to Adams as early as the Stamp Act controversy. In the final installation of *A Dissertation on the Canon and the Feudal Law*, Adams got to the real danger posed by the Stamp Act. It seems "very manifest from the S---p A-t itself, that a design is form'd to strip us in a great measure of the means of knowledge." The additional cost of stamped diplomas, books, and other college documents would limit access to Harvard and Yale to the wealthiest. This would destroy one of the principal avenues of social mobility and undermine the enlightened ideal of the career open to talents rather than birth. But the Stamp Act did more than that. It also assaulted some of the principal means by which learning and knowledge were diffused to the general public. The tax would "load" the press, Adams complained, the book and pamphlet industries, and "even an Almanack and a News-Paper, with restraints and duties" that would ratchet their prices beyond the resources of most consumers. The common people—especially the lower sort—would have no choice but to wallow in ignorance or give "their little subsistence" in pursuit of knowledge to "a set of stamp officers, distributors, and their deputies." Higher, lower, and popular education were all under assault from a phalanx of British officials and their local minions who sought to destroy the spirit of liberty by undermining the diffusion of learning and knowledge among the people.[41]

The British and their local henchmen also sought to displace and corrupt the American learned community by means of places and pensions. Placemen literally displaced the learned elite from positions of legislative and judicial authority. Rather than going to Harvard-educated Yankees, such positions were filled by clients of metropolitan patrons or pensioners of the local Tory leader Thomas Hutchinson. Once in power, Adams insisted, these placemen had an interest in further debasing the liberty and learning of the colony so that they might retain their authority.[42]

Adams directed his harshest criticism at Thomas Hutchinson, whose accumulation of offices and places, more than any other single initiative, threatened the public role of the enlightened philosophes in Massachusetts. When Adams himself was approached with the rather lucrative post of advocate general in the Court of Admiralty in 1768—a position he promptly refused—he readily understood what was afoot. With such overtures and pensions, Tories purchased support among the learned while denying "places" of public service and authority to truly independent patriot philosophes. Those who supported Hutchinson in his "new-regulating" of the colonies were "promoted to some place of honor and profit," while anyone who dared to defend popular liberty from "those innovations, was depressed, degraded, and persecuted, so far as it was in the power of the government to do it." Indeed, Governor Francis Bernard's veto of the popular patriot James Otis's election as speaker of the House in the aftermath of the repeal of the Stamp Act made it abundantly clear, at least to Adams, that "every man who should dare to oppose such projects" would "surely be cut off from all hopes of advancement."[43]

Adams was forthright in acknowledging that his fellow Whigs were animated by "ambition, a desire for profit, and other passions, like other men." His honesty and conscience demanded as much. Nonetheless, he could state without reservation that when these Whigs—like himself—had been given the opportunity to betray the liberties of the people for their own aggrandizement, they "sacrificed their private interest to the nation's honor and the public good in so remarkable a manner" that he could find no parallel "in the whole British empire."[44]

Even the press had been subject to attempts at corruption by Hutchinson and his clique. Adams replied to charges that the Whigs had censored dissenting voices in the press by noting the "constant reward of every scribbler who has taken up the pen on the side of the ministry." The sums Adams reported were staggering: "two, three, four, five, six, eight, fifteen hundred pounds sterling a year" were the rewards doled out for "the most wretched productions of dullness itself." As a point of reference, Adams's income from his legal practice at its high point was about three hundred pounds per year, and his was one of the most successful in the province. Clearly, such corruption of one of the principal means of diffusing learning and knowledge was no trivial matter. It threatened a vital pillar of public liberty. Without an independent and critical role for the learned political attorneys of the people and a truly free press, how could the public mind ever remain informed—much less instructed—on those matters that were vital to its interests and liberties? The Tory/ministerial assault on the independence of learning and the learned not only threatened the public understanding and character of the American people; it robbed them of the cultural resources essential for defending their liberties. Without these resources, they could never hope to maintain an enlightened political order.[45]

With the coming of independence, Adams began to detect a danger to learning and liberty from another, more local source. Independence had meant the reconstitution of the new states along more popular and republican lines. As the people came into power, they began to question the old authorities and elites that had previously presumed a right to lead them. Most notably, this involved a vastly weakened executive in the new state governments since executives had generally been appointed by the crown in the years before independence. But it also took the form of a suspicion of educated elites who claimed superior political insight based on their high cultural expertise. Nonetheless, throughout the revolutionary period Adams remained committed to the belief that liberty depended on learning and that the learned ought to serve as disinterested political attorneys and pedagogues of public opinion. In fact, Adams placed much of the blame for popular anti-intellectualism on the learned themselves. He urged Jonathan Dickinson Sergeant "to persuade Gentlemen of Education to lay aside Some of their Airs" and avoid ridiculing the people's "favourite Notions" if they were merely innocent prejudices which might easily be indulged "without the least deviation from Honour or Virtue." The educated elite could not "expect the Confidence of the common People if they treat them ill" or wear their high cultural endowments like a badge of exclusive privilege.[46]

For Adams, the dependence of liberty on learning was the sine qua non of enlightened government. It was the modern scientific learning of the Enlightenment that revealed the laws and lessons of history that were essential to the preservation and progress of popular liberty. Without broad public education and the ready diffusion of knowledge, the common people would be incapable of intelligently exercising, much less defending, their rights. And the sort of erudition gained at institutions of higher education in turn helped inculcate the high cultural expertise necessary for disinterested and prudent statecraft. It was this critical reliance of liberty on learning that, for Adams at least, revealed the truly frightening aspect of the policies of the ministry and its Tory allies. These policies were more than an attempt to tax the colonists without their consent. By undermining learning itself, they sought to pull up the American tree of liberty by its enlightened cultural roots.

In the years following the close of the revolution, however, Adams's thought underwent a transformation. He came to reconsider the relationship of liberty and learning. The possibilities of spreading Enlightenment seemed less propitious, and its reception among the people less certain. Adams also began to entertain doubts about the disinterestedness and virtue of the learned, questioning whether they really were merely political attorneys of the public. Even learning itself seemed as potentially dangerous as it was liberating. The John Adams who returned from his diplomatic service in Europe at the end of the 1780s was a noticeably changed man. His faith in the politics of Enlightenment had been shaken. From one of its most vociferous champions, he had become its most outspoken skeptic. John Adams had become the political gadfly of the early republic.[47]

The Nature of the Change: The Dangers of Learning

In his postrevolutionary writings, John Adams's understanding of the politics of Enlightenment underwent a profound transformation. Where his previous position had been progressive and optimistic, he now evinced a growing skepticism—if not pessimism—about the role of learning and the learned in the republican public sphere. He came to appreciate their limits and pitfalls, and ultimately he raised critical questions about the course of development of enlightened thought in the final decades of the eighteenth century. During his presidency, Adams was charged with a fundamental hostility to the Enlightenment and the whole notion of progress, a charge he bristled at with great indignation. Adams did not, of course, reject the Enlightenment or the belief in its potentially salutary impact on republican government. He remained committed to what he considered the scientific mode of political analysis and continued to enjoin the value of public education and learned statesmanship. But he did come to appreciate that the process of Enlightenment and progress faced real limits, and that the advance of learning and the influence of the learned were not as straightforwardly salutary as he had previously assumed.

Adams continued to believe, for example, in the importance of disseminating learning through public education and the press. In his *Discourses on Davila* (1790), he insisted that it was "scarcely possible" that there could be "too many or too great" efforts made on behalf of "general education." He did, however, insist that such efforts could expect only a limited return. Despite all possible "encouragement, public and private," for the education of the public, Adams acknowledged that "the laboring part of the people can never be learned." The dream of universal Enlightenment was just that, a dream. It ignored the "great question" that "will forever remain," namely *who shall work?*" The realities of the need to earn wages for the propertyless bulk of humanity entailed that "Leisure for study must ever be the portion of a few."[48]

In his reassessment of the potential for the broad dissemination of learning, Adams was actually moving closer to the mainstream of enlightened opinion, which, throughout the eighteenth century, had seen the diffusion of high culture as a necessarily limited phenomenon. Indeed, part of the appeal of early enlightened discourse was its relative inaccessibility and consequent snob appeal. Both Lord Shaftesbury's *Characteristics of Men, Manners, Opinions, Times* and Joseph Addison and Richard Steele's *Spectator*—two of the most prominent works of the early Enlightenment—were pitched to a relatively small "polite" audience with the clear presumption that part of the pleasure they provided was an awareness of their refined exclusivity. In comparison to such Augustan worthies, Adams's mature views were relatively progressive. Yet to John Taylor, an older and wiser Adams insisted that "there can never be, in any nation, more than one fifth—no, not one tenth of the men, regularly educated to science and letters." This was admittedly a small minority, though still far larger than the tiny erudite circle envisioned by Voltaire, who had surmised that 95 percent of the human species were constrained to lives of manual labor and thus would "never know that there is a Locke in the world." Regardless of the degree of dissemination attainable, Adams insisted that the reality and lesson of its limits were unavoidable. Since knowledge was a source of distinction, some people will always have "more influence in society than others; and consequently, that some will always be aristocrats, and others democrats." The dissemination of knowledge certainly helped enlighten the public, but its limits assured that it was a source of inequality and division as well as a pillar of liberty.[49]

The mature Adams also expressed a growing skepticism about the advance of learning in matters of political theory. Where Adams had previously waxed rhapsodic about the spreading application of the scientific method to the great questions of free government, he was now struck by the almost complete absence of progress in modern political thought. "Is it not unaccountable," Adams asked, "that the knowledge of all the principles and construction of free governments should have remained at a full stand for two or three thousand years?" This failure was all the more striking in that all the other "arts and sciences, in general, during the last three or four centuries, have had a regular course of progressive improvement." All the more shocking then that "the science of government has received very little improvement since the Greeks and Romans." Even the great Machiavelli had merely "revived the ancient politics," while the celebrated Montesquieu had "borrowed the best part of his book" from the Florentine purveyor of classical wisdom. Such great seventeenth-century republicans as "Milton, Harrington, Sidney" had in turn simply drawn on the ancients and Machiavelli and were in this regard closely "followed by Locke, Hoadley, &c."[50]

Even such advances in learning as had occurred were hardly an unambiguous boon to the commonweal. This is not to say that Adams took a reactionary position against the process of Enlightenment. During the onset of the French Revolution he continued to hold that "the progress of reason, letters, and science, has weakened the church and strengthened the common people" throughout Europe, and he optimistically hoped that if the people were "honestly and prudently conducted by those who have their confidence," they "will infallibly obtain a share in every legislature." But for Adams, the conditional and qualifying phrase became the operative one. The advance of political science could benefit the cause of republican liberty *only* if its enlightened purveyors could be constrained to behave "honestly and prudently." Increasingly, Adams had great anxieties about this condition. "Bad men increase in knowledge as fast as good men," he warned, "and science, arts, taste, sense, and letters are employed for the purpose of injustice and tyranny as well as those of law and liberty; for corruption, as well as for virtue." The high cultural means of political emancipation could evidently be as poisonous as the fruit of the biblical tree of knowledge.[51]

Adams's greatest reservations about the politics of Enlightenment, however, were directed at the political agency of the learned. Where

Adams had previously championed the empowerment of philosophe statesmen as a necessary bulwark of republican liberty, he was now far less sanguine about their influence. Hardly the disinterested public attorneys he had once described, the learned were no less sordid than their less enlightened neighbors. While scholars admittedly "renounce their pleasures, neglect their exercises, and destroy their health," their motive was far from disinterested. "The universal object and idol of men of letters is *reputation*," Adams insisted. Nor did men of learning necessarily abjure the more temporal pleasures of life. Although "men of letters must have a great deal of praise," Adams claimed, they also demand "some of the necessaries, conveniences, and ornaments of life." Indeed, it was precisely because "the people have almost always expected to be served gratis" that "democracy, simple democracy, never had a patron among men of letters." Like everyone else, the learned had their price. Wise they might be, but disinterested they assuredly were not.[52]

Nor did the character of the learned inspire any more confidence than their motives. Ancient history gave ample proof that learned priests selfishly "monopolized learning" and had consequently "really governed all mankind." This jealous possession of knowledge was matched among the learned by a thoroughgoing pugnacious dogmatism and intolerance, both in ancient and modern times. "You may read the history of all the universities, academies, monasteries of the world," Adams informed John Taylor, and "you will find in them as many parties and factions, as much jealousy and envy, hatred and malice, revenge and intrigue, as you will in any legislative assembly or executive council, in the most ignorant city or village." Whatever advantages study did confer on the learned, they clearly did not include moral or personal rectitude. Given the "perpetual strife" within the republic of letters and the "hatred and malice" that characterized the interactions of the learned, it was only natural that Adams would have some reservations about the value of their leadership both in the realm of public opinion and in the councils of government.[53]

Hardly a source of superior virtue and humanity, learning was in fact the principal source of social inequality. In a remarkable passage on the nature of class distinctions written after his turning, Adams reduced all class differences to that between the "gentlemen and the simplemen." The gentlemen were neither the wealthy nor the well born; rather, they were "all those who have received a liberal education, an ordinary degree of erudition in liberal arts and sciences." The learned enjoyed this privileged status "whether by birth they be descended from magistrates and officers of government, or from husbandmen, merchants, mechanics or laborers, or whether they be rich or poor." Nonetheless, given the expense of education, Adams noted that "*generally* those who are rich, and descended from families in public life, will have the best education in arts and sciences."[54]

Not only did learning confer an "aristocratic" distinction on gentlemen, history demonstrated that learned gentlemen were filled by "a constant energy and effort" to further "increase the advantages they possess over" the common folk so as "to augment their wealth and influence at their expense." Adams had once celebrated the learned character of Massachusetts's founders and political leaders. Now he pointedly asked, "are they not aristocrats?" The obvious answer was an unequivocal yes. Not only had "these men governed the province from its first settlement," they "have governed, and still govern, the state" regardless of the demise of monarchy and the rise of a purely enlightened republican order. To the charge of "erecting an aristocratic order of thinking men, in contradiction to the democratical order of unthinking men," Adams pleaded a loud and defiant nolo contendere: "Well! Is there not such a distinction in nature?" Clearly, John Adams had come a long way since his optimistic musings about liberty and learning in the 1760s and 1770s. His thinking about the politics of Enlightenment had undergone a profound sea change.[55]

The Sources of Disillusionment

That John Adams's views changed in the course of the 1780s was hardly a secret. His friend and correspondent Mercy Otis Warren noted in her history of the American Revolution that, upon his return from Europe,

Adams "was implicated by a large portion of his countrymen, as having relinquished the republican system, and forgotten the principles of the American revolution, which he had advocated for near twenty years." Adams bristled at the charge, yet while he had not abandoned "the republican system," he had reevaluated the politics of Enlightenment that underlay it. Several factors combined to prompt this reevaluation, one so profound that Warren found it "inconsistent with his former professions of republicanism."[56]

Troubles at Home, Troubles Abroad

Domestic developments during the struggle for independence gave Adams little cheer. With the exception of Gates's stunning victory at Saratoga in the autumn of 1777, news of the war was overwhelmingly discouraging. Even more disturbing, however, was the failure of the nation's political leadership to address the problems besetting the revolutionary cause and threatening the stability of American republican government. Like Hamilton, Adams quickly came to see that the biggest crises facing the early republic were financial. Runaway inflation and a rapidly "depreciating Currency," Adams informed the president of the Continental Congress in early 1779, were clearly "the greatest Source of Danger and Unhappiness to the States." The solution seemed equally obvious. A combination of vigorous taxes and decreases in discretionary spending would both finance the war and reduce inflation by taking much of the currency out of circulation.[57]

But instead of following such common sense, Adams saw the states spend like drunken sailors without enhancing their revenues one whit. His hope that the influence of middling farmers on the government would "after a little while, take Care of the Coxcombs and Coquettes," proved groundless. Several years later Adams was forced to acknowledge that in the course of the war and its inflationary cycle, his countrymen had "rushed headlong into a greater degree of luxury than ought to have crept in for a hundred years."[58]

By the early 1780s it had become evident to Adams that the states were both unwilling and unable to address the fiscal needs of the nation. The failures of the states were not simply the result of a dearth of public virtue and enlightened leadership. Their governments were deeply flawed constitutionally. Most lacked powerful executives to check the legislative branch, and in some cases the legislatures lacked an upper body to balance the popular assembly, a form of government under which "no country will ever be long happy, or ever entirely safe and free."[59]

Given the failures of the states, it fell upon the shoulders of the national Congress to redress the crisis of currency by assuming the power of taxation. By 1783 Adams had become convinced that if Congress did not take this measure "to satisfy their creditors at home and abroad," the United States would soon "be so far despised, that it will be but a few years, perhaps but a few months only, before we are involved in another war" with a European power eager to exploit the new nation's glaring weakness. What hope could he or any other emissary have to raise money from the Dutch, Europe's principal lenders, in such circumstances? What could he possibly say to potential creditors "if a doubt is started whether we can repay the money we wish to borrow?" A trip to The Hague to secure such money confirmed Adams's worst fears. "I find I am here only to be a witness that American credit in this Republic is dead," he told Franklin. And dead it would remain "until the United States shall all agree upon some plan of revenue, and make it certain that interest and principal will be paid."[60]

It was not simply its lack of revenue that weakened the American position abroad; Congress also lacked the authority to regulate trade. Instead, each state was left to pass its own tariffs and restrictions. Such a chaotic and weak position invited mercantile aggression from the powerful, centrally governed nation-states of Europe. Those states, and England in particular, had no motive to sign a treaty of commerce with the United States when they could simply seize commercial advantage unilaterally. The result could only be the destruction of American shipping and trade.[61]

At bottom, Adams saw that America suffered from the very malady that Hamilton had diagnosed in the early 1780s: a lack of central governmental authority. "There is no question more frequently asked me," Adams wrote to congressional secretary of foreign affairs John Jay, "than what can be the reason of such frequent divisions of States in America, and of the disposition to crumble into little separate societies." While in Europe during the 1780s, Adams followed the initiatives of congressional nationalists like Robert Morris, Alexander Hamilton, and James Madison with rapt attention as they sought to buttress the authority of the national government. He wholeheartedly supported their attempts to secure a national revenue and commercial policy. Without such powers, the United States was a nation in name only, easy prey to depredations from abroad and divisions within.[62]

Despite his warnings, the states did not effect "a union in America." Congress was denied a revenue, no unified commercial policy was adopted, and the states even ignored the provisions of the treaty of peace that Adams had helped to negotiate with Great Britain. Not until the ratification of the federal Constitution in 1788 were Adams's concerns finally addressed.

It was not only domestic developments that disheartened Adams. His diplomatic experience in Europe also had a chastening effect. Adams had been profoundly optimistic about the prospects of garnering European support for American independence. He had been among the first in the Continental Congress to argue that French, and perhaps even Spanish, backing could be secured once independence had been declared. Indeed, it was Adams who first advised dispatching ambassadors to Paris, just as it was Adams who drafted the congressional plan of treaties. Given his leading position in these initiatives, it was only natural that Congress would turn to him to join Benjamin Franklin and Arthur Lee in their diplomatic mission to the French court at Versailles. By the time he arrived in 1778, many of his hopes had already been realized. France had recognized the independence of the United States, entered into a military alliance with the fledgling nation, and signed a treaty of commerce. Adams could not have been more pleased, and his elation bubbled over in his correspondence. In the summer of 1778 he wrote to his friend

James Warren that the French alliance and the friendship of the court of Versailles were "a Rock upon which we may safely build."[63]

Within the course of a few months, however, Adams's hopes gave way to doubts. The American diplomatic mission, he discovered, was hampered by division and mutual dislike (if not hatred) between the easygoing Franklin and the prickly Lee. Caught between "two Gentlemen of opposite tempers," he confessed to his cousin Samuel Adams that "this is an ugly situation for me." Lee, though a man of integrity, was "too rigid, and Severe upon some occasions." Franklin, on the other hand, was "too easy and good natured," with the consequence that he "may perhaps overlook an Instance of Roguery, from Inadvertence and too much Confidence." Such polar opposites found it impossible to cooperate. Funds had been expended without receipts, and the diplomatic correspondence and other bookkeeping tasks of the American mission were in a shambles. Lee's recalcitrance and suspicions made meetings difficult; worse, at least for the hardworking Yankee Adams, was the dissipation of Franklin. "He loves his ease, hates to offend and seldom gives an Opinion until obliged to do it," Adams complained. For a man with as little patience as John Adams, these were trying circumstances indeed.[64]

Even more troubling were Adams's changing perceptions of the alliance with France. The French minister of foreign affairs, the Comte de Vergennes, treated the American ambassadors like representatives of a second-rate and dependent power. Their wishes might be indulged, but they clearly did not demand respect. The French court appeared "to have too much Diffidence of Us," he complained to Elbridge Gerry. This problem was only exacerbated by the slavish way the Congress followed the diplomatic bidding of their French ally. "There is Danger that the People and their Representatives, may have too much Timidity in their Conduct towards this Power," Adams warned Congress in December 1778, "and that your Ministers here may have too much Diffidence of themselves and too much Complaisance for the Court." The failure to insist on the independence of American diplomacy and a too-great reliance on France opened up the further danger "that French Councils and Emissaries and Correspondents may have too much Influence in our Deliberations."[65]

Adams's fears proved all too prescient. His attempt to take a firm, dignified stand with Vergennes resulted in his humiliating recall from Paris by Congress in early 1778. When he returned to Europe later that year with a commission to negotiate treaties of peace and commerce with Great Britain, he found himself once again hamstrung by the French stranglehold on the Continental Congress. In 1781 Vergennes succeeded in securing the revocation of Adams's commission to negotiate a commercial treaty, and Congress named four additional commissioners to "assist" him in negotiating a treaty of peace. To make matters worse, Adams was unable to open the negotiations with England without French support and approval—approval which was not forthcoming—because of explicit congressional instructions that bound him to adhere to the counsel and advice of the French ministry. That Adams did eventually succeed in negotiating a treaty of peace with Great Britain was due solely to the fact that he and his colleagues wisely chose to ignore those instructions.[66]

It was not that the French court opposed American independence. On the contrary, Adams knew that they wanted a sovereign United States and would never consider abandoning that goal or countenancing a British reacquisition of their former colonies. But France supported America not out of altruism or friendship but out of national self-interest. American independence was a means of weakening their principal rival, Great Britain. No stronger motive for the sovereignty of the United States could be imagined. That the French court would support a strong United States, however, was an entirely different matter. A strong America would never be pliable to the demands of France and might even emerge as a rival to its own colonial aspirations in the new world.

When Congress assured Adams of their unflinching confidence in the goodwill of France, Adams bristled with contempt. "If by confidence in the French Court is meant an opinion, that the French office of foreign affairs would be advocates with the English for our right to the fisheries [in Newfoundland], or to the Mississippi River, or to our

Western territory," he wrote in the midst of negotiations with Great Britain, "I own I have no such confidence, and never had." France had in fact been a hindrance in the pursuit of each of these American goals and had done everything possible to frustrate Adams's negotiations with Great Britain.[67]

The French were simply acting in their national self-interest, a reality that seemed to entirely elude Congress, with its naïve fixation on friendship, gratitude, and international goodwill. Years of diplomatic experience had disabused Adams of such illusions: "I have lived long enough, and had experience enough of the conduct of governments and people, nations and courts, to be convinced that gratitude, friendship, unsuspecting confidence, and all the most amiable passions in human nature, are the most dangerous guides in politics" between nations. That Congress failed to see such an obvious truth, despite Adams's regular reports and all the evidence of years of diplomacy, could not help but raise doubts in his mind about their capacity for enlightened leadership.[68]

"Philosophy itself has become a fop gamboling in a balloon":
The Enlightenment in Crisis

More than any domestic or foreign development, what changed Adams's assessment of the politics of Enlightenment was his exposure to the Parisian republic of letters. Adams witnessed a high cultural scene in disarray, one whose internal struggles threatened to undermine the very ideals of Enlightened discourse and rationality. Parisian intellectual life in the 1780s was characterized by the breakdown of established modes of enlightened sociability and politesse and the emergence of a new proto-Romantic sensibility. This sensibility was inspired by the writings of the Physiocratic "sect" and, above all, the figure of Jean-Jacques Rousseau. What made this new mode of discourse and its doctrines so troubling was that it drew on central threads of the Enlightenment itself, thus raising the possibility that the Enlightenment contained the seeds of its own undoing. It was the realization of this possibility that bred a new skepticism in Adams about the relationship of liberty and learning in general and the desirability of European revolutionary transformation in particular.

The Enlightenment in Paris reached its apogee in terms of productivity and visibility in the years between 1765 and the outbreak of the American Revolution. Governed by its "master institution," the salon—one of which was in session each night of the week—the republic of letters achieved a remarkable series of successes, from Voltaire's efforts in the Calas affair (a case of religious persecution of a Protestant family) to the Herculean task of completing the *Encyclopédie*. The defining characteristics of this republic were what historian Dena Goodman has called the "reciprocal exchange" of ideas and the polite "principle of governance" enforced by the female *salonnière*. Indeed, David Hume considered the female *salonnières* of Paris the true "Sovereigns of the learned World." Yet this republic was facing a growing insurrection from within. In the years immediately surrounding 1760, two significant challenges emerged to the doctrines and practices of the Enlightenment in Paris. In 1759 the French court physician François Quesnay published his great Physiocratic masterwork, the *Economic Tableau*. Shortly thereafter Rousseau followed up with his famous trilogy, *On the Social Contract, Émile*, and the *Nouvelle Héloïse*. Both the Physiocrats and Rousseau challenged the ideal of the salon and the values that had become conventional wisdom among the *lumières*.[69]

The most obvious feature of the Enlightenment that Rousseau and the Physiocrats rejected was its urbanity. The Enlightenment was very much a creature of the growing urban centers of the Atlantic world. This was in part because the cities were the loci of the great institutions associated with the diffusion of Enlightenment, such as coffeehouses, clubs, salons, academies, lodges, newspapers, and journals. But it was also because of a deep-rooted conviction that the city was a civilizing space whose commerce helped produce both progress in the arts and sciences and the wealth of nations. In Paris figures from Voltaire to Montesquieu and Diderot situated the progress of learning and enlightenment of public opinion in a decidedly urban context.[70]

Both the Physiocrats and Rousseau rejected the urbanity of the

Enlightenment. Behind all its purportedly scientific and mathematical rationality, Physiocratic thought ultimately expressed the rural worldview of the landowning class, an alternative "economic morality" that "was opposed to the urban and commercial order point by point." For his part, Rousseau rejected Paris and the urban scene in high dudgeon, denouncing it as one great den of vice and folly. The young hero of his didactic novel *Émile* would learn moeurs and morality from good, sturdy, illiterate peasants, unpolluted by the false pride and venality of the city and its unwholesome spirit of commerce and politesse.[71]

The challenge to enlightened urbanity was more than a critique of commerce. The Physiocrats and Rousseau also rejected the style of intellectual sociability associated with urban Enlightenment and its ideal of mannerly discourse. Hume had attributed the development of this new mode of intellectual sociability to the "league betwixt the learned and conversible Worlds," which edified the discourse of the latter while imposing mannered politeness on the former. The natural dogmatic pugnacity of the learned was thus curbed by the requirements of polite behavior within the urban *bon ton*. In France this identification of "culture with sociability and sociability with the polite society of men and women" reached its culmination in the salon.[72]

Rousseau, however, rejected the regime of the salons as "effeminate" and denounced their code of mannered discourse as inauthentic and hypocritical posturing. Where Hume spoke in defense of the rule of the *salonnière*—"no polite Writer pretends to venture upon the Public, without the Approbation of some celebrated Judges of that Sex"— Rousseau bridled at her female governance as an unnatural rule over "a harem of men more womanish than she." In place of the ideal of *la bonne compagnie*, Rousseau and his acolytes proffered a new ideal of open-hearted sincerity exemplified in his *Confessions*. In place of Enlightened politeness stood a new Romantic ideal of emotional sensibility—"tears were especially prized as evidence not of weakness but sublimity"—whose "overwrought manner of expression" would become "the standard voice" of the French Revolution.[73]

The assault on enlightened sociability went beyond a critique of social conventions. The mannered and polite discourse of the eighteenth century *bon ton* was the social expression of the Enlightenment's rejection of the dogmatic spirit of "system" associated with the rationalist thought of the previous century. This spirit of system had been overturned by the emergence of empiricism, whose central lesson was that "there is a degree of doubt, and caution, and modesty, which, in all kinds of scrutiny and decision, ought ever to accompany a just reasoner." The ideal of open dialogue, free from party "cant" and enthusiasm, found expression in the popular dialogues of writers as diverse as Shaftesbury, Mandeville, Berkeley, Hume, Voltaire, and Diderot. Yet one of the most distinctive features of Physiocratic thought was its systematic character. Hardly a series of hypotheses drawn from empirical observation, Physiocratic doctrine was, in Daniel Roche's phrase, "a science, based on natural, absolute, universal, immutable laws." It was the dogmatic pugnacity or "true belief" with which the Physiocrats maintained their "science" that led the philosophes to characterize them as a "sect."[74]

Moderate Physiocrat though he was, Anne-Robert Turgot was no fan of Humean doubt and caution. Turgot was convinced that the "certainty" and infallibility of mathematics was "attainable in all Sciences," and that "there is no dispute on which, in time, men cannot come to an agreement." As a member of the "sect," he deeply resented the charge of being "a man of systems," which "has become a favourite epithet against all who propose reform." Those leveling the charge were "prejudiced men" who were amazed that "they meet with a man inwardly convinced of a truth, and deducing from it consequences with the rigor of an exact logic."[75]

This charge of "fanaticism" lay at the heart of the rupture between the older modes of enlightened discourse and the new proto-Romantic ethos of authenticity. The combination of doctrinaire, systematic belief and the self-righteous conviction of sincerity produced a new secular spirit of enthusiasm. Adams would come to refer to this new enthusiasm—one he explicitly associated with Turgot, La Rochefoucauld, and Condorcet—by the word "ideology." More than simply an "obscure metaphysics," the ideology of the Physiocrats and the Romantic disciples of Rousseau was the art of political misrule and folly through inflexible dogmatism and fanatical devotion to principle, a devotion that Adams ultimately held responsible for the bloody missteps of the French Revolution. "We know the crimes that fanaticism in religion has caused," Frederick the Great of Prussia had warned. "Let us be careful not to introduce it into philosophy." When Adams read those words in 1799, he wrote in the margins of the page, "This was foresight." Instead of a force for reason and reform, it had become a danger to public order. In place of the older code of the *bon ton* came a new gestural and dramatic mode of self-representation and discourse.[76]

This was the cultural context that Adams found in Europe. Adams rejected the views of Rousseau as absurd and found the works of the Physiocrats indecipherable. But he also bristled at their challenge to the spirit of polite discourse and modest reasoning he associated with his own beloved empiricism. Upon reaching Paris, Adams immediately perceived the dramatically charged intellectual atmosphere. He found the new Romantic spirit of gesture and sensibility thoroughly repellent. In his autobiography, he recalled an evening he spent at the Academy of Sciences in 1778. After a series of elegies by D'Alembert, Adams witnessed the following spectacle:

> Voltaire and Franklin were both present, and there presently arose a general Cry that Monsieur Voltaire and Monsieur Franklin should be introduced to each other. This was done and they bowed and spoke to each other. This was no Satisfaction. There must be something more. Neither of our Philosophers seemed to divine what was wished or expected. They however took each other by the hand . . . But this was not enough. The Clamour continued, until the explanation came out "Il faut s'embracer, a la française." The two Aged Actors upon this great Theatre of Philosophy and frivolity then embraced each other by hugging one another in their Arms and kissing each others cheeks, and then the tumult subsided.

The dramatic intimacy of the posed embrace between unwitting and perfect strangers was exactly the kind of gesture that characterized the new Romantic zeitgeist, and it was through the careful staging of such "spontaneous happenings" in the not-too-distant future that figures like Jacques-Louis David would choreograph the symbolism of Revolution and Terror. That Adams did not share in this zeitgeist is clear from his derisive reference to its "dramatic" artificiality and utter "frivolity." Nor was he any less biting in his sarcasm about the resulting frisson in Parisian high society: "and the Cry immediately spread through the whole Kingdom," Adams recalled, "How charming it was! Oh! It was enchanting to see Solon and Sophocles embracing!"[77]

In fact, no small part of Adams's growing disenchantment with Franklin was the result of the aged "Solon's" immersion in the culture of sensibility. Adams dated his dissension from the Parisian high cultural scene to Franklin's arrival in the city of light in 1776 with Pennsylvania's newly drafted unicameral constitution. This radical document, incorrectly attributed to Franklin, led to his lionization by Turgot and his circle of Physiocratic reformers as the man who "seized fire from the heavens and the scepter from tyrants." Franklin himself self-consciously played up this image of the simple and virtuous *bonhomme* right down to his beaver cap, "derived directly from earlier images of Jean-Jacques Rousseau." It was in part the cultivation of this image by Franklin that so troubled Adams.[78]

Not only did the sage of Philadelphia rise late, he spent the bulk of his day with "Phylosophers, Accademicians, and Economists [Physiocrats]" and "some of his small tribe of humble friends in the literary Way." Whole days were wasted entertaining visitors who came "to have the honour to see the great Franklin, and to have the pleasure of telling Stories about his Simplicity, his bald head and scattering strait hairs, among their Acquaintances." Such levees may have been critical to the public relations campaign that Franklin used to advance his diplomacy, but to Adams they exemplified the "frivolity" of the emerging Romantic ethos. "Philosophy itself," Adams complained, "has become a fop gamboling in a balloon, 'idling in wanton summer's air,' like the gossamer."[79]

For Adams, the most disturbing tenet of the proto-Romantics was their rejection of the ideal of mixed and balanced government as exemplified in the British Constitution. Anglomania had been a persistent and unifying feature in the French Enlightenment, and figures from Montesquieu and Voltaire to Diderot and D'Alembert had been of one mind in their admiration of the way the British Parliament combined the voice of the people as found in the House of Commons with that of the aristocracy in the House of Lords. Combining these diverse interests in the legislature had a moderating effect on both parties; the nobility were "great without arrogance" and the people were afforded a vital "share in the government without confusion." It was this balancing of social interests, implicit in the bicameral constitutional forms that Adams championed, that Montesquieu thought made "political liberty" in England the "direct end of the constitution."[80]

Yet it was precisely this balancing of interests in the British and American constitutions that Turgot and his disciples rejected. Following Rousseau, they insisted that there was only one legitimate source of political authority, the *general will*. Unlike the interests of various social groups and classes, the general will spoke for "the people as a whole" and thus "is always right and always tends toward the public utility." The mixed government of England simply ensured that "the private interest of two orders is given first and second place" while the "public interest is merely third place."[81]

That the whole notion of a general will was an abstract philosophical posit did not in the least lessen its reality for its adherents. As the only source of legitimate authority, there was no need for checks and balances in government. It was for that reason that Turgot and his disciples such as the Marquis de Condorcet and Samuel du Pont de Nemours celebrated the unicameral legislature of Franklin's Pennsylvania Constitution, whose single chamber represented the general will or "the people." It was for the same reason that they disparaged the more complex and balanced constitutional forms of the other states. In early 1778 Turgot wrote to the English radical Richard Price about this thoughtless mimicry of "the usages of England" in the American state constitutions. "Instead of radiating all the authorities to one centre," he complained, "different bodies have been established, a body of representatives, a council [senate], a governor, just because England has a House of Commons, a higher chamber, and a king." This attempt at "balancing the different powers" of society was absurd "in republics founded on the equality of all the citizens" and could therefore only be "a source of so many divisions." In ignoring the unifying force of the general will, the Americans had sought to "prevent chimerical dangers" and had in fact "created real ones."[82]

Adams was naturally troubled by these sentiments when Price published them in 1784. He was even more troubled when he heard them reiterated in conversations with Lafayette, Condorcet, Du Pont, and La Rochefoucauld. Years later he wrote to Jefferson that it was these French notables' "Ignorance of Gover[n]ment and History" and their "gross Ideology" that first inspired him to write against these errors. But it was only when "every western wind brought us news of town and county meetings in Massachusetts, adopting Mr. Turgot's ideas, condemning my Constitution, reprobating the office of governor and the assembly of the Senate as expensive, useless and pernicious," that he finally took up his pen.[83]

The chaos of the French republic of letters threatened to spill over to the American strand, destabilizing its mixed republics and the politics of Enlightenment upon which they had been erected. This was a danger Adams simply could not ignore. In early October 1786 he feverishly began composing what would ultimately be a three-volume vindication of American constitutionalism. "To defend the separation of the legislative, executive, and judicial powers from each other, and the division of the legislative" along bicameral lines "will be the burden of my song." Since these divisions were the "*unum necessarium* of liberty, safety, and good order," he would spare "no pains" in their defense. "It is an hazardous Enterprize, and will be an unpopular Work in America for a long time," he confessed to Jefferson, "but as I have made it early in life and all along a Rule to conceal nothing from the People which appeared to me material for their Happiness and Prosperity, however unpopular it might be," he would not shirk his responsibility. His Yankee conscience would not permit it. By early 1787 the first volume of his *Defense* had been published.[84]

THE ADAMSIAN VISION:
THE ENLIGHTENMENT TRANSCENDED

Adams's mature works, published in the mid-1780s and thereafter, were so long-winded and convoluted as to be almost unreadable. Yet stylistic failings alone were not responsible for Adams's retrospective belief that they did little other than "to destroy his popularity." In these works Adams took it upon himself to debunk the most cherished notions of his countrymen. Especially after the outbreak of the French Revolution, many Americans came to believe that the Enlightenment had ushered in a new era of human equality that would result in the eradication of aristocracy, the rule of the people, and the perfection of humanity and its political institutions. In opposing the "universal opinion of America," Adams, like all gadflies, made himself an object of hostility and derision.[85]

Adams's mature political vision was the most complex and profound in the early republic. In fact, its very complexity invited miscomprehension. His critique of popular democracy led many readers to wrongly conclude that he favored hereditary monarchy and aristocracy. Similarly, his doubts about the inevitability of progress and the perfectibility of man prompted others to view him as a crusty intellectual reactionary who had lost all faith in the project of Enlightenment. The subtlety of Adams's vision prompted such misreading. His position was one of studied ambivalence. On the one hand, he personally favored equality, popular sovereignty, and the eradication of all aristocratic distinctions. On the other, his reading of history and human psychology forced him to acknowledge the permanence of social distinctions and the impossibility of truly democratic government.[86]

Adams hoped for progress and human improvement but despaired of their realization. He sincerely admired Jefferson's soaring optimism but ultimately shared Hamilton's worldly realism, just as he preferred

Jefferson's principles while agreeing with Hamilton's policies. Indeed, if anything, Adams was an even more hard-core realist than Hamilton, for while he shared the New Yorker's objectives, he remained skeptical about their ultimate consequences. For all its worldliness, Hamilton's vision was basically heroic: an unflinching embrace of commerce and modernity would be an unmitigated boon for the body politic. By contrast, Adams's view was tragic: commerce and modernity were the best game in town, but they were fraught with their own flaws and pitfalls, and any boon they produced would be decidedly mixed. Where Hamilton was worldly, Adams was world-weary.

What was distinctive in Adams's vision was that while he embraced and practiced the politics of Enlightenment, he remained skeptical about them. Skepticism had been an important element in eighteenth-century thought, especially in the Scottish Enlightenment and in the writings of David Hume. In directing that skepticism at the Enlightenment itself, Adams was both fulfilling and rejecting the Enlightenment. In fact, he was transcending the Enlightenment, acknowledging its insights while revealing its limits. Such a nuanced posture was inevitably misunderstood in the fiercely partisan atmosphere of early American politics.

Much of Adams's vision was purely critical. He debunked the popular beliefs of his countrymen, puncturing their exalted hopes and deflating their almost chiliastic expectations. It was this side of the Adamsian vision that evoked hostility and charges of betrayal. Like the great Athenian skeptic Socrates, Adams raised disturbing questions and promulgated unnerving doubts about the democratic and egalitarian prejudices of his fellow citizens. In this sense, his critics were right to claim that Adams had changed his views, for prior to the mid-1780s he had been thoroughly sanguine in his republicanism and his confidence in the politics of Enlightenment. His Socratic turn was a new departure, unheralded in his earlier writings and actions. Yet there was another, constructive side to the Adamsian vision. Having raised his skeptical doubts, Adams drew important political lessons from them.

Ironically, the lessons he drew were largely identical to those he had reached prior to his Socratic turn of the mid-1780s. Adams continued to believe in the necessity of a mixed and balanced government with a separation of powers among the "three independent branches." What had changed were the reasons behind this belief. His original reasons struck him in hindsight as visionary and naïve. "I own that at that time I understood very little of the subject," he later acknowledged. His newfound conviction was based instead on "awful experience" as well as "extensive reading and reflection." Adams's political convictions were now drawn from disillusionment rather than hope, growing from anxiety rather than aspiration. If his core convictions remained intact, the vision that supported them had changed dramatically.[87]

The Critical Side

It was the Socratic, or critical, side of the Adamsian vision that garnered hostility. Adams undermined many of the most cherished beliefs of his countrymen. But it was not merely the fact of opposition that roiled his detractors. What made his skepticism truly troubling was the means he used to establish it. Adams drew on the very sources of the Enlightenment that his more optimistic critics claimed to defend. The difference lay in the elements of the enlightened canon that Adams deployed, elements that marked him as both a purveyor of modern learning and a critic of its excesses. Where the new enthusiasts embraced self-evident truths and irrefutable first principles to establish the reality of human equality, the rectitude of popular sovereignty, the evils of aristocracy, the inevitability of progress in the arts and sciences, and the perfectibility of humanity, Adams cited the facts of human psychology and history to refute each of these claims.[88]

Like Hamilton, Adams drew heavily on the Scottish Enlightenment. But where Hamilton embraced Scottish political economy with its celebration of commerce and optimistic assessment of modernity, Adams was attracted to the less sanguine fields of history and psychology. It was not Hume's cheerful defense of corruption that drew Adams, but his profoundly revisionist—and decidedly anti-Whig—history. Indeed, it was Hume, along with his acolyte Edward Gibbon and the celebrated

William Robertson, who formed the core of Adams's notions of early modern European history and his revised understanding of the nature of feudalism. Similarly, his knowledge of ancient, especially Roman, history was culled from Adam Ferguson, the famed Scottish philosophe who, like Adams, embraced the Enlightenment with notable misgivings. It was not Adam Smith's *Wealth of Nations* that influenced Adams's thought so much as that author's spectatorial theory of morality and worldly understanding of human psychology found in *Theory of Moral Sentiments*.[89]

By pitting the facts of human psychology against the faith in human perfectibility, and human history against political theory, Adams debunked the cherished illusions of his age. In so doing, he showed that the politics of Enlightenment ought to be neither unflinchingly embraced nor shunted aside. Rather, their salutary truths needed to be extracted in a spirit of skepticism that incorporated their insights without falling victim to their excesses. Neither fulfilled nor rejected, the Enlightenment was transcended in the Adamsian vision.

The Human Condition: Unequal and Imperfect

The belief that "all men are created equal" was, for most Americans, self-evident. Adams was no exception to this consensus. Yet such agreement was predicated on the studied ambiguity of Jefferson's famed phrase. Did such equality extend to the impoverished as well as the propertied, to blacks as well as whites, and to women as well as men? Once this level of specificity was sought, consensus quickly broke down. Nor was there any more agreement on the precise nature of such equality. For Adams, it was the fact of a common nature issuing from a shared divine creator that gave the proposition its self-evidence. All men equally partook of the same human nature, had the same moral obligations, and were equal in the sight of God. From this common nature he was willing to infer the justice of equal rights and equal treatment under the laws. But when philosophes like Helvétius and Rousseau sought to prove "the natural Equality of Mankind" in a more profound and complete sense, Adams bristled with contempt. He had never heard "Reasoning more absurd" or "Sophistry more gross."[90]

Even the most casual acquaintance with his own beloved New England revealed the fallacy of thinking of equality as pertaining to more than moral duties and legal rights. Despite "the freest election of the people" in the United States, all the major offices in "every village" had, with few exceptions, "descended from generation to generation, in three or four families at most." What was true of New England was even more true of other regions and states, from the great manor lords and merchant princes who ruled New York to the small clique of slave-owning planters who dominated the southern states. Given these obvious realities, Adams considered it worse than mere delusion to "teach that all men are born with equal power and faculties," much less "equal property and advantages through life." Such rhetoric was simply "fraud," and those duped were almost as culpable as their manipulators, for it was not true egalitarianism that inspired them so much as personal and class envy. "No love of equality," Adams insisted "ever existed in human nature." Instead, people were animated by a burning "desire of bringing others down" to their own level, a yearning "which implies a desire of raising ourselves above them, or depressing them below us." The rhetoric of equality was a cover for base political ambition and petty social resentment. As such it was a danger to an enlightened republican order. "For honor's Sake," implored Adams, "let American philosophers and politicians despise it."[91]

For Adams, the roots of inequality lay in the very nature of man. Rhetorical champions of equality such as the radical philosophe the Marquis de Condorcet (a disciple of Turgot) saw human nature as essentially malleable. As knowledge and reason grew, progress would improve both human institutions and humanity itself, resulting ultimately in the perfection of men. The error in this line of thinking was its naïve faith in the power of reason. Adams, like Scottish philosophers from Hutcheson to Hume and Smith, insisted that man was ruled by his emotions or "passions" rather than by his rational faculty. The former formulated the ends of endeavor; the latter merely chose between means.

Statesmen and legislators might manipulate those passions, instituting rewards and punishments to channel them for the public good, but they could not eradicate them. Humanity might be improved, but such improvement was constrained by the inalterable nature of the human heart.[92]

Human nature was comprised of a variety of passions, some selfless, others selfish. Among the former was "*benevolence*, or an affection for the good of others." Unfortunately, such selfless passions were never a "balance" for their selfish counterparts. What did balance human selfishness, and thus made people "useful to each other in their social connections," was their "*passion for distinction*." Lifting from Adam Smith's celebrated ethical treatise, *Theory of Moral Sentiments*, Adams argued that it was the universal desire for the approval and applause of our fellow men that prompted both political ambition and the quest for social improvement. Nor was this passion for distinction the exclusive preserve of the rich and famous. In every human setting, people vied for preeminence and reputation among their fellows. "If anyone should doubt the existence of this propensity," Adams urged them to "attentively observe the journeyman and apprentices in the first workshop, the oarsmen in a cockboat, a family or a neighborhood." Whether in a "hospital or a church, the bar or the exchange, a camp or a court," the human passion for distinction governed the behavior of men.[93]

Though value-neutral in itself, this universal "desire of reputation," Adams believed, not only made us "good members of society" but could "alone command effectual obedience to laws." It was the fear of public obloquy more than legal punishment that restrained the vices of citizens. The regulation of this passion was thus one of the principal tasks of government; indeed, when carefully channeled by constitutional arrangements, it became "a principal means of government." Yet by its very nature, the passion for distinction is a source of inequality. Reputation is, after all, a zero-sum game. To be exalted in the eyes of others implies a position of superiority and preeminence above them. This inequality was further amplified by the existence of property rights in civilized communities, which allowed families to pass along their accumulated advantages—and thus inequalities—across generations. The inevitable consequence was a division in all societies between the educated, propertied, and celebrated few and the less fortunate and obscure many. The very constitution of the human mind and its governing passions entailed the social division between the common people and the aristocracy.[94]

The People: "Democracy . . . is always short-lived"

During his revolutionary career, John Adams had held the people in high regard. Preternaturally prudent, they were incapable of erring in the long run. In the very first "Novanglus" essay he had appealed to "universal history" to find a single case in which popular leaders had been able to make their followers "think themselves wronged, injured, and oppressed, unless they really were." Even after independence had been declared, Adams felt that the salutary influence of the people would "Cure" the "Follies and Frivolities" of the nation's "Gamblers and stockjobbers." The political power of the virtuous and honest "Yeomanry," he assured Mercy Otis Warren, "will, after a little while, take Care of the Coxcombs and Cocquettes." Honest, prudent, and virtuous, the people were the surest safeguard of republican liberty. "A democratic despotism," he insisted, "is a contradiction in terms."[95]

Years of "awful experience and reflection," however, had altered Adams's opinion, dashing his faith in the judgment and virtue of the people. Far from prudent, the people were all too easily led astray. When pitted against the cunning and "unbounded Ambition" of the elite, Adams was stunned by "the Stupidity with which the more numerous multitude, not only become their Dupes, but even love to be Taken in by their Tricks." Adams pointed to these failings of the people out of compassion rather than spite. These were hard truths, but they needed to be said, if only to protect the people from a mistaken sense of their own abilities. "Flattery has done more mischief to society, when addressed to the people," he argued, "than when offered to kings."[96]

It was not solely sagacity that the people lacked. They were also sorely deficient in virtue. Like all men, they were ruled by their selfish passions and if "not restrained" would transgress "the law of nature, the Decalogue, and all the civil laws." Adams cited historical case after case to show that in those instances where the people had held political sway, they had "been as unjust, tyrannical, brutal, barbarous, and cruel, as any king or senate." Once they had gained the upper hand, "the majority has eternally, and without one exception, usurped over the rights of the minority." Adams fully acknowledged that the elite was no better in that regard and was just as tyrannical as the people when afforded the opportunity. But at a time when the dominant rhetorical trend was the valorization of the many and their "general will" as the only authentic expression of the public good, Adams urged impartiality: the people might be no worse than nobles or kings, but they were certainly no better. And flattering them with virtues and duties they could never hope to fulfill was not the way of wisdom.[97]

To many Americans, Adams's critique of the people was downright reactionary. Even with their foibles and flaws, surely the people were a safer source of political authority than the "well born few" or an arbitrary monarch. Was not the rule of the majority the very essence of a popular republican government? For Adams, such protodemocratic views were hopelessly naïve and visionary, betraying a bent of mind he would later label "ideological." The problem with such majoritarianism was its Romantic faith in the unity of the people. But who were the people? The defenders of majoritarian democracy imagined them as *"the middling people"* who, Adams acknowledged, "have been in all ages and countries the most industrious and frugal, and every way the most virtuous part of the community." Yet in reality, a large percentage of every nation was propertyless, indeed the vast majority in European states. Even in America, "if we take into account the women and children," the majority of citizens were clearly "destitute of property, except for a small quantity of clothes, and a few trifles of other movables." Given the vote, would these people "not think of usurping the rights" of their more fortunate fellow citizens? Nor were the middling sort any more disposed to treat the lower classes more justly. Citing the case of

Renaissance Florence, Adams showed that the middle classes had "the same disposition to tyrannize over all above and all below them, as clearly as ever kings, nobles or mobs." Indeed, the lower classes had responded to this tyranny of the middling sort by instituting the princely government of the Medici and thus destroyed the republican government of Florence.[98]

Adams's critics were mistaken in assuming that his criticism of the people was animated by hostility. Quite the contrary, Adams attacked the pretensions of popular rule in order to protect its existence. He feared that the people would become giddy with their own sense of power and transgress the limits of prudence. Since myriad historical examples proved that the elite, when pushed to the wall, was always an overmatch for the people, such transgression would signal the end of America's noble experiment in popular government. If not restrained within its limited sphere, the power of the people would thus always prove its own undoing. True "democracy," Adams explained to his friend Benjamin Rush, "is always short-lived, and its atrocious cruelties are never checked but by extinguishing all popular elections to the great offices of state."[99]

The Aristocracy: "A Division Which Nature has Made, and We Cannot Abolish"

The critical treatment of the aristocracy was the most important element in the Adamsian vision. It was also the most misunderstood. Adams's doctrines were taken as a call for a titled and hereditary nobility in the early republic and a defense of aristocracy in general. Such a position was anathema to all right-minded Americans. It ran counter to enlightened thought on both sides of the Atlantic; hereditary nobility was a reactionary and irrational residue of the ancien régime, to be eradicated along with religious intolerance and persecution. In fact, however, Adams was no more enamored of aristocratic government in the 1780s than he had been in the 1770s. Quite the contrary, Adams sought to prevent the emergence of an American nobility. It was his fervent hope that the "many headed beast, the people, will, some time or other, have wit enough to throw their riders; and, if they should, they will put an end to an abundance of tricks, with which they are now curbed and bitted, whipped and spurred" by their aristocratic overlords. Indeed, Adams announced his intention in early 1786 to "devote the next ten years to the making of a book upon the subject of nobility" to achieve this very liberation. Despite the censure of his critics, Adams's attitude toward the aristocracy had not changed one whit.[100]

What had changed was his understanding of the aristocracy's historical role. From Hume, Gibbon, and Robertson he learned that feudalism was not, as he had previously believed, a system of monarchical despotism. Rather, the feudal epoch was an age of baronial domination where the great lords held the people in virtual thralldom and intimidated their titular monarchs. It was the coalition of the monarchy and the people, rather than the people and the nobility, that brought the epoch of feudalism to a close. The prime movers were those kings who, by "incorporating cities and granting privileges to the people, set them up against the nobles." Popular liberty, then, was ultimately a boon granted by kings to check their overgreat vassals. In return, the people granted their kings revenues in the form of taxes, which allowed the latter to build "standing armies, sufficient to control both nobles and commons." More powerful than the people and more cunning than their kings, the nobility everywhere had reduced the power of their titular monarchs to "a mere ceremony" except in those cases where those monarchs had entered into an "alliance with the people to support him against it." "What is the whole history of the wars of the barons but one demonstration of this truth?" asked Adams. It was precisely because of their unique role in political history that Adams made the aristocracy the centerpiece of his critical vision.[101]

The roots of aristocracy lay in human nature. Those with the greatest abilities and the most soaring passion for distinction sought recognition from and elevation above the mass of their neighbors. In a letter to his friend Thomas Jefferson, Adams identified what he called "the five pillars of Aristocracy" as "Beauty, Wealth, Birth, Genius and Virtues." There are two critical features of this list of the bases of aristocratic distinctions. First, birth is only one characteristic among many and is not given any particular priority. The second critical feature was Adams's inclusion of "Genius and Virtues." Genius and virtue were the markings of what many of Adams's critics called the "natural aristocracy," those individuals whose leadership was based on their superior learning, insight, and character. Even the most virulent critics of aristocracy drew a distinction between its pernicious "artificial" form and the benevolent "natural" variety. Purportedly a member of this benevolent elite himself, Adams acknowledged that the "natural aristocracy" was a republic's "brightest ornament" and the very "glory of the nation."[102]

Yet the natural aristocracy was also "the most dangerous element" in the polity and needed to be "judiciously managed." If this was not done, "it never fails to be the destruction of the commonwealth." Despite their vaunted talents, the natural aristocrats were no less avaricious and no more trustworthy than their "artificial" counterparts. Either would increase their power and wealth at the expense of the many if given the opportunity. At bottom, then, Adams insisted that the "distinction between the aristoi and pseudo aristoi" was illusory.[103]

Who, then, were the aristocrats for John Adams? Simply put, they were the elite. They were those individuals whose prominence, prestige, and power allowed them to influence public opinion and the course of government. "By an aristocrat," he informed John Taylor, "I mean every man who can command TWO VOTES," namely "ONE BESIDES HIS OWN." Such an elite was endemic to all civilized societies. Indeed, despite the much ballyhooed decline of hereditary or titled nobility, the political history of the eighteenth century was characterized by the consolidation of power by just such "aristocratic" elites. In England, it took the form of that coalition of financiers, merchants, and leading peers known as the Whig Oligarchy. In France it was characterized by the fusion of modernizing nobles and leading bureaucrats commonly referred to as "the notability." In America each region generated its own ruling elite. In the South it was made up of the large-scale slave-owning planters like Jefferson, Madison, and Washington; there "the descent of land and goods and chattels" did clearly, in Adams's poignant phrase, "constitute a hereditary order as decidedly as the descent of stars and garters." The mid-Atlantic states were ruled by the merchant princes of the Quaker party in Pennsylvania and the Philipse and Delancey families of New York as well as great proprietary landlords like the Penns, Schuylers, and Livingstons. In his own Massachusetts, it was Harvard-educated elites like himself who had "governed the province from its first settlement" and "still govern the state."[104]

An aristocratic elite—either natural or artificial—was an ineradicable component of any political community. Indeed, the very practice of representative government was inherently elitist. "Is not representation an essential and fundamental departure from democracy?" he demanded of John Taylor. "Is not every representative government in the universe an aristocracy?" The elite's power and guile made it a force to be reckoned with. For Adams, reckoning with that force was the principal task of an enlightened statesman. The aristocrats were "the most difficult Animals to manage, of anything in the whole Theory and practice of Government," he told Jefferson, "they not only exert all their own Subtilty Industry and courage, but they employ the Commonalty, to knock to pieces every Plan and Model that the most honest Architects in Legislation can invent to keep them within bounds." Yet they were also an immense resource of talent and skill. A source of political danger, they were nonetheless capable of great good. Animadversions against them were ineffective and unjust. The distinction between the elite and the people was "a division which nature has made, and we cannot abolish." Nor were the aristocrats any worse than the people, for both had the same tyrannical urges. The only difference lay in the elite's superior skills and abilities. "Blind, undistinguishing reproaches against the aristocratical part of mankind," he insisted, "are neither pious nor benevolent." Wisdom and justice required an evenhanded treatment, one that acknowledged virtues as well as vices. Unfortunately, such evenhandedness did not enamor Adams in the hearts and minds of his countrymen.[105]

The Constructive Side

Adams's critical vision, his debunking of human equality and perfectibility, earned his countrymen's opprobrium. His critique of popular sovereignty and avowal of the permanence of aristocratic power and influence ran counter to public sentiment. Although hardly pleased, Adams was not surprised at this result. He had predicted to Jefferson that his *Defense* would "be an unpopular Work in America for a long time." Having resolved long ago "to conceal nothing from the People which appeared to me material to their Happiness and Prosperity, however unpopular it might be at the time," Adams was prepared for the public censure that accrued to those who refused "to flatter popular Prejudices and Party Passions." He was not disappointed.[106]

Yet Adams's debunking of "popular prejudices" was not the sum and substance of his vision. His critical treatment of social inequality and the distinctions arising from it was merely the first, preparatory part of his constructive political teaching. Adams's critical musings established the basic facts of social existence, the great "science of society" that was merely a prolegomena to the more vital study of politics itself. The scientific study of society disclosed the true nature of political life, its essential problems and core issues. Having come to grips with these problems and issues, Adams could then ascend to the highest level of political reflection, the mastery of "the principles of government." This mastery allowed him to formulate specific measures to address the problems and dangers that confronted any political community, but particularly an enlightened republican government.[107]

The Nature of Politics: "The Essence of a Free Government Consists in an Effectual Control of Rivalries"

The most important lesson Adams drew from the fact of social inequality was the inevitability of political struggles. And while the forms political rivalries took were as varied as the social distinctions they

189

drew on, the most common one was between the aristocratic elite and the people. When the former sought to "increase the advantages they possess over the latter," the result was inevitably mutual "resentments and jealousies, contempt, hatred and fear." The political consequence was "parties, divisions, tumults and war." But there were other sources of division as well. In America, sectional differences fomented partisan rivalries. So too did regional sources of wealth. Where Jefferson saw the distinction of Whig and Tory as emanating from different casts of mind, Adams located it in different social classes. "Landed gentlemen are generally not only aristocrats," he observed, "but tories." Nor, in America at least, were these Tory squires opposed by the people. Their real rivals were the urban men of business whom Hamilton championed. It was only "commerce, manufactures, navigation, and naval power, supported by a moneyed interest," that restrained the landed gentry "from establishing aristocracies or oligarchies, as absolute, arbitrary, oppressive, and cruel, as any monarchy ever was."[108]

Whatever form these struggles took, however, the impact was the same. Whether North against South, rural against urban, landed against moneyed, or the more traditional social distinctions "between the rich and poor, the laborious and the idle, the learned and the ignorant," the various social interests will vie for power and political "rivalries will spring out of them." In a republican government, these rivalries form the bases of partisan divisions, and "these parties will be represented in the legislature." It was because rivalries and factional struggles were endemic to political life that Adams made them such a dominant theme in his political writings.[109]

Adams's conviction that politics was inherently rife with clashing interests was hardly unique. What was distinctive in his conception, however, was his belief that political strife could not, indeed *should* not, be eliminated. Partisan conflicts were ineradicable precisely because they were grounded in social distinctions that were themselves natural and fixed. While most men of his time sought to reconcile these disparate urges and achieve political harmony, Adams was convinced that such an endeavor could never bear fruit. "The predominant passion of all men in power" was to increase that power "whether kings, nobles, or plebeians," Adams claimed. "Tyranny will be the effect" if any party or social group ever gained ascendancy. It was for this reason that, despite the antiparty feelings of his contemporaries, and despite the absence of the very notion of a loyal or legitimate opposition in early American political culture, Adams nonetheless insisted that "all nations, under all governments, must have parties."[110]

Partisan political strife was not only ineradicable, it was actually desirable. When carefully managed and contained, political strife could "bring the truth to light, and justice to prevail." Political struggles were far more, however, than a benefit to a free government—they were its very essence. A free and republican government could last only as long as the class struggles within it remained unresolved. The victory of the elite signaled the end of popular participation and the onset of oligarchic or baronial domination. The ascendancy of the people would give rise to "everlasting fluctuations, revolutions, and horrors, until a standing army, with a general at its head, commands the people," a prognosis all too grimly borne out in the course of the French Revolution. This was Adams's greatest insight: political liberty is the residue of ongoing political and class struggles. "The great secret" to protecting that order was to control those struggles without extinguishing them. Thus "neither the poor nor the rich should ever be suffered to be masters" in the realm of government. Instead, "they should have equal power to defend themselves" and keep their struggle alive and unresolved. The very "essence of a free government," Adams concluded, "consists in an effectual control of rivalries," not their elimination.[111]

The Principle of Balance

Containing the perennial struggle between the common people and the aristocratic elite without extinguishing it was thus the fundamental problem facing an enlightened, republican political order. Adams's solution to this problem was his doctrine of balance. It was the core of his vision, and preserving that balance was the fundamental object of his principles of political architecture.

The people could only protect themselves against the elite by having a popular and democratic voice in the legislature. Such had been the lesson of English political history, where the House of Commons had formed "an impregnable barrier" against aristocratic domination. Indeed, for all the charges that Adams had betrayed the ideal of popular sovereignty, he continued to believe that "there can be no free government without a democratic branch in the constitution." Unfortunately, a simple and pure democracy was both unstable and dangerous. The people were likely to overreach themselves, attacking the elite and their property. "Property must be secured," Adams warned, "or liberty cannot exist."[112]

To balance the power of the people, Adams called for the creation of a senate to represent the elite. Armed with their own branch of the legislature, they could defend their interests and property against the assaults of their less-advantaged countrymen. An elite upper chamber in the legislature would also benefit the government by affording a safe and controlled venue for the exercise of that elite's unique talents. After all, the aristocracy—both natural and artificial—"forms a body of men which contains the greatest collection of virtues and abilities in a free government."[113]

Ironically, an aristocratic senate not only safeguarded the property of the few, it also protected the people from the elite. Adams was convinced that a unicameral or purely "popular" legislature would fall under the sway of the very elites it was meant to contain. The wealthy and educated would invariably "acquire an influence among the people" by dint of their superior abilities and learning that would "soon be too much for simple honesty and plain sense, in a house of representatives." The only way to preserve the democratic character of that house was to exile the elite from it. They must be "separated from the mass" of the people "and placed by themselves in a senate." For Adams, this was "to all honest and useful intents, an ostracism." Failure to ostracize the elite would lead to their domination of the house and corruption of the legislature, and "when the legislature is corrupted, the people are undone." Far from being a champion of aristocracy, Adams was its greatest foe. It was not fear for but fear of them that led him to call for their separate political establishment in the legislature.[114]

The establishment of the people and the elite in separate branches of the legislature was necessary but not sufficient to ensure political balance. Left to itself, the struggle between the people and the elite would simply spiral out of control. The key to controlling this rivalry was a powerful and independent executive "of sufficient strength and weight to compel both these parties, in turn, to submit to the laws." Adams called this third power monarchical, for which he was roundly denounced as a hopeless reactionary, yet he was remarkably clear in defining it as nothing more than "the executive power in a single person."[115]

By Adams's reckoning, the American president was nothing less than an elected monarch with a limited term of office, rather like a Venetian doge or a contemporary Polish king. And while Americans then and now have been reluctant to recognize the kingly status of the chief executives, their stature as heads of the nation's "first family" and their unlimited power to pardon suggest otherwise. Indeed, it is the failure of European commentators to recognize this kingly status that leaves them befuddled at the American propensity to hold their presidents responsible for personal scandals that—while routinely besmirching royals—would never have much impact on a prime minister.

The president thus represented a third principal aside from the people and the elite, one "always ready and inclined to throw weights into the lightest scale, to preserve or restore the equilibrium." This equilibrium was obviously dynamic rather than static, and it was the executive's primary political duty to monitor the shifting balance of power between the many and the few and to buttress whichever was weaker at any given moment. For their part, both the people and the elite would jealously guard against the aggrandizement of the executive power. It was this system of dynamic equilibrium that Adams envisioned as the only means to contain the great class struggles of political society without extinguishing the spark of liberty, a truth "as eternal and unchangeable as the earth and its inhabitants."[116]

The separation of powers between the executive and legislative branches, and the balance within the legislature between the few and the many, comprised Adams's great political teaching and his greatest legacy for his nation. "Our only Security," he lectured his friend and rival Thomas Jefferson years after their retirement from the public stage, lay in his dynamic system of "Checks and Ballances."[117]

THE ADAMSIAN PRACTICE

Theory as Practice

Adams was in Europe when the delegates gathered in Philadelphia in the summer of 1787. Writing from afar, he described that assemblage as a collection of "heroes, sages, and demigods," one requiring "no assistance from me in forming the best possible plan." In fact, they not only needed his help, but embraced it eagerly.[118]

The first volume of *Defense of the Constitutions* had reached America "at a very critical moment," in the words of one Massachusetts correspondent. Arriving "just before the meeting of the grand Convention of Philadelphia," Richard Cranch predicted that it "will naturally be much talked of, and attended to by many of the greatest States-men from all parts of the United States." The demand for Adams's book was considerable; running rapidly through several editions, it was for its day a bestseller. From South Carolina, Thomas Pinckney told Adams that his first volume had "arrived in time to be of utility" for the "deliberations of the Federal Convention now sitting at Philadelphia." The *Defense* "circulates and does good," reported John Jay, precisely because "it conveys much information on a subject with which we cannot be too intimately acquainted." Benjamin Rush of Philadelphia thought the work had "diffused such excellent principles among us, that there is little doubt of our adopting a vigorous and compounded federal legislature." Adams's old revolutionary comrade Richard Henry Lee was even more effusive. Adams's "judicious collection" of political history and theory would assuredly have "a proper influence in forming the federal government now under consideration." "I think there is no doubt," he predicted, "but that this legislature will be recommended to consist of the triple balance" that Adams championed. Even the disdainful James Madison acknowledged that the book "has merit" and would certainly "become a powerful engine in forming public opinion."[119]

Adams's arguments were routinely invoked in Philadelphia that summer to justify the new frame of government. Particularly on the nature and composition of the Senate, Alexander Hamilton, Charles Pinckney, and Gouverneur Morris all proposed Adamsian justifications for the upper branch of the legislature. Indeed, Morris's arguments were "so close to Adams's as to be indistinguishable." Even James Madison drew on the *Defense* in his discussion of the role of the Senate, arguing that it afforded the elite a fundamental barrier against the people's representatives in the House. And while the diminutive Virginian has often been credited as the father of the United States Constitution, that document bears far more similarity to the prescriptions in Adams's *Defense* and his previously drafted Massachusetts Constitution of 1780 than to Madison's own Virginia Plan.[120]

The strongest evidence of Adams's influence on the federal Constitution may have come, ironically, from its opponents. Several prominent Antifederalists credited the *Defense* as the blueprint for the newly proposed frame of government. "I am fearful that the principles of government inculcated in Mr. Adams's treatise," wrote Samuel Bryan in the *Independent Gazetteer* of Philadelphia, "have misled some well designing members of the late Convention." Some three weeks later "John Humble" echoed Bryan's charge in the same newspaper. That the constitutional delegates had "found out and discovered, that nothing but a new government consisting of three different branches" could save the nation "from inevitable destruction" was achieved largely "through the assistance of John Adams, Esquire." Most caustic of all was a poem in the *State Gazette of South Carolina*:

> *In evil hour his pen 'squire Adams drew*
> *Claiming dominion to his well born few:*

In the gay circle of St. James plac'd
He wrote, and writing, has his work disgrac'd.
Smit with the splendor of a British King
The crown prevailed, so once despis'd a thing!
Shelburne and Pitt approv'd of all he wrote
While Rush and Wilson echo back his note.

According to the poet, it was Adams's *Defense* that had inspired the framers to abandon the purity of American republicanism for a monarchical and aristocratic plan of government.[121]

Not all assessments of Adams's influence were so dire, of course. Once the Constitution was adopted and it became clear that freedom had not been interred, others were more congratulatory. Francis Adrian Vanderkemp assured the sage of Braintree that he had been the guiding light of the new constitutional movement and "the soul of the Philadelphia Convention." Even the Antifederalist Richard Henry Lee assured his old friend that his efforts on behalf of the Constitution would "have its rewards in the thanks of this and future generations." The influence of Adams's *Defense* on the framing and adoption of the federal Constitution was substantial, and despite his initial modesty, he knew it all too well. "Our new Constitution is formed, in part, upon its principles," he wrote to Richard Price, "and the enlightened part of our communities are generally convinced of the necessity of adopting it, by degrees, more completely."[122]

Balancing Forces: The Diplomacy of John Adams

Adams spent the decade before the adoption of the Constitution in Europe. Unfailingly, he strove to achieve a dignified and independent position for his fledgling country within the international community. This required navigating the tempestuous American mission to France, extracting a greater French naval commitment in America, and jousting frequently with the French minister of foreign affairs, Charles Gravier, the Comte de Vergennes. More than anything, however, it required a constant effort to ensure that the French did not "have too much Influence in our Deliberations." Adams feared that the French court had "too much Diffidence of the People of America" and were disposed to treat that nation diplomatically as a dependent satellite rather than as a sovereign equal.[123]

Adams's fears were well founded. Commissioned to negotiate treaties of peace and commerce with Great Britain in 1779, Adams was nonetheless instructed to act only with the advice and prior approval of Vergennes. The French foreign minister forbade the American minister to enter into any peace discussions and would not even allow him to communicate his commercial commission to his British counterparts. A series of testy letters between the diplomats in the summer of 1780 were used by Vergennes to prompt Congress to strip Adams of his commercial commission and subsequently add four colleagues to the peace mission.[124]

By the summer of 1780 Adams had reached a crossroads. The revolutionary struggle was on the point of collapse. Washington was unable to take the field due to a lack of funds. The British army was rapidly subduing the southern states. Congressional authority, like its currency, had largely collapsed. Even the states were gripped with lassitude. The United States was still diplomatically isolated with naught but a French ally that increasingly treated her as a subordinate rather than an equal. Adams railed against the supine surrender of American sovereignty to the machinations of Vergennes and his agents, castigating congressmen "who suffered themselves to become the Instruments of the Count, and His Minister the Chevalier De La Luzerne." Yet he knew that this submission was ultimately due to the weakness of the American position. Without any other source of support, Congress had little choice but to follow the promptings of her French benefactor.[125]

The only way to regain an independent American position was to find another source of support and supply that would afford vital resources and serve as a counterweight to the imperious court of Versailles. Such an alliance would balance the power of France, protecting America's diplomatic sovereignty and standing among the community of nations. In the summer of 1780 John Adams sought that balance in the Netherlands. Even before he received congressional authorization—his commission as interim representative to the Dutch did not arrive until September 17—Adams set out for Holland to see "whether something might not be done to render us less dependent on France." It was to be the scene of his greatest diplomatic triumph.[126]

No longer the great power they had been in the seventeenth century, the Dutch were now clients of Great Britain and her Prussian ally. The once-mighty republic had fallen under the sway of the titular monarch or stadtholder Willem V, whose power rested on English and Prussian influence. Yet the Netherlands remained a considerable commercial and maritime power, and Amsterdam was still one of the foremost banking and financial centers in the world. As early as 1778 Adams had lamented that those maritime and financial resources "have been employed against" the United States by a British ally who "could not possibly do without them." If only "something may turn up," he mused, "to awaken the old Batavian Spirit," the Dutch might be torn from their British alliance and their wealth deployed on behalf of the American cause. In fact, Adams considered an alliance with the Netherlands far more natural than that with France. The Dutch and Americans shared a "Similitude of Manners, of Religion and in Some Respects of Constitution," both being confederated republics. Beyond that, both countries had achieved their independence through revolutionary struggle against a foreign power. Most important of all, however, were the "attractions of Commercial Interests" that Adams felt confident would "infallibly draw them together."[127]

Adams's diplomatic activities in the Netherlands were highly unconventional. Knowing there was little hope of establishing relations with the stadtholder's pro-British regime in The Hague, Adams ignored it entirely. Instead he traveled to Amsterdam, the center of both Dutch finance and, more important, the republican or "patriot" opposition to the stadtholder. He promptly contacted the leading patriot politicians there and sought out a venue to turn the political balance of the nation against the pro-British policies of The Hague. To this end he practiced a radically new form of ambassadorial activism that has since become known as public diplomacy. Adams used both private conversations and public forums to appeal directly to the Dutch people on behalf of the American cause. He supplied Jan Luzac, editor of the well-respected anti-British *Gazette de Leyde*, with a stream of documents demonstrating both the tenacity of the American struggle and the justice of its cause. Luzac's publication of the Massachusetts constitution—drafted by Adams—in early October established the author's reputation among the Dutch as a statesman and demonstrated the depth of America's commitment to enlightened republicanism. Through the agency of the Amsterdam attorney Hendrick Calkoen, Adams secured the publication of *Thirty Questions*, a series of letters he had written justifying the American cause, predicting its ultimate success, and intimating his desire for Dutch financial assistance. With the help of the patriot Baron van der Capellen, Adams had the Declaration of Independence translated and published. Both Calkoen and Capellen helped Adams establish his first contacts with the Dutch financial community.[128]

Despite this flurry of activity, Adams took no steps to initiate formal diplomatic relations in 1780. The pro-British posture of The Hague precluded any hope of success. Adams was waiting for a break, something to "awaken the old Batavian Spirit" of independent republicanism. Adams got that break in late December when the British declared war on the Netherlands. The roots of this fourth Anglo-Dutch war lay in conflicts over Dutch shipping to America through its colony of St. Eustasia in the Caribbean. The British naturally proscribed this commerce as trading with the enemy and consequently attacked Dutch shipping. When the Dutch sought to circumvent these depredations by joining the Russian-sponsored League of Armed Neutrality, the British preempted Russian involvement by declaring war on the Dutch. Ironically, the pretext that the British used was American. On September 3 the British had captured Henry Laurens, the man Adams replaced as emissary to the Netherlands. Laurens was carrying the draft of a treaty that William Lee had written with the Amsterdam merchant Jean de Neufville and that had been approved by that city's pensionary, Engelhart van Berckel, some two years earlier. Despite the fact that neither Lee, Neufville, nor van Berckel was an accredited agent of his respective government, the

British demanded that all the parties involved—including the city of Amsterdam—be punished by The Hague. When that government understandably refused to accede to this demand, the British used it as a pretext to declare war, thus officially placing the United States at the center of the struggle.[129]

In February 1781 Adams tried to open a loan of one million guilders through Jean de Neufville, but his endeavor was a complete bust, attracting a paltry number of subscribers. He learned a valuable lesson from this failure, however. In the realm of Dutch banking, foreign loans were political gestures every bit as much as financial transactions. Adams realized that without diplomatic recognition there was little chance of extracting funds from a major financial house. No sooner did he receive his full commission as minister plenipotentiary to the Netherlands on February 15 than Adams sought to rectify this situation. He immediately began drafting a memorial to the States General at The Hague, presenting his credentials and formally requesting diplomatic recognition of the United States. After completing a second draft, Adams submitted it on April 19, 1781, the sixth anniversary of the battles of Lexington and Concord.[130]

Adams's memorial was more than a diplomatic dispatch. It was a carefully crafted piece of propaganda meant to sway public opinion every bit as much as to present his credentials to the government of the Netherlands. Indeed, no sooner had the delegates of the States General decided to ignore Adams's missive than they discovered he had secured publication of thousands of copies of the document in English, Dutch, and French, many of which were sent directly to leading political figures and newspapers. The core argument of the memorial was that the Dutch and Americans shared a common heritage, having both been born from revolutionary struggles for independence. "If there was ever among nations a natural alliance," Adams claimed, surely it "may be formed between" the United States and the Netherlands. "The origins of the two Republics are so much alike," he noted, "that the history of the one seems but a transcript of the other." Thus, Dutch failure to acknowledge the justice and necessity of the American Revolution was tantamount to "a censure upon the greatest actions" of that nation's "immortal ancestors," actions that had "been approved and applauded by mankind and justified by the decision of heaven." Such failure, then, was more than a betrayal of republican principles; it was an abrogation of past glories and national identity. As Simon Schama has noted, "by identifying America with the historical memory of the first Dutch revolt," Adams's memorial "stigmatized the British interest not merely as anti-American but anti-Dutch."[131]

Adams's public diplomacy took a heavy toll on him. Politically, his endless propagandizing infuriated the French, who opposed his initiatives at every step. In the summer of 1781 they successfully cajoled Congress to strip him of his commissions to negotiate with Great Britain, instead placing him at the head of a five-man peace mission that included his nemesis Benjamin Franklin. Further, they insisted that he secure French approval of his future diplomatic efforts in the Netherlands. At a personal level, his ceaseless action and frequent travel in the Netherlands—he toured most of the principal cities in the spring—left him dangerously weak. In August he suffered a serious collapse. Diagnosed with malaria, Adams lapsed into a coma for over a week, and it was several months before he felt strong enough to move about and resume his duties.[132]

Once fully recovered, Adams sprang back into action. Buoyed by the news of the American victory at Yorktown, he descended on the president of the States General in early January 1782 and requested action on the memorial he had presented the previous spring. This time Adams was not ignored. His request was forwarded to the States General, whose members returned to their provinces to seek the opinion of their constituents. Leaving nothing to chance, Adams set out on another tour of the major cities of Holland. Politicians were lobbied, petitions circulated, town meetings held, and public opinion galvanized, on behalf of recognition of the United States. By the end of February, the province of Friesland had committed to recognition, and by mid-March an "extraordinary Town Council" in Amsterdam did likewise. All the states of Holland were on board as March came to a close, and by April only "the most intransigently Orangist" or stadtholderian province of Zeeland remained outside the fold. Finally, on April 19, 1782, one year to the day after the submission of his memorial and seven years after the outbreak of the war for independence, John Adams was officially recognized as the representative of the United States of America and duly received by "His Most Serene Highness the Prince of Orange," Stadtholder Willem V. Adams, at last, had opened official relations with America's "natural ally," the Netherlands.[133]

Adams wasted no time. Immediately he submitted a proposed treaty of amity and commerce. The negotiations moved slowly, but by September 17 the final details had been agreed upon, and on October 8 the treaty was formally signed at The Hague. In the interim he began negotiating terms for a loan with a consortium of houses including Willink, Van Staphurst, De la Lande, and Fynje, all substantial financiers with strong patriot credentials. The basic terms were set by July. The Americans would borrow five million guilders at the rate of five percent interest plus a brokerage commission repayable over fifteen years. Once he had brokered this first loan, Adams was able to secure additional ones in 1784, 1787, and 1788, netting an additional nine million guilders. At long last, Adams's arduous labor in the Netherlands had been crowned with success.[134]

Adams's Dutch initiative had profound consequences. Personally, he finally received the accolades and celebrity that had eluded him in Paris. To the Dutch, he was the embodiment of the American revolution and held a public status fully "equal to that of Franklin in France." Indeed, even in Paris he enjoyed a newfound respect, now recognized as the "Washington de la Negotiation." Churlishly, he confided in his diary that "a few of these Compliments would kill Franklin if they should come to his Ears." Diplomatically, Adams had immeasurably improved the international stature of the United States. Having broken the ice with the Dutch, he was able—with the aid of Franklin's replacement, Thomas Jefferson—to negotiate similar treaties with Prussia and Portugal in the ensuing years. More than that, the Dutch treaties afforded the United States a critical balance to those held with France. Without them it is at best debatable whether Adams's colleagues on the peace commission would have dared join him in defying their instructions and negotiating with Great Britain without the guidance of the French foreign office. Financially, Adams's Dutch loans came too late to affect the course of the Revolutionary War. Nonetheless, Dutch finance proved vital in sustaining both the confederation government and the federal regime that replaced it. Without the contacts Adams established, the Hamiltonian scheme of funding and assumption would have been inconceivable. Moreover, nothing did more to sustain American credit during its years of fiscal crisis than the fact that it had been found creditworthy by several of the leading Dutch banking houses. Adams's efforts in the Netherlands ultimately proved vital to the future of his nation.[135]

Ironically, one of the most dramatic results of Adams's initiative was entirely unintended. His radical public diplomacy did far more than swing public opinion—and with it, the States General—behind the American cause. It sparked a reassessment by the Dutch of their own political situation. His propagandizing had reawakened memories of Dutch republicanism, of an age when the nation was dominated by neither the stadtholder nor the British. Shortly after Adams left the Netherlands, the Dutch initiated their own "Patriot" revolution. Its most noted historian claimed that the "decisive moment in the development of Patriot politics" was the public diplomacy of Adams and his petitioning campaign on behalf of American recognition. "America had held up a mirror" for the Dutch, "in which they had glimpsed an idealized image of heroic patriotism" and were thus "on the point of inaugurating Europe's revolutionary generation." Adams had yearned for something "to awaken the old Batavian Spirit." That thing turned out to be John Adams himself.[136]

A Test of Balance: John Adams and the Quasi-War

On March 4, 1797, John Adams was inaugurated President of the United States of America. He took justifiable pride in his rise from the son of a middling Massachusetts farmer and shoemaker to the highest office in the land. At last he had received the recognition due his many years of service to the nation. Undoubtedly this great honor assuaged his burning vanity and need for public applause. Yet even as he ascended to the zenith of his political career, he felt a twinge of misgiving. As he looked over at his predecessor, he thought he saw in Washington's mien a stern warning. "Ay! I am fairly out and you fairly in," the tall Virginian seemed to say. "See which of us will be happiest." If Washington had, in fact, been thinking the dour thoughts Adams ascribed to him, he had good reason. The legacy he left his successor included a nation torn by bitter partisan strife, a cabinet of studied mediocrity, and a growing crisis with France that would occupy the entirety of the Adams administration.[137]

By the end of Washington's second term, partisan divisions had reached a fevered pitch. Adams's election had been remarkably close, a mere three electoral votes separating him from his rival, Thomas Jefferson. The campaign had been a rancorous affair whose tone was set by the increasingly scurrilous nature of partisan newspapers on both sides. The political waters were further roiled by the intrusion of foreign powers. At the behest of his government, French ambassador Pierre Adet actively campaigned for Jefferson and his party. He issued a series of proclamations published in the newspapers blaming the Federalists for the deterioration of Franco-American relations and threatening retribution if Jefferson was not elected and Washington's mistaken policies were not duly reversed.[138]

Perhaps even more disturbing to Adams were the divisions within the Federalist party itself. A faction of ultra or "High" Federalists were uncomfortable with Adams and his reputation for stubborn independence. Rumors swirled that Hamilton had tried to tamper with the Federalist electors to replace the aged New Englander with his running mate, Thomas Pinckney of South Carolina. Hamilton's scheme backfired badly, nearly resulted in the election of Thomas Jefferson, and deeply wounded Adams. To be replaced on the ticket by an established worthy like John Jay would have been one thing, but to be superseded by "such a character as Jefferson, and much more such an unknown being as Pinckney," Adams complained, would have "mortified my vanity" and "filled me with apprehensions for the safety of us all." If such chicanery had succeeded, Adams was convinced that "our constitution could not have lasted four years."[139]

Further complicating matters was the lackluster cabinet Adams inherited. After the resignations of Hamilton and Jefferson, Washington found it increasingly difficult to attract qualified men to serve in his administration. Ultimately, he was forced to accept second-rate figures to head the various departments of the executive branch. Attorney General Charles Lee and Treasury Secretary Oliver Wolcott were more or less competent if unimaginative, but Secretary of War James McHenry was a complete nonentity. Worst of all, however, was Secretary of State Timothy Pickering, a supercilious and self-important schemer who had been at the bottom of Washington's list of potential candidates. When all the others refused, though, Pickering was reluctantly awarded the post.

Adams's decision to retain these men was one of the most fateful of his term in office and is puzzling to contemporary minds accustomed to incoming presidents choosing their own cabinet officers. Yet such choices were unprecedented when Adams assumed office, particularly for a president who shared the same party affiliation as his predecessor. Moreover, Adams had never conceived of the president as the head of a ruling party, as we currently do. Instead, he saw the role of the chief executive as an independent political force who balanced the shifting partisan and sectional forces within the government. "If any one entertains the idea, that, because I am a President of three votes only, I am in the power of party," he told Attorney General Charles Lee, "they shall find that I am no more so than the Constitution forces upon me." Given his conception of his presidential role as an extrapartisan arbiter, it was thus understandable that Adams would retain his predecessor's cabinet as a sign of continuity in government.[140]

Unfortunately, Adams's decision to retain Washington's cabinet, combined with his independent executive style, proved disastrous. Lacking clear direction and leadership from Adams, most of them turned to Hamilton for advice and fell to intrigue among themselves. With the exception of Charles Lee, they ultimately proved disloyal to the president and "came to be the bane of John Adams's existence." Adams eventually had no choice but to dismiss them. In the interim, they immensely complicated his term in office.[141]

By far the greatest burden Adams inherited from his predecessor was an acute and rapidly escalating crisis in foreign relations. The Jay Treaty—which Adams had warmly supported—had avoided a dangerous conflict with Great Britain. In so doing, however, it raised the ire of the French. The French Directory—the five-man executive that succeeded Robespierre's Jacobin rule—considered the Jay Treaty a betrayal of revolutionary solidarity and the earlier Franco-American treaties of 1778. In their eyes it appeared that the Americans had basely capitulated under the pressure of British naval might. If it was naval depredations that moved American foreign policy, then the French were prepared to oblige. In the summer of 1796, prior to the election of Adams, the Directory issued two decrees stating that—in place of the stipulated agreement of 1778 with the United States that the "free ships" of neutral nations made their cargoes "free goods"—they would henceforth treat the vessels of neutral nations in the same fashion that they allowed the British to treat them. These decrees were further elaborated in early March of the next year, when it was declared that a neutral ship carrying any British property whatsoever was a fair prize for seizure. This amounted to open season on American shipping in the West Indies, the prize jewel of America's burgeoning commerce. The result was an undeclared naval struggle known as the Quasi-War between France and the United States that began eight months before Adams took office and lasted throughout his tenure.[142]

The roots of the Quasi-War ultimately lay in American weakness. The French did not desire a full-scale war with the United States; they merely sought to force the Americans to accept a favorable treaty, one that would undo the damage of the Jay Treaty and establish the new republic as a duly subservient ally. They were convinced that, given American weakness (the United States had no navy to speak of), they could achieve this fairly easily by flexing their superior might in the Atlantic and Caribbean. The naval depredations that ensued were devastating to America's burgeoning commerce. In the year following the French decrees of 1796, more than three hundred American vessels were seized by the French, almost half the number sent to Saint Domingue (now Haiti) annually from American ports. Shipping insurance rates doubled from six percent to twelve in the first six months of the Quasi-War, then skyrocketed to over a third of the value of a cargo by early 1798. By that time French naval vessels could be seen prowling American waters as far north as the Delaware Bay and Long Island Sound.[143]

Although largely forgotten now, the Quasi-War of 1796–1800 was the greatest foreign crisis the nation had faced since gaining its independence. Its economic impact was devastating, particularly for the commercial seaports, and it might easily have degenerated into a full-scale war like the one that erupted with Great Britain in 1812. That it did not reach that point was due largely to the enlightened statecraft of John Adams. This feat was all the more remarkable given the rancorous partisanship within the government and the disloyalty of his own cabinet.

Adams's First Initiatives

The Quasi-War may have begun on Washington's watch, but it was on Adams's that it threatened to spiral out of control. Within weeks of assuming office, Adams learned that the French had refused to recognize Charles Cotesworth Pinckney as the replacement of ambassador James Monroe, ordering him to leave the country. Shorn of any diplomatic contact in France, Adams grew increasingly alarmed as fresh reports of French seizures in the Caribbean filtered into Philadelphia. Even worse was word of new decrees further targeting American shipping, declaring the Franco-American treaties of 1778 null and void, and even threatening to hang American sailors seized on British naval vessels as pirates.[144]

Adams's initial response to the crisis was to seek a diplomatic accommodation with France, just as Washington had with Great Britain. The best way to achieve this pacification was to send a fresh peace embassy to Paris. To offset American weakness, Adams hoped to present a united diplomatic front by filling his peace commission with one Federalist and two Republicans, Elbridge Gerry and James Madison. Such a bipartisan commission would impress the French with the unity of the United States in the face of foreign depredation, while the inclusion of two Republicans known to be friendly to French aspirations would ameliorate their anger. Even before taking office, Adams approached Jefferson with his plan. At first Jefferson was open to the suggestion, but Madison simply refused. He had no intention of helping his partisan foes, foreign crisis or no. In the first decade of the federal government, politics decidedly did not end at the water's edge, and the Republican opposition led by Madison had no desire to cooperate with a Federalist administration. Nor did Adams's bipartisan approach fare any better within his own party. When he broached it to Treasury Secretary Oliver Wolcott in early March, the latter threatened the resignation of the entire cabinet if Adams did not drop the proposal. The president had little choice but to comply.[145]

Despite the absence of cooperation across the partisan divide, Adams still hoped to pacify relations with France. In mid-May he addressed a special session of Congress, apprising the legislators of the crisis with France and stressing the dangers of further escalation. The French refusal to deal with Pinckney "until we have acceded to their demands without discussion" was not merely "the denial of a right" but an attempt "to treat us neither as allies, nor as friends, nor as a sovereign State." Nonetheless, Adams stressed the need to settle the conflict diplomatically. He judged it "expedient" to dispatch a fresh embassy "fully instructed to enter on such amicable discussions, and to give such candid explanations, as might happily remove the discontents and suspicion of the French government" and end the hostilities. At the same time, however, the United States should strengthen its position by enhancing its defenses. The nation was, after all, under attack and experiencing "depredations on our commerce" as well as "personal injuries to our citizens." As such, Adams considered it his "indispensable duty" to urge upon Congress "effectual measures of defense." Diplomatic engagement abroad and preparedness at home were the two prongs of Adams's policy of pacification.[146]

Within two weeks Adams had settled on his commissioners. Pinckney, who had remained in Holland after his expulsion from France, would be joined by fellow Federalists John Marshall of Virginia and Francis Dana, the chief justice of the Massachusetts Supreme Court. On May 31 he submitted their names to the Senate, which promptly ratified them. The commissioners were empowered to abandon the principle of "free ships, free goods" contained in the Franco-American treaties of 1778 and to seek a treaty giving France the same trade privileges that Great Britain enjoyed under the Jay Treaty. In return, the French would agree to abrogate the defensive military alliance of 1778 and end all hostilities. When Dana begged off on account of ill health, Adams sought to further mollify the French by tapping the Francophile New Englander Elbridge Gerry as his replacement. Though Gerry was a Republican viewed with suspicion by most Federalists, especially those in Adams's cabinet, Adams trusted him implicitly, and that trust was repaid with diligent and invaluable diplomatic service. Despite High Federalist reservations, by mid-September the commissioners had assembled in Holland and begun their journey to Paris.[147]

Adams's military strategy was overwhelmingly naval. Since the Quasi-War had so far been limited to the seas, Adams chose to respond to it in that quarter alone. He urged the speedy building of a viable American navy (the United States had only three frigates at that time, all under construction). Merchant vessels should be armed and harbor defenses fortified. An aggressive program of naval armament and a vigorous cruising of the Atlantic and Caribbean would check the French threat and force a negotiated settlement. "Talleyrand," he was convinced, "could not be for war with this country"; nor could he imagine any ruling group in France favoring "a measure so decided." The French were jockeying for diplomatic advantage, and the Americans should jostle right back.[148]

Adams's defensive program ran into stiff opposition in Congress. Republicans opposed it almost in its entirety, agreeing to harbor fortifications but little else. Funds were appropriated to complete the three frigates under construction, but beyond that no further naval expansion was authorized. Merchant vessels could arm, but only if they were bound for the Mediterranean or East Indies, thus leaving the nation's vital Atlantic commerce utterly unprotected. Adams also faced opposition from within his own party. Many High Federalists preferred a large army for defense and urged reliance on British naval convoys for commercial protection.[149]

Adams persisted, however, and his cajoling, coupled with increasing French captures, moved Congress to agree to build another dozen frigates in early July. Even so, merchant vessels were still forbidden to defend themselves, and a Federalist attempt to raise an army of fifteen thousand men was narrowly defeated. Adams, of course, was not particularly troubled by the failure to raise this force. For him the critical thing was naval expansion. Since his days in the Continental Congress, he had been a champion of American sea power. From this small but significant beginning, he would nurture the American navy, giving it full cabinet status in 1798. By the end of his tenure it was a formidable force. Adams always considered himself the father of the American navy; to his credit, there is a good deal more to this claim than his legendary vanity.[150]

The Gathering Storm: The XYZ Affair and Its Aftermath

As his first year in office came to a close, Adams anxiously awaited news from his peace commissioners. Intimations from William Vans Murray, the American minister to The Hague, were hardly encouraging; nor was the continued French cruising of the Atlantic and the Caribbean. Adams had little ground for optimism, but nothing could have prepared him for the dispatches he received in early March 1798. After a perfunctory brief meeting with Talleyrand (the French minister of external affairs) in early October, the American commissioners were visited by three of his emissaries, Jean Conrad Hottinguer, Pierre Bellamy, and Lucien Hauteval, who laid out the essential preconditions for any accommodation. The Americans would have to disavow several "objectionable" remarks the president had made the previous spring. The United States government must pay all debts owed by France to American shippers as well as compensate American merchants for French depredations. In addition, they must loan the French government at least thirty-two million guilders in a show of revolutionary solidarity. Finally, the Americans must pay Talleyrand a bribe of fifty thousand pounds sterling. Once these preconditions had been met, the French would consider entering into negotiations.[151]

In defense of Talleyrand and the Directory to which he belonged, such treatment was routine in their dealings with weak satellite states under their military sway. He had no way of anticipating that the American commissioners would take such umbrage at his efforts to impose his diplomatic will on them, or that his attempt to extract a modest "gratuity" would result in a full-scale imbroglio. But the XYZ Affair, as it came to be known (it was named after the pseudonyms X, Y, and Z that Adams applied to protect the identities of Talleyrand's emissaries), precipitated a complete collapse of Franco-American relations. Marshall and Pinckney left in high dudgeon. Only Gerry remained behind at the request of Talleyrand, trying to salvage some prospect of reconciliation from the diplomatic shipwreck. America tottered on the brink of a full-scale military conflict and a thoroughgoing immersion in the global struggle between France and her enemies.

With full-scale war seemingly imminent, Adams wrote to his cabinet on March 13: Should he submit the dispatches to Congress? If so, should he then call for "an immediate declaration of war"? Secretary of State Pickering strongly favored both, and Adams was sorely tempted to follow his advice. Yet he knew that his desire to vindicate his earlier warnings about the French by disclosing the dispatches would enrage public opinion and thus make a peaceful reconciliation much more difficult. Adams swallowed his rage and sent Congress a brief missive on March 19, apprising them that negotiations had failed and requesting additional defensive preparations. Although Adams did not even mention the word *war*, the Republicans accused him of fomenting enmity with France and warmongering. They demanded the dispatches. This proved a dreadful mistake. Several Federalist congressmen, apprised of the content of the XYZ papers, joined the Republican chorus. On April 2 the House of Representatives formally called for President Adams to surrender Marshall's papers. The very next day he sent them to the Capitol, expunging only "some names and a few expressions descriptive" of the individuals involved.[152]

The disclosure of the XYZ Affair utterly transformed the public landscape. For the first—and only—time in his public career, John Adams was wildly popular. Republican attempts to downplay the conflict with France now sounded patently absurd. Adams's warnings of the previous year had been vindicated and his previous calls for defensive measures seemed almost prophetic. Borne up on a groundswell of patriotic resentment at French perfidy, Adams was buoyed to truly heroic status. His admirable restraint in both his message of March 19 and those of the previous year now revealed a dispassionate and prudent statesman.

High Federalist Theodore Sedgwick—no fan of the moderate president—acknowledged that, contrary to the "infamous attacks that have been made on his character by his opponents," Adams had "exhibited a manly fortitude and dignified composure." The Reverend Nathanael Emmons preached the Christian duty of submission to civil rulers, and Timothy Dwight identified the atheistical French Directory as an agent of the Anti-Christ. Young men sporting black, anti-Jacobin cockades in their hats rallied in cities across the land in a show of patriotic support for the president; Abigail Adams reported that one such gathering in Philadelphia numbered roughly a quarter of the city or "ten thousand Persons." Most gratifying of all, however, were the patriotic addresses and pledges of support that flooded the president from across the country.[153]

Adams carefully replied to each one, and many of these replies—along with the original addresses—were published in newspapers throughout the nation. Adams used his new bully pulpit to warn of the unique dangers posed by the French. "I know of no government ancient or modern that ever betrayed so universal and decided a contempt of the people of all nations, as the present rulers of France," he informed the Cincinnati of South Carolina. "They have manifested a settled opinion that the people have neither sense nor integrity in any country, and they have acted accordingly." Yet the dominant theme of his replies was the need for patriotic unity. In surprisingly dispassionate prose, Adams continued to urge peaceful reconciliation, rarely raising the prospect of full-scale war. Indeed, a content analysis of thirty-one of these addresses has led one scholar to conclude that Adams "looked upon his role as that of an educator or leader who must carefully think through situations and pass on information and evaluations to the people." At long last, John Adams had come into his political own.[154]

Bowed by public opinion, the Republican opposition in Congress collapsed. Adams got his naval program through, and merchant vessels were armed and harbors and coastal defenses were fortified. In early May the Navy Department was established, and Adams chose Benjamin Stoddert of Baltimore to head it. Stoddert proved an excellent choice, remarkably capable and fiercely loyal to Adams. When he assumed office, he had but one seaworthy vessel; within three years he had fifty-four. Congress promptly authorized the construction of a dozen sloops of war and ten galleys to join the three frigates nearing completion. Twelve more ships were added on June 30, and another three the following month. The impact on American commerce was immediate. Beginning in the summer of 1798, French seizures of American ships began to decline, a trend that accelerated over the next eighteen months. As insurance rates fell, American shipping rebounded. Indeed, according to a congressional estimate in early 1799, insurance savings alone were three times larger than all American naval expenditures since 1794. By the beginning of 1799, American patrols had largely achieved ascendancy over the French in the Atlantic and Caribbean, a victory symbolized in the public mind by the capture of the *Insurgente*—reputedly the fastest frigate under French colors—by Captain Thomas Truxtun's *Constellation* on February 9. The creation of a powerful American navy was the greatest administrative triumph of Adams's presidency. In fact, it was one of the more impressive achievements of the early republic.[155]

Adams used his new naval might to lash out at French interests in the Caribbean. Saint Domingue (Haiti) was the prize jewel of France's new world empire. Its slave-manned sugar plantations produced enormous wealth, far outstripping any of its island rivals. The revolution in France, however, had inspired slaves to seize on the ideal of *liberté* for themselves. What ensued was a protracted civil war between revolutionary slaves led by the redoubtable Toussaint L'Ouverture, free mulatto *gens de couleur*, and white masters hoping to reestablish plantation slavery. Both French and British forces had tried to subdue the Haitian Revolution and seize the sugar island for their new world dominions. American trade with the island, as a purported French possession, was proscribed by the Non-Intercourse Act of June 1798. But in the fall of 1798 Adams received word from Toussaint promising to protect American shipping and ensure payment for American cargoes. Resumption of trade under L'Ouverture's protection would practically amount to recognition of a slave revolutionary as a legitimate head of state, something no other nation had even considered. Moreover, such trade would clearly strengthen that revolutionary both in his civil war and in his struggle for independence from France.[156]

Despite the radical implications, Adams did not hesitate. On January 16, 1799, he issued a proclamation officially ending the embargo on Haiti. He appointed Edward Stevens (Hamilton's boyhood friend) American consul general to the government of Toussaint in the port of Cap François. That June he issued another proclamation explicitly authorizing American shipping bound for the Toussaint-held ports of Cap François and Port Republicain (Port-au-Prince).[157]

Adams's Haitian initiative had profound effects, not least of which was France's newfound respect for American power. Domestically, the resumption of shipping to Haiti was a welcome tonic for American commerce. Perhaps most important, it proved decisive for Toussaint's struggle. Not only was American commerce a source of vital supplies, but the American navy's increasingly effective patrols in the Atlantic and

Caribbean denied his foes both matériel and reinforcement. As L'Ouverture gained firmer control over the island's ports in the second half of 1799, Adams was able to happily report to Congress that "our citizens trading to those ports, with their property, have been duly respected" and French privateering had been squelched. For Toussaint, the turning point came that winter, when American Captain Raymond Perry of the *General Greene* cut off his opponents' supplies in the besieged port of Jacmel and, at L'Ouverture's request, bombarded its fortifications. By the end of February, the city had been taken and Toussaint's foes forced to flee in retreat. Adams's support for Toussaint had been critical. By the end of his term in office Adams was moving rapidly toward full-scale diplomatic engagement with the revolutionary government of Haiti, a process that would be abruptly reversed by his Republican successors.[158]

Much to Adams's chagrin, the suddenly hawkish Congress delivered a good deal more than he requested or desired. In the summer of 1798 it passed a series of war measures that ultimately undermined the Federalist cause. The most notorious of these have become known as the Alien and Sedition Acts. These infringements of civil liberties have often been credited with costing Adams his reelection. In fact, however, their political impact and draconian nature have been vastly exaggerated. The three "alien" acts extended the residence period for naturalized citizens to fourteen years; they also empowered the president to deport enemy aliens deemed "dangerous to the peace and safety of the United States." Admittedly harsh, this latter measure is not unique in the history of American wars. In any event, it had little impact. Although he signed the legislation, Adams refused to enforce it, insisting on the "strictest interpretation" of the measure. When it expired two years later not one alien had been apprehended, much less deported, although many chose to leave voluntarily.[159]

The Sedition Act was another matter. The law imposed stiff penalties of up to five years' imprisonment and a $5,000 fine on those convicted of "printing, writing, or speaking in a scandalous or malicious way against the government of the United States." Nor was Adams reluctant to enforce this law. Some fourteen indictments were handed down under his tenure, among them five of the six leading Republican editors. Even so, the Sedition Act was hardly the cause célèbre conjured by some historians. For one thing, the law actually liberalized the existing common law in use in the states. Truth was a legitimate ground of defense, prosecutors had to establish malicious intent, and juries could judge both fact and law. None of these safeguards existed in the state courts. Nor did the Republican opposition, as embodied in the Virginia and Kentucky Resolutions, object to the Sedition Act as an abridgment of the freedom of the press. Instead they argued that it infringed on states' rights, specifically the right of each state to punish seditious libel. And in fact, once in office Jefferson eagerly urged Republican governors to use the state courts to silence Federalist critics, often with great effect.[160]

What did hurt Adams was the army that Congress foisted on him. Adams had called for a modest expansion of the nation's ground forces, putting his trust in the "floating batteries and wooden walls" of the navy. What he got was a huge army of twelve thousand men, with an additional ten thousand in a "Provisional Army" to be deployed in the event of a declaration of war or an imminent French invasion. Adams was still old-fashioned Whig enough to fear standing armies as a potential threat to liberty. Nor did he see the necessity of such a conspicuous force in a nation protected from the armies of its enemies by thousands of miles of ocean. Worst of all, however, was the expense. Navies were hardly cheap, but for a commercial nation like the United States, they more than paid for themselves by lowering insurance rates, which in turn promoted revenue-generating commerce. A large army, however, was a fiscal black hole, consuming funds without any tangible economic return. A necessary evil for combating enemy forces, its presence—and the dramatic increase in taxes required to support it—was inevitably unpopular in a nation whose land was, at least as yet, unmolested and unthreatened.[161]

When three men (two of German descent) were jailed in early 1799 for refusing to pay those taxes in the crucial swing state of Pennsylvania, an auctioneer named John Fries led a party of 150 men to Bethlehem and sprung them from jail. Fries's Rebellion, as it became known, was a meager affair. Adams issued a proclamation denouncing it, and Fries and his accomplices were quickly arrested. Along with two associates, Fries was promptly convicted of treason and sentenced to death. Such heavy-handed punishment for what had been no more than a tempest in a teapot turned German-speaking public opinion in Pennsylvania, formerly solidly Federalist, in a pro-Republican direction and transformed Fries from a miscreant to a martyr for liberty. Fortunately, Adams chose to ignore the unanimous advice of his cabinet and pardoned all parties involved in May 1800. But the political damage had been done. A once-solid phalanx of support had been lost, and the Federalist party took on a menacing aspect in the public mind.[162]

The Crisis Defused: John Adams and the Treaty of Mortefontaine

In the months following the disclosure of the XYZ Affair, hostilities with France intensified. As the public exploded in paroxysms of patriotic rage, many High Federalists pressured Adams for a formal declaration of war, an act that would devastate their Francophile Republican opposition and almost assure the victory of the president and his party in the next election. At first appearance, Adams seemed eager to comply. In June he had informed Congress that he would "never send another minister to France" unless given prior "assurances that he will be received, respected, and honored as the representative of a great, free, powerful, and independent nation." Six months later Adams remained every bit as bellicose. The Directory's refusal to rescind its orders of the previous January targeting American shipping convinced him that only "an efficient preparation for war" could possibly "ensure peace." With the solid support of his party and an opposition in retreat, Adams seemed poised to lead his country into its first large-scale war since its founding. The Federalist ship dominated the political seas, and a truculent President Adams was securely at the helm.[163]

Then without warning, John Adams transformed the political landscape. On February 18, 1799, he nominated William Vans Murray as "envoy Extraordinary" to the French Directory. Adams took this dramatic measure entirely on his own initiative, without even consulting his own cabinet. The political impact was enormous. Republicans were rejuvenated and Federalists divided. The moderate wing of his party embraced Adams's initiative. Attorney General Charles Lee and Navy Secretary Benjamin Stoddert congratulated the president on his statesmanship, and John Marshall praised his "wisdom and courage." High Federalists, however, were apoplectic. Less than one month earlier Hamilton—now their undisputed leader—had urged a formal declaration of war. They now saw Adams's abrupt nomination of Murray as both pusillanimous and politically suicidal. A delegation of five High Federalist senators, led by Theodore Sedgwick, called on Adams, threatening to block the nomination. Adams was adamant. If Murray's nomination was blocked, he threatened to resign the presidency to Thomas Jefferson. He did, nonetheless, agree to add two additional envoys to join Murray. Two days later, on February 25, he nominated Oliver Ellsworth and Patrick Henry—the latter replaced, when he declined, by Federalist governor William Davie of North Carolina—to join Murray as members of a fresh peace commission, a nomination that was shortly ratified.[164]

At first glance, Adams's abrupt about-face seems impulsive, if not foolhardy. His heroic defiance of the previous year sounded hollow as he proposed to sue for peace once again after promising to never do so without prior assurances from Talleyrand, assurances that had not been officially received as yet. Feeling betrayed, High Federalists lashed out, rejecting Adams's leadership of the party and actively opposing his measures. Yet on closer inspection, Adams's change of mind seems far less precipitous. He had always favored a diplomatic solution to the Quasi-War. In fact, he had broached the idea of a fresh embassy to Secretary of State Pickering in late October 1798 and the rest of the cabinet the following month. In early January he ordered Pickering to draft a "project of a treaty and consular convention" that would be acceptable "if proposed by France." The nominations did not themselves make the embassy imminent; Adams did not dispatch his envoys for another seven months. Nor was it so politically disastrous as the High Federalists feared. In fact, Federalist political strength increased across the country in the immediate aftermath of Adams's nominations. Nonetheless, it was a dramatic decision, one that, by alienating the High Federalists, probably cost Adams his reelection.[165]

Adams was too acute a political observer not to be aware of the likely results of his action. He knew he was placing his political career in jeopardy. Yet he also knew that a full-scale war would have a devastating political impact. "Tranquility upon just and honorable terms," he wrote to Washington shortly after his nomination of Murray, "is undoubtedly the ardent desire of the friends of the country." Adams personally paid a high price to achieve that tranquillity, and the reasons he did so reveal the greatness of his statesmanship.[166]

Assuredly, Adams's assessment of the international situation played a significant role in his decision to renew diplomacy. He had always believed that the French did not really want a full-scale war with the United States and had merely miscalculated in assuming that they could bully the new republic into submission. Adams's belief was echoed by John Marshall when he arrived in Philadelphia in June 1798. Elbridge Gerry, who had remained in France at Talleryand's insistence until August 8, similarly assured the president that France ultimately wanted a pacific resolution. He had received promises from Talleyrand that the previous demands for an American loan, apologies, and gratuities were all mistakes and that negotiations could be fruitfully resumed. From The Hague, Murray confirmed these pledges after speaking with Talleyrand's emissary Louis Pichon, though he remained suspicious.[167]

In early February Adams got word from Murray that the latter had received a letter from Talleyrand the previous October promising any fresh embassy "the respect due to the representative of a free, independent, and powerful nation." Two weeks later he learned that France had revoked several of the more obnoxious decrees against American shipping. Within three days Adams nominated Murray as envoy extraordinary. The signals from France all indicated that peace was at least possible.[168]

Ultimately, however, it was domestic concerns that prompted Adams's decision to send a fresh embassy. The jockeying for place within the new army deeply alarmed him. The choice of Washington to head it was obvious yet raised troubling issues. At his advanced age, the Virginian could serve only as the titular head; actual organizational command would fall to his ranking major general. According to the current standings in the army lists, "General Knox is legally entitled to rank next to General Washington," Adams told Secretary of War McHenry, "and no other arrangement will give satisfaction." McHenry, however, had other ideas. He approached Washington behind Adams's back, claiming that only Hamilton could carry the burden of second in command. He urged the aged general to insist on Hamilton's promotion above Knox.[169]

Washington had initially been disposed to defer the decision of rank beneath him to Adams, who was, after all, commander in chief. Animated by the underhanded machinations of McHenry, however, he now demanded Hamilton as his immediate subordinate. When he intimated that the advance of Hamilton was the sine qua non of his assuming command, Adams was forced to relent and assure Washington on October 9, 1798, that he had final say over his subordinates in the army. Outmaneuvered, Adams would henceforth treat Washington and the High Federalists within his own cabinet with great circumspection. His greatest suspicions, however, were reserved for Hamilton. Previously he had thought quite highly of the New Yorker, admiring his firm response to the Whiskey Rebellion and his sure grasp of finance and politics. "The Secretary of the Treasury is all that you think him," he had written to John Trumbull in early 1791. "There is no office in the government better filled." Now he saw him as an enemy, a feeling that was more than reciprocated by the New Yorker after Adams's nomination of Murray.[170]

Far more dangerous than the machinations for position within the army, however, were the potential uses to which it might be put. Not least of these were imperialist adventures. Many High Federalists, Hamilton among them, hoped to use a declaration of war against France as a pretext to seize by force Louisiana and the gulf states of Alabama, Mississippi, and Florida (known at the time as West and East Florida). Even more grandiose was a plan to join the British in a military campaign to "liberate" all of South America. This scheme was first broached to the British prime minister William Pitt in January 1798 by Francisco de Miranda. After receiving a favorable reception, Miranda—an exiled Venezualan nationalist who had spent several years in the United States—consulted with Rufus King, the American minister to the Court of St. James. With King's encouragement, Miranda wrote twice to Hamilton. Hamilton was deeply intrigued, and by the end of 1798 he was convinced that the United States should declare war on France and immediately seize Louisiana, the Floridas, and South America with British support.[171]

Adams was, of course, aware of these schemes. That summer he had been visited by British ambassador Robert Liston at his summer retreat in Quincy (formerly Braintree), Massachusetts. Liston proposed a joint military campaign that would take both Spain's possessions in South America and France's colonies in the Caribbean. Adams was diplomatically astute enough to gently turn Liston's proposals aside, yet he was deeply troubled by this spirit of military adventurism within his party and his army. A joint military action with Great Britain would be tantamount to a full-scale political alliance that would draw the United States deeper into the maelstrom of European politics and war. Because of its relative weakness, the United States would become a dependent satellite of the British, losing both its international independence and its much-desired "tranquility." More than that, the domestic political consequences of such adventures were appalling. American public opinion had barely swallowed the army and the taxes necessary to support it. If that army were now used to fulfill imperial ambitions, Adams feared it would "produce an instantaneous insurrection of the whole nation from Georgia to New Hampshire." Avoiding imperial adventures and their domestic ramifications was a powerful factor in Adams's decision to renew diplomacy with France.[172]

Adams's greatest concern, however, was that the army would be used domestically. If war were formally declared, many Federalists might charge antiwar Republicans with treason and use the army to squelch domestic dissent. Such fears were not without foundation. In early February Hamilton wrote to Sedgwick, urging that the army "be drawn toward Virginia." Seizing upon the Virginia and Kentucky Resolutions as a pretext, the army should deploy on Virginia's borders while measures were taken "to act upon the laws" in that state and thus "put Virginia to the test of resistance." Such sentiments struck Adams as sheer madness that obviously threatened civil war. They convinced him of the need to defuse the crisis diplomatically and dismantle the army as soon as possible.[173]

Indeed, the prospect of civil war did seem increasingly likely at the time. While Hamilton was organizing his army, Virginia began its own military preparations. The state ordered five thousand guns and ammunition. It also established three arsenals of ten thousand weapons apiece and ordered the construction of a weapons factory in Richmond, all paid for by a hefty 25 percent increase in taxes. Although Hamilton's army might have been able to subdue Virginia, Adams was mortified at the prospect. The Federalist party was clearly overreaching the limits of constitutional authority, and unabated conflict with France, much less a full-scale war, would have made them oppressively powerful. Adams thus played the essential balancing role he had always envisioned for the president. He threw his weight behind the weaker party against the stronger when the latter threatened to sweep the field. Such an act was all the more principled—indeed, heroic—when that stronger power was his own party and the weaker sought his political demise.[174]

Determined to defuse the Quasi-War diplomatically, Adams did not hastily dispatch his envoys. Instead, he delayed for much of 1799, patiently allowing his naval buildup and diplomatic initiative with Haiti to work on the French and soften their position. Adams's patience bore fruit. That summer he obtained fresh assurances from Murray that the American commissioners would be duly received by the Directory, followed shortly thereafter by a letter to the same effect from Talleyrand himself. Chastened, the French seemed eager to reach an agreement. At last Adams felt the moment had arrived to resume diplomacy. Accordingly, he requested the secretary of state to prepare the commissioners' instructions "that they might be finished and signed, and everything prepared" for their departure.[175]

Adams was not cheered by the response he got. Purportedly writing on behalf of the cabinet in early September, Pickering demurred. Citing recent changes in the Directory—four of its five members had been purged in June—Pickering argued that the current French government was unstable and would likely undergo "further and essential changes." The army might well reinstate the monarchy, "probably at no great distance." In such circumstances, Pickering claimed, it was the duty of the cabinet "to submit to your consideration the question of a temporary suspension of the mission." Five days later Pickering sent the president another letter, this time arguing that, instead of a revived monarchy, the Directory was likely to degenerate into "another reign of democratic fury and sanguinary anarchy." Either eventuality, he insisted, would "justify a relaxation of our zeal for the sudden and hasty departure of our envoys."[176]

Adams knew from Stoddert that Pickering did not, in fact, speak for the entire cabinet. The secretary of the navy had warned Adams that a cabal of "artful designing men" were plotting against him to undermine his peace initiative and "make your next election less honorable" and more precarious "than it would otherwise be." Adams should immediately come to Trenton, where the government had fled from an outbreak of yellow fever in Philadelphia, and assume direct control over his administration. Adams was reluctant to leave Quincy—Abigail was seriously ill—but when he received a letter from one of the envoys, Oliver Ellsworth, suggesting the exact same plan of delay as Pickering, Stoddert's warnings of conspiracy began to resonate. By October 10 he was in Trenton.[177]

During the following week Adams met with his cabinet to "confer with them coolly on the subject, and convince them, or be convinced by them, if I could." Pickering, Wolcott, and McHenry all argued that the instability of the Directory precluded meaningful and lasting diplomatic settlement. Supported by Lee and Stoddert, however, Adams remained unconvinced. The best-laid plans of the High Federalists within the cabinet and without seemed about to go astray. Peace would jeopardize their plans for a closer relationship with Great Britain as well as their current political dominance. In a last-gasp effort to salvage the situation, Alexander Hamilton paid the president a visit.[178]

The meeting between Hamilton and Adams was brief but dramatic. The contrast between the two could not have been greater. Adams was on top of his game. Though deeply passionate by nature, he had always been able to rise above himself in moments of great crisis, subduing his passions and acting with a stoic clarity. This was one such moment. By his own account, he was "in a very happy temper, and very good humor," and welcomed the New Yorker "with great civility." In contrast, Hamilton often responded to crises with violent despair and truculence. Combining "eloquence and vehemence," he urged the president to delay his mission. The Bourbon monarchy would soon be restored and would look askance at any government that had curried favor with its revolutionary foe. Moreover, the restoration of the Bourbons would place Great Britain in a position of unrivaled hegemony. It was foolish to enter a pact that would clearly alienate the victorious British prime minister Pitt.[179]

Hamilton harangued Adams with a considerable "degree of heat and effervescence"; Adams listened with "great mildness and civility." The president was struck by Hamilton's "total ignorance" of European affairs. A Bourbon restoration was both unlikely and irrelevant. France would make peace with the United States because it was in her interest to do so, a fact that would govern the deliberations of any regime that held power. Moreover, Adams believed that Pitt and his war were highly unpopular in England, a belief that was vindicated when he was driven from office and made peace at Amiens in the years ahead. Adams tried to reason with Hamilton, "but to no purpose." Caught in the throes of despair, Hamilton was not in a reasonable mood. He left the meeting filled with contempt for Adams, convinced that he was unfit to occupy the Presidency. For his part, Adams was even more convinced that the commissioners should depart as soon as possible and that the only danger in the mission lay in "the disturbed imagination of Alexander Hamilton." On October 16 he ordered Pickering to send Ellsworth and Davie copies of their instructions and arrange for their departure "by the 1 of November, or sooner."[180]

As it turned out, Adams may have been too tardy, rather than hasty, in sending his envoys. French military victories in Switzerland and Holland in the autumn of 1799, coupled with Napoleon's ascension to power in November, dramatically strengthened the French position. By the time the envoys were received in Paris in early March 1800, Napoleon was securely in power and the tide of war was turning in his favor. Subsequent victories in Italy and the Levant alarmed the American emissaries, inducing them to make further concessions and, by late summer, largely abandon their instructions. According to the terms of the Treaty of Mortefontaine (signed on October 3, 1800), the French offered neither compensation for commercial depredations during the Quasi-War nor recognition of congressional abnegations of the earlier treaties of 1778, both of which had been demanded by Adams. Yet they did recognize American neutral shipping rights, and the treaty reopened the lucrative trade with France and her colonies. More important, it ended the Quasi-War.[181]

Like the Jay Treaty before it, the Treaty of Mortefontaine did not give the Americans all they desired, but it did resolve the crisis, and as the principal scholars of the Federalist era have argued, it was probably the best accommodation that could have been reached. Adams recognized it as such. When a testy Federalist Senate rejected it on January 23, 1801, Adams stood his ground. He resubmitted it and with some minor changes, the Senate ratified it on February 3, just ten days after rejecting it. At last the Quasi-War was over. Peace had been secured and civil war avoided. Adams considered this achievement the greatest of his public life. By the time he had succeeded, he knew it would be his last. In just one month Thomas Jefferson would replace him as President of the United States.[182]

The election of 1800 was, if anything, more scurrilous than the previous one. One pamphlet painted Adams as a champion of "privileged orders and distinctions in society," a tool of aristocracy whose "principles would wrest the government from the hands of the people, and vest its dominion and prerogatives in the distinguished and 'well born few.'" In *The Prospect Before Us*, Republican hatchet man extraordinaire James Callender indicted Adams for corruption, nepotism, and financial malfeasance. The most damning calumnies, however, came from a Federalist source. In October 1800 Alexander Hamilton circulated a fifty-two-page printed letter lambasting Adams. The president combined "an imagination sublimated and eccentric" with "a vanity without bounds, and a jealousy capable of discoloring every object." Adams was subject to "paroxysms of anger, which deprive him of self-command," outbursts witnessed by several congressmen as well as "most, if not all his ministers." In addition to these failings—flaws that "tend naturally to the detriment of any cause of which he is the chief"—Adams had throughout his presidency "committed some positive and serious errors of administration." Indeed, his entire handling of the pacification of the Quasi-War was, in Hamilton's view, an exercise in fantasy and amateur bungling. Having violently excoriated Adams for some fifty-odd pages, Hamilton closed his diatribe with a backhanded endorsement. Convinced of Adams's "unfitness" for the presidency, nonetheless the "great importance of cultivating harmony among the supporters of the government" compelled him, however "reluctantly," to "refrain from a decided opposition" to his reelection.[183]

Republicans, who immediately reprinted Hamilton's screed, cackled with glee while even Hamilton's most ardent supporters were filled with dismay at his monumentally poor judgment. Frustrated by a crisis, Hamilton had gone off half-cocked before, most notably in 1783, when he schemed to use a threatened military coup to force nationalist concessions from the Confederation Congress. Back then Hamilton had his "aegis" Washington to reel him in. Now he was on his own, Washington having died the previous year. In the twelve months following his meeting with Adams in Trenton, he became increasingly anxious and disheartened. In April, under Hamilton's very nose, Aaron Burr narrowly captured all of solidly Federalist New York City's twelve seats in the state assembly for the Republicans, thus assuring their control over the legislature which would choose the presidential electors for the state. Feverishly, Hamilton wrote to Governor Jay, urging him to call a special session of the legislature to enact popular district balloting for the presidential electors. Jay, however, refused. In early May Adams dismissed McHenry and Pickering, replacing the latter with John Marshall. Much to Hamilton's dismay, Adams immediately began dismantling the New Yorker's army. Finally, when he heard from McHenry that Adams purportedly preferred losing to Jefferson to being "indebted to such a being as Hamilton for the Presidency," Hamilton snapped. He sent Adams an angry letter, demanding an explanation and, by implication, satisfaction. Recognizing Hamilton's oblique challenge to a duel, Adams simply ignored the missive. Denied an opportunity to defend his honor, he lashed out at Adams with his pen. The Federalist party would never recover from his outburst.[184]

In stark contrast to Hamilton, Adams faced the election of 1800 with surprising equanimity. Even Hamilton's tirade elicited more regret "on account of its author than on my own," Adams claimed. Adams was no fan of Hamilton, as he readily acknowledged, yet he recognized him as a man of "talents" that, if carefully governed, "might be useful." Nonetheless, he knew that his chances of reelection were jeopardized by the divisions within the Federalist party that Hamilton's outburst had revealed. He also knew that those divisions had been exacerbated by his own peace initiatives and his rapid demobilization of the army. In fact, he was convinced that, as one scholar has noted, "the danger from the extreme Federalists was greater than that from the Republicans." It was the extremism of the High Federalist cabal that threatened the party, Adams believed, because they were entirely out of touch with the more moderate mainstream of public opinion. As things turned out, Adams's assessment was quite accurate. Adams proved far more popular than his High Federalist foes, running well ahead of his party in the polling of 1800.[185]

In fact, despite all the obstacles he faced, and in contrast to Jefferson's subsequent talk of a "revolution of 1800," Adams almost won the election. Where popular polling took place, Adams actually did better than he had four years earlier. Indeed, Adams almost certainly garnered a majority of actual popular votes. Unfortunately, most states in 1800 left the choice of electors to their legislatures. Even so, the election was remarkably close. Ironically, New York's twelve electoral votes proved the margin of victory. Burr's capture of New York City in April had proven decisive; with the switch of but a few hundred votes there, Adams would have been reelected president. While Hamilton's assault on the character of the president hurt the aged Yankee's campaign, it was his bungling of the assembly election in his own bailiwick that cost his party the White House and, ultimately, its viability and survival in the early republic.[186]

Eight years later Adams would publicly bemoan Hamilton's botched political machinations and his "fatal" campaign against him, deployed "with the express purpose of destroying" his public career. Nonetheless, he was remarkably philosophical about the outcome. Forced retirement had "given me eight years, incomparably the happiest of my life, whereas, had I been chosen President again, I am certain I could not have lived another year." The first American president to be voted out of office, Adams still took great pride in his accomplishments. He had guided the nation through its greatest crisis to date, one that had threatened both war abroad and civil discord at home. He had balanced the forces of foreign powers and domestic factions. His achievement had cost him his own political career. It was a sacrifice that, to his credit, he never regretted. Indeed, it was probably his greatest source of pride.[187]

"MONUMENTS WILL NEVER BE ERECTED TO ME"—THE LEGACY OF JOHN ADAMS

John Adams lived twenty-six years in retirement. The first half were spent fretting about his legacy. Throughout his career he had courted unpopularity by taking principled stands in opposition to public opinion. Whether defending the British soldiers charged in the Boston Massacre, denying the "natural" equality of man, decrying the excesses of the French

Revolution, or making peace in opposition to the war hawks in his own party, Adams took a peculiar pride in his posture as an independent gadfly. He fully expected to alienate many of his countrymen by these acts, and it was in part that expectation that made his actions seem heroic to himself. Faced with the calumny of his contemporaries, he salved his aching vanity with the hope that posterity would recognize his greatness. In his retirement, however, he began to lose faith in this hope. History would not vindicate him because history itself was hopelessly corrupt. "I doubt whether faithful history ever was or ever can be written," he complained to his old friend Benjamin Rush. His legacy was in doubt. For a man of Adams's soaring vanity and accomplishment, such a fate was unendurable.[188]

What Adams could not stomach was a growing suspicion that he was being robbed in the public mind of credit for his accomplishments by other, less worthy figures. For two years he had labored in the Continental Congress for independence, the one man most responsible for its eventual adoption. Yet his historical role had been upstaged by "the theatrical show" of the Declaration of Independence; Jefferson "ran away with all the stage effect of that . . . and all the glory of it." He spent the better part of a decade in vital diplomatic service, none of which could compete with the popular image of Franklin as America's great diplomatic genius. His *Thoughts on Government* was eclipsed by Paine's *Common Sense*, just as his *Defense of the Constitutions* and *Discourses on Davila* were dwarfed by *The Federalist*. Washington's administration was already immortalized by what Adams called the "impious idolatry to Washington" and Jefferson's "will be quoted by Philosophers, as a model, of profound wisdom." His own, by contrast, "will have no character at all."[189]

"Mausoleums, statues, monuments will never be erected to me," he complained. "Panegyrical romances will never be written, nor flattering orations spoken, to transmit me to posterity in brilliant colors." As ever, Adams's vision proved prescient. He has no monument or holiday to commemorate him. His face does not even appear on our currency.[190]

In the first dozen years of his retirement, Adams vainly struggled against his fate. In 1802 he began writing his autobiography. He got as far as the beginning of his diplomatic tenure when he abandoned the project. In 1809 he commenced publication of a series of essays and documents in the *Boston Patriot* in defense of his handling of the Quasi-War, "one of the wisest, most virtuous, most successful and most important actions of my life." Within a few years, however, his interest flagged and he stopped writing. Adams never could tell his own story. Lacking the ability to control his emotions, he often fell into tangential asides of strident self-justification and equally strident accusations of his adversaries. More than that, he was simply too honest to sing his own praises in a sustained fashion. "I look so much like a small boy in my own eyes," he told Rush, "that with all my vanity I cannot endure the sight of the picture."[191]

Adams did, at last, find his path to fame. On January 1, 1812, he resumed his correspondence with Thomas Jefferson. The bitter election of 1800 had doused the already-flickering embers of their old friendship. Jefferson considered Adams an apostate to the revolutionary creed; Adams saw the Virginian as a political "intriguer." For years Benjamin Rush, a Philadelphia physician and mutual friend from the days before independence, had been trying to reconcile the two old comrades he considered "the North and South Poles of the American Revolution." Renewed correspondence with Jefferson would not only "do great honor" to Adams, Rush assured him; it would afford him the opportunity to examine "the scenes of business in which they had been engaged" and "all the errors of opinion and conduct into which they had fallen." In short, it was a perfect venue for stating his case to future generations. At the very outset of 1812, Adams sent Jefferson as "a Friend to American Manufactures" a brief letter with "two Pieces of Homespun" (two volumes of his son's *Lectures on Rhetoric and Oratory*). Thus began the most remarkable correspondence in American political history.[192]

Perhaps the greatest work of early American letters, the Adams-Jefferson correspondence was clearly written for posterity. Both pretended otherwise. Jefferson feigned shock that "a printer has had the effrontery" to propose publication. Adams claimed indifference. Jefferson's letters, he assured him, would "do you no dishonor," while in his own case "my reputation has been so much the Sport of the public for fifty years, and will be with Posterity, that I hold it, a bubble, a Gossamer, that idles in the Wanton Summer air." Nothing could have been further from the truth, however. Each sought to direct the correspondence into channels that would best serve his reputation. Thus Jefferson resisted Adams's subtle attempts in the first year of their exchanges to broach their political differences. Jefferson preferred to present himself in a posture of serene retirement, above the fray of partisan political squabbles. Adams would have none of it. He fired back a volley of letters stating his political position and poignantly demanding that "you and I ought not to die, before we have explained ourselves to each other." Sensing his old friend's desperate need to speak his mind and state his case, Jefferson relented and allowed himself to be led on this epistolary excursion by the bumptious Yankee.[193]

He was in for a wild ride. In addition to discussing politics past and present and history ancient and modern, Adams cajoled Jefferson into debates on ethics, religion and theology, metaphysics and epistemology, Indian affairs, Hindu cosmology, and literary criticism. No set of documents can match this correspondence in revealing the minds of these two men.

After breaking the ice, Adams dominated their ensuing correspondence. Part of this dominance came from sheer effort; Adams wrote over two-thirds of the roughly 160 letters they exchanged. Adams was also the better epistolary stylist. Jefferson's stately and lofty missives seemed almost pedantic in contrast to what Rush called Adams's "elevated and nervous style." Where Jefferson was ponderous and earnest, Adams was playful, humorous, and even mischievous; Rush had warned Jefferson that "some of his thoughts electrify me." Most of all, however, Adams dominated the correspondence by force of argument. Jefferson may have had more intellectual breadth than the older Yankee, but on those matters he cared about, Adams had a depth of knowledge and insight that the Virginian could not hope to match. And since Jefferson graciously allowed Adams to steer the discourse, Adams selected those topics he was strongest at.[194]

The correspondence with Jefferson was a tonic for Adams's frayed self-esteem. As his principal modern biographer has noted, he "was no longer the bitter, vindictive man he had been when he departed Washington." Adams had mellowed, secure in the knowledge that he had at least secured some legacy for posterity. The correspondence with Jefferson was his monument, albeit a literary one. It associated his name with that of Jefferson and served to remind Americans of his contribution to the two men's mighty collaboration in securing independence in the Continental Congress. This association was only strengthened by the fortuitous fact that they both died on the same day, July 4, 1826, the fiftieth anniversary of the Declaration of Independence. With Jefferson and Washington, he was one of the eternal heroes of 1776.[195]

Although primarily associated with American independence in popular consciousness, Adams has had far more profound, if subtle, legacies. Not the least of these have been cultural. Adams was the first of a long line of Yankee gadflies, men with a strong contrarian streak who stood against the overwhelmingly optimistic strain of American culture. As a youth, Adams had been charged by his friends Jonathan Sewall and Daniel Leonard with "a little capillary vein of satire, meandering about in my soul, and it broke out so strangely, suddenly, and irregularly that it was impossible ever to foresee when it would come and how it would appear." That same "vein of satire" can be found in the writings of subsequent Yankee contrarians like Herman Melville, William Gaddis, and Thomas Pynchon. Their "system novels" mimic Adams's insufferably long-winded and tangential style, just as they share Adams's ironic vision that life and history disclose critical truths to which those living and making history will ever be oblivious. This ironic and skeptical strain in American thought, first exemplified by Adams, has supplied the national culture with what Friedrich Nietzsche called the intellectual conscience. Curmudgeonly gadflies like Adams have kept our culture at least minimally honest. The truth is out there, Adams tells us, if only we have the courage to pursue it.[196]

John Adams's greatest legacy, however, was political. The great apostle of balance, Adams's constitutional musings were predicated on his conviction that no political party, movement, or leader was immune to the corruptions of human nature. He did not deny the existence of virtuous and disinterested public leaders; he simply insisted that "they are not enough in any age or any country to fill all the necessary offices" of state. *Trust no one* was his creed, especially those whose "hypocritical pretence of disinterestedness" and public virtue were "set up to deceive" the people and take advantage of their ignorance and credulity. To protect the people from such intriguers, Adams championed the ornate systems of checks and balances and separation of powers that inform American constitutional government.[197]

In the years since his death, American voters have seen these constitutional checks and balances transformed by an imperial presidency and an active judiciary. The direct election of senators has reduced the difference between the two branches of the legislature to one of duration in office. Instinctually, the American people have compensated by devising an electoral strategy to achieve Adamsian balance. The American penchant for divided government, unique among western democracies, has served as an extraconstitutional means of checking political power. What critics decry as gridlock is in fact American government working exactly as Adams desired. American voters divide power within the federal government precisely because, like Adams, they know that neither party is entirely right or disinterested. They divide power because they know that neither party has a monopoly on virtue or can be completely trusted. They divide power because they know that the ensuing interminable partisan strife checks the worst excesses of the most powerful. Most important, they divide power because they know, as Adams insisted, that as long as neither party achieves true dominance, republican government persists, and with it our most precious liberties. This is John Adams's greatest legacy. All in all, not bad for a curmudgeon.

❧

CHAPTER THREE

THOMAS JEFFERSON: ROMANTIC AMERICA

THE STATESMAN AS ARTIST

A Natural Aristocrat

WITH BUT ONE "possible exception," John F. Kennedy pronounced an assemblage of Nobel laureates "the most extraordinary collection of talents" to ever grace the White House. The exception: "when Thomas Jefferson dined alone." Patriotic hyperbole aside, Kennedy's point was well taken. Jefferson was much more than simply a revolutionary statesman and political theorist. The American Da Vinci, he truly was the universal man idealized by the Renaissance. The breadth of his mind was stunning, his intellectual appetite canine and omnivorous. In addition to political philosophy, Jefferson read widely in metaphysics, epistemology, and moral and aesthetic philosophy. One of the few early Americans who could actually do the calculus associated with Newton's mechanics, he was an avid student of the sciences, conversant with the most recent developments in chemistry, biology, zoology, and botany, and he had a more than passing interest in meteorology (he kept a fastidious log of atmospheric conditions wherever he went). Widely read in classical and modern history, he was equally fascinated by the emerging social sciences of political economy and sociology and proved himself a fairly accomplished amateur anthropologist. A devoted philologist, Jefferson's expertise spanned both classical and modern Romance languages, and he devoted considerable study to the languages of Amerindians and medieval Anglo-Saxons. Jefferson was also an eager and sophisticated connoisseur of the arts. An accomplished draftsman and violinist, he was a devotee of the theater and opera, a knowledgeable collector of artifacts, paintings, and statuary, and the greatest architectural genius of the early republic. Quite simply, Thomas Jefferson thought about more in one week than occurs to us mere mortals in a year. He was indeed an "extraordinary collection of talents."[1]

His accomplishments were just as legion and varied. Jefferson's greatest talent was as a revolutionary propagandist. His *Summary View of the Rights of British America* was the most radical, eloquent, and impassioned articulation of the American constitutional position in the period before independence and, as a stirring statement of the American cause, second only to his own Declaration of Independence. His pungent political correspondence in the 1790s supplied the ideological and rhetorical glue that held the Republican opposition together through the era of Federalist dominance.

Jefferson was also an extremely able legislator. As a member of Virginia's House of Burgesses, he was a consistent and radical supporter of colonial resistance. After independence he used his legal training to draft a revision of the state's legal code for his fellow legislators. In the Continental Congress he was an early advocate of independence, and in the Confederation Congress he drafted the famous Northwest Ordinance of 1784, a progressive and perhaps visionary plan for the settlement of the American West. As a constitutional theorist, he drafted two constitutions for his state (one in 1776, the other in 1783), maintained a regular exchange of views with James Madison while the latter was drafting the federal Constitution, and later became the principal spokesman for the "strict" construction of that document.

In the realm of foreign affairs, Jefferson spent the better part of five years in Paris as Benjamin Franklin's replacement as well as minister plenipotentiary to the rest of Europe before returning to serve as Washington's secretary of state. As an executive, Jefferson presided over the

American Philosophical Society, the state of Virginia, and the United States of America. In the latter office he doubled the size of the nation, dramatically curtailed its debt, destroyed his partisan opposition, and inaugurated the "Era of Good Feelings," one of those rare interludes of political tranquillity in American history. A master builder, Jefferson took an active role in the planning, layout, and architecture of the new national capital on the Potomac and personally designed the new state capital at Richmond and the University of Virginia. He built the oldest surviving political party in history and promulgated the lineaments of what would become the democratic creed. In his spare time he performed scientific experiments and observations, wrote *Notes on the State of Virginia*—a classic of contemporary natural history, anthropology, and political thought—invented several mechanical devices (most notably a lighter moldboard plow), and organized the curriculum and vetted the faculty for the University of Virginia that he created in Charlottesville.

Given this résumé, it is little wonder that Thomas Jefferson has captured the American imagination. But he has done far more than that. The patron saint of both political parties, Jefferson is a source of inspiration for both radicals and reactionaries, progressives and conservatives. He is a national icon who hovers far above the other members of his celebrated generation. More than a founding father, Jefferson is the spokesman of the American creed, the prophet of democracy who reminds us that "all men are created equal," that "the earth belongs in usufruct to the living," and that "the tree of liberty must be refreshed from time to time with the blood of patriots and tyrants." It was not so much what he said or did as what he was or represented. Jefferson embodied an ideal, an ideal that exemplifies the politics of Enlightenment in early America in which political power would be conferred on those with superior "virtue and talent." He, like his colleagues, called this ideal "natural aristocracy." And Thomas Jefferson was the natural aristocrat par excellence.[2]

He certainly looked the part. Unusually tall and slim, he combined a graceful manner with a strikingly erect posture. His was just the sort of physique that would seem most at home on horseback. His face was handsome without being pretty, his long fine nose and alert eyes offset by a strong protruding jaw and framed by abundant sandy red hair. His manners were both impeccably correct and gracious, combining "all the winning softness of politeness, without the artificial polish of courts." Although he was somewhat shy in large gatherings, in more private settings his charm could be overwhelming. There was a beguiling softness to Jefferson's manner. "Before I had been two hours with him" noted the French general Marquis de Chastellux, "we were as intimate as if we had passed our whole lives together." After just one meeting, Margaret Bayard Smith was struck by "something in his manner, his countenance and voice that at once unlocked my heart."[3]

Jefferson's persona and demeanor were overwhelmingly sunny. He hated conflict and studiously avoided personal confrontations—no mean feat for a revolutionary statesman and political leader. Moreover, he was an avowed optimist: "I steer my bark with Hope in the head," he told Adams, "leaving Fear astern." He was also a man of profound public integrity. His political career exemplified the ideal of disinterestedness. He entered public service with immense wealth and retired well on the road to bankruptcy. These virtues, charms, accomplishments, and talents all made Jefferson the embodiment of natural aristocracy in the new nation. He was that most exalted elite, an elite by dint of merit and talent, virtue and accomplishment. That he used that exalted status to champion democracy and popular rights transformed him from his nation's most noted natural aristocrat to one of its most beloved heroes.[4]

To the Manor Born

Aristocracy came naturally to Jefferson. Unlike Hamilton and Adams, he was born into a world of privilege and ease. His manners had the polish of a refined gentleman precisely because he had been trained to be one since earliest childhood. If his tastes were remarkably sophisticated, it was because he had the wealth and leisure to cultivate them. Indeed, the enlightened eclecticism of his mind had the aristocratic quality of an expert collector of fine intellectual artifacts. One thing is certain; when

Thomas Jefferson wrote that "those who labor in the earth are the chosen people of God," he was speaking from observation, not experience.
Aside from a small whip, Jefferson never lifted a farm implement in
his life.[5]

Peter Jefferson, Thomas's father, was, like his own father, a substantial figure in the slaveholding squirearchy of his county. Both senior
Jeffersons had amassed sizable estates—Peter's was possibly the largest
in Albemarle County at the time—and held the prestigious county offices of sheriff and justice of the peace. But Jefferson's mother, Jane,
was a Randolph. The Randolphs were arguably the first family of Virginia, rivaled only by the Lees, Carters, and Byrds. "One must be fa-
tigued with hearing the name of Randolph," complained Chastellux of
his travels in Viriginia. They were not only "ancient" and "numerous,"
they also controlled immense wealth. The Randolphs traced their lin-
eage back to such European monarchs as David I of Scotland, Hugh
Magnus of France, Charlemagne, and Alfred the Great. Jefferson poked
fun at his Randolph genealogy in his *Autobiography*, yet he took it seriously enough to order his agent in London to "search the Herald's office
for the arms of my family."[6]

In fact, Jefferson took great pride in his Randolph ancestry, as well
he should. When he entered politics, it would be under the protective
wing of Speaker of the House of Burgesses Peyton Randolph. When he
struggled against Hamilton in Washington's cabinet, his sole ally was
Attorney General Edmund Randolph. And when his eldest daughter
married, it would be to future governor and congressman Thomas Mann
Randolph. If ever a revolutionary statesman was to the manor born, it
was Thomas Jefferson.

Jefferson received an education befitting a gentleman. He was taught
by private tutors until the age of five, when he entered an "English"
school. Four years later he began his training in French and the classical
languages. By sixteen he had sufficiently mastered Greek and Latin
grammar to enter the College of William and Mary, which he attended
for two years. Jefferson learned more than dead tongues, however. He
was instructed in mathematics, literature, and history. He was also

taught deportment, correct table manners, and elocution. Even grace was imparted through dancing minuets and reels.[7]

As with Hamilton and Adams, it was Jefferson's education, his mastery of the received canon, that marked him as an enlightened statesman. Yet there was one huge difference between the education of Jefferson and that of Hamilton and Adams. For the latter, education was first and foremost a vital means of financial support and social status, only secondarily a potential source of political authority. Although professionally trained, Jefferson was, in the best sense of the term, an amateur intellectual who pursued higher learning for the sheer joy of it. Jefferson never expected to earn his bread with his books.

Like a true aristocrat, he sought the widest possible perspective and the most thorough immersion in all the varieties of high cultural fare. Such breadth of mind and universality of vision naturally came at a price, namely the attention to detail that characterizes "merely" scholarly minds. Put another way, the lack of depth that many scholars have noted in Jefferson's political philosophy was not weakness so much as a different intellectual style. What scholars call depth was just the sort of minor matters that the aristocratic Jefferson happily left to the professionals once he had discovered the essential principles of an issue. He had better things to do.

Upon maturity Jefferson came into a tidy fortune. His father had left him nearly four thousand acres, more than twenty-five slaves, and the bulk of his movable property. Jefferson's marriage more than doubled his holdings, catapulting him from a man of substantial wealth to one of the richest men in British North America. He collected thoroughbred racehorses and fine musical instruments, rare books and Indian artifacts, French wines and English scientific apparatuses. He traveled in style, arriving at the Continental Congress in a coach and four with two liveried slaves. He lived nicely: while serving as a diplomat in Paris, he rented a large house and had a staff of six servants to attend him when he was not visiting in the fashionable Faubourg Saint-Germain. When he returned home, he completed construction of the most impressive mansion in early America. And of course, he entertained well. His celebrated dinner parties were always elegant and extravagant, his knowledge of fine cuisine almost as extensive as his scientific and architectural expertise. The wine bill alone for his first term in the Oval Office was nearly ten thousand dollars. A man of great style and discernment, he enjoyed the pleasures and beauties that money could supply. Indeed, given his eventual bankruptcy, he may have enjoyed them a bit too much.[8]

"Virginian Geese are all Swans"

Thomas Jefferson was more than an aristocratic gentleman. He was a Virginia aristocrat, a landed gentleman of the Old Dominion. He was fiercely loyal to his native state—his only published book was devoted to it. Of the three accomplishments he had listed on his tombstone, two—author of the statute "for Religious Freedom" and "Father of the University of Virginia"—dealt exclusively with his home state. When he spoke of "his country," he invariably had Virginia in mind. Most Americans at the time identified primarily with their immediate community, state, or region, but Virginians were different. Notoriously local in their orientation, the leaders of the Old Dominion were downright tribal in their solidarities. "Not a bairn in Scotland" nor "a lad upon the highland," insisted a knowing John Adams, "is more clannish than every Virginian I have ever known." Virginia was the oldest, largest, and most populous colony in what would become the United States of America, and its leaders took an understandable, if ferocious, pride in it.[9]

Virginia's elite also took an inordinate pride in itself. As Adams ruefully put it, "Virginian Geese are all Swans," and to hail from the Old Dominion was fully "equivalent to five talents." The slaveholding squirearchy of Virginia was the most cohesive and politically entrenched elite in early America. "In no colony was there greater solidarity in the ruling class," notes Jeffersonian scholar Merrill Peterson, "or greater deference in the mass of the people." From such security came the confidence to lead and command; even before the Continental Army had been created, George Washington arrived at the Continental Congress in a full-dress military uniform.[10]

Virginia supplied the most distinguished delegation to the Continental Congress, the basic plan for the federal Constitution, and three of the nation's first four presidents. The Virginia elite combined the education and well-bred manners of entrenched wealth with the confidence and self-assurance born of their command over their slaves and their less fortunate white neighbors. Jefferson exemplified these traits, so much so that for most of his political career he was the principal leader of Virginia's planter class. To lead a political elite that included such luminaries as George Washington, Richard Henry Lee, Patrick Henry, George Mason, Peyton Randolph, and James Madison was itself no small accomplishment.

The Chesapeake society that molded Jefferson was distinctive in many ways. Its extremely diffuse agrarian settlement pattern—the capital, Williamsburg, was no more than a large village—left residents isolated on remote farmsteads. To compensate, the Virginia gentry would host and visit relatives and friends, cultivating the gracious hospitality for which they were so justly famed. Comparatively high mortality rates meant that many children lost one or both parents before reaching maturity, resulting in youths spent in "alien" households with extended relatives. When Jefferson was two years old, his father's best friend (and his mother's first cousin), William Randolph, died, and the Jeffersons moved to the Randolph's Tuckahoe plantation where Peter could supervise Thomas's orphaned cousins. Because displays of the normal range of passions could critically endanger family peace, life in such extended households inculcated habits of emotional reserve. This was especially true for children like George Washington, who lost their father and therefore their protector. Such circumstances bred a certain stoic demeanor, and Jefferson was no exception. Peter Jefferson died when his son was only fourteen, just as his own father had died when he was eight. "Perfect happiness I believe was never intended by the deity to be the lot of any one of his creatures in the world," young Thomas wrote to his friend John Page. The best that could be achieved was to "fortify our minds against the attacks" of life and "assume a perfect resignation to the divine will, to consider that whatever does happen, must happen."

Predictably, Jefferson responded by hiding his emotions behind a mask of stoic reserve and polite manners. "Politeness is artificial good humor," he told his grandson. "It covers the natural want of it, and ends by rendering habitual a substitute nearly equivalent to the real virtue." Unlike the gloomy New Yorker and the volatile Yankee, the Virginian was bred from childhood to a polite demeanor and a steady disposition.[11]

The most distinctive feature of Jefferson's region, however, was the predominance of plantation slavery. It was slavery that afforded the Virginia gentry the wealth and leisure to pursue cultivation and higher learning. It was plantation slavery that gave them the economic independence to leave their holdings in the hands of overseers and managers while they attended to affairs of state. For some squires, slavery inculcated the leadership qualities of self-assurance and command, especially masters who combined their complete control over the lives of the enslaved with a sense of responsibility or noblesse oblige toward them. By all accounts, Jefferson was just such a slave-owner, reluctant to submit his "people" to the lash or sell them without their consent. Throughout his life he felt keenly his duty to "those whom fortune has thrown into our hands, to feed and clothe them well, protect them from all ill usage," while demanding no more labor than that "performed voluntarily by freemen." Slavery molded Jefferson's character, just as it did those of his comrades among the Old Dominion's ruling class.[12]

The Virginia influence was not, of course, all roses and sunshine. Not all aristocratic wealth was spent on refined cultivation. Virginia gentlemen were avid and often reckless gamblers, sometimes losing whole fortunes on the result of a horserace or the turn of a card. Others lavished huge sums on modish clothing, fine furniture, well-bred horses, and magnificent houses. Jefferson was not the only member of his generation to squander in conspicuous consumption an estate that had taken several lifetimes to amass. Not all leisure was spent in quiet study, and hospitality was not the only salve for rural isolation. Starved for society, Virginians could turn any gathering—court days, election days, even Sunday church—into an occasion for festivities. These were often boisterous events with aristocratic horseraces, plebeian "rough and tumble"

(a form of personal combat whose object was to disfigure one's opponent), and always a copious stream of liquor supplied by the squires to
their common white neighbors. The confidence and self-assurance of
the slaveholding elite also made them intensely competitive, their polite
manners covering an extremely sensitive, indeed pugnacious, sense of
honor that could be assuaged only by the code duello.

Planter family life taught young gentlemen far more than emotional
restraint. Even by the standards of their day, Virginia gentlemen were
inordinately patriarchal in their views of women and sexually predatory.
The death of Jefferson's father in his early adolescence filled him with a
"patriarchal rage" toward his mother. Charming and gallant, he was always dismissive in his attitude toward women. Their proper sphere was
the home and hearth, their participation in the public sphere anathema.
He could not stomach French female intrusion into matters of state and
applauded American women as "too wise to wrinkle their foreheads with
politics," content instead to "soothe and calm the minds of their husbands
returning ruffled from political debate." Nor was Jefferson immune to
the sexual attitudes of his class. Why endure the hardships and sacrifices
of marriage, he asked in his early twenties, when sex could be readily obtained elsewhere? "St. Paul only says that it is better to be married than to
burn" in the fires of lust, he argued. If that saint had known that "providence would at an after day be so kind to any particular set of people as to
furnish them with other means of extinguishing their fire than those of
matrimony, he would have earnestly recommended their practice."[13]

What "means" Jefferson "practiced" to extinguish his "fire" is unknown. At the time he was living in Williamsburg, where prostitutes
were available. Perhaps he sought the attentions of a married woman.
Four years later he would try to seduce Elizabeth Walker, the young wife
of his absent friend John, an unsuccessful suit that he purportedly pursued for over a decade, well after his own marriage to Martha Wayles
Skelton. Then, of course, there was always the possibility of an assigna-
tion in the slave quarters. In 1802 Jefferson would be accused of father-
ing several children by his slave Sally Hemings. Recent DNA evidence
has rendered this charge probable but not certain since Thomas had a

younger brother who lived nearby. A remarkably private man, Jefferson jealously guarded his personal life. (He burned his correspondence with his wife after her death.) What is certain is that such practices were part of the life of the Virginia gentry. If Jefferson did not indulge in them, it was by means of an act of restraint that many of his fellow squires chose not to exercise.[14]

The most damning blight on Virginia was, however, the institution of slavery. Slavery could inculcate in some masters like Jefferson a surety in command and a sense of responsibility to others. It could also give vent to what Jefferson himself eloquently described as an "exercise of the most boisterous passions" between those practicing "the most unremitting despotism" and those suffering "the most degrading submissions." "The man must be a prodigy," he wrote, "who can retain his manners and morals undepraved by such circumstances."[15]

Slavery retarded the economic development of Virginia, drawing capital away from commerce and manufactures toward the almost exclusive cultivation of tobacco. Slavery also distorted Virginia society, producing vast disparities in wealth. The greatest disparity, of course, was that between the slaves, who comprised almost half the population of the colony, and their gentry owners. Slavery also skewed the distribution of wealth within the white community. No more than one-tenth of the white population owned roughly two-thirds of the colony's wealth. At least half of all white families were landless, a fact that barred them from voting. The lack of commercial centers rendered the remainder of whites—those who owned a handful of slaves or hoped to one day—dependent on their gentry neighbors and patrons for credit, vital marketing services, and the hire of the odd slave laborer.[16]

Slavery concentrated wealth because those who owned the labor of others could operate at a scope and scale, and with minimal labor costs, that family farmers could not hope to compete with. But slaves were more than labor. They were also capital, capital that increased naturally. "A child raised every 2 years is of more profit," Jefferson calculated, "than the crop of the best laboring man." The value of land might improve with cultivation, but slaves multiplied of their own accord, one of those rare instances, Jefferson thought, where "providence has made our interest and our duties coincide perfectly."[17]

Despite his own rather substantial investment in it—by the time of the American Revolution, he held nearly two hundred people in bondage—Jefferson despised slavery. No one was more aware of how slavery marred the mores and manners of his class, how it retarded his region's economy and stultified its society. Slavery was the great stain on Virginia's character, threatening to turn its political leaders into a gaggle of base hypocrites. "How is it that we hear the loudest yelps for liberty," asked the sardonic Samuel Johnson, "among the drivers of Negroes?" Worse yet, slavery undermined the image of Virginia itself, suggesting that the purported frontier of enlightened freedom was in reality a backward bastion of brutality. For a man like Jefferson, who identified so deeply with his region and was so sensitive to image and reputation, the issues and implications raised by slavery were intolerable. Slavery was Jefferson's personal bête noire; it would haunt him throughout his career. In his final years, it awoke him "like a firebell in the night," filling him "with terror." "We have the wolf by the ears," he complained, "and we can neither hold him, nor safely let him go." That would ultimately be Jefferson's fate, unable to hold on or fully let go of an institution he loathed. Being a Virginia aristocrat like Thomas Jefferson carried its own unique psychic burdens.[18]

Jefferson the Visionary

Natural aristocrat and Virginia squire, enlightened statesman and southern slavemaster: these were the features and roles that defined Jefferson and molded his character. They do not, however, explain his greatness or his contribution to American culture. The key to that lay in the remarkable quality of his mind. Jefferson was uniquely able to synthesize vast amounts of information and learning into overarching worldviews informed by an imagination that was both powerful and disciplined. His synthetic imagination or "vision" was unmatched in his time and has few peers in American history; his articulation of that vision transformed the politics of the early republic.

The power of Jefferson's imagination lay in his rather distinctive cultural training and tastes. The Sage of Monticello was unique among the founding fathers in the depth of his immersion in the realm of the aesthetic. None of his political allies or rivals could remotely match his knowledge of or interest in the fine arts, music, literature, drama, or design. It was in the arts that Jefferson "refined" his imagination, disciplining and focusing its powers. When he supplied Robert Skipwith with "A List of Books for a Private Library" in 1771, the largest group of entries (eighty-four in all) dealt with literature and the arts. By contrast, a mere eight were devoted to politics and commerce. Indeed, of all his remarkable skills, his surest mastery was in architecture. Great as his political writings were, they pale in comparison to the glittering designs of Monticello and the University of Virginia, leading one scholar to describe him as "first of all an artist." Jefferson seamlessly combined an artistic temperament and a finely developed aesthetic sensibility with the theory and practice of politics.[19]

Glimpses of Jefferson's political artistry first emerged in the 1770s. Much of his 1774 pamphlet *A Summary View of the Rights of British America* was thoroughly pedantic. His claim that the colonies were sovereign political entities united with the realm through a common monarch was admittedly radical but hardly unique, and his claim that the colonies had been established without any contribution "from the public treasures of his majesty, or his ancestors, for their assistance," was palpably absurd. But the opening and closing paragraphs were rhetorical gold.[20]

Abandoning the technicalities of constitutional casuistry, Jefferson assumed, by his own description, "that freedom of language and sentiment which becomes a free people, claiming their rights, as derived from the laws of nature, and not as the gift of their chief magistrate." "Let those flatter who fear," he thundered, "it is not an American art." It was his ringing phrases and his defiant insistence that "kings are the servants, not the proprietors of the people," and that "the God who gave us life gave us liberty at the same time; the hand of force may destroy, but cannot disjoin them," that gained Jefferson fame, not the careful recitation of facts and legal principles. The same artistry is evident in the Declaration of Independence. Few Americans today can recall any of the body of that work, but the introductory and concluding paragraphs are another matter. The powerful evocation of the "laws of nature and nature's god" and the "self-evident" truths that "all men are created equal" and enjoy from "their creator" the "inalienable rights" to "life, liberty, and the pursuit of happiness" transforms the Declaration from a state paper designed to facilitate French diplomatic recognition into a fundamental statement of principles, perhaps the core statement of the liberal democratic creed in modern times. The powerful statement of the right of revolution in the introduction is rhetorically fulfilled in the final sentence by the mutual pledge of "our lives, our fortunes, and our sacred honor." The effect is stunning and has captured the imagination of peoples around the world ever since. Jefferson intentionally designed it that way. In fact, as one scholar has recently demonstrated, Jefferson conceived of the Declaration as a performance piece; what were once thought to be misplaced punctuation marks were actually gestural cues for the delivery of the text as an oration. By 1776, Jefferson was gaining a reputation for a political artistry and felicity of expression that bordered on the sublime.[21]

Beginning in the early 1780s, Jefferson truly gave vent to his political imagination. A series of crises transformed his relationship to the politics of Enlightenment, freeing him from its limitations and constraints. Jefferson at last unleashed his aesthetic sensibility and allowed his fertile imagination to soar where few could follow. Where other statesmen continued to articulate the enlightened politics of programs and policies, Jefferson articulated a new politics of worldviews and principles. Where others sought to methodically link means to prescribed ends, Jefferson evoked a vision of America, its destiny and essential character, then laid out the steps necessary to safeguard it from the dangers it faced.

The Jeffersonian vision was progressive, radical, and democratic. It was also, and perhaps above all, dramatic and imaginative. More than that, its articulation transformed the nature of politics in early America, giving it a character that was thoroughly ideological and antideferential.

Politics became less a matter of credentials and administrative accomplishments than a function of the ability to communicate passionately held and widely shared ideals in a unifying vision. Politics became less a matter of the head and more one of the heart, and political rhetoric was transformed at its highest level from erudite disputation to Romantic poetry. His greatest political work of art was a vision that was so compelling and alluring that it has gripped the minds and hearts of Americans ever since. Ultimately, Jefferson was America's first great Romantic artist. It had not always been so.

THE TURNING

Thomas Jefferson had not always been a Romantic visionary. In the years leading up to and during the American struggle for independence, he practiced the politics of Enlightenment in his native state of Virginia. Like Adams, he worked to enlighten the public mind through public education, the establishment of religious freedom, and the creation of an intellectual atmosphere that was open and free from constraint. He also labored to reform the government and society of Virginia along modern and progressive lines. It was not only his goals that were imbued with the principles of the philosophes, however; Jefferson's reforms were offered in the spirit of moderation and compromise that were central to enlightened political activism from Addison and Hume to Voltaire and Diderot.

Beginning in the early 1780s, however, a subtle but discernible change in Jefferson's intellectual outlook took place. Not breaking with the doctrines of the philosophes, wholesale, Jefferson shifted emphases within those compromises that typified enlightened thought in fields as diverse as metaphysics, ethics, and aesthetics. These shifting emphases were part of a larger proto-Romantic movement on both sides of the Atlantic in the last quarter of the eighteenth century, a movement "from classification to imagination." As central terms took on new meanings and conceptual relations were reworked, the compromises that established the moderate character of enlightened thought became problematic and, eventually, untenable. The polite world of enlightened intellectual refinement gave way to the first glimmerings of Romanticism, and Jefferson became its herald in the politics of the new nation.[22]

As with Hamilton and Adams, Jefferson's values and beliefs were challenged by political developments during the struggle for independence. Virginians turned out to be far less public minded and virtuous than the Sage of Monticello had hoped. The Old Dominion proved impervious to efforts at reform, a source of immense frustration to a practitioner of the politics of Enlightenment like Thomas Jefferson. The political crises of Virginia also took on a personal dimension for the lanky statesman. When the British invaded and overran Virginia during his tenure as governor, his political career reached its absolute nadir. The Virginia legislature seriously considered censuring him for his official conduct. Compounding his despair, shortly after leaving his office his wife died after a difficult childbirth, making him an emotionally devastated and lifelong widower. As tragedy followed tragedy, each contradicting his aspirations and ideals, Jefferson began to reassess those ideals. Under the pressure of recalcitrant realities, he modified his beliefs to accommodate them. The result was the unfettering of the Romantic spirit in the Jeffersonian vision.

The Enlightenment of Thomas Jefferson

"Bold in Pursuit of Knowledge": The Education of Thomas Jefferson

For a man of his place and time, Thomas Jefferson received a remarkably thorough training in the scientific, philosophical, and literary canon of the Enlightenment. Shortly after his father's death, the fourteen-year-old began boarding with the Reverend James Maury at the latter's Edgeworth plantation. A gentleman in his own right, Maury was both a respected clergyman and, in Jefferson's words, "a correct classical scholar." One of the best-educated men in the province, whose interests included natural philosophy or science as well as classical tongues, James Maury began Thomas Jefferson's journey on the path of enlightened learning.[23]

The man who led Jefferson down the length of that path was William Small. A recent graduate of the University of Aberdeen, Scotland, Small began teaching mathematics and physics at William and Mary in 1758, just two years before Jefferson enrolled in the college. One of the two professors assigned to Jefferson, Small was the only layman on a faculty of hard-drinking and quarrelsome clergymen, and after Jefferson's other instructor, the Reverend John Rowe, was dismissed for drunken brawling, he became the young student's only pedagogue.[24]

Jefferson was extremely fortunate. He did not exaggerate when he described Small as "a man profound in most of the useful branches of science." It was from Small that he "got [his] first views of the expansion of science" as well as his first taste of higher mathematics; Jefferson's love for math and science would be a lifelong affair. A remarkable polymath, Small, who was the first member of the faculty to give "regular lectures in Ethics, Rhetoric and Belles Lettres," immersed his teenage charge in the full panoply of modern learning, especially the ethical and sociological theories of the Scottish Enlightenment. Taken with his serious young student, the twenty-six-year-old professor made him "his daily companion when not engaged" in the classroom.[25]

From their daily conversations, Jefferson first began to discern the lineaments of the enlightened worldview, the overarching synthesis of "the system of things in which we are placed." Jefferson hardly exaggerated when he claimed that his relationship with Small "probably fixed the destinies of my life."[26]

After two years of collegiate instruction, the nineteen-year-old Jefferson began five years of legal training with George Wythe, a good friend of Small's. The first professor of law in early America, the self-taught Wythe trained some of the most important legal and political minds in the early republic, including future Chief Justice John Marshall, President James Monroe, and noted statesman Henry Clay. Under Wythe's tutelage, Jefferson pored over the tedious pages of Edward Coke and the voluminous William Blackstone. His studies went far beyond the technical mastery of the common law and procedures, however. He studied the political implications of the law in authors like John Locke, Joseph Priestley, and the Baron de Montesquieu, just as he explored its ethical basis in the writings of Francis Hutcheson, Lord Kames, and the Marquis de Condorcet. This was an intellectually exciting period in Jefferson's life, a time when "I was bold in pursuit of knowledge," he recalled with fondness, "never fearing to follow truth and reason to whatever results they led and bearding every authority which stood in their way."[27]

The years of close reading under the direction of Small and Wythe steeped Jefferson in the learning of the Enlightenment, leaving him deeply committed to its values. Indeed, the booklist he supplied for Robert Skipwith's private library in 1771 reads like a who's who list of eighteenth-century learning. Bayle, Bolingbroke, Buffon, Burke, Franklin, Hume, Kames, Locke, Montesquieu, Reid, Robertson, Rousseau, Smith, Stewart, and Voltaire were all prominently listed among a bevy of "modern" literary figures such as Addison, Congreve, Fielding, Goldsmith, and Sterne, to name just a few. Although only in his early twenties when he finished his studies, Thomas Jefferson was fully a man of the Enlightenment.[28]

Jefferson had also been initiated into the mores of enlightened sociability. Small and Wythe introduced their charge to a tiny circle of learned cultivation in Williamsburg. Presiding over this circle was Royal Governor Francis Fauquier. A man of great taste, breeding, and scientific interest—he was a member of the Royal Society in London—the middle-aged governor personified enlightened politeness and refinement and was, in Jefferson's estimation, "the ablest man who had ever filled that office." Evenings at the governor's palace were a finishing school of sorts for Jefferson, refining his enlightened tastes, sharpening his wits, and teaching him the finer points of learned and polite discourse. The twenty-something-year-old squire emerged from this conversational milieu as one of the most polished and cultured men of his generation, a man who was, in the words of Dumas Malone, "the fullest American embodiment of the ideals of the Enlightenment" this side of Benjamin Franklin.[29]

"The Time to Guard Against Corruption and Tyranny, is Before they
Shall Have Gotten Hold of Us": Reforming the State of Virginia

From his earliest entry into political life until the end of the 1770s, Jefferson practiced the politics of Enlightenment in his native state. Like Adams in Massachusetts, he labored diligently to enlighten the public mind of his province through education and religious disestablishment. He also strove to reform the political life of Virginia, drafting constitutional and legal provisions to render it more republican and humane. Most important, however, were Jefferson's efforts at social reconstruction. He tried to redress the economic underdevelopment of his state as well as eliminate its root cause, the institution of slavery. His goals were enlightened; so too were his methods. Reflecting the enlightened ideal of moderation, he sought in all realms to leaven progressive change with the stabilizing force of tradition. Thoroughly modern in both means and ends, Jefferson's practice of the politics of Enlightenment was intended to transform the Old Dominion from an underdeveloped slave society into an enlightened and liberal state, one that a learned natural aristocrat like Jefferson could take justifiable pride in.

Like the other philosophes of the eighteenth century, Thomas Jefferson was convinced that liberty depended on the broad diffusion of enlightened learning. This conviction became all the more vital after independence, when Virginia adopted a purely republican form of government. "The most effectual means of preventing" the growth of tyranny, Jefferson insisted, "would be, to illuminate, as far as practicable, the minds of the people at large." An ill-informed and unenlightened public (much of Virginia was illiterate) would be inattentive to their liberties and unable to detect threats in a timely fashion. To alleviate this danger, Jefferson proposed a bold and thorough plan of public education, the first comprehensive scheme of its type for his state.[30]

Jefferson's scheme would divide each county into smaller administrative units called hundreds. Each hundred would erect a public school where "all the free children, male and female, resident in this respective hundred, shall be intitled to receive tuition gratis" for three years. In addition to literacy and basic mathematics, students would be instructed in "the most useful facts from Grecian, Roman, European and American history." The study of history was critical for Jefferson, just as it was for Adams. Only by intimate knowledge of "the experiences of other ages and countries" could the future citizens of Virginia "be enabled to know ambition under all its shapes, and prompt to exert their natural powers to defeat its purposes." Every year one gifted but poor student would be selected from each of these hundred schools to attend, at taxpayers' expense, the county's publicly built grammar school. After one year of studying the classical languages, geography, and "the higher part of numerical arithmetick," the bottom third of the "public foundationers" would be winnowed out and sent home. After the second year, all but the one truly outstanding poor scholar in each grammar school would end their public education. The lone student, the "best in genius and disposition," would receive an additional four years of advanced instruction at the public charge. Assuming just twenty such grammar schools were erected, Jefferson later argued that "by this means twenty of the best geniuses will be raked from the rubbish annually." Finally, one of these twenty scholars would be selected every other year to obtain a free college education at the College of William and Mary.[31]

Jefferson's meritocratic scheme not only benefited its gifted and diligent charges, it was also intended to assure the health of the body politic. "The publick happiness," Jefferson argued, could be protected only when those "whom nature hath endowed with genius and virtue," regardless of "wealth, birth, or other accidental condition," received the thorough and "liberal education" that would qualify them "to guard the sacred deposit of the rights and liberties of their fellow citizens" in their public and political careers.[32]

Jefferson also tried to reform the College of William and Mary along modern, enlightened lines. The college would be shorn of its sectarian affiliation with the Church of England and placed under the secular control of the political authorities. The curriculum would also undergo extensive revision. An expanded and up-to-date program in mathematics and the physical and life sciences, history, and languages ancient and modern would replace the study of theology. An additional department would offer courses on philosophy, ethics, literature, and the fine arts. Instead of training future divines for the Anglican ministry, Jefferson envisioned university-level professional instruction in medicine and the law. Remodeled along these lines, Virginia's sole institution of higher learning would serve as the perfect capstone to Jefferson's edifice of enlightened education.[33]

For Jefferson, the enlightenment of "the people at large" was not simply a matter of classroom instruction: to bring the fruits of enlightenment to those lacking means, he proposed that Virginia erect a public library as a deposit of higher learning. He also sought to ensure the greatest possible freedom of the press. If forced to "decide whether we should have a government without newspapers or newspapers without a government," Jefferson claimed, "I should not hesitate a moment to prefer the latter." To that end, he included in his draft of a constitution for his state a clause explicitly providing that newspapers be exempted from all restraint save private actions for libel. Far more controversially, he added a further proviso disestablishing the Anglican church and assuring the "full and free liberty of religious opinion." Everywhere in the Atlantic world, the struggle for religious toleration was a central goal of the politics of Enlightenment. Jefferson was no exception.[34]

These were radical sentiments in a state that still had a fully established church. Dissenters (Protestant and otherwise) were barred from office and forced to support the Anglican ministry. Indeed, in the decade before independence, the authorities of church and state in Virginia had responded to the evangelical challenge posed by the growing number of Baptists with persecution and violence. Jefferson struggled valiantly to eradicate this infamy. To bar a man from office for his religious opinions was a gross violation of his "natural right" to civic participation. "Our civil rights have no dependence on our religious opinions," he insisted, "any more than our opinions in physics or geometry." Nor was it necessary for the state to protect the sacred truths of Christianity. "It is error alone which needs the support of government," Jefferson wryly observed.

"Truth can stand by itself." Far in advance of their time, Jefferson's efforts were bitterly resisted by his fellow planters. Notwithstanding, he continued to insist on an immediate and strict separation of church and state. "The time to guard against corruption and tyranny," he declared, "is before they shall have gotten hold of us." When Jefferson's labors finally bore fruit in the 1780s, he considered it one of the greatest accomplishments of his life. Religious freedom, like public education and freedom of the press, was an essential precondition for illuminating "the minds of the people at large."[35]

For Thomas Jefferson, achieving independence meant far more than merely severing political ties with Great Britain. It was a golden opportunity for reform in Virginia. Even before he began drafting the Declaration of Independence, he worked feverishly on a new state constitution. Although never adopted, the plan of government he composed in the spring and early summer of 1776—it took him two drafts—was a model of enlightened statecraft. Powers were strictly separated between an independent judiciary, an annually elected executive, and a bicameral legislature. Most judiciary officers were appointed by the chief executive (known as the "administrator"), who lacked both prerogatives and a legislative veto, but the highest court of the state would be chosen by the popularly elected House of Representatives. That body in turn was balanced by an upper chamber or Senate whose members served far longer terms. Jefferson did not entirely abandon property qualifications for the franchise in his constitution. Only those with one-quarter of an acre in town or twenty-five "in the country" could vote, although he did propose expanding the electorate to those who had paid a municipal rate known as "scot and lot" for two years in a row. But another of his constitutional provisions would have obviated the requirement entirely. Jefferson attempted to achieve this through his boldest constitutional proposal, government-mandated land reform: "Every person of full age neither owning nor having owned 50 acres of land, shall be entitled to an appropriation of 50 acres" or enough to make up an estate of that size. Too radical for his contemporaries, Jefferson's land reform would have given Virginia's republican frame of government a strongly democratic tincture, one made even more pronounced by his insistence that "every person qualified to elect shall be capable of being elected." Few constitutionalists of his day were willing to go as far as Jefferson in putting power in the hands of an enlightened and informed people.[36]

Jefferson also rewrote the legal code of Virginia. In 1776 he was elected by the Virginia legislature to a small committee charged with revising the laws of the state. He did the lion's share of the work, and over the next three years he produced a complete revision of the legal code. Jefferson called for the abolition of primogeniture and entail—laws that devolved intestate property on the eldest male heir and prohibited breaking up "entailed" estates by sale or deed—as relics of feudalism and tools of privilege that contributed to the concentration of wealth in the hands of the few. Aristocratic vices like gambling and dueling were strictly proscribed, and such procedural safeguards as trial by jury and habeas corpus were written into fundamental law. The laws were also secularized. Witches and prophets were no longer to be burned at the stake but rather treated as public nuisances. Most important, Jefferson sought to humanize the law. Drawing on the legal writings of the Italian philosophe Cesare Beccaria, he eliminated the death penalty for all but the most heinous crimes. Liberal and humane, Jefferson's revision of the laws of Virginia was, like his constitutional schemes, a model of enlightened political activism.[37]

Jefferson's social reforms were no less enlightened. As both legislator and governor, he sought to diversify Virginia's underdeveloped staple economy by promoting commerce and manufactures. A student of political economy, Jefferson was fully versed in the Enlightenment's celebration of commerce. Trade not only produced the wealth of modern nations, it also "has taught the world more humanity." Indeed, Jefferson's first public act, even before his election to the House of Burgesses, was to mount a successful campaign to promote commerce and navigation on the Rivanna River by clearing it of obstructions. In his *Summary View of the Rights of British America* he urged a policy of free trade. As both governor and legislator he pursued a variety of measures designed to "regulate and promote commercial intercourse between Virginia and the international community." During his first year as governor he succeeded in obtaining authorization from the legislature to contract with a French firm to establish both a foundry and a weapons factory on the James River. In later years he would erect a successful naillery at Monticello. Commerce and manufactures would help redress the economic imbalances of Virginia's monocrop agriculture, creating new opportunities and avenues for labor and enrichment. They would thus modernize Virginia society, relieving its inequality and poverty.[38]

The root cause of Virginia's underdevelopment and inequality, however, was slavery. Jefferson recognized that humanizing his native land would ultimately require eradicating that evil. "The abolition of domestic slavery is the great object of desire in those colonies" like Virginia, "where it was unhappily introduced in their infant state," he declared in his *Summary View*, an object repeatedly frustrated by the crown's veto of colonial legislation to ban further importations of African bondsmen. Jefferson repeated this charge in the culminating passage of the Declaration of Independence—to his mortification, it was deleted by his fellow congressmen—castigating the British monarch for waging "cruel war against human nature itself, violating its most sacred right of life and liberty in the persons of a distant people who never offended him." One of his very first acts as a legislator was to urge Colonel Richard Bland to introduce a provision to ameliorate the condition of slaves and facilitate their emancipation in the county courts. Unfortunately the measure failed and Bland was rudely "denounced as an enemy of his country." Undaunted, Jefferson continued to struggle against the perpetuation of bondage in the Old Dominion. In 1777 he drafted a Bill to Prevent the Importation of Slaves and apparently proposed a measure the following year granting full civil and political equality to those free blacks "who enlisted or shall enlist, to serve in the army during the war" for independence. As part of his revision of Virginia's legal code, he would have banned all importation of slaves into Virginia; those illegally brought into the state and resident there for one year "shall be free." Far more radical was an amendment to that bill he purportedly prepared for submission once it was to be taken up by the legislature. This amendment would have abolished slavery gradually, ordering the emancipation of "all slaves born after passing the act" and further mandating the freedmen's training "at the public expense" in agriculture and "arts or science, according to their geniuses." Coupled with commercial and manufacturing development, Jefferson's efforts at abolition were part and parcel of his vision of an enlightened state of Virginia.[39]

Jefferson was a progressive modernizer who sought to reform his state in keeping with the strictures of the politics of Enlightenment. He was not, however, a radical zealot. Like all politically minded philosophes, he was governed by the ideal of enlightened moderation.

It was their moderation that made philosophes "the best defenders of the sovereign," claimed the famed Denis Diderot, precisely because, like "those buckets of water hanging up in the corridors of our police commissioners," they were always "ready to be thrown over the flames of fanaticism." It was only through "moderate opinions" observed David Hume, that statesmen could "find the proper medium in all disputes" and thus abate party zeal. The essential "lesson of moderation" for all radical zealots was "that its antagonist might possibly be sometimes in the right." Moderation and balance were the watchwords of the politics of Enlightenment, and they were words Jefferson lived by. In every avenue of reform, he balanced change with the stabilizing, if not conservative, force of continuity.[40]

Jefferson's program of public education exemplified this ideal of moderate balance. It would assuredly afford the common people the rudiments of literacy, numeracy, and the historical knowledge necessary to safeguard their liberties. It would also benefit the gentry, as Jefferson readily acknowledged, providing them with "convenient schools, at which their children may be educated," albeit "at their own expense." Jefferson was under no illusion that his limited plan of primary education would level the social and cultural differences between the slave-holding squires and their common white neighbors. Although his meritocratic scheme of scholarships would have lifted some poor geniuses from the ranks of the latter, the actual numbers involved—one every two years—were quite limited. Nor did Jefferson, in his private musings, expect that these socially mobile scholars would ever achieve the political power and authority he heralded in his proposal. Ultimately they were "destined for learned professions, as means of livelihood." The poor scholars would "need those branches" of learning that "are the basis of their future profession," while the squires' high cultural training must "qualify them for either public or private life." Hardly the work of a utopian radical, Jefferson's plan of education was a carefully balanced and thoroughly moderate proposal that benefited all segments of white society.[41]

The same spirit of balance and moderation can be seen in Jefferson's constitutional reforms. On the one hand, his proposed land reform had a decidedly populist import and would have resulted in the enfranchisement of all adult white males. On the other hand, the electoral power of the people was restricted to their choice of gentry representatives to the lower house of the legislature. That body in turn would elect both the executive and the Senate. Indeed, as he informed Edmund Pendleton, he could accept any provision for the selection of senators—he later embraced the notion of an electoral college—"rather than a mere creation by and dependence on the people." Aside from high sheriffs and coroners, all the principal county officers would continue to be appointed by the executive as they had been in the colonial period, thus ensuring the continued control of the squirearchy over local government and politics. In short, the gains in popular power in Jefferson's constitutional reforms were balanced by the stabilizing force of gentry rule.[42]

Much of Jefferson's legal revision was also decidedly moderate. Primogeniture and entail were rarely invoked in Jefferson's day, and witches had not been burned in Virginia in anyone's memory. Even his humanization of the penal code was balanced. Although he did attempt to curtail the use of capital punishment, his solution to the problem of crime was to replace capital with corporal punishment. Sexual crimes like "rape, polygamy, or sodomy" would result in castration or, in the case of a female offender, "by boring through the cartilage of her nose a hole one half inch in diameter in the least." Those plebeians who disfigured their opponents in rough and tumble would suffer disfigurement by the law "in like sort" or "in some other part of at least equal value and estimation, in the opinion of a jury," as well as restitution to the victim in the form of "one half of his lands and goods." Jefferson himself was rather uncomfortable with his use of "the lex talionis." The principle of "an eye for an eye, and a hand for a hand will exhibit spectacles in execution whose moral effect would be questionable," he wrote to his old legal instructor George Wythe. At the same time, he knew that his humanitarian impulses could not run roughshod over accepted opinion and practice.[43]

Even Jefferson's crusade against slavery was moderate in both tone and substance. His call to end the importation of slaves was not nearly as radical as it first appeared. True, those illegally brought into the state would be freed after one year, but if they did not leave Virginia within the following year, they would be placed "out of the protection of the laws." Nor were such efforts at suppressing the importation of African bondsmen necessarily a first step to the eradication of slavery itself. Many planters supported such measures to keep up the value of the slaves they already held, as a hedge against falling prices for tobacco on the international market.[44]

The one genuine effort at abolition that Jefferson proposed took the form of a planned rider to a bill that had yet to see the legislative light of day. That measure would not have emancipated any of Jefferson's roughly two hundred slaves, though it would have gradually freed their future children when they reached the age of maturity. Once freed, they would have been subject to forced repatriation "to such places as the circumstances at the time should render most proper." Gradual emancipation would ultimately end the curse of slavery, but it would also eradicate any African-American presence in the Chesapeake. And in fact, the abolition of slavery itself did not necessarily entail an end to the social inequalities that institution had produced. Jefferson's scheme of abolition also called for the state "to send vessels at the same time to other parts of the world for an equal number of white inhabitants" who would replace the enslaved African Americans, presumably serving as tenants on the vast estates of the Virginia squires.[45]

Like his attempts to educate his fellow citizens and reform their political life, Jefferson's efforts at abolition were often progressive but rarely truly radical. His very moderation itself was emblematic of his deep and abiding commitment to the values and politics of Enlightenment.

The Nature of the Change: The Enlightenment Unraveled

The spirit of compromise was not only a vital part of the politics of the philosophes; it was also emblematic of the worldview of the Enlightenment itself. Indeed, moderation was one of the essential virtues of the enlightened, whether in the realm of politics or philosophy. In the early 1780s, however, Jefferson began to reassess these compromises. While never rejecting them entirely, he pushed them to their limits, changing the locus of key terms and reconfiguring the relations of central concepts. In so doing, he and other proto-Romantic thinkers of the late eighteenth century unraveled the Enlightenment, deconstructing it from within. Understanding how they did so reveals the way in which Romanticism arose from what were once complementary principles and notions that had now become antinomies. In Jefferson's able hands, these transformations effected the liberation of the Romantic spirit, a spirit that would fully blossom in his mature vision.

Enlightened Compromises: Metaphysics, Ethics, and Aesthetics

Few concepts were as central to the Enlightenment as that of nature, which the philosophes had interpreted along Newtonian lines. The universe was comprised of corporeal bodies whose motions—like the striking of billiard balls—were described by the mathematical formulas of mechanical force. This view of nature had been critical in the struggle against enthusiasm and superstition. Newtonianism left no room for sympathetic magic, demonic possession, or divine providences and prophecies. Only enlightened naturalism and philosophy, claimed David Hume, was "able entirely to conquer" the "unaccountable terrors" of the superstitious mind. And the presence of the divine was to be found not in miraculous portents but rather in the orderly and mathematical structure of the cosmos, one that clearly implied a rational designer.[46]

The problem with this mechanistic view of nature was that it not only disenchanted the world, it also deanimated it. As seventeenth-century rationalists from Bacon and Hobbes to Gassendi and Descartes had recognized, nature as conceived by modern physics was a rational system, but one that lacked overarching unity and purpose. "Nature has no fixed goal," declared the infamous Baruch Spinoza, and "all final causes are but figments of the human imagination." Voltaire agreed wholeheartedly. Explaining a natural phenomenon by its "primary" cause or underlying purpose was like claiming that "noses were made to support spectacles." Not only did mechanistic nature lack purposes, but its determinism undermined any role for freedom and innovation in the universe. Coldly rational and impersonal, the Newtonian universe was governed by immutable laws whose very fixity suggested a static metaphysical order without change, development, or growth. Such a cosmos was hardly an alluring backdrop for human endeavor or life.[47]

The philosophes solved this problem by invoking what we today call culture. It was the "arts and sciences" that supplied humans with purposes and goals. Insofar as those goals arose from the reflection of a rational animal on its needs and environment—both physical and social—they might themselves be described as natural. More important, culture introduced a dynamic element into the enlightened worldview. As Francis Bacon had taught, breakthroughs in the sciences led to a greater mastery over nature and gave rise to remarkable advances in technology and the "mechanical arts." The refinement of learning in the "arts" or humanities helped promote politeness, civility, and public Enlightenment. Such "ages of refinement," Hume argued, were "both the happiest and most virtuous," in part because "a progress in the arts is rather favourable to liberty, and has a natural tendency to preserve, if not produce, a free government." Culture thus complemented nature, for the philosophes, completing it as it were and supplying it with the purpose and progress so central to mankind's hopes and dreams. The importance placed on the progress of the arts and sciences thus served to moderate the radical implications of the Enlightenment's metaphysical naturalism, softening its determinism and obscuring its reductive materialism.[48]

The same strategy of moderation can be seen in the Enlightenment's treatment of ethics. Consequentialism, the doctrine that the value of an act lies in its effects rather than in the intentions of its agent, was central to the moral theory of the philosophes. Seventeenth-century Rationalists like Thomas Hobbes in his *Leviathan* had first deployed consequential reasoning in their political philosophy, arguing that political obligations were rooted in the rational self-interest of individuals who sought to avoid the dangers inherent in life in the anarchic and violent "state of nature." Locke's *Second Treatise of Government* had extended Hobbes's formula in a republican direction while softening its depiction of the state of nature. But not until Bernard Mandeville's influential and infamous *Fable of the Bees* was consequentialism extended over the entire realm of ethical phenomena. Mandeville's enlightened consequentialism opened a whole new "liberal" avenue for action by arguing that, in a modern commercial society, such vices as greed, vanity, and self-love ought to be given free rein by the state as long as they produced public benefits.

Ethical consequentialism was rational as well as worldly because judging consequences required careful instrumental calculations of cause and effect. Assessing acts on the utility of their outcomes also transformed the very nature of virtue itself, replacing the older classical goals of honor, courage, and self-sacrifice with such humdrum middle-class traits as frugality, industry, and temperance. Where the older classical and Christian ideals had been austere, the modern virtues were "softer" and more "amiable," noted Adam Smith, and more conducive to "candid condescension and indulgent humanity." Enlightened consequentialism, with its stress on the rational calculation of public utilities, was an essential part of the modern and liberal worldview of the eighteenth century.[49]

The problem with enlightened consequentialism was its arid rationalism. Judging actions on the basis of their tendency to produce public benefits turned morality into a matter of cold calculation utterly devoid of existential commitment or heroic engagement. More than that, the moral rationalism of the appeal to public utility threatened to reduce moral action to enlightened self-interest or *amour propre*. The moral psychology of such an approach was clearly selfish and decidedly unflattering. Morally speaking, man was a selfish, albeit rational, egoist whose actions were motivated by self-love rather than fellow-feeling. This was, in fact, precisely the conclusion that Mandeville had reached: the ancient lawgivers and moralists were prudent politicians but intellectual charlatans who tried "to make the People they were to govern, believe, that it was more beneficial for every Body to conquer than indulge his Appetites, and much better to mind the Publick than what seem'd his private interest." Man was a rational but selfish animal whose talk of virtue served as sheep's clothing to cover his wolfish character.[50]

Enlightened philosophes softened the character of ethical consequentialism by balancing reason with the passions or, as Jefferson put it, the "head and the heart." The Scottish moral philosopher Francis Hutcheson argued that man was endowed with both benevolent affections and a moral sense. It was these benevolent instincts, rather than vanity, that explained virtuous actions, and our ethical judgments of those actions were grounded in a moral sense that apprehended those affections in the actor. David Hume elaborated Hutcheson's theory, grounding our benevolent affections in an empathic fellow-feeling or "sympathy." Hume's friend Adam Smith further extended the doctrine of sympathy in his own *Theory of Moral Sentiments*, arguing that our ability to sympathize with others allowed us to consider our own moral actions from the perspective of an imaginary spectator, and it was from that perspective that we came to judge the moral "propriety" of our behavior.

The doctrine of moral sense thus tamed ethical consequentialism, eliminating its wolfish, egotistical character. People were instinctually propelled both to act for the good of others and to approve of all actors who evidenced those instincts. These instincts were not violent but "calm" passions, as moral philosophers from Hutcheson to Hume and

Smith all insisted. At the same time, moral sense philosophy preserved the essential insight of Mandeville: "Usefulness," as Hume observed, was the "source of moral sentiment" and therefore "every thing, which contributes to the happiness of society, recommends itself directly to our approbation and good will." Indeed, actors might be judged by their intentions and affections, but the acts themselves were still evaluated by the standard of utility. The calm passions of benevolence made agents morally virtuous, Hutcheson claimed, but "that action is best, which procures the greatest happiness for the greatest numbers." Moral sense doctrine thus ensured the respectability of consequentialism, restraining its excesses while retaining its core insight.[51]

The very same spirit of moderation and compromise can be seen in the development of the enlightened theory of aesthetic cultivation. In a series of essays entitled "The Pleasures of the Imagination," the famed Augustan writer Joseph Addison had applied Lockean empiricism to the realm of the beautiful. Aesthetic taste was ultimately grounded in sensory experience, but it was capable of refinement and cultivation through rational reflection and study. Exposure to the fine arts and criticism fostered an increased sensitivity to the finer shadings of beauty, affording cultivated aesthetes the ability to "converse with a picture, and find an agreeable companion in a statue." Hume shared Addison's perspective. Beauty might be in the eye of the beholder, but that eye could be trained by regular exposure to the arts and careful study of works of criticism about them. Guided by reason, an enlightened consumer of the arts was capable of enjoying aesthetic pleasures denied his unsophisticated peers.[52]

Like ethical consequentialism, the problem with the doctrine of aesthetic cultivation was its arid rationalism. Beauty became a matter of sense rather than sensibility, and informed aesthetic judgments arose from a process of rational comparison between given works and "correct," largely classical, forms. Despite its virtues, such a doctrine did not necessarily square with the actual experience of beauty by many people, an experience that was capable of producing powerful emotional effects rather than reasonable ruminations. Moreover, the doctrine of aesthetic cultivation was inherently elitist since most people lacked both the means and the leisure to refine their tastes through study and contemplation. Hutcheson had tried to redress these problems by positing an aesthetic sense, distinct from but allied to the moral sense, that allowed all people to apprehend the beautiful by a universal internal standard. Hutcheson's posit solved the problem of elitism, but not the arid rationalism of enlightened aesthetics. When art was not purely imitative, what appealed to our aesthetic sense was its regularity or ability to reveal the unifying and harmonious elements in an apparently discordant context. "The figures which excite in us the ideas of beauty," he declared, "seem to be those in which there is *uniformity amidst variety.*" That such beauty was ultimately a matter of rational system and proportion was evinced by his discussion of "the beauty of theorems."[53]

The solution to the rationalism of the enlightened doctrine of cultivation came in the form of Edmund Burke's landmark treatise, *A Philosophical Enquiry into the Origins of our Ideas of the Sublime and Beautiful.* The experience of beauty was rooted in pleasant sensations of a delicate nature that "induce in us a sense of affection and tenderness." By contrast, the sublime was evoked by painful sensations and produced the powerful emotions of terror, horror, and astonishment; "whatever is qualified to cause terror, is a foundation capable of the sublime."[54]

The sublime thus complemented the beautiful both by serving as a stark counterpoint to highlight the latter's pleasures and by adding emotional and psychological depth to an aesthetic experience that might otherwise appear insipid and dull. And while the experience of the sublime might at first appear stormy and irrational, Burke insisted that it ultimately served the purposes of calm, rational understanding. The sublime did this by "exercising" the "finer organs" of our imagination and rational faculties. Since the mind itself probably depended on "some fine corporeal instruments in its operation," Burke concluded that "to have them in proper order, they must be shaken and worked to a proper degree" and nothing more effectively shook them than the terrors of the sublime. Just as culture completed nature and the moral sense balanced the rational calculation of consequences, so the sublime complemented the enlightened cultivation of the beautiful, safeguarding its contemplative pleasures while moderating its potentially elitist and rationalist excesses.[55]

Deconstructing Enlightened Moderation

Jefferson never rejected these enlightened compromises per se. As late as 1788 he commissioned John Trumbull to paint a joint portrait of "the three greatest men that have ever lived, without any exception": Francis Bacon, John Locke, and Isaac Newton, the founding trinity of the English-speaking Enlightenment. But beginning in the 1780s, Jefferson's understanding of these compromises was subtly but profoundly altered. Like the other great proto-Romantics of the late eighteenth century, Jefferson did not reject the Enlightenment so much as unravel it. By changing the precise signification of key concepts and stressing one moderating element over another, the proto-Romantics ultimately undermined the compromises that lay at the very heart of the philosophes' worldview. The center could not hold, and the age of Enlightenment gave way to the first glimmerings of the Romantic spirit.[56]

Perhaps the first critical notion of enlightened thought to undergo transformation was that of nature. Beginning at the middle of the eighteenth century, the mechanistic Newtonian universe of tranquil and fixed mathematical laws was challenged by the organicism of the emerging life sciences. As a student, Jefferson had been captivated by mathematical physics, but for most of his life his deepest scientific affinities and interests were in what he called "natural history." Unlike Newtonian physics, the life sciences rehabilitated an organic sense of nature, one characterized by dynamism and change that led Jefferson to conceive of "external nature as stormy and unruly." More than that, the organic nature of the life sciences rehabilitated the notion that natural processes developed toward fixed ends. Nature was, after all, purposeful. Unlike the conception of most philosophes, Jefferson's nature was not an impersonal and mathematical order but rather "a source of value and a standard of truth."[57]

This organic conception of nature had profound implications for the Enlightenment's conception of culture as "the arts and sciences." If nature was itself purposeful, then what need was there for culture to complement or complete it by adding additional goals and ends? Indeed, what was to preclude the possibility that the goals of culture did not contradict those of nature? This was exactly the position the great proto-Romantic Jean-Jacques Rousseau had taken in his *Discourse on the Arts and Sciences*. Far from meliorative, the march of higher learning had corrupted man, robbing him of his pristine natural innocence and virtue. The enlightened cult of progress was an illusion, and the growth of urbanity and sophistication was a sign of moral and social decay. In his *Notes on the State of Virginia*, written in the 1780s, Jefferson argued that "the natural progress and consequences of the arts" promoted a corruption of natural human goodness that "suffocates the germ of virtue, and prepares fit tools for the designs of ambition." Culture no longer completed nature, in Jefferson's understanding. Instead it undermined its pristine innocence and inherent goodness. The Enlightenment's cosmological compromise was torn asunder.[58]

A similar change occurred in the realm of ethics. In the works of novelists like Henry Brooke, Samuel Richardson, and Oliver Goldsmith, the calm passions of the moral sense were transformed into the emotional transports of sentimentality. James Macpherson's "discovery" of the Gaelic epic poem *Ossian*—fraudulent as it turned out—helped spark a literary Gothic revival. Jefferson adored *Ossian*. "The tender, and the sublime emotions of the mind were never before so finely wrought," he wrote to Macpherson's brother Charles, adding that "I am not ashamed to own that I think this rude bard of the North the greatest Poet that has ever existed." The *honnête homme* of Voltaire's *Candide* became Henry Mackenzie's *Man of Feeling*. Rousseau's *Nouvelle Héloïse* and *Émile* were suffused with overwrought emotion and sensibility: characters shed effusive tears, and as Robert Darnton has shown, so too did readers. Laurence Sterne, Jefferson's favorite author, was at the forefront of the proto-Romantic "counterculture" that valued vulnerability, sensitivity, and tender-heartedness over calculation, rationality, and calm deliberation. Jefferson considered Sterne's works "the best course of morality that ever was written."[59]

The transition from moral sense to Romantic sensibility undermined the relationship between reason and the calm passions that enlightened philosophes had labored to establish. Sentimental novelists taught that morality was entirely a matter of feeling, an internal process that resided in the sincere and authentic promptings of the human breast. This was exactly the way Jefferson came to reconceptualize the doctrine of the moral sense. In his famous letter "The Head and the Heart" that he wrote to Maria Cosway, an Italian-born British painter with whom he had an amorous dalliance in Paris, Jefferson's "heart" informs his head that nature had given them "a divided empire." "To you she allotted the field of science," he declared, "to me that of morals." Ethics were too critical to leave to the vagaries of human reason, and thus nature had "laid their foundation" exclusively "in sentiment, not in science." The moral sense was the voice of conscience, Jefferson informed his daughter, "and if you always obey it," regardless of consequences, "you will always be prepared for the end of the world: or for a much more certain event which is death."[60]

Jefferson's privileging of heart over head, like that of other sentimental proto-Romantics, turned morality from a matter of rational judgment to one of internal authenticity. To be truly moral meant to be sincere, and to be morally sincere meant "to be pure in thought, free of doubt, close and affectionate." Ethical consequentialism gave way to the ethos of the sensitive and pure heart, one filled by the unerring sense of its own purity and sincerity.[61]

In the realm of aesthetics, proto-Romantics undermined the enlightened doctrine of cultivation by stressing the sublime over the beautiful. The former was no longer simply a point of contrast to highlight the pleasures of the latter, but rather a desirable aesthetic experience in its own right that made the beautiful seem pale and languid in comparison. Jefferson was very much a part of this movement. In contrast to the pastoral idyll of his contemporary Virginians, Jefferson chose to build his mansion not in a pleasant vale but atop a mountain. His landscape designs reflected a vision of nature that was "irregular, waving and rustic in outline," one that was "romantic rather than classical." The nearby "Natural bridge," a geological formation in Virginia, so captivated him that he purchased it. The bridge was "the most sublime of Nature's works." The awe and terror inspired by its massive height "gave me a violent head ach," he claimed in his *Notes*, a pain "relieved by a short, but pleasing view of the Blue ridge." Indeed, by the end of his treatment of this spectacle, Jefferson's sublime had ceased being a contrast to the beautiful and instead became its highest culmination and fulfillment. "It is impossible for the emotions, arising from the sublime, to be felt beyond what they are here," he positively gushed, "so beautiful an arch, so elevated, so light, and springing, as it were, up to heaven, the rapture of the Spectator is really indiscribable!" The exquisite taste of the beautiful, cultivated by reflection and study, gave way to the raptures of the sublime.[62]

The cult of stormy and organic nature, the embrace of sentimentality, and the aesthetic appreciation of the sublime, then, were the categories by which Jefferson unraveled the moderating compromises of the Enlightenment and cleared the ground for the newly emerging Romantic ethos of sensibility. Jefferson was not alone in making this transformation. Rather, he was part of a trans-Atlantic "transition from neoclassical to romantic" that occurred in the closing decades of the eighteenth century. John Adams's exposure to this transformation in Paris repelled him, filling him with anxiety and dread for the sustainability and rationality of the politics of Enlightenment. By contrast, Jefferson was enraptured by it during his years in the City of Light, becoming the American herald of Romantic sensibility at home and abroad.[63]

"A wound on my spirit which will only be cured by the all-healing grave": The Sources of Disillusionment

The causes of Thomas Jefferson's intellectual transformation in the 1780s lay in his previous experience of the struggle for independence. Like Hamilton and Adams, Jefferson embraced the American Revolution filled with high hopes and great expectations, encouraged by his faith in the politics of Enlightenment. And as with Hamilton and Adams, his sanguine expectations were dashed by historical realities. The virtue of the people proved illusory and the wisdom of their leaders suspect. The revolutionary cause was not the glorious one that Jefferson had envisioned but rather a bitter and unseemly struggle against political incompetence and public selfishness. That in itself would have prompted a man as thoughtful as Jefferson to reassess his convictions. Compounding this disillusionment were developments within Virginia itself, which remained impervious to reform. Worse, some of the greatest revolutionary failures of Virginia occurred during Jefferson's two one-year terms as governor of the Old Dominion. Put simply, Virginia failed to meet the challenge of revolutionary armed struggle. So too did Jefferson.

The failures of Virginia under his watch, as well as the resultant criticism he bore for them, cut Jefferson to the core. "These injuries," he wrote to James Monroe, "had inflicted a wound on my spirit which will only be cured by the all-healing grave." Few American founders experienced the personal and political devastation that Jefferson endured during the struggle for independence. Few experienced a disillusionment so crushing. It was therefore understandable that few would respond with as thorough and radical an intellectual reassessment and transformation.[64]

The Troubling State of Virginia

Jefferson worked hard and long to reform the state of Virginia. The revolutionary moment offered an ideal opportunity to remodel his state, enlightening its culture, redesigning its political institutions and laws, and promoting progressive, modern social changes. No utopian schemer, Jefferson presented a program that was moderate rather than radical and made ample compromise with entrenched interests and popular opinion. This very moderation must have made the failure of reform in Virginia all the more galling to the young philosophe. Try as he would, and try he did, after years of dogged diligence, Jefferson's endeavors to enlighten Virginia proved fruitless.

His progressive plan of public education was rejected outright. The call for public libraries went unheeded. So too did his demand for liberty of the press. The Anglican church was ultimately disestablished, but this achievement owed more to the political weight and activism of Baptists and other dissenters than to the high-minded idealism of enlightened statesmanship. Even so, it did not occur until the latter half of the 1780s, when Jefferson was serving as a diplomat in Paris.

Jefferson's political reforms fared no better than his cultural ones. His constitution of 1776 was rejected out of hand, presumably on the grounds that it arrived too late. A similar fate befell a subsequent draft he prepared in 1783, when the convention for which it was composed never materialized. Land was not distributed to the common freemen, and the franchise remained restricted, as it had been before the revolution. The unfairness and injustice of these measures appalled Jefferson. Most common Virginians "who pay and fight for its support," he complained, "are unrepresented in the legislature," an odd state of affairs for a political community whose motto was "no taxation without representation." Yet in the years after independence those with the franchise in the Old Dominion comprised less than "half of those on the roll of the militia, or of the tax gatherers." And among those with the right to participate in political life, their actual representation was "very equal." For example, Warwick County, "with only one hundred fighting men," sent the same number of delegates to the state assembly as Loudon, which fielded 1,746 men under arms. Thus he concluded that "every man in Warwick has as much influence in the government as 17 men in Loudon." Jefferson's legal revision fared little better than his constitutional reform. Virginia's penal code remained just as harsh as it had previously been. Even the abolition of primogeniture and entail took nearly a decade to effect, by which time Jefferson was no longer in his native state to take credit for its accomplishment.[65]

Jefferson's efforts to modernize his society also foundered. His attempts to promote commercial development were thwarted by the war, which curtailed the international trade of the Chesapeake and left tobacco without available markets. Internal trade was hampered both by the closing of courts and by the runaway inflation that promptly transformed Virginia's currency into a nearly worthless medium of exchange. By the end of his second term in office, the state's currency had been devalued to a shocking ratio of 250 to one. Jefferson's attempts to promote manufactures suffered a similar fate. Interminable delays in executing the contracts with the French firm of Penet, Windel & Co. brought the whole project to a standstill. Most disturbing of all, however, was the absence of any meaningful action against slavery.[66]

Except for desultory measures simplifying voluntary manumissions, nothing was done to address the problem of slavery in Virginia. No plan of emancipation, however gradual or modest, was even seriously proposed. The enslaved received no more legal protections than they had previously been afforded. Nor was the legal and social status of free blacks in any way ameliorated. Like all of Jefferson's reform initiatives, his hopes to redress Virginia's greatest failing, the practice of chattel slavery, was left utterly unfulfilled. The revolutionary moment had passed, and Virginia had not been improved or reformed one whit.

Compounding this failure were Jefferson's own failures of leadership. As wartime governor of Virginia, he saw his state invaded three times. In each case he was unable to offer much in the way of resistance, despite commanding the resources of the largest and most populous state in the nation, one that boasted a militia of fifty thousand men and that prided itself on its military valor and accomplishment. Accounting for Jefferson's failure to protect his state from invasion, several historians have plausibly argued that the lack of constitutional authority vested in the executive and the desolate state of its finances precluded any real hopes of success. Indeed, it is entirely possible that he could have done nothing to spare Virginia its ignominious fate. Unfortunately, nothing is precisely what Thomas Jefferson did.[67]

By the time Jefferson assumed office in early June 1779, the British had already captured Georgia and were beginning their siege of Charleston. That city fell early in the following year, exposing the interior of the southern states to invasion from the British forces. Jefferson received urgent requests from the southern commander Horatio Gates for men and supplies to augment his woefully overmatched army. What Gates got was a mere fifteen hundred militiamen. Worse yet, most arrived with neither arms, food, nor supplies of any kind. Eventually, Gates pleaded with Jefferson not to "send any Men into the Field, or even into this camp" if they were "intirely unequiped, and unprovided, with everything that is necessary for the Service they are intended to perform."[68]

Jefferson's succors had shocked Gates. Rather than setting a good example for the "backwardness" of her recalcitrant neighbor North Carolina, Virginia's paltry efforts "rather Countenances, than disgraces, their Sister State." "What can the Executive Councils of Both States believe will be the consequences," he demanded, "of such unpardonable neglect?" The answer was not long in coming. In mid-August, Gates was routed at the battle of Camden; his army was dispersed and, with it, any semblance of opposition to the British commander Lord Cornwallis in the South.[69]

In September 1780, just three months into his second term, Jefferson was warned by Gates of a planned British invasion of Portsmouth, at the mouth of the James River, the principal port of Virginia. Jefferson had received similar reports the previous year and had chosen to disregard them. When those invasions never occurred, Jefferson was vindicated as a man of cool and cautious judgment. Jefferson displayed the same cool demeanor in this case. Unfortunately, this invasion was all too real. On October 20, 2,500 British soldiers disembarked in Portsmouth under the command of Major General Alexander Leslie. In short order they reduced the town and the nearby ports of Newport News and Hampton Roads. Little or no organized opposition stood between them and the newly established state capital of Richmond, just one hundred miles up the James River. Only orders from Cornwallis that Leslie recall his forces and rendezvous with him in North Carolina in mid-November saved Jefferson and his state from being overrun by this modest force.[70]

This reprieve did not last long. At the end of the previous year, Washington had apprised Jefferson of a rumored enemy naval expedition to the Old Dominion from New York. Again, Jefferson resisted any rash moves. Even after British vessels were seen headed for the James River on December 31, 1780, Jefferson remained calm and composed. News that the British had landed troops and were advancing on the interior found Jefferson serenely strolling in his garden. He had, of course, heard these reports, but he had also heard others suggesting "they were nothing more than a foraging party." Until he received more definitive information, he declined to "disturb the Country by calling out the Militia" and sounding the tocsin of alarm. By that point, alas, it was too late. Within a few short days the notorious traitor Benedict Arnold sailed with a tiny force of nine hundred men up the James River past Williamsburg and right up to the state capital at Richmond. Unopposed, he entered the town on January 5. After burning the state's paltry foundry and seven other buildings, he retired unmolested on January 7 to bases farther downriver. Virginia had been invaded and overrun, its capital sacked and razed by a puny force that had not been compelled to fire a shot in anger.[71]

Worse followed bad for Jefferson and his fellow Virginians. In late March Major General William Phillips arrived with 2,600 soldiers and replaced Arnold as head of the local British forces. By mid-April he had seized Williamsburg and was on the march to Petersburg, just south of Richmond. He entered Petersburg on the twenty-fifth after a brief battle with state militia led by "Baron" von Steuben, who had been forced to retire after running out of ammunition. Phillips burned several public buildings and warehouses, and then marched to Richmond before returning to his ships on the James, all the way leaving a trail of fire and destruction. Finally, Cornwallis arrived in Petersburg on May 20 with an army he had marched unopposed from North Carolina through the very heart of Virginia. By this point, Jefferson and his council had decided to evacuate Richmond and reconvene the government in Charlottesville, at the foot of the Blue Ridge Mountains, near his Monticello estate.

With a force of over seven thousand troops, Cornwallis easily dislodged Lafayette—he had been dispatched by Washington with a few thousand troops to shore up the collapsing state of Virginia—from Richmond and sent him scurrying for cover to the north. He then dispatched a small raiding party under the command of Banastre Tarleton to capture the rebellious government in Charlottesville. Tarleton succeeded in capturing several members of the legislature and narrowly missed nabbing Jefferson himself on June 4. His official term of office had ended just two days before.

When the remnants of Virginia's government assembled in Staunton on June 12, Jefferson was nowhere to be seen. Despite the ongoing crisis, he decided that since his official term had ended on the second, he was no longer responsible for the executive department and, as of that date, stopped meeting with his executive council. That the legislature had been dislodged from its seat of government and was thus unable to elect his successor was none of his concern. He had discharged his duty by the letter of the law. The legislators felt otherwise. Stunned by the swiftness of their state's military collapse and the seeming equanimity with which its chief executive had faced it, they immediately resolved that "at the next Session of Assembly An Enquirey be made into the Conduct of the Executive for the last twelve Months." Jefferson had reached the nadir of his pubic career, a man under threat of censure by his fellow Virginians.[72]

Jefferson bristled at the charges against him. He never denied that he was ill equipped by his "line of life and education for the command of armies." Indeed, he had sought to resign his office to more capable military hands in late 1780 and in the spring of 1781, only to be rebuffed both times by suggestions that this would appear to be quitting his post at a time of troubles. Errors he undoubtedly made, but they were honest mistakes. Nor could he have done much differently, given his limited powers and the pitiful resources at his command. After more than a dozen years of sacrifice on behalf of his beloved state, he now "stood arraigned for treason of the heart and not merely weakness of the head." Jefferson choked at the injustice of it all.[73]

Jefferson was not wrong in listing the restraints under which he labored. The powers of his office were narrowly circumscribed by the state's constitution. Virginia's tiny foundry was utterly inadequate to supply—much less service and repair—the necessary weaponry for its forces, and the British control of the seas combined with the collapse of the state's credit made the procurement of matériel from other states next to impossible. The taxes assessed by the legislature were utterly inadequate and often went uncollected (in 1779 some 50 percent of counties were delinquent); regardless, Virginia's planters and yeomen refused to exchange provisions and supplies for the militia for the state's valueless money. Even calling out the militia was a dodgy business. Counties repeatedly refused to meet their quotas, some quite vociferously. John Taylor reported that in Lancaster the militia "assembled in a Mob, and disarmed the Officers as they came to the field." Given these constraints, what more could the philosophe governor have done?[74]

The problems facing the chief executive of Virginia, however, were hardly unique. All of the revolutionary state constitutions dramatically curtailed the powers of the executive, and all of those governors had faced identical crises of supply and public indifference and defiance. Successful war governors overcame these challenges by being innovative and bold, occasionally transgressing the letter of the law to keep resistance alive. Nor was Jefferson entirely without administrative redress. As early as May 1780, he and his council had been granted impressive emergency powers. Under threat of invasion, they could seize all necessary supplies, call out and dispatch up to twenty thousand men to any theater of their choosing, and imprison all resisters and recalcitrants without legal restraint, effectively exercising the power to impose martial law. Nor was the dearth of weapons as dire as it seemed. Interdiction of supplies to the Continental Army combined with the arrival of French provisions had actually left the state with a fairly ample supply by May 1781. The problem with Jefferson's tenure was not so much a lack of authority and resources as the way he used, or all too often failed to use, them.[75]

After Leslie's incursion in the fall of 1780, Steuben, whom the new southern commander Nathanael Greene had dispatched to aid in the defense of Virginia, urged the governor to erect a fortification at Hoods, a site that controlled the approaches to Richmond and would thus aid in its defense against enemy raids. All he required to execute the work was the labor of forty slaves and ten artisans. Jefferson, however, was unmoved. Even after Benedict Arnold sacked that city with his measly force of nine hundred in early January, little if anything was done. With his honor and reputation on the line, Steuben implored Jefferson to act boldly to protect against future invasions, "as I can do nothing without the Assistance of the Government." Jefferson's reply was hardly encouraging. True, he and his council had approved the project, but they could not possibly have agreed to furnish him with the necessary workmen. "The Executives have not by the laws of this State," he explained, "any power to call a freeman to labour even for the Public without his consent, nor a Slave without that of his Master." Steuben was obviously mistaken in his recollection.[76]

No further work on the fort was done. When Phillips and Cornwallis returned in the following months, they were not encumbered by it in their marches to Richmond.

Jefferson had not, of course, been utterly passive in his tenure as wartime governor. Just one week before Arnold's arrival in Virginia, he had mobilized the militia of nine different counties. Unfortunately, the object of this call was not to repel future British incursions but to subdue the Amerindians on the frontier "by carrying the war into their country." Thus while Gates's army languished to the south, Virginia's best-equipped, crack troops were busy effecting the "total suppression of Savage Insolence and Cruelties," far from the ever-advancing British lines. Amazingly, Jefferson continued to augment these forces even after Arnold's daring raid. "History affords no instance of a nation being so engaged in conquest abroad," wrote a thoroughly disgusted Nathanael Greene, "as Virginia is at a time when all her powers were necessary to secure herself from ruin at home." The governor's priorities had obviously been misplaced and his judgment lacking.[77]

Jefferson was not entirely to blame for Virginia's failures. Equally complicit was his council, which if anything was even more dilatory than he. Nor could the legislature be absolved of all responsibility. It had, after all, been in session during the invasion of Leslie and Arnold and, as Jefferson pointed out, fully approved of his actions at the time. Perhaps most guilty of all were the citizens of the Old Dominion who had continually refused to pay their taxes, assume their military duties, or part with those supplies the war effort demanded. By all measure, there was more than enough blame to go around. Nonetheless, Jefferson was the easiest and, given some of his curious decisions, most obvious scapegoat. And scapegoat he might well have been, had a Franco-American expedition not arrived in the Chesapeake in the autumn of 1781 and secured a decisive victory at Yorktown. After that joyous event, there seemed little purpose in pursuing the well-meaning ex-governor. On December 12 the legislature officially cleared Jefferson of all charges and voted its thanks to him, affirming "the high opinion which they entertain of Mr. Jefferson's Ability, Rectitude, and Integrity as chief Magistrate of this Commonwealth."[78]

This vindication brought little relief to the wounded *philosophe*. Leaving office under a cloud, Jefferson vowed to quit the public stage and never return. But fate had one more trick to play on the patriarch of Monticello. Three months into his retirement his beloved wife, Martha, died from complications following a difficult childbirth the previous spring. Devastated, Jefferson fell into a deep depression. His whole world had fallen apart, and his relatives were fearful for both his sense and his sanity. Slowly, Jefferson became himself again and in the closing months of 1781 threw himself into a new project, one that would consume his energies and absorb his attention.

Jefferson had actually begun this project the previous year. In the autumn of 1780 he had received a questionnaire from François Marbois, the secretary to the French minister to Congress. Marbois's inquiries concerned the political, demographic, and economic arrangements of the Old Dominion, precisely those issues necessary to facilitate commercial and consular relations with the state. Arnold's incursion had forced him to put his effort to answer aside, but in the aftermath of his tragedies he took up his pen again. What emerged from Jefferson's literary efforts was the first expression of his altered worldview, one in which the Romantic spirit was at last unfettered from the shackles of enlightened moderation and compromise. *Notes on the State of Virginia* affords the first glimpse of the soaring lineaments of the Jeffersonian vision.[79]

THE JEFFERSONIAN VISION: ROMANTIC AMERICA

A prolific writer, Thomas Jefferson published just one book in his lifetime. *Notes on the State of Virginia* was the Sage of Monticello's great literary testament, the statement of his political and philosophical creed. Far more than a review of his state's natural, commercial, and political conditions, *Notes* was primarily concerned with the character and ethical worth of Virginia evaluated in the aftermath of its revolutionary struggle for independence. Nor was it concerned solely with Virginia per se. Virginia, in Jefferson's mind, was an exemplar, if not a symbol, for America writ large. *Notes on the State of Virginia* was Jefferson's considered judgment on the moral and political state of America.

That Jefferson's appraisal was overwhelmingly positive is hardly surprising, but it was necessary. Despite their initial enthusiasm for the American cause, many European philosophes had raised troubling criticisms about the course of subsequent American political and social development. The British press issued a torrent of damning reports and commentaries, and even radical friends of the American cause developed doubts. Richard Price had been one of the most ardent champions of an independent and republican United States, but the failures of America, particularly with regard to the problem of slavery, led him to "fear that I have made myself ridiculous by Speaking of the American Revolution in the manner I have done." The great achievement of Jefferson's *Notes* was to refute those aspersions and vindicate the character of America. He did so by inaugurating a new style of political discourse in early America, one that broke decisively with the older politics of Enlightenment. Where eighteenth-century philosophes had drawn on enlightened social science to craft practical programs of legislation, Jefferson reasoned from Romantic principles, whose self-evidence issued from the authentic urges of the moral sense. These idealistic principles were the core of Jefferson's vision of America. It was a vision that captured the hearts and minds of his countrymen. It continues to do so to this day.[80]

The Lessons of *Notes on the State of Virginia*

Jefferson faced a daunting challenge in *Notes on the State of Virginia*. The Old Dominion suffered from several obvious failings. Its agriculture was primitive and depleted the soil with disturbing rapidity. Its population was painfully ill educated. Its laws were draconian, and its government dominated by a tiny, elite squirearchy. Two flaws, however, towered above all the others. Virginia's economy and society were alarmingly underdeveloped by eighteenth-century standards. Staple production had produced a rustic society lacking urban refinement and commerce. Even more troubling was the persistence of chattel slavery. Partisans of America might have excused this failing in the years before 1776, as Jefferson himself did, by arguing that British interference hamstrung Virginia's attempts to redress it. In the years after independence, however, that argument sounded decidedly hollow. To the contrary, it appeared all too evident that, as Richard Price noted, "the people who have been struggling so earnestly to save *themselves* from Slavery are very ready to enslave *others*."[81]

Jefferson vindicated the state of Virginia by offering a far more favorable scale of judgment for assessing the character of his country. His agrarian idyll turned Virginia's rusticity into its greatest moral and political asset, and his doctrine of racial difference, while never justifying slavery, demonstrated that its persistence was due to logistical difficulties rather than moral failure. Jefferson's principles did far more than defend the character of Virginia, however. In place of the old programmatic politics of Enlightenment, Jefferson proffered a new Romantic politics of principle, one focused on internal sensibility rather than empirical realities.

The Agrarian Idyll: The Problem of Rusticity

From an enlightened point of view, one of Virginia's most glaring flaws was its rusticity. The Enlightenment was a remarkably urban affair; urban sociability refined manners and promoted polite cultivation. More than that, it inculcated an ethos of benevolence. "It is impossible," Hume insisted, for cultured townfolk to help but "feel an encrease of humanity, from the very habit of conversing together, and contributing to each other's pleasure and entertainment." The urban setting also produced orderly government and personal liberty, Adam Smith argued, and had established them in the late medieval period, "when the occupiers of land in the country were exposed to every sort of violence." Cities were thus civilizing spaces. The countryside, by contrast, was an uncultured and ignorant backwater filled with bumpkins, boors, and booby squires.[82]

Cities and towns were also the sites of commercial activity, the valorization of which was an essential component of the politics of Enlightenment. It was trade, the free exchange of surplus goods, that "knit mankind together in a mutual intercourse of good offices," Addison argued, and for that reason insisted that "there are not more useful members in a commonwealth than merchants." Voltaire agreed wholeheartedly; more than a source of personal and national wealth, commerce "contributes to the well-being of the world" by fulfilling mutual wants and needs across vast distances. Commerce also promoted manufactures, which afforded employment for the needy and the pleasures of consumption for the fortunate. Adam Smith demonstrated that trade and manufactures contribute vitally to the wealth of nations, the former by promoting a greater division of labor and the latter by using machinery and technology to reach levels of productivity far beyond what was possible in the countryside. Hume was hardly unique in concluding that "the greatness of the sovereign and the happiness of the state are, in a great measure, united with regard to trade and manufactures." Virginia, alas, lacked both.[83]

Jefferson's handling of the problem of rusticity was bold and brilliant. In his chapter on "Counties and Towns" he acknowledged that Virginia had tried to promote urban development, with results that "remain unworthy of enumeration." Yet the absence of towns was due less to a failure of policy than to the supervening hand of nature. Filled with numerous and intersecting waterways, Virginians had no need to create commercial entrepôts when trade was so easily brought "to our doors." Thus where "the laws have said that there shall be towns," Jefferson observed, "*Nature* has said there shall not." The rustic life of Virginia was thus natural. By contrast, Jefferson claimed "that rise and fall of towns" was one of those rare cases where "accidental circumstances" were able to "controul the indications of nature." Towns and cities thus violated the ordinances of nature, and Virginia was fortunate to be free of them.[84]

Jefferson's discussion of towns was only the opening motif of his agrarian idyll that emerged in full in his subsequent chapter on "Manufactures." Far from being a failing, the rural rusticity of the Old Dominion was its greatest glory. Agriculture was natural, and for Jefferson, nature was an organic entity that disclosed its own beneficent ends. Living in harmony with nature and its ends, rustic farmers were able to retain their natural virtue, goodness, and innocence. "Those who labour in the earth are the chosen people of God," Jefferson declaimed, "whose breasts he has made his peculiar deposit for substantial and genuine virtue." The exemplars of this agrarian idyll were, of course, the yeomen, those independent and self-reliant husbandmen who look "to their soil and industry" for their sustenance. By contrast, urban tradesmen were dependent on "the casualties and caprice of customers," a dependence that "begets subservience and venality, suffocates the germ of virtue, and prepares fit tools for the designs of ambition." What the so-called Enlightened took for urbane refinement and cultivation was really a cancer on the body politic. "The mobs of great cities add just so much to the support of pure government," he wrote with obvious sarcasm, "as sores do to the strength of the human body." Virginia was well rid of them.[85]

Jefferson's agrarian idyll had a variety of virtues. Focusing his idyll on the figure of the sturdy and independent yeoman allowed Jefferson to obscure the vast disparities in rural Virginia between a small elite of immensely wealthy squires on the one hand and the far larger numbers of poor landless whites and enslaved blacks on the other. It also concealed the real differences in other states between frontier subsistence farmers and their coastal, commercially oriented counterparts. Most important of all, Jefferson's agrarian idyll had an immense appeal to the vast majority of Americans who were, at this time, agriculturalists. Theirs was not merely one special interest among many; rather, theirs was the true and authentic public interest. Indeed, they were endowed with a superior virtue by the very nature of their vocation.

Jefferson's agrarian idyll also had the virtue of sounding very familiar. "The glorification of the yeoman" had been, as historian Edmund Morgan notes, a staple of republican "country" politics for well over a century before the American Revolution, as well as a "central ideological tenet of deferential politics," by means of which certain landed elites politically mobilized "the many against the rest of the few." This country or "real whig" discourse—derived from the Florentine Renaissance and further articulated by seventeenth-century republicans like James Harrington and Algernon Sidney—had been a standard rhetorical justification for colonial resistance in the years leading to independence, and Jefferson's seeming invocation of it made him seem a true believer in the old, glorious cause.[86]

In reality, however, Jefferson's agrarianism differed dramatically from the older country ideal. Ever since the writings of Machiavelli, classical republicanism had been organized around the problem of war. The yeoman was valorized as the sturdy hoplite citizen-soldier. Commerce corrupted him by softening his martial spirit with luxuries, thus rendering him "effeminate." The republican antitype of this luxury was the simplicity and austerity of the Spartan phalanx or the early Roman legion. By contrast, Jefferson's Romantic agrarian idyll was pacific. Where classical republicans had seen wars as the natural expression of a people's martial virtue and *amor patriae*, Jefferson saw them as idiotic and tragic "efforts of mutual destruction." America's policy should be "to cultivate the peace and friendship of every nation." For Jefferson, the virtue of the yeomanry lay not in their martial Spartan simplicity but instead in their approximation of natural "primitivism."[87]

The context for Jefferson's celebration of rural life was not the warlike polities of the ancient world but the noble savages of North America. In his chapter on "Aborigines," Jefferson extolled the pure liberty and innocence of Amerindian societies. Untainted by the corrupting influence of civilization, "their only controuls are their manners and that moral sense of right and wrong" that "every man makes a part of his nature." Although Americans could not, of course, be expected to revert to this purer and more natural state of social organization, Jefferson embraced agrarian rusticity as the closest possible approximation to it in a civilized context. Rural America was not virtuous despite its primitive underdevelopment but because of it. Commerce, manufactures, and the trappings of modern refinement and "civilization" brought war and oppression. Rusticity promoted peace and preserved natural virtue in the human breast. Jefferson's agrarian idyll made rustic Virginia appear a veritable promised land.[88]

"The real distinction which nature has made": Race and the Problem of Slavery

Far more damning than the rustic nature of Virginia society was its practice of slavery. How could Virginia claim to be at the forefront of a new American empire of liberty when it held vast throngs in thralldom without the most elemental rights? Jefferson's handling of this problem in *Notes on the State of Virginia* was subtle and far-reaching. He did not deny the iniquity of slavery; to the contrary, his chapter on "Manners" contained a stunning and passionate indictment of the institution that John Adams thought "worth diamonds." Unfortunately, as desirable as abolition clearly was, its achievement was complicated by "the real distinction which nature has made" between blacks and whites. By no means did Jefferson believe that racial differences justified slavery; nonetheless, he was forced to admit that they were "a powerful obstacle to the emancipation" of the enslaved.[89]

Jefferson's discussion of race immediately followed his proposed scheme of emancipation in the chapter on "Laws." Some six pages long, it is frankly painful, sometimes shocking, reading for contemporary sensibilities. It was only marginally less so in his own day. More than three decades ago Winthrop Jordan pronounced it "the strongest suggestion of inferiority" expressed by any American "until well into the nineteenth century," a judgment that has since stood the test of time. Jefferson's catalog of racial difference served two purposes. Although it did not justify slavery, it did tend to minimize the wrongs it inflicted on the enslaved. Indeed, a careful reading of Jefferson's indictment of slavery in "Manners" suggests that the greatest evils of slavery were visited on whites rather than blacks. More important, Jefferson's discussion of race sought to demonstrate that emancipation could not occur without the forced expatriation of the freemen. Jefferson thus implied that it was the logistical and financial complexities of colonizing the enslaved, rather than any attachment to slavery itself, that explained why so little had been done to eradicate the baleful institution. Both of these purposes served the higher end of vindicating Virginia—and by implication, America—from the moral stain of slavery.[90]

Perhaps the most obvious differences between blacks and whites were physical. Simply put, blacks were ugly. Their faces were marred by an "eternal monotony" caused by their pigmentation, "that veil of black which covers all the emotions." Nor were blacks disadvantaged solely by their visages. They also lacked the "elegant symmetry of form" that Jefferson found among whites. Moreover, they emitted "a very strong and disagreeable odor," which was the result of the fact that "they secrete less by the kidneys and more by the glands of the skin" rather than a regimen of hard labor with few opportunities to bathe. Overall then, blacks were simply far less physically attractive than whites. That his judgment was natural rather than subjective was proven, Jefferson claimed, by blacks' "own judgment in favor of the whites" as sexual partners, a preference analogous to that of the male "Oran-ootan [*sic*] for the black woman over those of his own species." Implicit in this analogy was the suggestion that blacks occupied a racially intermediate position between higher simians and white humans, a position predicated in part at least on purported physical resemblances.[91]

The failings of blacks were not, unfortunately, skin deep. Jefferson found the minds of blacks "much inferior" to those of whites. They were utterly devoid of any but the most rudimentary powers of ratiocination, so much so that "one could scarcely be found capable of tracing and comprehending the investigations of Euclid." Even their acts of bravery were the result, not of native courage, but of "a want of forethought, which prevents their seeing a danger till it be present." Nor were they any more favorably endowed in the aesthetic realm. Jefferson found their powers of imagination thoroughly "dull, tasteless, and anomalous." Phillis Wheatley's much-celebrated poetry was simply "below the dignity of criticism." The letters of Ignatius Sancho—a contemporary and famous black man of letters in London and a correspondent of Jefferson's favorite author, Laurence Sterne—betrayed an imagination that was "wild and extravagant" and "escapes incessantly from every restraint of reason and taste." Although exceptional for a black, compared to whites among "the epistolary class," Sancho would have to be ranked "at the bottom of the column." Even that assessment presumed that he had in fact authored the letters in question without "amendment" from an abler white hand, a presumption Jefferson pointedly noted "would not be of easy investigation."[92]

The one realm of aesthetic expression in which blacks evinced some small capacity was music, where Jefferson acknowledged "they are more generally gifted than the whites with accurate ears for tune and time." This gift, however, was physical rather than aesthetic, as the mimicry of parrots demonstrates. The true measure of musical ability was composition, and while some few blacks "have been found capable of imagining a small catch," Jefferson doubted that "they will be equal to the composition of a more extensive run of melody, or of complex harmony."[93]

That the degradation of the black mind might be due to the incapacitating effects of slavery itself, Jefferson utterly denied. Many blacks had been "so situated that they might have availed themselves of the conversation of their masters," and some had even been "liberally educated." Despite these advantages, Jefferson insisted that blacks showed no evidence of intellectual aptitude, much less genius; "never could I find that a black had uttered a thought above the level of plain narration." By contrast, Amerindians who lacked the exposure to white civilization were able to "astonish you with strokes of the most sublime oratory," strokes that demonstrated the strength of their "reason and sentiment." Moreover, the physical and intellectual superiority of mulattos over "pure" blacks—an improvement Jefferson claimed "has been observed by every one"—proved that black mental "inferiority is not the effect merely of the condition of life." Certainly the Romans of the "Augustan age" practiced a far harsher slave regime than that of Virginia, yet "their slaves were often the rarest artists" as well as "exceptional men of science." For Jefferson, the conclusion was inescapable. The mental and cultural inferiority of blacks was not due to slavery at all. Rather, it was "nature which has produced this distinction," a distinction which no merely human policy could alter.[94]

The overall impact of Jefferson's discussion of race was to depict blacks as bestial. Admittedly human, their form did not have the beauties of the species, just as their minds lacked the higher faculties of reason that were its dignity. Jefferson's treatment of black sexuality further suggested the primacy of animal urges over human attachments. Although "more ardent" than whites, blacks' sexual drive was "an eager desire" rather than a "tender mixture of sentiment and sensation." Similarly, despite a power of memory fully "equal to the whites," the "griefs" of blacks "are transient," their "numberless afflictions" both "less felt, and sooner forgotten," than they would be among the more sensitive and sentient whites. Blacks, Jefferson insisted, were creatures of "sensation" rather than "reflection," a fact evidenced by the "disposition to sleep when abstracted from their diversions, and unemployed in labor." Jefferson could not help but note that this disposition was shared by other beasts of burden: "an animal whose body is at rest, and who does not reflect, must be disposed to sleep of course." Apparently blacks were just such animals.[95]

Jefferson's assessment of black racial capacities was not entirely negative. Despite their other failings, blacks had a fully functioning moral sense. Nature may have been "less bountiful to them in the endowments of the head," but "in those of the heart," Jefferson claimed, "she will be found to have done them justice." Several scholars, following Gary Wills, have seized on this passage to demonstrate the utter irrelevance of the rest of Jefferson's racial diatribe. Unfortunately, what Jefferson gave he also took away. His intended audience of philosophes would surely have recognized that Jefferson's own account made his posit of a black moral sense problematic at best.[96]

Part of the problem lay in Jefferson's insistence that blacks lacked a sense of beauty. Yet for moral-sense theorists, from Shaftesbury and Hutcheson to Hume and Kames, the posit of a moral sense is part and parcel of a general aestheticization of ethical experience. Without an aesthetic sense, it is not clear how blacks could possibly have the sensibility to recognize what Hutcheson called the "moral beauty in actions." Even more troubling was their lack of reason. Although the "several rights of mankind are first made known, by the natural feeling of their hearts," Hutcheson insisted that these rights were "to be regulated by right reason." It was because of this that children were not afforded rights until the age of majority, when "they come to the mature use of reason." Unfortunately, Jefferson denied that blacks could ever achieve that state. Indeed, black mental inferiority might be one of those "rare cases" where Hutcheson acknowledged that enslavement might be "necessary" in "the interest of a society." The black moral sense was not, apparently, a particularly equalizing endowment.[97]

Jefferson did not, of course, use race or any other factor to justify slavery in *Notes on the State of Virginia* or elsewhere. He did, however, minimize the suffering it imposed on blacks. Slaves in the Old Dominion were subject to thoroughly "mild treatment," as evidenced by the fact that their population "increases as fast, or faster, than the whites." Moreover, such misery as did occur was mitigated by the "transient" nature of blacks' grief. Indeed, when Jefferson did iterate the evils of slavery in "Manners," the thrust of the passage was the institution's baleful effects on white society.[98]

Comprised of a single rather long paragraph, this chapter contained three distinct arguments against slavery separated by the conjunctive "and." The first refers to the "unhappy influence on the manners of our people produced by the existence of slavery among us." Slavery gave rise to the "most boisterous passions," with whites exercising "the most unremitting despotism" and blacks responding with "degrading submissions." Yet it was not this degradation that concerned Jefferson—he never mentioned it again—so much as the negative impact of mastery on whites. Absolute power and the necessity of imposing discipline coarsened the moral sensibilities of slave-owners. Particularly troubling was its effect on white children who, being imitative by nature, were morally disfigured by witnessing the "despotism" of their fathers over their slaves.[99]

Jefferson's second argument dealt with the political impact of slavery. Slavery transformed whites into "despots" and blacks "into enemies," thus destroying "the morals of the one part, and the amor patriae of the other." Again, the most baneful effect of slavery here was on whites, who have their morals degraded and are faced with black enmity. That Jefferson was primarily concerned with the impact of slavery on whites was further suggested by the sentences that conclude this argument. Slavery further impaired white morality by destroying their industry. "In a warm climate no man will labor for himself who can make another labour for him," Jefferson claimed, and thus "of the proprietors of slaves a very small proportion are ever seen to labor."[100]

Jefferson's third argument dealt with the religious impact of slavery. Slavery endangered the "liberties of a nation" by undermining the public's belief in the divine origins of such liberties as well as the conviction that these gifts of God "are not to be violated but with his wrath." This was by far the weakest of Jefferson's critiques. Although his charge that slavery endangered the people's faith is credible—he had claimed that God endowed men with rights in the Declaration of Independence—it is not particularly damning. Far less credible is his subsequent invocation of divine retribution. His claim to "tremble for my country" at the thought that "God is just" and that "his justice cannot sleep forever" is overwrought, and his fear that divine punishment might take the form of a slave insurrection guided by "supernatural interference!" simply cannot be taken seriously. A freethinker and outspoken materialist, discussions of divine providence are conspicuously absent from the rest of Jefferson's writings. Its dramatic inclusion here was simply Jefferson demonstrating his antislavery bona fides to the republic of letters. That, after all, had been the point of the exercise.[101]

The real point of Jefferson's discussion of race was that racial differences required that any plan of abolition include the forced expatriation of the freedmen. Emancipation opened the prospect of miscegenation, which was clearly an affront to the "dignity and beauty" of human nature. Even more troubling was the likelihood of a postemancipatory racial war of extermination, one that Jefferson and his readers surely knew blacks would lose. The "deep rooted prejudices" of whites, and blacks' resentment "of the injuries they have sustained," would, when combined with "the real distinctions nature has made," undoubtedly "divide us into parties, and produce convulsions that will probably never end but in the extermination of the one or the other race." A political and moral necessity, colonization was the sine qua non of abolition.[102]

The moral necessity of colonization was vital to Jefferson's defense of Virginia. It demonstrated that the failure of emancipation in the Old Dominion was due to the difficulties of colonization rather than a lack of sincerity in its condemnation of slavery. And these difficulties were considerable. Slave children would have to be separated from their parents and raised "at the public expense, to tillage, arts or sciences." At the age of majority they would be sent abroad "with arms, implements of household and of the handicraft arts, seeds, pairs of the usual domestic animals" and all the other supplies and aids necessary to establish them as "a free and independent people." To these staggering logistical and financial burdens was added the necessary expense of procuring "an equal number of white inhabitants" from Europe who could only be induced to "migrate hither" by additional and costly "proper encouragements." Given these almost overwhelming obstacles to colonization, Virginia's failure to abolish slavery could be seen as the result of an understandable reticence to take on an immense logistical responsibility by a war-weary state rather than of a lack of moral principle.[103]

Colonization and racism established the authenticity of Jefferson's—and by extension, Virginia's—loathing of slavery, as well as his/its commitment to the core principles of freedom and human dignity that lay behind the American Revolution despite the persistence of bondage. In essence, Jefferson's discourse of racial difference and the consequent need for colonization meant never having to say he was sorry about slavery.

The Politics of Principle

Jefferson did far more than vindicate that state of Virginia in his *Notes*. His agrarian idyll and his invocation of racial difference heralded a new mode of political discourse in early America, one that broke with the Enlightenment in decisive ways. The politics of Enlightenment had been, in practice, programmatic. In its stead, Jefferson proffered a Romantic politics of principle.

Jefferson's politics of principle had several advantages over its enlightened predecessor. Precisely because they were ideals, Romantic principles were relatively insulated from empirical realities that might contradict them. This insulation also had the effect of complicating the relationship between rhetoric and action. Jefferson's principles often sounded radical, but their application to practical politics was underdetermined by given realities. This afforded a decidedly flexible and pragmatic thrust to political action and choice. Because principles revealed the fundamental political character of agents, they could be used to form political alliances and communities based on shared ideals.

Moreover, these principles also had the advantage of being integrative; they could be synthesized into a larger ideological vision.

What made the politics of Enlightenment programmatic was its central concern with matching specific means to agreed-upon ends. Thus when Alexander Hamilton sought to promote commercial and industrial development, he proposed a program of specific measures to secure the public credit, expand the money supply, and induce individuals to invest in mercantile and manufacturing ventures. Similarly, John Adams tried to secure the blessings of a free republican government through specific constitutional measures that balanced social forces, separated powers within the government, and precluded the ultimate victory of one faction over another. By way of contrast, Jeffersonian principles were not so much instrumental plans of action as normative ideals that demanded moral, if not existential, commitment.

Principles revealed the true character of a political actor, whose test of virtue lay in zealotry on behalf of sincerely held ideals rather than tangible results from particular initiatives. Hence the importance of racial difference for Jefferson. Racial difference, and the consequent need for colonization, vouchsafed the purity of Jefferson's—and Virginia's—antislavery convictions despite their failure to eradicate the institution. That colonization itself was, as the Duc de La Rochefoucauld-Liancourt observed in the 1790s, "attended with so many unpleasant consequences that it cannot possibly be carried into effect," was hardly a legitimate basis to question the authenticity of Jefferson and his fellow squires' antipathy to slavery. Indeed, it was this devotion to principled and sincere convictions that led Jefferson to react to "the Missouri question" that arose in his retirement as if awakened by "a fire bell in the night." When the inhabitants of the Missouri territory applied for statehood in 1818, James Tallmadge, congressman from New York, moved to amend the petition so that the further introduction of slavery into Missouri would be prohibited "and that all children born in that State after its admission to the Union shall be free at the age of twenty-five years." By sectionalizing the issue—investing it in "a geographic line"—Talmadge and his northern cohorts were denying that southerners like Jefferson truly shared the principle that slavery was a cancer on the American body politic that should not be allowed to spread, thus questioning the sincerity of their stated convictions.[104]

In Jefferson's Romantic politics of principle, American identity was bound by shared convictions. When one section questioned the authenticity of the other on core principles, Jefferson could only conclude that the "knell of the Union" was at hand. His only consolation was "that I live not to weep over it." In Jefferson's new Romantic politics, principles were not means to ends—they were ends in themselves.[105]

Precisely because of its programmatic character, the politics of Enlightenment had been firmly rooted in empirical reality. Hamilton's various reports drew on an immense range of enlightened social-scientific works on political economy, public revenue, and international commerce. For his part, Adams absorbed (and recapitulated) an even larger corpus of political theory, history, and philosophy. Jeffersonian principles, by comparison, seemed to float above the realm of the factual. As normative ideals, they were the evaluative prism through which experience was organized and were therefore insulated from empirical refutation. This allowed Jefferson, as Joseph Ellis has remarked, to view "the disjunction between his ideas and worldly imperfection as the world's problem rather than his own."[106]

This disjuncture between rhetoric and reality gave the Jeffersonian politics of principle a decidedly radical tone. Insulated from evidentiary refutation, ideals could be articulated in a thoroughgoing and uncompromising fashion. At the same time, they afforded those practicing the politics of principle a remarkable flexibility in operation. Since principles indicated ideal commitments rather than prescribing specific programs, there was no direct relation between a given ideal and a particular policy. Principle led Jefferson, in his chapter on "Public Revenue and Finance," to call on his countrymen to eschew commerce entirely and focus exclusively on agricultural development. Not only were farmers "the most virtuous and independent citizens," but avoiding maritime trade would eliminate an inevitable source of future wars, a course that

Jefferson hoped "will be our wisdom." In the very same passage, however, Jefferson acknowledged that his principled hopes bore very little relationship to reality. "The actual habits of our countrymen attach them to commerce," he noted, and consequently "they will exercise it for themselves." America, then, would undoubtedly be party to commercial wars, "and all the wise can do, will be to avoid that half of them which would be produced by our own follies, and our own acts of injustice" and ensure the nation had sufficient forces to fight the other half.[107]

Perhaps the most dramatic asset of the politics of principle was its ability to generate powerful political solidarities. Shared principles made for communities of the like-minded who were bound by common ideals rather than narrowly defined agendas. Jefferson's agrarian republican party united "the whole landed interest," he told Philip Mazzei, against the Federalist forces of corruption represented by "British merchants and Americans trading on British capitals." Moreover, unlike the particularistic character of enlightened political programs, Romantic ideals could interact. Both agrarianism and racial difference worked to obscure apparent differences between northern family farmers and southern planters. Agrarianism elided real differences in wealth and status between these groups, while racial difference assured northern Jeffersonians that their southern comrades shared their principled opposition to slavery despite their failure to eradicate it. Most important of all, principles could be combined to form a unified and comprehensive ideological worldview.[108]

In the years Jefferson spent abroad following his drafting of *Notes*, he articulated a number of distinctly radical principles. He would mold these principles, together with his agrarian idyll and his doctrine of racial difference, into an ideological whole that idealized America and its revolutionary heritage as the central moment in a world-historical movement toward self-government and freedom. Jefferson's ideals spoke to the most elemental human needs for dignity and liberation. Addressing those needs, if only on an ideal level, was one of the most alluring achievements of Jefferson's Romantic vision of America.

The Principles of Jeffersonian Democracy

Jefferson's retirement after the completion of *Notes on the State of Virginia* was remarkably short-lived. The years 1783–84 saw him in the Confederation Congress. The following five years were spent as Franklin's replacement at Versailles. In neither of these offices was he particularly effective, despite his best efforts.

In Congress he drafted a comprehensive plan for the organization and government of the Northwest Territories that ultimately proved unworkable and had to be replaced by a more practical scheme. His prodigious diplomatic labors to achieve a more comprehensive and thoroughgoing commercial compact with France fell victim to the latter's overall indifference to the project. Notwithstanding, these were remarkably productive years for Jefferson, especially those spent abroad. It was in the midst of Parisian high society that he first formulated the principles of Jeffersonian democracy. When Thomas Jefferson returned to America to serve as George Washington's secretary of state, he was a man intellectually transformed.

The Romantic revolution that had transpired in his thought would soon similarly transform the nature of politics in the early republic. Indeed, American politics still bears the imprint of this transformation. After Jefferson, no political movement or leader could hope to succeed without the kind of broad-reaching and inspiring vision that the Sage of Monticello offered. More than any other founding father—perhaps more than any other statesman in American history—Jefferson had "the vision thing."

"The True Foundation of Republican Government": *Participatory Democracy and Liberty*

Perhaps the most novel departure in Jefferson's Romantic vision was his new understanding of the role of popular power in republican government. Prior to his turning, Jefferson's republicanism had been colored by a strong tincture of elitism. He had opposed the popular election of senators in Virginia because he had "ever observed that a choice by the people themselves is not generally distinguished for its wisdom." Beginning in the 1780s, however, he eschewed such enlightened moderation and wholeheartedly embraced the ideal of popular sovereignty. Where Jefferson had once sought to ensure that legislators were "perfectly independent when chosen," he now sought to collapse entirely the distinction between the government and the governed. "The whole body of the nations is the sovereign legislative, judiciary, and executive power for itself," he informed Edmund Randolph. "It is the will of the nation which makes the law obligatory." It was precisely because the true source of all political authority was the will of the people that Jefferson believed the execution of Louis XVI in no way abrogated the treaties he had signed with the United States. Treaties and alliances were compacts between sovereign peoples; their governments were merely their agents.[109]

At first glance, Jefferson's belief in popular sovereignty looks a lot like Rousseau's majoritarian doctrine of the "general will." In fact, however, it was far more radical. Even Rousseau had acknowledged that the majority could transcend the limits of natural right. Madison in particular sought to point out the failings of majority rule to his friend and mentor. The people were not a solitary entity. Rather, they were a collection of interests and factions, and in "a simple Democracy" it was doubtful whether "a majority having any common interest, or feeling any common passion, will find sufficient motives to restrain them from oppressing the minority." By contrast, Jefferson was remarkably sanguine. The majority "may sometimes err," yet those "errors are honest, solitary, and short-lived." It was therefore best to "bow down to the general reason of the society," for "even in its deviations" from the course of justice it always "soon returns again to the right way."[110]

What made Jefferson's vision so radical was that he combined majority rule with a profound sense of civic humanism. This resulted in a political posture that "specifically calls for mass participatory democracy." For Jefferson, systems of popular representation merely approximated the republican ideal. Its true essence was "a government by its citizens in mass, acting directly and personally." Only by his direct involvement in the business of government could the citizen feel "that he is a direct participator in the government of affairs, not merely at an election one day in the year, but every day." Once so engaged, he would be a bulwark of his country's freedom with an interest in the health of his republican government and eager to exercise his political virtues and talents.[111]

The problem was, of course, the impossibility of direct political involvement by the people in any but the most local venues. Jefferson acknowledged that his ideal would never "be practicable beyond the extent of a New England township." His solution was to devolve power among localities rather than concentrate it in centralized governments. "The way to have good and safe government," he insisted, "is not to trust it all to one, but divide it among the many." Once energized by direct involvement in their local governments, the people would be infinitely more vigilant against usurpation by state and national authorities.[112]

In his retirement, Jefferson sought to achieve this political devolution in Virginia through his so-called ward scheme. Adopting his old educational division of counties into wards, Jefferson now proposed turning them into political units. Each ward would be small enough so that "every citizen can attend, when called on, and act in person." Each district would then elect local officers who would "manage all its concerns." Modeled on the New England towns—"the wisest invention ever devised by the wit of man for the perfect exercise of self-government"—the wards would also be electoral districts, creating a strong sense of local community among the citizenry. Moreover, the wards would "relieve the county administration of nearly all its business," a decided boon since county officials were invariably "self-appointed" and "self-continuing" squires who held "their authorities for life." By stimulating the political interest and civic awareness of the common folk, local ward government would produce a more informed and active citizenry. "These little republics" would thus not only thwart the oligarchic usurpations of county and state officials, they would also "be the main strength of the great one."[113]

What made Jeffersonian direct democracy far less radical than it appeared was his strong streak of what we today call libertarianism. The essence of republican government may have been mass participation, but its "true foundation" was "the equal right of every citizen, in his person and property, and in their management." These were, of course, negative rights in the sense that they set limits to the state's intervention in the affairs of individuals rather than positive rights that enjoined government action on behalf of community goals. Jefferson had, after all, embraced the primitive ideal of Amerindian societies because they lacked any government at all and therefore "enjoyed in their general mass an infinitely greater degree of happiness" than their overgoverned European counterparts. Government was an inherently coercive, necessary evil that had to be strictly contained. Although organized on the basis of broad and active participation by an energized citizenry, Jefferson's idealized democracy governed best by governing least.[114]

It was this combination of libertarianism and localism that explains Jefferson's initial hostility to the federal Constitution. Jefferson had been critically aware of the failings of the Confederation government, both from his tenure as a member of the Congress and through his subsequent correspondence from Europe. And he was sympathetic to efforts to cement the rapidly dissolving bonds of union. When poor attendance undermined the Annapolis convention of 1786, Jefferson told Madison that he hoped it might be followed by another meeting that would "make us one nation as to foreign concerns, and keep us distinct in Domestic ones." Jefferson's goal was to strengthen the existing confederation rather than create a new federal frame of government. He told John Adams that all that was truly useful in the new federal scheme could have been distilled into a handful of amendments "to the good, old, and venerable fabrick, which should have been preserved even as a religious relique." Jefferson saw no need for the full-scale remodeling that occurred in Philadelphia, the results of which "stagger all my disposition to subscribe to what such an assembly has proposed."[115]

Separated by an ocean, Madison tried to explain himself to his friend. Any revision of the union had to go beyond a mere confederation of states. The problem was not only the weakness of the central government; it was also the popular degeneration of the state governments themselves. The new federal government would thus have to be a compact of the people "as will render it clearly paramount" to the states. Moreover, it must not only regulate trade and foreign affairs; it also required "a negative *in all cases whatsoever* on the local legislature" in order to check the rising tide of popular licentiousness in the states. Madison's explanations had little effect. "Not more than 1 out of 100 state acts concern the confederacy," Jefferson argued, yet the federal veto "proposes to mend a small hole by covering the whole garment."[116]

Jefferson clearly failed to grasp the need for a truly federal scheme of union. Nor did he seem to even register Madison's claim that the popular degeneration of the states required a central government capable of checking their internal abuses. Neither object, Madison insisted, could be achieved by "a confederation of sovereign States," in no small measure because any "*voluntary* observance of the federal law by all the members could never be hoped for." Madison's arguments fell on deaf ears. Jefferson simply dropped the issue.[117]

As was so often the case during his diplomatic tenure in Paris in the latter half of the 1780s, Jefferson's correspondence with Madison was curiously disconnected, as if the two were arguing past each other. Still immersed in the politics of Enlightenment, Madison failed to recognize that Jefferson had embraced the principled politics of Romanticism. Thus when Jefferson raised principled objections to the newly proposed Constitution, Madison urged its practical necessity. When Jefferson championed the adoption of a bill of rights, Madison insisted such a bill was both inconsequential and ineffective. "Experience proves the inefficacy of a bill of rights on those occasions when its controul is most needed," as their "repeated violation" by "overbearing majorities in every State" demonstrated. Madison's practical observations were beside the point, however. The inclusion of a bill of rights was a matter of principle, and what might seem an empty rhetorical gesture to the worldly Madison was, for Jefferson, a vital display of republican sentiment and disposition. Only when Jefferson returned to America would Madison come to understand the transformation in his mentor's rhetoric and the flexibility it afforded his political practice.[118]

Jefferson's localism, libertarianism, and participatory democracy were visionary ideals, not programs of action that bound statesmen to specific policies. Ironically, no one seems to have understood this more clearly than his arch-nemesis, Alexander Hamilton. "A true estimate of Mr. Jefferson's character," he observed while urging his fellow Federalists to swing their support from Burr to Jefferson during the contested election of 1800, "warrants the expectation of a temporizing rather than a violent system." Even the Sage of Monticello's opposition to energetic government and the concentration of power within the executive branch, Hamilton believed, would have little effect on his own behavior once ensconced in the Oval Office. Hamilton knew his man. Jefferson proved an energetic executive, and he acted decisively in purchasing Louisiana and suppressing the Burr conspiracy and northern defiance of his embargo, despite the fact that each of these actions violated his own principles of strict construction of constitutional powers.[119]

"A strict observance of the written laws is doubtless *one* of the high duties of a good citizen," he explained to John Colvin after his retirement, "but it is not *the highest*." The highest duty was to pursue what was sincerely perceived to be the "public advantage." Where that required "the transgression of the law" in its literal and narrow sense, Jefferson believed a true statesman, sincerely motivated by public sentiment, should pursue it nonetheless. This might, of course, open a republican executive to charges of legal usurpation, not to speak of inconsistency or hypocrisy, but "his station makes it his duty to incur that risk."[120]

"The Earth Belongs in Usufruct to the Living": Equality and Independence

One of the most alluring features of Jefferson's vision was his commitment to liberty, equality, and personal independence. In his years abroad, he extended his concern for these ideals to society as well as government.

301

The remarkable poverty and social inequality he saw in Europe shocked him and led him to reassess the nature of property rights. In 1785 he wrote to Madison that "the earth is given as a common stock for man to labor and live on." In itself this was not a particularly radical position. Locke had argued as much in his *Second Treatise of Government.* Yet Locke had insisted that the labor of individuals gave them a natural right to appropriate the earth and its products as their private property. Indeed, even the gross inequalities that emerged after the growth of commerce and the use of money, both of which allowed the wealthy to appropriate ever larger amounts of property, were consistent with natural right because the use of money was a tacitly agreed upon social convention. Jefferson, by contrast, denied that property was a natural right at all. For him, as for Rousseau, the right to property was political rather than natural. This is not to suggest that Jefferson was a proto-socialist; far from it, he freely acknowledged that "an equal division of property is impracticable." His point, rather, was that whenever the allocation of property resulted in both landless poverty and uncultivated estates, "it is clear that the laws of property have been so far extended as to violate natural right." In such a state of affairs, he insisted, "the fundamental right to labor the earth returns to the unemployed," and a just government must ensure their access to the land.[121]

Jefferson's principle of social equality and independence not only applied to individuals. It also entailed a reassessment of the relation between entire generations of men. "The question Whether one generation of men has a right to bind another," he wrote to Madison from Paris, "seems never to have been started [*sic*] either on this or our side of the water." Nonetheless, Jefferson considered it "among the fundamental principles of every government." Convinced that "no such obligation can be transmitted," he proposed a principle "which I suppose to be self-evident, *'that the earth belongs in usufruct to the living.'*" To deny this principle was to subject the earth to the dead hand of the past.[122]

Jefferson's principle of generational independence had far-reaching implications. On a purely personal level, it represented what one scholar has called a "piquant" protest against the oppressive debts he had inherited from his father-in-law, John Wayles. But it also applied to the problem of debt on a national scale. Suppose, for example, previous French monarchs had contracted debts so large that the payment of interest alone would absorb the entire gross domestic product of the nation. "Must the present generation" forfeit all to their previous monarchs' creditors for the accident of having been born in France? Such a position was palpably absurd. The failure of most thinkers to consider this conundrum and recognize the principle of generational independence that it violated was the result of the common experience of individuals assuming the debts they inherited along with lands and other properties. Yet this assumption of personal debts was entirely the result of "the will of the society," which had judged that the inheritance of land should be accompanied by that of personal debts as well. But in the case of entire generations, there was "no umpire but the law of nature," and the law of nature taught that "one generation is to another as one independent nation to another." Thus no debts could bind a society for more than nineteen years, the span Jefferson estimated for the passage of a generation.[123]

This principle also extended beyond the realm of debt. Patents, copyrights, and state-sanctioned privileges could not justly be extended beyond nineteen years. Indeed, even laws and constitutions could not last past a generation. Each generation is master of its persons and property which "make the sum of the objects of government." Thus, Jefferson concluded, each frame of government "and every law, naturally expires at the end of 19 years. If it be enforced longer," he informed Madison, "it is an act of force and not of right."[124]

Alarmed by the radical musings of his friend, Madison tried to convince Jefferson of the impracticality of his principles. Drawing on Bernard Mandeville's argument in *The Fable of the Bees*, Madison showed that agrarian simplicity and republican virtue would actually decimate the poor of Europe by eliminating sources of gainful employment. "From a more equal partition of property must result a greater simplicity of manners," which in turn would lead to "less consumption of manufactured superfluities" or luxuries. The independence of generations was even more problematic. The living might well have title to the earth, but surely not to "the *improvements* made by the dead" upon it. These improvements "form a charge against the living who take the benefit of them," a charge that "can no otherwise be satisfyed than by executing the will of the dead accompanying the improvements." Moreover, requiring "some positive and authentic" act to continue a frame of government beyond nineteen years would render it "too subject to the casualty and consequences of an actual interregnum." Whatever the theoretical merits of Jefferson's principle of generational independence, in practical terms it was likely to result in the periodic collapse of government with all the perils of a potentially anarchic return to the state of nature. Although sympathetic to his friend's idealistic feelings, he could not help but politely suggest that they were "not in *all* respects compatible with the course of human affairs."[125]

Once again Madison had misunderstood his fellow Virginian. Jefferson's principles were the expression of his moral sensibility, not a blueprint for legislation. For all his criticism of the inequality of property, the actual measures he proposed to redress it—the replacement of primogeniture and entail with partible inheritance and a graduated tax on property—were, while progressive, hardly radical. Despite his rhetoric, Jefferson did not envision a large-scale scheme of land reform for America or Europe. Nor was his principle of generational independence as absolute as Madison had feared. Jefferson never even considered defaulting on the Revolutionary War debt of the United States, much less his own inherited burden. Indeed, when it came to certain issues, Jefferson was more than willing to pass on the burdens of the past and present. There was no greater burden than the problem of slavery in Virginia. But it was "to the rising generation, and not to the one in power," that he looked for the fulfillment of the great desideratum of abolition. This was, in fact, the posture that Jefferson took for the remainder of his life, a posture that justified his refusal to publicly advocate that worthy goal. Madison had little to fear.[126]

"A Little Rebellion Now and Then is a Good Thing": *Revolutionary Activism*

There was one element of Jefferson's vision that was unreservedly and unabashedly radical: his unqualified commitment to revolutionary activism. In the 1770s he had been a reluctant revolutionary who was forced to sunder the ties binding the colonies to the British Empire only by the latter's infringements of the former's natural rights. In the years after his turning, however, he embraced insurrectionary activity with a fervor unrivaled by his countrymen. Armed uprisings were not merely necessary to achieve constitutional reforms; they were, of themselves, vital outpourings of public sentiment and commitment. "A little rebellion now and then is a good thing" he wrote to Madison. "It is a medicine necessary for the sound health of government." Periodic revolts, successful or otherwise, renewed the republican spirit of the people and kept their leaders on a tight leash. "The tree of liberty must be refreshed from time to time with the blood of patriots and tyrants," he wrote to William Smith. "It is its natural manure." Where others shrank from the violence of the angry "mobocracy," Jefferson positively thrilled to the eruption of crowd action. He was "America's first and foremost advocate of permanent revolution."[127]

Jefferson's commitment to revolutionary activism explains his curious reaction to Shays's Rebellion. An armed tax revolt by indebted farmers in western Massachusetts, Shays's Rebellion was the single most important catalyst behind the drafting and adoption of the federal Constitution. That citizens could take up arms against their own duly elected republican government was proof of both popular degeneracy and the alarming impotence of the states in restraining it. Shays's Rebellion galvanized reluctant Federalists like George Washington, convincing him that "we are fast verging to anarchy and confusion." The prospect that such anarchy would spread to the other colonies thoroughly alarmed him. When the Constitutional Convention finally met in Philadelphia, Washington gladly chaired the gathering. His reaction was typical of most leading American statesmen at the time.[128]

Jefferson was almost alone in downplaying the significance of Shays's Rebellion. Far from proving the weakness of American government, the Yankee revolt was an isolated and rare event. Drawing on his love of mathematics, Jefferson calculated roughly "a century and a half" per uprising, hardly a high rate of instability. Such periodic eruptions were in fact crucial to republican government. No country "can preserve its liberties if their rulers are not warned from time to time that their people preserve the spirit of resistance," he insisted, and the tax revolt in western Massachusetts was just such a salutary reminder. Moreover, the resistance in question had been "founded in ignorance, not wickedness." "The people cannot be all, and always, well informed," he reasoned, and when such misapprehension led to discontent, it was far better that they "take arms" than simply acquiesce in the face of perceived oppression. The proper response to such upheavals was not to repress them and make constitutional revisions but to "set them right as to facts, pardon and pacify them." Because rebellions were vital to the health of the body politic, "honest republican governors" ought to be "so mild in their punishment" of them "as not to discourage them too much." Surely the isolated events in New England did not warrant a full-scale transformation of revolutionary governments.[129]

The greatest instance of Jefferson's insurrectionary ardor, however, was his profound solidarity with the French revolutionary cause. Jefferson had borne witness to the early stages of that world-historical upheaval. He had observed the gathering of the Assembly of Notables in 1787 with calm optimism, predicting for France "a tolerably free constitution, and that without it's [*sic*] having cost them a drop of blood." He was present at the opening of the Estates General in 1789 and helped Lafayette with early drafts of the Declaration of the Rights of Man. When blood was at last shed, Jefferson did not shy away from it. In fact, as Conor Cruise O'Brien has argued, Jefferson's commitment to the French Revolution actually grew as it became more radical and violent. "The present disquiet will end well," Jefferson assured Washington, because the people were aroused, enlightened, and "they will not retrograde."[130]

What made Jefferson's identification with the French Revolution so intense was his understanding of its relation to the previous American cause. The American Revolution had been the opening salvo in a global campaign for liberty that was now spreading to Europe. The French have been "awaked by our revolution," he wrote to Washington in 1788. Even more gratifying was the remarkable esteem in which the French revolutionaries held their American predecessors such as Thomas Jefferson himself. American revolutionary principles and examples were treated with a sacred reverence. Like the prescriptions of holy writ, their authority was claimed by all parties, and their revealed teachings were "open to explanation, but not question." Resting squarely on the previous American example, the French Revolution extended the glorious cause from the new world to the old.[131]

Once back on American shores, Jefferson continued to champion the cause of revolution in France, and identification with revolutionary France became one of the central tenets of the Jeffersonian opposition during the administrations of both Washington and Adams. If anything, Jefferson's devotion to the struggle for liberty in America's old revolutionary ally deepened in the years after his return to the United States. Indeed, the "monocratic" Anglophile posture of the Federalist majority in the new government led him to reverse the roles of the two revolutions. Under siege from a Tory fifth column at home, the secretary of state now saw the success of revolution abroad as critical to safeguarding the republican character and revolutionary heritage of the United States. Only French victories against foes foreign and domestic could protect America "from falling back to that kind of Half-way house, the English constitution."[132]

Even the execution of Louis XVI and the ensuing Jacobin reign of terror failed to shake Jefferson's revolutionary ardor. He displayed obvious displeasure when his disciple and ex-secretary William Short detailed the massacres committed by Robespierre and his fellow Jacobins. "The tone of your letters had for some time given me pain," he complained in early 1793, "on account of the extreme warmth with which they censured the proceedings of the Jacobins." Only the Jacobins had the vision and will to use the guillotine to eradicate the threat of a royal restoration. Undoubtedly in the ensuing struggle "many guilty persons fell without the forms of trial, and with them some innocent." These losses were truly regrettable, and he would "deplore some of them to the day of my death." Yet they had been sacrificed to the noble cause of liberty. The revolution had of necessity fallen on the ultimate resource, "the arm of the people." Unfortunately that resource was "a machine" that was "not quite so blind as balls and bombs, but blind to a certain degree" nonetheless.[133]

Having worked himself up into a fevered pitch of revolutionary enthusiasm, Jefferson culminated his complaint with an almost apocalyptic reckoning of the stakes involved:

> The liberty of the whole earth was depending on the issue of the contest, and was ever such a prize won with so little innocent blood? My own affections have been deeply wounded by some of the martyrs to this cause, but rather than it should have failed, I would have seen half the earth desolated. Were there but an Adam and an Eve left in every country, and left free, it would be better than as it now is.

Jefferson's "Adam and Eve" letter was the most extreme statement of his commitment to the French Revolution and to the principle of revolutionary activism that highlighted the radical nature of his vision.[134]

Rhetorical flourishes aside, however, Thomas Jefferson was no Pol Pot. Permanent revolution was an ideal, not a prescription for practice. Despite the fears of his Federalist foes, Jefferson's Jacobinism was largely theoretical. As Hamilton shrewdly surmised, the Virginian's political "system," once he was in office, was "temporizing" rather than "violent." Indeed, even his affection for and solidarity with revolutionary France had its limits. During John Adams's Quasi-War with France in the closing years of the eighteenth century, Jefferson's identification with French revolutionary activism became a distinct political liability.

Given the state of political affairs, the Sage of Monticello did not hesitate to denounce "the atrocious proceedings of France towards this country." In fact, he now insisted that the association of "the cause of France with that of freedom" had never been a central position of his opposition party. To the contrary, that affiliation was "artfully confounded" by Federalist "Anglomen and monocrats." Jefferson did not renounce his affection for "the progress of liberty in all nations," but his core position was founded on American independence in the world: "Commerce with all nations, alliance with none."[135]

The essential fungibility of Jefferson's politics of principle was, in practice, one of the most alluring and effective features of his vision. Principled politics informed action, but did not prescribe it. Changed political realities led to a refining of principles rather than to either a doctrinaire and dogmatic loyalty to previous postures or a cynical and callous flip-flop. Jefferson's rejection of the cause of France in 1799 was every bit as authentic and heartfelt as his previous embrace of it, apparent inconsistencies notwithstanding. Both convictions were sincere, and if he seemed duplicitous in his opportunistic transformation, it was, as historian Joseph Ellis has remarked, "the kind of duplicity possible only in the pure heart."[136]

THE PRACTICE OF JEFFERSONIANISM

Once he returned to America at the end of the 1780s, Thomas Jefferson devoted the rest of his life to fighting for his Romantic vision of America against Hamilton's Federalist politics of Enlightenment. Jefferson drew on his entire range of political principles during this struggle, but three were central: agrarianism, participatory democracy, and revolutionary activism. The most appealing elements of the Jeffersonian vision, these principles were the guiding star of the Republican party. By their light Jefferson steered the course of his nation's destiny during both terms of his presidency. Often just beneath the surface, however, was the least attractive of his principles, his doctrine of racial inferiority and its tortured complication of the slavery question. Only late in life would this principle come to the fore in his thinking and, combining with the other three, prompt him to organize one more opposition.

In both opposition and office, Jefferson's politics of principle were remarkably flexible. But while his principles never generated consistent programs, they did entail broad policy preferences. The agrarian character of American society could be preserved only by devoting the nation's energies to westward expansion. This in turn meant limiting urban commerce to the export of American agricultural goods, a course Jefferson avidly but unsuccessfully advocated as secretary of state. Participatory democracy at the grassroots level was assured by setting strict bounds to the power of the central government, as Jefferson did by arguing for "strict" construction of the Constitution during the debate over Hamilton's proposed bank. To further check the "consolidating" usurpations of the Federalist regime, he championed states' rights and nullification in his famous Kentucky Resolutions of 1798. Revolutionary activism took the form of solidarity with the cause of republican France and implacable hostility to reactionary and monarchical Great Britain. These republican sensibilities on foreign relations molded Jefferson's responses to the Genet Affair, the Jay Treaty, the Quasi-War, and the English maritime intrusions that provoked his embargo policy. Jefferson's politics were nothing if not principled.

At the same time, however, his politics also worked at a more mundane and practical level. After all, Jefferson may have been a Romantic visionary, but he was first and foremost a Virginia squire. His politics were just as firmly rooted in sectional interests as they were devoted to abstract principles. Agrarian expansion would weaken the North by diverting population and capital from urban and commercial development. Faced with this dilemma, few northern leaders hesitated to choose commerce over agrarianism. When John Jay negotiated a favorable commercial treaty with Spain in 1786 that would have sacrificed American navigation of the Mississippi, the northern states uniformly embraced it and would have ratified it but for southern intransigence and threats of disunion. Moreover, the trajectory of Jeffersonian western expansion had a decidedly southern shift. The first new states admitted to the federal union, Kentucky and Tennessee, were both slave states, and the Louisiana Purchase opened up an even wider venue for the spread of the "peculiar institution." Jefferson's agrarian vision encompassed Florida, Texas, and even Cuba and Mexico, but never Canada. States' rights and strict construction also had an important sectional component. On the one hand, northern commerce and industry depended on a strong central government for its protection. On the other hand, a strong federal government was a threat to southerners who feared that their northern neighbors might interfere with or even abolish slavery on a national level. Patrick Henry warned his fellow squires before the adoption of the Constitution that among the "ten thousand implied powers" that the proposed federal government might assume could well be the authority to "liberate every one of your slaves if they please." Finally, friendship for France and enmity for England would have a devastating impact on northern merchants, many of whose imports and capital came from Great Britain.[137]

Implicit within the struggle for Jeffersonian democracy was a thinly veiled "southern" strategy. Republican newspapers in the North denounced the "aristocratic" pretensions and "monarchical" principles of Federalist elites and championed a spirit of political leveling against them. Once in power, Republicans denied those elites any access to federal office. In so doing, they destroyed the legitimacy of the North's political ruling classes and the deference that had supported them. But as New England Federalist Fisher Ames ruefully noted, Jeffersonian democracy was exclusively intended for export north of the Potomac: within the Old Dominion this leveling spirit had no impact whatsoever. Despite "their abstract theories," the Virginia squirearchy's "state policy is that of a genuine aristocracy or oligarchy." At a purely sectional level, Jeffersonian democracy brought southern hegemony to the new nation by fomenting a political insurgency against the ruling elites of the North. It was a brilliant strategy.[138]

Forming an Opposition

When Thomas Jefferson arrived in Norfolk from Paris in late November 1789, forming a national opposition was the farthest thing from his mind. His plan was to quickly settle his debts, return to Paris, and resume his diplomatic duties. News that he had been nominated and confirmed as secretary of state surprised and dismayed him. Despite the honor, Jefferson was reluctant to accept. Only the importunate pleadings of Madison and Washington, and the latter's assurance that his duties would not be too onerous, overcame his reservations. Jefferson reentered the national political scene reticently, expecting his role to be brief and uneventful.

Jefferson arrived in New York City early in the spring of 1790. Political temperatures in the new national capital were just beginning to boil. John Adams's campaign for titles had already alienated those congressmen who harbored anti-Federalist misgivings. Debate over petitions to abolish the slave trade stoked sectional animosities, tensions further exacerbated by the question of the permanent location of the federal government. The most serious conflict, however, was over Alexander Hamilton's financial scheme to handle the Revolutionary War debt. The Treasury secretary's plan for funding the debt at par had passed fairly easily, notwithstanding Madison's puerile efforts to impose "discrimination." But the assumption of state debts faced stiffer opposition. Indeed, the passage of time made its fate seem even more dire. Southerners saw it as an immense boondoggle, while northerners insisted on its adoption as the sine qua non of the union. When assumption failed in the House in mid-April, northern supporters of the Treasury plan reached a state of near panic. That panic only deepened after the measure was rejected once again in June.

Jefferson soared serenely above the fray. A loyal member of the administration, he maintained amicable relations with his fellow cabinet officers and cooperated fully with them in establishing the new administration. In fact, it was Jefferson who rescued assumption for Hamilton and, in the process, settled the divisive issue of the permanent location of the government. Shortly after assumption failed for the second time, he bumped into the Treasury secretary in front of the president's house. Years later he recalled that the neurotic New Yorker, while pacing and fulminating, appealed to him in a moment of despair. Jefferson proposed a dinner with Madison. The following day, after supper, Jefferson brokered the first great compromise of the new federal government. To "save the Union," Madison would secure the votes necessary to assure the assumption of state debts. In exchange, Hamilton must help arrange for the permanent location of the government in Georgetown on the Potomac after a ten-year hiatus in Philadelphia. This latter arrangement was made solely "as an anodyne" to "calm in some degree the ferment which might be excited by the other measure alone."[139]

Jefferson downplayed his role in the negotiation and subsequently claimed the canny New Yorker got the best of him. The Virginian was far too modest. His was the critical agency in bringing the negotiation to fruition. He also drove a very hard bargain. In addition to securing the capital on the Potomac, Jefferson also extracted a revision of Virginia's balance of debts that netted his state over $13 million. That Jefferson had served his state's interest was undeniable. He had also, however, helped secure the single most important object of the new national government and its energetic Treasury secretary. Jefferson's collaboration with Hamilton exemplified the spirit of cooperation and compromise that would be necessary to navigate the new federal ship of state through the shoals of sectional and partisan conflict. Yet it was a collaboration based solely on political expediency. Jefferson did not share Hamilton's modernizing vision of an enlightened central government pursuing commercial, urban, and industrial development. Such a vision ran directly counter to Jefferson's Romantic faith in agrarian simplicity and limited government. He rescued assumption because it was necessary to keep the wheels of government turning and the finances of the nation afloat. Understandably, then, his cooperation with Hamilton was short-lived. Less than a year later he had begun forming an opposition party.[140]

What led Jefferson to abandon compromise for conflict was his growing realization of the scope of Hamilton's plans for the young republic. The Bank of the United States—proposed by Hamilton in mid-December—would enrich northern financiers and speculators and thus enhance the power of the North in the federal government. Additionally, the stimulation of commerce and manufactures resulting from an increased money supply would draw capital to northern urban development and away from westward agricultural expansion. Moreover, the need for a steady source of revenue to finance the debt and ensure that bank stock traded at par would preclude any measures that might hamper commerce with Great Britain, whose trade and tonnage in the former colonies generated the vast bulk of federal taxes. In short, Hamilton's program represented the complete negation of the Jeffersonian vision.

Every bit as troubling as Hamilton's policies was his remarkable ability to see them enacted. A brilliant polemicist and political tactician, the New Yorker seemed to sweep his foes from the field. Despite the recalcitrant grumbling of the southern opposition, Hamilton promptly secured passage of his controversial bank legislation. In February 1791 Jefferson, Madison, and Attorney General Edmund Randolph all urged the president to veto the bill, and Jefferson authored a brief arguing that the power to create corporations, much less banks, was not specifically authorized by the Constitution; nor was it in any strict sense of the term "necessary." To treat such a power as "implied," as Hamilton and his fellow Federalists did, was "to take possession of a boundless field of power, no longer susceptible of any definition" or limitation. The carefully reasoned brief gave Washington pause, and he seemed genuinely disposed to veto the bill. Then Hamilton sent the president his famed defense of implied powers and promptly secured Washington's signature. At roughly the same time, Jefferson presented three commercial reports to Congress urging a policy of discriminatory tariffs. Hamilton opposed discrimination on the grounds that it would jeopardize British trade and thus deprive the Treasury of vital revenue. Despite popular hostility to Great Britain, Hamilton secured the defeat of Jefferson's proposals in Congress, which tabled the question and asked the secretary of state to

314

draft a more studied report. Hamilton even intruded into foreign affairs, most notably in his secret meetings with British diplomats, meetings that, for the secretary of state, had the bitterly galling approval of George Washington himself. By early 1791 Hamilton had emerged as the single most influential statesman in the new republic.[141]

By the spring of 1791 Jefferson had seen enough. In May he and Madison took an extended "botanizing" expedition up the Hudson valley. Hamilton soon learned that the Virginians had been meeting with his political rivals in New York, such as Robert R. Livingston, Aaron Burr, and anti-Federalist Governor George Clinton. Jefferson's northern embassy established the first lineaments of the famed axis between Virginia and New York that would fix the national character of the emerging Republican party and, with the "revolution of 1800," win him the presidency. In the ensuing months and years, Jefferson would continue to recruit new allies in the North among discontented tradesmen and farmers as well as elites such as Thomas Mifflin and Albert Gallatin of Pennsylvania and Elbridge Gerry of Massachusetts. Jefferson had begun organizing what has become the oldest political party in modern history.[142]

The most important measure Jefferson took in forming the Republican party, however, was the establishment of a national party newspaper. There was no shortage of anti-Hamiltonian local papers, but there were no national weeklies to rival John Fenno's *Gazette of the United States*, the official vehicle of the Federalist administration and, Jefferson charged, "a paper of pure Toryism." In early 1791 Madison, Jefferson, and fellow Virginian Henry Lee began courting Philip Freneau, a respected poet and one of the most accomplished journalists in the nation. Newspaper publication was a risky venture, and it took almost seven months of relentless urgings and negotiations before he finally acquiesced. To allay the financial risks, Madison and Lee procured investment capital, and Freneau's new *National Gazette* could rely on a steady stream of income from printing documents and notices from the State Department. To supplement his income, Jefferson also hired Freneau as a translator at the State Department at a salary of $250 per year and assurances that his duties would be sufficiently light as to not interfere with his journalistic interests. Further, Jefferson took great pains to ensure that the federal postal service distributed the weekly throughout the length of the nation.[143]

The *National Gazette* quickly became the Republican standard bearer. Its unrelenting criticism of the Federalist party, its administration, and even its chief executive, and its unfailing devotion to Jeffersonian principles, galvanized the Republican opposition and unified it around a common creed. Pseudonymous essays in its pages by party luminaries like James Madison established a common party line on policies foreign and domestic. Combined with the regional alliances first established that spring, Jefferson and Madison's hiring of Freneau laid the cornerstone of the Republican edifice.

Jefferson's role in the newly established Republican party put him in an awkward position. Ever conflict averse, he shied from political confrontation and unpleasantness. When an edition of Thomas Paine's recent *Rights of Man* appeared in the spring of 1791 with a brief prefatory note by the secretary of state extolling the work as an excellent antidote to "the political heresies which have sprung up among us," Jefferson was thoroughly appalled. Jefferson did not deny writing the note or that the heresies in question were those broached by John Adams in his *Discourses on Davila*, but he insisted that his comments had not been intended for publication. Jefferson's faux pas was innocent enough, and when he finally screwed up the courage to write to his old friend Adams in mid-July, the elderly Yankee readily accepted his explanation. Yet Jefferson could not leave well enough alone. He attempted to dodge the charge of traducing the reputation of his old comrade by insisting that a pamphlet by John Quincy Adams defending his father had led to the attacks on the vice president.[144]

"My note produced nothing to the production of these disagreeable pieces," he assured Adams. Instead it was "to *Publicola*" solely that "the whole contest is to be ascribed and all its consequences." Jefferson's attempt to minimize the effect of his attack on his old friend clearly strained the limits of credulity, just as did his mendacious claim to

Adams that he "had not in view any writings which I might suppose to be yours" when he spoke about "heresies." This much the elder statesman was willing to overlook for the sake of friendship. But when Jefferson claimed that their political differences were "well known to us both," Adams could not keep his peace. "You and I have never had a serious conversation together I can recollect concerning the nature of government," he pointedly reminded Jefferson. Jefferson's apparent duplicity in this exchange suggests the extreme discomfort he took in openly partisan behavior. The Sage of Monticello was still a reluctant opposition leader.[145]

Jefferson had good reason to be reluctant. To privately oppose the views and policies of various Federalist officeholders was one thing, but to organize an opposition to the very administration he served was another. As a member of Washington's cabinet, Jefferson was free to oppose the proposals of Hamilton or Adams. But once those proposals had been adopted by the president, it was Jefferson's duty to support them. To organize a political opposition—worse, to establish an opposition newspaper devoted to attacking the administration (including the president himself)—seemed downright perfidious. These were in fact precisely the charges that Hamilton leveled against him in the summer of 1792.

Writing as "T. L." and "An American," Hamilton exposed the relationship between Jefferson, Madison, and Freneau. No "independent editor," Freneau was "the faithful and devoted servant of the head of a party" who drew a salary from the State Department. His willingness to thus "bite the hand that puts bread in his mouth" by criticizing the administration that employed him could be explained only by the fact that "the man is hired to do it" by the secretary of state. For his part, Jefferson was not only "emulous of being the head of a party" but was "the declared opponent of almost all the important measures of the administration" he purportedly served. That the secretary of state had "too little scruple to embarrass and disparage the government, of which he is a member," Hamilton ascribed to the Virginian's desire to elevate "State-power upon the ruins of National Authority." The New Yorker's merciless pen cast Jefferson as a political intriguer and defamer "who has been the prompter open or secret of unwarrantable aspersions on men" whose "patriotism and integrity need never decline a comparison of him." For a man of such private inclinations and delicate sensibilities as Jefferson, the harsh glare of public scrutiny that Hamilton threw upon him must have been excruciating.[146]

Hamilton's political "outing" of Jefferson in the summer of 1792 finally steeled the shy Virginian for political combat. The secretary of state resolved to resign his office by March of the following year, eliminating any apparent conflict of interest and thus freeing the great visionary to lead the forces of agrarian virtue against the corrupt legion of Hamiltonian bank jobbers. Calls for reconciliation from Washington fell on deaf ears. Jefferson utterly denied Hamilton's charges. His own opposition to Hamilton's "system" was private and principled. Hamilton's system was patently designed "to demolish the republic" and reflected the corrupt influence of congressmen who were "out to profit by his plans." Opposing such a system, then, could in no way be an act of disloyalty to the administration since it had been enacted by votes illegally purchased.[147]

Jefferson's rage clearly got the better of him as he wrote to Washington, for the president had ultimately endorsed Hamilton's program as his own. But Jefferson had worked himself into a fit of righteous indignation. Where his own opposition had been muted and principled, Hamilton's attacks were direct and scurrilous. Jefferson had not started the feud with Hamilton, but he would not back down. Nor would he suffer slander from "a man whose history from the moment of which history can stoop to notice him, is a tissue of machination against the liberty of the country which has not only received and given him bread, but heaped its honors on his head." It was Hamilton who was disloyal, a traitor to the American people who had adopted him. There would be no rapprochement. Jefferson was in the fight in earnest.[148]

For his part, Jefferson had no intention of ceding the field to Hamilton. If he must resign his office to pursue his role in the opposition, he would ensure that the New Yorker was not left to mold the administration to his will. In early 1793 he helped prepare a set of resolutions that William Branch Giles introduced in the House calling for a

strict accounting of Treasury transactions and charging the secretary
with malfeasance in office. In mid-February he prepared another set insisting that Hamilton "be removed from his office by the President of
the United States." When Hamilton was vindicated in early March,
Jefferson postponed his retirement.[149]

For the next ten months the battle with Hamilton shifted to the field
of foreign affairs. Initially, Jefferson's prospects looked promising.
When news of war between France and England arrived in March, the
Republicans seized on the popular enthusiasm for the revolutionary
cause of France. The Federalists were cast as "Anglomen" who would
abandon their sister republic in her hour of need to the reactionary
clutches of Great Britain. The treaties of 1778 bound America to her old
ally, a bond that was now strengthened by both gratitude and shared political principles. Riding the tide of public opinion, Jefferson easily
squelched Hamilton's efforts in the cabinet to declare the Franco-
American alliance null and void. While the exact wording of the president's neutrality proclamation was not to his taste, Jefferson approved of
its overall thrust. Washington was now following Jefferson's advice, eschewing Hamilton's Anglophilia, and the secretary of state looked at the
political prospects unfolding before him with confidence. The French
Revolution had galvanized the American people and revealed their true
divisions. On the one hand were the pro-British urban Federalists, self-
styled "natural aristocrats," "paper men," and "old tories." On the other
were the Francophile Republicans comprising independent merchants,
"tradesmen, mechanics, farmers and every other possible description of
our citizens." Jefferson had reason to be sanguine.[150]

Citizen Edmund Genet's arrival that spring galvanized public opinion in a Republican direction. The new French minister's triumphal tour
from Charleston to Philadelphia contrasted sharply with what Jefferson
called "the cold caution of the government." Genet was lionized in the
Republican press while the administration was charged with wearing an
"anglified complexion." Even Washington was not immune. Jefferson
sincerely regretted the calumny heaped on the president, but when
Washington angrily hinted that Jefferson should call off Freneau's as-

saults, he balked. Freneau's paper had helped put the Republican opposition in the ascendant and "saved our Constitution." Riding high on the wave of public sentiment, Jefferson gushed with praise for the French ambassador. "It is impossible to be more affectionate, more magnanimous than the purport of his mission," he declared in mid-May. "He offers everything and asks nothing."[151]

Unfortunately, Genet asked a great deal. By illicitly commissioning privateers, he threatened to draw the United States into war with Great Britain; his attempts to organize filibustering operations in the American West were likely to embroil relations with Spanish Louisiana. Where Hamilton bristled at the effrontery of the French emissary and his obvious contempt for the sovereignty of the federal government, Jefferson viewed his actions through the Romantic lens of shared convictions. If Genet was at times indiscreet, it was no doubt due to his honest zeal and authentic devotion to the sacred cause of revolution and human emancipation. Understandably, the secretary of state did what he could to protect the young emissary. Despite his disapproval of the privateering enterprises, Jefferson argued in the cabinet against the use of force or the law to make Genet desist. He warned the Frenchman that Americans caught filibustering would be tried for treason, but he failed to apprise Washington of those schemes. Indeed, when Genet received a rather frosty reception from the president, Jefferson assured him that Washington's mien and policies did not reflect the sentiments of Congress or the nation. Alas, Genet took Jefferson's reassurance literally. When Washington insisted that he cease outfitting privateers and disposing of British prizes captured in American waters, Genet threatened to appeal over his head to Congress and the American people. Jefferson was flabbergasted.

Genet had gone too far. The elected president of the United States, Washington commanded the loyalty and respect of the nation. "Never in my opinion was so calamitous an appointment made," Jefferson wrote in an about-face to Madison in early July, "as that of the present minister of F[rance] here." Genet was "hotheaded" and utterly lacking in "judgment." His dealings with the president were "disrespectful and even indecent." Worst of all, however, were his threats to appeal to Congress and "from them to the people." If news of these outrages ever reached the public, Jefferson feared "they will excite universal indignation" against Genet and the Republican opposition that had embraced him.[152]

Jefferson's worst fears were realized that summer. In late June Hamilton began his "Pacificus" essays, defending Washington's policy of neutrality against its Francophile critics. At the end of July he began his "No Jacobin" series, which detailed the entire record of Genet's contemptuous behavior. The impact of Hamilton's writings was staggering. The public now vilified Genet, and neutrality now seemed an act of independent and prudential statecraft rather than a betrayal of republican principles. Jefferson saw the writing on the wall. With public opinion against them, the Republicans must drop all opposition to Washington's neutrality proclamation and "abandon G[enet] entirely." Once again Hamilton had stanched the rising tide of Republicanism. Wisely, Jefferson sounded a tactical retreat.[153]

Just before leaving office at the end of 1793, Jefferson took one last parting shot at the Federalist "colossus." On December 16 he submitted the report on commerce that Congress had requested two years before. After a brief review of the state of American trade, Jefferson proposed a set of "principles" to govern the nation's commercial diplomacy. "Founded in reciprocity," these were the very principles of discriminatory tariffs that he and Madison had previously championed. Using access to American markets as its leverage, discrimination would extract favorable terms of trade by making them in the best interests of other nations. If a nation like France was in a reciprocal treaty with the United States, she would enjoy unfettered access at duties no higher than those paid by Americans. If, on the other hand, a nation like Great Britain "imposes high duties on our production, or prohibits them altogether, it may be proper for us to do the same by theirs." Denied the all-important American market for their manufactures, the English would have no choice but to capitulate. The problem with Jefferson's plan was that it vastly overrated the importance of America's trade. The American market was simply not that critical to England, nor its economy sufficiently strong, to impose its will on Great Britain. Discriminatory tariffs would in fact destroy trade with Great Britain, resulting in America's economic devastation, especially for the urban centers of commerce. Armed with the relevant facts by Hamilton, Federalist congressman William Loughton Smith of South Carolina easily shelved the program.[154]

Jefferson had been bested yet again by Hamilton. After nearly four years in office, Jefferson had few achievements. During his tenure, as historian Merrill Peterson has wryly observed, "the advance in foreign relations could be measured in inches." The Republican opposition he had helped form had been checked at every critical point. For the second time in his life, Jefferson left executive office under a cloud of frustrating failures. For the second time in his life, he responded to these failures by retiring from public life and vowing never to return.[155]

Leading the Opposition

Jefferson did not, of course, make his final exit from the public stage in early 1794. He did, however, take a sabbatical. For a full year he avoided politics and devoted his energies to domestic affairs at Monticello. When he returned to the fray in 1795, it would be in a different role. Heretofore Jefferson had helped organize the Republican opposition, but Madison had been its primary leader. Henceforth their roles were reversed. Meticulous and diligent, Jefferson was a brilliant political tactician whose political judgment helped sustain the party through the dark years of Federalist ascendancy. It would ultimately lead them to victory in the election of 1800.

Madison had been a bold but conventional leader, leading his Republicans into legislative battle behind a cannonade of constitutional arguments, usually to dispiriting defeat. Jefferson, by contrast, fought a ruthless guerrilla struggle, constantly probing for weakness in the Federalist position and using the press to harass the foe with so constant a barrage of criticism that it drew the ire of Washington: "Every act of my Administration" had been "tortured" in the Republican press and subject to "the grossest, and most insidious misrepresentations," he said. Unlike Madison, Jefferson preferred to skirmish, offering amendments and raising quibbles with administration policies rather than to risk defeat in set battles over high constitutional ground. Jefferson's greatest political skill, however, may have been his mastery of the tactical retreat. Whenever he sensed that public opinion was drifting away from Republican positions, he promptly abandoned them, as he had when Hamilton's "No Jacobin" essays turned the public against Genet. At the time, many members of the opposition had spent precious political capital praising and justifying the French ambassador and were reluctant to give him up. Monroe noted that many Republicans still "applaud him [Genet] for his zeal in pressing the cause of his country" and feared that to throw him over entirely "would create a despondency" in the party ranks "that would complete the triumph" of the Francophobe Federalists. But Jefferson's was a cooler and more strategic political mind. Genet simply had to go, he told Madison; "he will sink the republican interest if they do not abandon him." Jefferson knew when it was time to cut his losses and regroup; as long as his forces remained intact, the Republicans could never be utterly vanquished.[156]

This pattern of attack and retreat can be seen in Jefferson's handling of the Republican opposition to the Jay Treaty of 1795 that settled commercial relations with England. The worldly Hamilton had endorsed the treaty as an enlightened piece of statecraft that, recognizing American weakness and dependence, extracted the best terms that could realistically be hoped for. By contrast, Jefferson the Romantic visionary railed against the pact as a betrayal of fundamental principle and revolutionary solidarity with France. From Monticello, Jefferson coordinated a furious and effective assault on it. Through most of 1795 the treaty was wildly unpopular; Jay was burned in effigy in several cities, and Hamilton was stoned by an angry crowd in Manhattan when he tried to defend it. Even after the treaty was ratified by the Senate and signed by the president in mid-August, Jefferson refused to relent. Rather than let the matter drop, he took the battle to the House of Representatives. With popular sentiment squarely behind him, Jefferson assured Edward Rutledge that Republican congressmen would "rid us of this infamous act" by refusing to pass measures to enact it on the dubious constitutional ground that, because the House had to appropriate funds to execute treaties, "the representatives are as free as the President and Senate" to approve or reject them. As the groundswell of clamor against the treaty remained strong in the early spring of 1796, Jefferson inflated this constitutional argument into a vital matter of principle; but when the cumulative effect of Hamilton's "Camillus" essays and the arrival of the popular Treaty of San Lorenzo—which ensured access to New Orleans and a favorable adjustment of southern borders with colonial Spain—swung public opinion behind the Jay Treaty, Jefferson abruptly dropped his opposition. Despite a Republican majority, the representatives put the treaty into effect.[157]

Madison was despondent. "A crisis which ought to have been so managed as to fortify the Republican cause," he wrote in late May, "has left it in a very crippled condition." Jefferson's view was far more sanguine. The Federalists had ultimately carried the day, "yet it has been to them a dear bought victory." He counseled "patience."[158]

The key to Jefferson's patience was his unshakable confidence in ultimate victory. Federalists were either corrupt financiers, British merchants, Americans trading on British capital, or timid men. Republicans, by contrast, comprised "the entire body of landholders" and laborers "whether in husbandry or the arts." All that was necessary was to awaken the public and "snap the Lilliputian cords with which" the monocratic few "have been entangling us." Jefferson had good reason for optimism. The electoral strength of New England was more than balanced by the Republican South and rising West. Federalism's viability hinged on control of the middle colonies of New York, New Jersey, and Pennsylvania. Jefferson's alliance with Burr and Livingston in New York and Republican sympathy for the Whiskey Rebels in western Pennsylvania had made serious inroads into both states, gains further consolidated by the furor over Genet and the Jay Treaty. Only Washington's immense popularity had sustained the Federalists in the face of relentless criticism, and with his second term coming to a close, Jefferson had every reason to believe that time was on his side. It was for that reason that he counseled patience to his fellow Virginians and urged them to avoid steps that might alienate opinion in the mid-Atlantic. Jefferson's judgment proved prescient. In the election of 1796 he came within three votes of capturing the presidency.[159]

For all his prowess, Jefferson was still a reluctant leader who loathed the glare of public scrutiny. In the spring of 1795 he wrote to Madison that he would not run for president the following year. What led him to change his mind is not certain, but Jefferson had intimated to Madison that he might relent if a different candidate would cause a "division or loss of votes, which might be fatal to the Southern interest." Jefferson was especially uncomfortable in 1796 because his adversary was his old friend John Adams. Nor was Jefferson's reticence entirely disinterested. The next president would inherit a foreign crisis. By the summer of 1796 the French had begun seizing American shipping in the Caribbean in response to the ratification of the Jay Treaty, threatening war. As he wryly told his son-in-law some months before the final presidential tally, "a well-weighted ambition" for high office would assuredly "wish to be the second on that vote rather than the first."[160]

The depths of Jefferson's discomfort with his role as the Republican "Generalissimo" (as the Federalists called him) became evident in a letter of congratulation he drafted to Adams in late December. In it he warned the Yankee of "the subtlety of your arch friend of New York," Alexander Hamilton. He also urged him to avoid a full-scale war with France. Touchingly, he concluded with one of his glorious sentimental effusions:

> [T]hat your administration may be filled with glory and happiness to yourself and advantage to us is the sincere wish of one who tho', in the course of our voyage thro' life, various little incidents have happened to have been contrived to separate us, retains still for you the solid esteem of the moments when we were working for our independence, and sentiments of respect and affectionate attachment.

For Jefferson, such effusions were never gratuitous. As he explained to Madison—Jefferson had sent him the letter to forward at his discretion—the purport of this letter was to offer an alliance with the new president. If Adams would abandon Hamilton, the Republicans should accept him as their leader and "come to a good understanding with him as to his future elections." Madison did not forward Jefferson's letter to Adams. Adams was notoriously independent-minded, and as Madison suspected, in the coming months and years it would become necessary for Jefferson to once again lead the Republican opposition against yet another monocratic Federalist administration. By that point, however, Jefferson would be free of all doubt and reservations. The struggle would be total. Before long he was paying scurrilous muckrakers like James Callender to denounce his old friend Adams in print.[161]

Jefferson was not alone in renewing partisan passions. After a honeymoon that barely lasted past Adams's inauguration, the Republicans turned on the new president with a frightening ferocity. Their Federalist opponents gladly reciprocated. By the summer of 1797 Jefferson reported that "men who have been intimate all their lives cross the street to avoid meeting, and turn their heads another way, lest they should be obliged to touch their hats."[162]

The cause of this rancor was the deepening crisis with France. In early 1797 word arrived that France had abrogated the old treaties of 1778 and ordered American minister Charles Cotesworth Pinckney to leave the country. As news of fresh seizures of American ships in the Caribbean filtered into the capital, Adams summoned Congress to fortify the nation's maritime forces and approve a fresh embassy to Paris. The prospect of a full-scale war with France was every bit as terrifying to Jefferson and his fellow Republicans as it was alluring to the High Federalists. War with the French republic would entail a dramatic enlargement of the federal military and the Treasury department, both of which could not help but concentrate even more power in the central government and away from the states. The cost of war would require a significant expansion of the national debt, further entrenching the financial system of Hamilton and making the Republican goal of eliminating it deeply problematic. Worst of all, Federalists would reap a harvest of patriotic war sentiment while the Republicans languished under the taint of their longstanding identification with the nation's enemy. The Quasi-War with France portended, potentially at least, the death knell of Republicanism.

Despite the gathering storm, Jefferson remained calm during the ensuing year. The Republicans still controlled the House of Representatives and could therefore deny Adams the resources to take any offensive actions in the Atlantic. Again, he counseled patience. The French Directory could not possibly desire war any more than Adams, and once friendly relations between the two sister republics were restored, the dark clouds on the political horizon would dissipate before the bright sky of Republican ascendancy. Jefferson's optimism was severely challenged, however, when John Adams informed Congress in mid-March that the embassy to France had failed and that additional military preparations were therefore necessary. Declaring the president's message "almost insane," Jefferson declared that its sole purpose was "to render the war party inveterate and more firm in their purpose without adding to their numbers." Jefferson simply refused to believe that the diplomatic exchanges of the previous year had been as dire and disrespectful as Adams represented. A full and complete disclosure of the dispatches would surely reveal the president's tortured misrepresentations.[163]

Jefferson blundered horribly. The revelation of the "XYZ Affair" that he had demanded dealt a severe blow to the Republican opposition. The evident contempt that France had shown to the American ministers buoyed the Federalists on a wave of patriotic resentment. Adams was flooded with addresses from across the nation praising his steady and firm leadership. Republicans were now in an untenable position: to turn on their sister republic would imply hypocrisy, but to stick with her smacked of giving comfort to the enemy. Jefferson tried to remain upbeat, but as Congress began preparing the so-called Alien and Sedition Acts, it became impossible. Jefferson and his fellow partisans could not fail to recognize that the intention of the sedition law was to silence their shock troops in the Republican press, a vital resource in Jefferson's partisan strategy. The pro-commercial and pro-British policies of Hamilton looked to expand unchecked. Amid ominous hints as to whether

Virginia's best interest lay in the union, Jefferson's southern strategy was on the verge of collapse.[164]

The proper response, Jefferson urged, was not "a scission of the union" but "a little patience." Partisan and sectional conflict were inherent in all republican governments, and "seeing that we must have somebody to quarrel with," the Yankees were perfect for that role. Lacking a western frontier, their population could not expand much more, and their character, like that of "the Jews," was so unpleasant "as to constitute from that circumstance the natural division of our parties." Given time, Jefferson claimed, "we shall see the reign of witches pass over, their spells dissolve, and the people recovering their true sight."[165]

Not all of his fellow southerners shared Jefferson's optimism. The Quasi-War had buttressed the Federalist party and emboldened it to take legal means to crush its Republican opposition. As talk of secession spread in the Chesapeake, Jefferson knew he had to take some dramatic measure to galvanize the southern opposition and draw it away from disunion. By early October 1798 he had completed drafting his famous Kentucky Resolutions.

The Kentucky Resolutions denounced the Alien and Sedition Acts as illegal and unconstitutional assaults on republican government. Jefferson's case was not that they infringed on vital liberties but rather that they usurped the rights of the states. Jefferson, of course, acknowledged that exporting aliens without benefit of trial violated due process, but that was a minor issue. The real problem was that aliens "are under the jurisdiction and protection of the laws of the state wherein they are," and since "no power over them has been delegated to the United States" by the Constitution, the Alien Act obviously violated that document. Similarly, the real problem with the Sedition Act was that it violated the Tenth Amendment, which reserved all undelegated powers "to the states respectively or to the people," rather than the First Amendment, which ensured freedom of the press. The regulation of the press was strictly reserved to the states, and it was in the state courts under state laws that seditious libel should be prosecuted. These constitutional infringements were by no means isolated incidents. They were part of a long pattern of Federalist usurpation that "goes to the destruction of all limits prescribed to their power by the government." The assault on "the friendless aliens" was but "a first experiment" that would soon be extended to "the citizen." Such acts must be promptly "arrested at the threshold" lest they "drive these states into revolution and blood." The Kentucky Resolutions were, then, a call for eternal vigilance against the consolidating intrigues of the Federalists against the liberty and sovereignty of the states. "Confidence is everywhere the parent of despotism," Jefferson declared. "Free government is founded in jealousy."[166]

The central principle of the Kentucky Resolutions was the classic doctrine of states' rights, namely that the federal Constitution was a compact of the states rather than the people. Whenever the federal government violated the terms of that pact, its acts were necessarily "void and of no force." Moreover, because each state was a party to the federal compact, each "has an equal right to judge for itself" both when its rights had been violated as well as "the mode and measure of redress." Jefferson was treading on dangerous ground here. If each state was a court of constitutional review, it was within their power to nullify whatever federal laws they found objectionable. This was exactly the position Jefferson took. As the only "parties to the compact," the states were "solely authorized to judge in the last resort of the powers exercised under it."[167]

When the delegates in Kentucky's General Assembly adopted Jefferson's resolves in early November, they prudently expunged his mention of nullification, just as Madison did in his subsequent Virginia Resolutions. To raise the issue at this point would unduly alarm Republican opinion in the North and alienate swing voters. Nonetheless, the doctrine of nullification was implicit in Jefferson's interpretation of the Constitution as a compact of the states.[168]

The Virginia and Kentucky resolves were intended to serve three distinct purposes. Denouncing the transgressions of the Federalists would mobilize Republican sentiment for the upcoming congressional elections. The invocation of states' rights would draw those political bodies into the struggle against the consolidating usurpations of the centralizing monocrats. Finally, they sent a warning shot to the rest of the nation: the South's hint of disunion would check the consolidating urges of Federalist warmongers and galvanize Republican feeling in the critical mid-Atlantic. "Firmness on our part, but a passive firmness, is the true course," Jefferson insisted.[169]

Unfortunately, the resolves Madison and Jefferson penned utterly failed to achieve their goals. Federalists scored impressive gains in the congressional election of 1799, even in Jefferson's native Virginia. Most states chose to ignore the pleas issued from Kentucky and Virginia, and some responded with great umbrage. In late February Congress approved a report defending the Alien and Sedition Acts and refuting Jefferson's arguments point by point. To make matters worse, Adams had opened diplomatic channels to the slave revolutionaries in Haiti that, Jefferson darkly surmised, could only encourage their "intercourse with their black brethren in these states." The effects of such an intercourse, Jefferson complained to Madison, threatened a racial "combustion."[170]

After nine long years of partisan struggle, the entwined Federalist projects of northern commercial expansion and federal consolidation had gone on unabated. After countless political battles the Republican party was no closer to victory than it had been when Jefferson first formed it. Now his old Yankee friend was pointing a racial dagger at the very heart of his beloved Virginia. At last Jefferson abandoned the politics of patience. In late August he wrote to Madison calling for a fresh set of resolutions to express the clear determination "to sever ourselves from that union we so much value, rather than give up the rights of self government which we have reserved, and in which alone we see liberty, safety, and happiness." Having reached the end of his tether, Jefferson braced for the coming storm. As Virginia quietly began arming herself, Hamilton laid ominous plans to move his army to the borders of that state and force a contest of wills. Thomas Jefferson's transcendent vision was on the verge of immolation in the fires of civil war. A lifetime of political labor was about to go up in smoke.[171]

Jefferson's political career did not, of course, culminate in secession. Little more than one year later he was elected President of the United States and commenced a full generation of Republican ascendancy in the early republic. The three men most responsible for that election were, ironically, his primary rivals, John Adams, Aaron Burr, and Alexander Hamilton. Horrified at the prospect of civil war and assured a favorable reception by France, John Adams dispatched a fresh peace delegation to Paris in October 1799, defusing the sectional crisis and splitting, as he knew it would, the ranks of his own party. Adams's actions swept over Jefferson like a cool breeze. By late November all talk of secession was replaced by "a sincere cultivation of the union" and a willingness to pursue peace "even with Great Britain." Jefferson's patience was restored. A divided Federalist party gave Jefferson the opportunity for which he had been waiting so long, and it was John Adams who created that division.[172]

If Adams created the conditions for Jefferson's victory, Burr realized them. Given the solid electoral support Jefferson expected from the South and the tiny margin of the previous election, he had good reason to believe that a sweep of New York's twelve electoral votes would put him over the top. In mid-January Burr assured Jefferson that he had the city in the bag and would therefore have a clear Republican majority in the statehouse. Burr's confidence proved as well founded as his tactics were effective. The twelve electoral votes he delivered in the election of 1800 finally put the Republican party in control.[173]

At last, when the inconceivable happened and an electoral tie between Burr and Jefferson threw the election into the Federalist House of Representatives, it was Hamilton who rescued his arch-nemesis. A caucus of Federalists decided to support Burr, but Hamilton ran a private campaign for Jefferson. Aaron Burr was "one of the most unprincipled men in the United States," he told John Rutledge. He warned James A. Bayard, the sole elector of Delaware, that if Burr should succeed, he "will certainly attempt to reform the government *a la Bonaparte*." Put simply, Burr was "the most unfit man in the United States for the office of President." Jefferson might be "tinctured with fanaticism," but at least he was incorruptible, "which is a security he will not go beyond certain limits." For thirty-five ballots over six days the Federalists denied Jefferson the nine states he needed to claim victory, but on the thirty-sixth, Bayard finally relented. Jefferson would, at last, be able to bring his vision of America to life.[174]

Governing the Nation

On March 4, 1801, the painfully shy president gave his first inaugural address so softly, he was barely audible in the first row. But the text he composed, reprinted in newspapers across the nation, was glorious. In a few short, staccato phrases, Jefferson evoked his glittering vision of America: "A rising nation spread over a wide and fruitful land, traversing all the seas with the rich productions of their industry, engaged in commerce with nations who feel power and forget right, advancing rapidly to destinies beyond the reach of mortal eye." It was a vision of "transcendent objects," to which Jefferson pledged "the honor, the happiness, and the hopes of this beloved country." So exalted were these objects that the new president was confessedly humbled "by the magnitude of the undertaking" thrust upon him. Nonetheless, with the support of his fellow countrymen and "the patronage of your good will," he stoically advanced "with obedience to the work" that his nation had assigned him in the hope that the "infinite power which rules the destinies of the universe" would "lead our counsels to what is best, and give a favorable issue for your peace and prosperity." Jefferson's inaugural was one for the ages.[175]

Thomas Jefferson inaugurated far more than his first presidential term on that day in early March. What he later referred to as the "revolution of 1800" marked a fundamental turning point in American history. In his eight years in office, he reversed the trajectory of Federalist policy, directing the energies of the central government away from urban commercial development and toward agrarian expansion. He also utterly routed the remnants of the Federalist party, instituting a generation of one-party rule known as the "era of good feelings" or "the Virginia dynasty." The pattern of constitutional government he established, characterized by states' rights and sharply limited federal intrusion, remained the dominant model of political practice right up to the Civil War, and his ideals of limited government and even more limited taxes remain popular desiderata to this day. Jefferson's achievements were among the most influential and impressive in all of American history.

Jefferson benefited from favorable circumstances. The Sage of Monticello inherited a nation at peace and in the flush of prosperity. His Federalist opposition was divided and lacked leadership. European wars assured a lucrative neutral commerce and induced Napoleon to sell Louisiana for a paltry $15 million. But fortune was only part of the equation. What made Jefferson so successful as a president was the way he matched luck with political skill. As Hamilton shrewdly surmised, Jefferson proved an extremely energetic and adept executive.

Few presidents have dominated their administrations as thoroughly as Jefferson did. Eschewing long-winded and contentious cabinet meetings, he preferred one-on-one meetings with his executive officers, which avoided both faction and dissent. Because his cabinet members reported directly to him (often on a daily basis), he was able to constantly monitor and steer all the activities of his administration. As undisputed head of his party, which enjoyed comfortable majorities in both the House and the Senate, he personally dictated Republican legislative agendas and almost invariably got from Congress what he wanted. As head of state, he wielded the power of patronage with a truly Walpolean mastery. Moderate Federalist officeholders might be retained—and absorbed within the Republican party—but high ranking and well-established leaders were removed from office at every available opportunity. When their appointments were not dependent on presidential pleasure, as in the judiciary and military, Jefferson simply had his lieutenants in Congress rescind or reorganize their offices. "No purge in nineteenth century American politics," notes one scholar, "not even those of the Jackson years, surpassed the thoroughness of Jefferson's house cleaning." When it came to governing the nation, Jefferson left little to chance.[176]

Jefferson used his political skills to achieve three basic objectives, each contained in his inaugural address. First and foremost was the pursuit of fiscal austerity. Government spending must be cut so "that labor may be lightly burthened" and the public debt honestly and speedily repaid. The second goal was the "encouragement of Agriculture." This entailed securing ample land for agrarian expansion through purchases from Amerindians and acquisition of fresh territories from foreign powers. Jefferson's final goal was to ensure that commerce remained the "handmaid" of agriculture rather than a potential source of urbanization and political corruption. This would be achieved by pursuing a commercial policy based on "honest friendship with all nations" but "entangling alliances with none." These were, Jefferson claimed, the fundamental principles of Republican America and "consequently those which ought to shape its administration." They would be the objects of his labors for the next eight years.[177]

"A Wise and Frugal Government": Jeffersonian Finance

If there was one thing "necessary to make us a happy and a prosperous people," Jefferson claimed in his inaugural, it was "a wise and frugal government." As Joseph Ellis notes, "simplicity and austerity, not equality or individualism," were the watchwords of his administration. Frugality would relieve the tax burden of the American people, whose government would no longer "take from the mouth of labor the bread it has earned." Austerity would also allow the government to finally begin retiring its expanding debt, a growing burden on the future of the new nation and whose "honest paiment" was, for Jefferson at least, every bit as important as the "sacred preservation of the public faith." Finally, a "wise and frugal government" would enhance the liberty of the people. Shorn of excess revenues and expenditures, the federal government would be reduced to a guardian of the nation's common interests, powerless to otherwise interfere in the lives of the American people.[178]

Once in office, Jefferson was as good as his word. At the very outset of his administration, he worked out a plan of strict fiscal austerity with his talented and diligent Treasury secretary, Albert Gallatin. In his first message to Congress, he issued a successful call for immediate tax relief. Specifically, Jefferson requested and received the repeal of all internal taxation. According to the plan he had worked out with Gallatin, tariffs alone would be "sufficient to provide for the government" and finance the debt. Jefferson was right. Further, eliminating all internal taxes was not only fiscally sound, it was also, not surprisingly, quite popular with the rural majority of Americans. Only the American people could judge "whether we have done well or ill" in repealing taxes, but Jefferson had little reason to doubt their approval.[179]

What made cutting taxes so impressive was that Jefferson did it at the same time that he paid off the national debt. He devoted almost $7.5 million, nearly three-quarters of the federal budget, to paying off the $83 million the United States owed when he took office. After interest, all of that sum was used to redeem principal, and by the end of his second term he reported that he had retired a little more than $33.5 million of the debt, the maximum amount permitted by law. Thus, despite tacking on an additional $15 million with the Louisiana Purchase, Jefferson had actually shrunk the national debt by one-third. Moreover, redeeming principal reduced future interest payments, allowing even greater payments of principal and thus even greater reductions in interest. By the end of his first term, this effect was becoming, as Jefferson noted, "already sensible" in the federal budget. Two years later it led Jefferson to urge Congress to begin planning for the budget surpluses that were inevitably on their way. This was the sort of fiscal problem that presidents dream about.[180]

To pay for his tax breaks and debt retirement, Jefferson slashed federal spending. In his first year in office he cut $1 million, a reduction of more than one-quarter of the domestic budget. "We are hunting out and abolishing multitudes of useless offices," Jefferson wrote his son-in-law in the summer of 1801. Jefferson slashed the diplomatic corps in Europe by half, closing embassies in Prussia, the Netherlands, and Portugal. The elimination of internal taxes eradicated nearly four hundred Treasury officers, and the repeal of judicial offices Adams had filled in the final weeks of his presidency further streamlined the federal payroll. The vast bulk of Jefferson's savings, however, came from the military. Instead of a costly standing army, the American people would rely on "a well-organized and armed militia" as "their best security" against both foreign invasion and domestic usurpation. As for the navy, Jefferson claimed that all that was needed was "a small force" of agile ships for "service in the Mediterranean" against North African piracy. If frugality was the mark of wisdom in government, Jefferson's administration was remarkably sagacious.[181]

The success of Jefferson's policy of fiscal austerity was rooted, in his mind at least, in its adherence to libertarian principle. A small government on a shoestring budget could not form designs on the liberty of the people. Government was a necessary evil, and that one which governed least governed best. This was true not only politically and socially but economically as well. "Agriculture, manufactures, commerce, and navigation," what Jefferson considered "the four pillars of our prosperity," were "most thriving when left most free to individual enterprise." It was his practice of laissez-faire, Jefferson believed, that sustained the economic growth of the nation, which in turn assured its government's fiscal solvency. It did not hurt that the early corporate and business structures of the nation had already taken firm root during the Federalist era, and that the resumption of the Napoleonic Wars in his first term sparked a dramatic expansion of the American neutral carrying trade. Nonetheless, his fiscal achievement was real and its results impressive.[182]

At the same time, Jeffersonian austerity had some troubling implications. In purely sectional terms, abolishing internal taxes meant shifting the entire tax burden of the nation to the commerce of the northern seaports. It was bad enough that the carriage tax had been repealed at the behest of the Old Dominion's squires, but the whiskey tax, finally being collected and promising "in some measure to equalize the northern and southern burdens," was also repealed. For how long could the free states of the North, "who possess so prodigious a preponderance of white population, of industry, commerce, and civilization over the Southern," be expected to "remain subject to Virginia"? These were the sorts of questions that Jeffersonian policies raised with northern Federalists, and at alarming frequency at that.[183]

Jefferson's frugality also had a powerful economic impact, especially on urban commerce. Although Jefferson made his deepest budget cuts in the military, the lion's share of those were in the new navy that Adams and Stoddert had so carefully nurtured. Indeed, so clearly was Jefferson bent on gutting the navy that he had a very hard time finding anyone willing to head it. Adams had bequeathed him a fleet of thirteen frigates with an additional six heavy men-of-war under construction. Jefferson immediately canceled construction of the new heavy ships, sold off all but six of the frigates, and left the remainder "to rot in drydock." Instead, Jefferson preferred light "sloops-of-war" and tiny gunboats for harbor defense. Eliminating any meaningful naval presence in the Atlantic and Caribbean meant denying American commerce any protection in those waters. That inevitably drove insurance costs up and profit margins down. In Jefferson's first three years in office, the value of American exports fell by roughly $40 million or 40 percent, and only the resumption of war in Europe revived American commerce during Jefferson's tenure.[184]

The most profound implication of Jeffersonian finance, however, was constitutional. When Hamilton had first projected an energetic and active federal government, his purpose was not merely to enact particular programs; he also sought to legitimize the government itself. Once the American people came to see that their central government provided them with tangible benefits without threatening their liberties, they would gradually accept the reality and legitimate authority of that state as the source of their prosperity and the bulwark of their freedom. Jeffersonian government completely reversed that process. Most benefits were once again relegated to the states, and people came to expect their central government to supply little and demand less.

In both relative and absolute terms, the federal government shrank dramatically under the rule of Jefferson and his successors in the Virginia dynasty. Indeed, by the 1830s the emasculated federal government had retired its debt and faced the problem of what to spend its revenues on; Jefferson had seen that day coming as early as 1806. Internal improvements and public education seemed the best objects in his eyes, but his hard-won diminution of federal authority in the domestic sphere led him to conclude that the Constitution would have to be amended first "because the objects now recommended are not among those enumerated in the constitution." As Hamilton had seen before, constitutional interpretation would ultimately hinge on public opinion, and that opinion would rest on experience and expectations. The experience of Jeffersonian government led the American people to expect little intrusion from their collective government and to see such intrusions as extraconstitutional. Those expectations would not give way until the Civil War. Some still persist to this day.[185]

Agrarian Expansion: The Louisiana Purchase

No principle was more vital to the Jeffersonian vision of America than agrarianism. Rural life was simple and natural, imbuing the breast with morally elevated sentiments. A society of self-reliant yeomen maximized human happiness and dignity in a civilized setting. Agrarianism was also vital to republican government itself, producing a vigilant and independent citizenry. "Our governments will remain virtuous," Jefferson assured Madison, "as long as they are chiefly agricultural." They would remain agricultural only "as long as there shall be vacant lands" for Americans to take up "in any part of America." To assure the availability of such "vacant lands," Jefferson devoted the considerable energies of his administration and the nation to westward expansion. The capstone of these efforts was, of course, the Louisiana Purchase of 1803, which doubled the size of the national domain. The greatest diplomatic triumph in the early republic, and possibly the biggest real estate bargain in recorded history, the Louisiana Purchase ensured the future agrarian character of Jefferson's empire of liberty. It was, without question, the greatest achievement of his presidency.[186]

There is a curious irony about the Louisiana Purchase. Jefferson's vast acquisition was, at first glance at least, largely fortuitous. He had not even considered purchasing fresh territory west of the Mississippi. Nor would Napoleon have ever consented to make the offer, had disease and insurgency not foiled his attempt to recapture Haiti, the key to his plans for a revived French empire in the Americas. As war with England loomed, Napoleon decided to unload his vast domains in North America to the United States for ready cash rather than see them fall to British arms poised in Canada. Yet to see Jefferson's triumph as solely the result of luck would be to woefully diminish his achievement. The Virginian got the bargain he did because he put his administration in a position to take advantage of it, and because he acted promptly and decisively when the opportunity presented itself. When it came to westward expansion, Thomas Jefferson made his own luck.[187]

In fact, the Louisiana Purchase was only part of Jefferson's policy of agrarian expansion, albeit a dramatic one. Much of his labor was directed at acquiring lands east of the Mississippi. At the time, most of the territory west of the Appalachians was "unsettled," which is to say occupied by Amerindians. In the first half of the 1790s, the Federalists had abandoned the project of conquest in the trans-Appalachian interior and adopted a policy of "civilization," which assured Amerindian land titles and offered tribal communities education as well as training in agriculture. Jefferson embraced the lineaments of the Federalist program—but as a means of Indian removal. Training Amerindians in husbandry was desirable because it "will enable them to live on smaller portions of land," happily freeing up land for white settlement. Trading posts were used to "promote this disposition" by getting Amerindians into debt. "That is the way I intend to git there countrey," Jefferson reportedly declared, for once they were in debt, they would have no choice but "to give there lands for payment." Jefferson's aggressive policies netted almost 200,000 square miles of Amerindian lands in trans-Appalachia, far more than necessary for "the immediate needs of the expanding white population." Nor was the pattern of these acquisitions random. Jefferson pursued what one historian has described as "essentially a military strategy." By focusing his purchases on the Ohio and Mississippi Rivers, Jefferson was able to "secure the supply lines and encircle the enemy." As the president put it, "our settlement will gradually circumscribe and approach the Indians," who would be forced to abandon their tribal identities and "incorporate with us" or face inevitable expulsion "beyond the Mississippi."[188]

Jefferson had once, like Rousseau, celebrated Amerindian society as a happier, golden age of noble savagery, but when its future hung in the balance with agrarian expansion, Jefferson promptly "divested his mind," in Dumas Malone's stately phrase, "of the sentimentality he had previously manifested toward the American aborigines." Jefferson had begun the process of Indian removal that Andrew Jackson would so tragically complete.[189]

As far as the Louisiana Purchase is concerned, Jefferson had not looked beyond the Mississippi, but he had for some time been keenly interested in New Orleans and West Florida (the gulf coast regions of Alabama and Mississippi). The former was particularly vital as the commercial bottleneck of the trans-Appalachian West. For all his paeans to the independent yeoman, Jefferson recognized that most American farmers could never be induced to settle the West without access to international markets. As early as 1786 he had insisted that "the navigation of the Mississippi we must have," and when it was finally secured by the Treaty of San Lorenzo in 1795, his worst fears for the West were allayed. Now possessed of the right to deposit goods in New Orleans without paying custom duties, western farmers would have easy access to European markets. As long as that city remained a possession of enfeebled Spain, Jefferson was sanguine for the future. As he informed his territorial governor of Mississippi, it would be a source of "extreme pain" should a more powerful state be "substituted for them." The fruit of the West could safely ripen on the Spanish vine until an expanding United States was ready to pluck it.[190]

Shortly after his inauguration, Jefferson's worst fears were realized. By late spring of 1801 he learned that Spain had secretly agreed to cede Louisiana, with its capital New Orleans, to France the previous October by the Treaty of San Ildefonso. While not yet executed, Jefferson considered this transfer "very ominous to us." France was a great world power, and wresting territorial concessions from her would be far more difficult than from the relatively weak and impotent Spanish. Jefferson's concerns turned to alarm that October when the Spanish Intendant of New Orleans revoked the right of deposit. The president wasted little time in getting congressional authorization to dispatch James Monroe to Paris to purchase New Orleans and the Floridas—the latter of which Jefferson erroneously assumed was part of the Spanish cession—for roughly $10 million. By the time Monroe arrived, Napoleon had countered with an offer of the entire Louisiana territory for a mere $5 million more.[191]

That Jefferson did not envision, much less propose, the bargain he received is undeniable. But he would never have secured it if he had not acted promptly to get prior congressional authorization to enter negotiations after the closure of New Orleans. Nor was the need for such negotiations so obvious as to be a foregone conclusion. The closure of New Orleans was an inconvenience, but it did not stop American commerce down the Mississippi; Americans could still legally trade directly with ships in the harbor, and Spanish custom officials were easily bribed. In any event, the closure was revoked by the following spring. Jefferson acted so decisively because the issue mattered deeply to him, and he saw an opportunity to take advantage of the delicate position France was in due to its failure to recapture Haiti. And if his negotiations had not borne fruit, he would have persisted in his extralegal efforts to secure New Orleans. Indeed, before he learned of the bonanza that Monroe and Robert R. Livingston, the American minister to France, had been offered in Paris, Jefferson confessed that his confidence lay not in negotiations but "in the policy of putting off the day of contention" until the nation "shall have planted such a population on the Mississippi as will be able to do their own business." That business was, of course, filibustering, whereby American settlers engaged in "unauthorized" conquest of foreign territory.[192]

A successful filibuster undoubtedly entered into the future French emperor's deliberations, and in the years following Jefferson's initial westward thrust, filibustering would become an honored strategy of territorial expansion, especially among southerners. Much of the Floridas was acquired by filibustering, and the entire settlement and incorporation of Texas was one grand filibuster. Even if Napoleon had utterly refused to enter into the negotiations with the American envoys, the United States would have eventually acquired most of Louisiana anyway, as long as the nation pursued Jeffersonian policies.

Great bargain that it was, the Louisiana Purchase was not without its costs, even for Jefferson. Adding even the marginal sum involved to the national debt was a painful act for a president as committed to fiscal austerity as he. The foreign customs of Louisianans and their lack of any experience with republican government forced him to abandon his democratic principles. The regime he imposed on that territory was thoroughly autocratic. Jefferson's chosen governor ruled with the advice of a council of notables comprised of thirteen wealthy individuals chosen by the president. There were no popular elections, and jury trials were reserved for capital cases. The greatest sacrifice Jefferson made for Louisiana, however, was in his principle of strict construction of the Constitution. That document was notably silent about the acquisition of fresh territories, and by his own reckoning his land transaction did not pass constitutional muster. Initially, Jefferson favored a constitutional amendment that would authorize the purchase ex post facto. But when he learned in August that Napoleon would rescind the treaty if it were not ratified within the next few months, Jefferson swallowed his constitutional scruples entirely. "I infer that the less we say about constitutional difficulties respecting Louisiana the better," he wrote to Madison, "and that what is necessary for surmounting them must be done sub silentio." Principle might inform, but it rarely dictated policy in Jefferson's Romantic political practice.[193]

The Louisiana Purchase may have been a remarkable diplomatic triumph, but it was not met with universal approval. Many northerners, especially those from New England, objected to the transaction. In his second inaugural, Jefferson tried to cast those northern fears as concern for the union and the effective operation of "the federative principle." In point of fact, however, northerners feared the effect that westward expansion would have on the nation's economy. Settlement of the trans-Mississippi West would draw population and capital away from commercial development and positively hinder industrialization. To many northerners, Federalist or otherwise, the Louisiana Purchase represented the complete negation of the enlightened, pro-urban, and commercial policies that Hamilton had championed during the previous decade, policies that had secured their prosperity and attached them to the union.[194]

It was not primarily the extent of the Louisiana Purchase that troubled northerners. Their most frequent and pointed objection—one that Jefferson never acknowledged—was that the incorporation of the new territories into the union would extend slavery and thereby upset the political balance between the free North and the slave South. This was no idle fear. Slavery had been a conspicuous element in the lower Mississippi valley since its first settlement, but only in the last decades of the eighteenth century did it give rise to a full-blown slave society. Spurred by booms in cotton and sugar cultivation, Louisiana's planter elite gobbled up huge tracts of land and imported throngs of African bondsmen to work them. Of the fifty thousand residents of the territory Jefferson acquired, at least half were slaves, and in the more settled areas near New Orleans they represented a clear majority of the population. Congressional attempts to limit slave importations into the new territory had to be promptly repealed in the face of local howls of protest and threats of secession. To make matters worse, Jefferson proposed turning the entire region north of the Arkansas River into a huge Indian reserve for the resettlement of those tribes remaining east of the Mississippi. The implication was patently clear. The future states carved out of the Louisiana Purchase would all be exclusively of the slave variety, ensuring both the spread of the peculiar institution and the dominance of the South in national affairs. "Louisiana is to be a field of blood before it is a cultured field," predicted one gloomy Federalist in the summer of 1803, "and indeed a field of blood while it is cultivated." Such prognostications were tragically prophetic.[195]

"Peaceable Coercion": The Great Embargo

Fiscal austerity, agrarian expansion, and a commercial policy of "honest friendship with all nations" without "entangling alliances" were the three principal goals Jefferson set for his administration when he took office. He achieved the first two goals in his first term. Both had been singular successes. Peace, prosperity, and low taxes had been the promise of a Republican administration, and Jefferson assuredly delivered. His reelection was one of the most lopsided in American history. The Sage of Monticello garnered all but fourteen of the 176 electoral votes. The practice of Jeffersonian government had been an unqualified success.[196]

Jefferson's last four years in office were devoted to achieving his third and final objective, an open and reciprocal trade with the world. The spreading Napoleonic Wars in Europe prompted both major belligerents to squeeze neutral shipping, and as more countries were drawn into the fray, the pressure on the American carrying trade became increasingly intense. By the middle of his second term, Jefferson faced a full-blown commercial and diplomatic crisis that endangered the nation's prosperity and threatened to draw it into war. The policy Jefferson pursued, the Great Embargo, was designed to gain recognition of American maritime rights without spilling blood. For the final fourteen months of his administration, American ports would be closed to the world. It was a principled course of action that drew on well-established Republican doctrine. It was also an unmitigated disaster.

Both belligerents infringed on American shipping in the years after 1803, but because Great Britain was the master of the seas—especially after Nelson's stunning victory at Trafalgar—she was the greater threat to American vessels. By far the most contentious issue with Britain concerned American rights to neutral shipping. The so-called carrying trade had been protected by the Jay Treaty, but when those provisions expired in 1805, a British Admiralty Court handed down a decision in the *Essex* case in late July that effectively banned the trade altogether. Even more stringent orders in council were issued in the following two years, clearly intended to drive American merchants from a lucrative trade that had buoyed the American economy. Almost as galling as British seizures of American ships was their practice of impressment. Madison estimated that between the outbreak of war in 1803 and March 1806, at least twenty-two hundred men had been seized from American vessels and held as "deserters" from the Royal Navy. Such acts of force, sometimes with loss of life to American sailors, were an invitation to war.[197]

Yet Jefferson avoided open conflict. A nonimportation act against Great Britain was passed in 1806, but Jefferson suspended its operation in the hope of a diplomatic settlement. Such hopes became dimmer, however, after the HMS *Leopard* fired on, boarded, and impressed four seamen from the United States frigate *Chesapeake* off Norfolk in June 1807. Jefferson responded with an angry proclamation banning all vessels of the British navy from American waters. In early autumn Jefferson's old nemesis, the British monarch George III, ordered his officers to "enforce impressments rigorously over neutral merchant vessels," most of which were American. Napoleon followed suit by extending his blockade of the British Isles to American shipping. As Jefferson saw it, the nation was faced with a terrible dilemma. If she submitted to this degrading treatment, she would lose all international standing and self-respect. If she took up arms, she would be dragged into an international struggle that would cost dearly in blood and treasure. Faced with these untenable alternatives, Jefferson chose a third course, one that would secure American rights without risking American lives. On December 18, 1807, he asked Congress to order an embargo on all American trade. Four days later he signed the measure into law. America was closed for business.[198]

Jefferson did have one other option: to try to make a commercial treaty with Great Britain. In the closing months of 1806 Jefferson's envoys to the Court of St. James had negotiated just such an agreement. Like the Jay Treaty before it, the Monroe-Pinckney Treaty was far from perfect. The British would tolerate American neutral commerce only for the duration of the present struggle, and there was no mention of impressments. An explanatory note, however, promised that the offensive practice would be restricted to British ports, which was a substantial concession.[199]

Jefferson rejected the treaty out of hand, refusing even to send it to the Senate. Impressment was the "sine qua non" of any agreement with

Great Britain, and he was convinced that the American people "would rather go on without a treaty than with one which does not settle this article." Why Jefferson should have laid such stress on impressment is not clear. The use of press gangs to fill the ranks of the Royal Navy was a time-honored practice, and Great Britain could hardly abandon it now that she was caught in a life-and-death struggle. Nor were these "habitual wrongs" quite so glaring as Jefferson declared. Many sailors on American vessels were, in fact, British deserters; his own secretary of the Treasury, Albert Gallatin, estimated that they comprised over one-third of the nation's sailors. All in all, the Monroe-Pinckney Treaty was a good pact, although not a great one. Jefferson rejected it because he thought he could get an even better one. The Virginian would extract concessions without firing a shot. Jefferson was ready to practice "peaceable coercion."[200]

An outgrowth of the doctrine of discriminatory tariffs that Madison had proposed at the outset of Washington's first administration, Jefferson's practice of peaceable coercion had a long and distinguished Republican pedigree. It was rooted in the conviction that the United States could impose trade policy on the major European powers, particularly Great Britain, by "withholding or restraining its commerce" with them. This was, of course, the tactic the patriots had used in their struggle against imperial oppression in the years before independence. That the Continental Association, using this tactic, had failed to move British policy in the mid-1770s was no reason to assume it wouldn't work now. American commerce had grown steadily, and the American market for British manufactures was even more vital to that country's economy since the Napoleonic Wars had interdicted its trade with the Continent. The commercial power of the United States became a more potent weapon with each passing year, if only the government had the wisdom to use it. If Jefferson could force a settlement "during the present paroxysm of the insanity of Europe" by withholding American trade, he would have secured the nation's future prosperity without hazarding the present peace. More important, his experiment would prove to all the world that the defense of the natural rights of commerce did not require the madness of war but could be secured by "those peaceable coercions which are in the power of every nation." It was a noble experiment that the great Romantic visionary entered into with the highest hopes.[201]

Perhaps the most glaring problem with Jefferson's peaceable coercion was its economic impact at home. Without question the Great Embargo hurt Britain, but not nearly as much as it hurt America. Closing American commerce sent all sectors of the American economy into a precipitous decline. Without the support of international demand, prices for agricultural products plummeted. Stay laws had to be passed in several states to keep farms from being seized for debts and mortgages foreclosed. Predictably, the suffering was worst in the urban seaports of the north. Grass reportedly grew along the desolate wharves of Boston. In May 1808 one visitor to Manhattan observed more than eighty bankruptcies in that month alone, with debtors imprisoned by the hundreds. Thousands more were unemployed. All told, some thirty thousand American sailors lost their jobs, as did another one hundred thousand workers in ancillary maritime trades. By the time the embargo of 1808–9 had run its course, business activity in the United States had declined by over 75 percent. In purely economic terms, Thomas Jefferson had cut off his nation's nose to spite Great Britain's face.[202]

Almost as troubling as the economic devastation wrought by the embargo was the difficulty of enforcing it. Sounding more than a bit like his old enemy Hamilton, Jefferson explained to his Treasury secretary that "Congress must legalize all *means* which may be necessary to obtain its *end.*" In all, Congress passed four more embargo acts in the course of 1808 to do so. In response to illicit trade, coastal shippers were required to post bond of double the value of their ships and cargo before clearing customs, and penalties were dramatically increased for those in violation of the law. When others circumvented these restrictions by transporting American produce by land—a lively trade with Canada was sprouting up in the Lake Champlain area of upstate New York—Jefferson responded with yet stiffer penalties and an additional act in March that explicitly outlawed the overland trade.[203]

When the residents of upstate New York, like the Whiskey Rebels before them, dared to resist federal Treasury officials with force, Jefferson responded on April 19 by declaring the entire Lake Champlain region in a state of insurrection. Gallatin promptly called in the army, and the area was placed under military rule, an occupation that lasted until Jefferson left office. By that point the president had been authorized by Congress to use military force whenever and however he thought expedient. Customs officials were empowered to search and seize property anywhere in the nation without warrant or any restraints of due process. In pursuit of peaceable coercion, Jefferson had been forced to intrude in the lives of Americans in a fashion that was far more draconian than anything Hamilton and his hated Federalists could ever have envisioned, much less attempted.

The biggest problem with Jefferson's Great Embargo, however, was that it was utterly ineffective. The president grossly overestimated the importance of American commerce to the British economy. Nor was that nation, in any event, even remotely likely to surrender a perceived advantage in a struggle for its very survival. The depths of Jefferson's miscalculation became evident after Congress authorized him in April 1808 to lift the embargo against whichever belligerent relented in its assault on American commerce. To sweeten the deal, Jefferson instructed his ministers in London and Paris to dangle the possibility of a military alliance with the first power to recognize America's commercial rights; if either party "shall have withdrawn, and the other not, we must declare war against the other." That summer he learned of Napoleon's response. In his humiliating Bayonne Decree, the French emperor announced that he would help the beleaguered president enforce his embargo by peremptorily seizing all American shipping.[204]

Peaceable coercion had been a complete fiasco. Unfortunately, the more obvious that conclusion became, the more deeply Jefferson committed himself to the embargo. Gripped by an idée fixe, the president buried himself in the minutiae of enforcement, personally inspecting each request for grain and flour shipments to famished American ports. If only the embargo could be more rigorously enforced, he thought, it would undoubtedly work its magic on the courts of Europe. Why Jefferson, who had been so pragmatic in his previous practice, should have resorted to rigid dogmatism now is a matter for speculation. Perhaps he felt the principle was so vital and central to his overall vision that to abandon it would violate his most cherished convictions. With his second term winding down, he may also have wanted one last great achievement to set as a capstone to his legacy. That the potential costs of the policy would have accrued primarily to northern commercial centers undoubtedly mitigated the risks in his mind. In any event, by the time he left office he seemed, to many Americans at least, more a narrow-minded crank than a visionary statesman.

Jefferson paid dearly for his disastrous embargo. Peaceable coercion breathed new life into the moribund Federalists, particularly in New England. The author of the Kentucky Resolutions was hoisted by his own petard by the legislature of Massachusetts, which resolved that the Embargo Acts were an egregious violation of the most basic civil liberties and therefore "unconstitutional, and not legally binding." Connecticut followed suit, pledging "to abstain from any agency in the execution" of laws that were clearly "unconstitutional and despotic." A small band of hyper-Republican purists from Virginia known as "Quids" and led by the mercurial John Randolph broke with the administration over its violation of civil rights during the embargo as well as its previous handling of a convoluted land deal in Georgia. Most ominous of all was the predicament of northern Republicans, who were forced to defend a policy that their constituents universally despised. Jefferson's southern strategy was sorely strained. The president compounded all these problems by abdicating all leadership and responsibility in November once he learned of Madison's electoral victory. Gallatin and President-elect Madison pleaded with him to take up the party reins and "point out to them some precise and distinct course," but Jefferson was intransigent.[205]

The most he would do was intimate that a repeal of the embargo effective the following summer would be acceptable. That would give the nation sufficient time to arm itself for war, for the nation would now have to defend "by force our right of navigation" against the British. At last the dam broke. Northern Republicans joined forces with Quids and Federalists to force repeal on March 4, the very day Jefferson's term expired. No measures were taken to prepare for war. Once Britain learned of the repeal and Jefferson was safely out of office, it relaxed the most stringent orders in April. The final and utter defeat of peaceable coercion marked the closing act of Jefferson's presidency.[206]

Jefferson never did acknowledge the failure of his embargo. Culpability lay exclusively with the handful of Federalists who, "during their short lived ascendancy," forced the repeal of the embargo and thus "inflicted a wound on our interests which can never be healed." Circumstances had conspired to undermine what he was convinced was a sound and humane policy. Fortune had abandoned him.[207]

As was so often the case in his career, however, Jefferson made his own luck. His dismantling of the navy positively invited foreign depredations. Had he embraced the Monroe-Pinckney Treaty, he could have spared his nation great economic suffering and secured terms far superior to those it was ultimately forced to accept. By rejecting it, he steered the nation on a pointless and insipid course of military collision with Great Britain that within a few years would leave the country's capital a burning ruin and New England on the verge of disunion. Had he relented once the failure of peaceable coercion was evident in the summer of 1808, he might still have been able to hold his party together and heal the wounds of his nation. Instead he pursued his course with dogged, if not fanatical, relentlessness. For all his characteristic vanity, John Adams was all too accurate when he told Benjamin Rush that their mutual friend, the great Romantic visionary Thomas Jefferson, "leaves the government infinitely worse than he found it, and that from his own error or ignorance." For once, Adams had the last laugh.[208]

The Last Campaign:
Slavery, States' Rights, and Southern Education

For Thomas Jefferson, the prospect of retirement was always more alluring than the reality. The years following his presidency were no exception. Surrounded by his grandchildren and his beloved daughter Martha, Jefferson was a loving if controlling patriarch. The Sage of

Monticello cherished his family circle, yet it was not a bed of roses. His two sons-in-law were not on speaking terms, and the husband of one granddaughter almost stabbed Jefferson's grandson, Jefferson Randolph, to death in a street brawl. His immense epistolary exchanges gave more pleasure than they generated. He devoted his energies to putting his plantations and finances in order, but a national financial collapse in 1819 ruined any prospect of rescuing his property from creditors after his death. More than anything, Jefferson missed the challenge and excitement of the political fray.

Even in retirement, of course, Jefferson was far from inactive. Five years into his retirement he was placed on the board of a proposed secondary school in Charlottesville. Within another five years he had transformed it into a proposed university, one whose magnificent buildings he designed and over whose subsequent inauguration he would preside as its rector. The Sage of Monticello also kept abreast of political affairs, offering counsel to his fellow dynasts Madison and Monroe while maintaining a truly staggering correspondence with political associates and disciples. Not all the developments in the young republic met with his approval. Madison's abandonment of the issue of impressment with the British in the Treaty of Ghent, which ended the War of 1812, and his rechartering of Hamilton's dreaded Bank of the United States were both disappointments, as was the unchecked reign of John Marshall's Federalist influence in the judiciary. Talk of federal internal improvements during Monroe's administration was hardly heartening, suggesting as it did a backsliding from the pure doctrines of strict construction. But throughout the first decade of his retirement, Jefferson's qualms and efforts were private. Well into his seventies and increasingly frail, he was happy to leave the politics of principle to the rising generation.

In 1819 Jefferson's complacency came to an abrupt end when the repose of his retirement was disturbed by "a fire bell in the night." That alarm "awakened and filled me with terror," he wrote in early 1820, because he "considered it at once as the knell of the Union." The "Missouri question," as he referred to it, was "the most portentous one which ever yet threatened our Union," and he bitterly confessed to Adams that

351

"I thank god that I shall not live to witness its issue." The refusal of northern congressmen to admit Missouri to the union as a slave state, and their extraction of a compromise that ostensibly set a limit to the expansion of slavery in the western territories of the Louisiana Purchase, shook the Sage of Monticello to the very roots of his being. The empire of liberty he had labored so hard to nurture and grow was now threatened by the hateful institution that he had failed to eradicate. The paradox he elided by rhetorical sleights of hand had come home to roost. Drowning in debt amid his contentious descendants, the Virginian gathered his waning energies for one last campaign.[209]

Jefferson utterly denied that the Missouri question had anything to do with slavery. "The cession of that kind of property," he assured one northern republican, "is a bagatelle" whose eradication "would not cost me a second thought." That was, of course, if it took the form of gradual emancipation and colonization. One thing was certain, however: "permitting the slaves of the south to spread into the west will not add one being to that unfortunate condition." As early as 1807, Jefferson had hailed the benefits of transporting slaves into the Louisiana territories. "By dividing that evil," he explained to John Dickinson, the diffusion of slavery "would lessen its danger" in the more established Atlantic states. Now he went further. Spreading slavery actually benefited the enslaved. Exactly how this forced separation from kith and kin would achieve such a result was never explained, but he was certain nonetheless that "their happiness would be increased." What was more, the diffusion of slavery would "facilitate the means of getting finally rid of it." Spreading slavery to the West "will dilute the evil everywhere," and "by dividing the burthen on a greater number of coadjutors," the expansion of slavery would "proportionally facilitate" its own eradication. Contrary to the hypocritical posturing of northern "anti-slavery" congressmen, the true opponents of slavery were those who opposed its containment. "If there were any morality in the question," Jefferson insisted, "it is on the other side."[210]

In Jefferson's view, the real object of opponents to Missouri's admission as a slave state was power, pure and simple. His old enemies the

Federalists—officially defunct—were the real culprits. Seizing on an issue with "just enough of the semblance of morality to throw dust into the eyes of the people and fanaticise them," northern Federalist wolves in Republican guise sought to ride the Missouri controversy back into power. In fact, the whole issue smacked of a sectional power grab by the northern states, a mere "trick of hypocrisy." The callous sectionalism of northern Federalists was endangering the future of the union. "A geographical line, coinciding with a marked principle, moral and political," Jefferson feared, "will never be obliterated." Indeed, "every new irritation will mark it deeper and deeper" until the nation was rent asunder. "My only consolation is," he sighed, "that I live not to weep over it."[211]

The Missouri controversy may have been a power grab by northerners, but for southerners like Jefferson "it is a question of existence." Once empowered to curtail the spread of slavery, the northern majority in Congress could next abolish slavery without colonizing the freedmen, ignoring the realities of racial difference that Jefferson had labored to establish. The inevitable result of such a dangerous and irresponsible act would be miscegenation and racial war. "The real question" for southerners then was "Are our slaves to be presented with freedom and a dagger?" For Jefferson, the Missouri question wasn't about slavery; it was about race. Disunion and civil war were looming, and with them the prospect of a racial conflagration. The Missouri controversy represented the culmination of all his darkest fears.[212]

The Missouri question roused the aged statesman from his retirement, but it was not the sole object of his concern. The hypocritical antislavery agitation was part of a larger scheme to undermine Republican principles and bring back the failed policies of Hamiltonianism. The ultimate "line of division," Jefferson claimed in 1823, was between the true Republicans committed to "the preservation of State rights as reserved in the constitution" and crypto-Federalists who seek "to merge all into a consolidated government." The principles of strict construction and states' rights that Jefferson held so vital to constitutional government were under assault once again. The "subtle corps of sappers and miners" in this nefarious campaign was the federal judiciary, which was "con-

stantly working under ground to undermine the foundations of our confederated fabric" by "construing our constitution from a co-ordination
of a general and special government to a general and supreme one
alone." If Congress could not stand up to this threat, "the States must
shield themselves, and meet the invader foot to foot." Congressional
warnings should be the first line of defense against the pretended independence of the judiciary, but if these were ignored the legislature
should immediately "impeach and set the whole adrift." Alternately,
it might limit future judicial appointments to a term of six years "with
a re-appointmentability by the president with the approbation of *both*
houses." In any event, Jefferson utterly denied the judiciary had any
special provenance in matters of constitutional interpretation. Each
branch of government had an "equal right" to interpret that document,
"especially where it is to act ultimately and without appeal." For Thomas Jefferson, John Marshall's decision in *Marbury v. Madison* had settled nothing.[213]

Within Congress, consolidators took up the cry of protective tariffs
and internal improvements. Both of these policies were popular in the
West, and that section's unnatural schism from "the agricultural States"
of the South had fortified "the manufacturing and consolidating parties"
of the North. Tariffs and internal improvements were, of course,
merely the opening wedge of the drive for complete federal consolidation. Once that wall had been breached, the northern crypto-Federalists
would soon enact "whatever they shall think, or pretend will be for the
general welfare." An aristocracy, "founded on banking institutions" and
other commercial and industrial combinations ruling over "the plun-
dered ploughman and beggared yeomanry," would be the result. Consolidation was thus "a next best blessing to the monarchy of their first
aim, and perhaps the surest stepping-stone to it." It represented the re-
suscitation of the Hamiltonian politics of Enlightenment that promoted
commercial and industrial development over agrarian expansion and urban plutocracy over rural egalitarianism. "I scarcely know myself which
is most to be deprecated," he wrote in 1822, "a consolidation, or disso-

lution of the States. The horrors of both are beyond the reach of human foresight." Three years later his doubts were gone: consolidation was the greater threat. As he had made clear in his Kentucky Resolutions of 1798, the purity of Republican government was always more important than the coalition of the independent states.[214]

The principles and positions Jefferson articulated in his last campaign were no longer merely Republican. Rent as that party was by northern heretics, Jefferson's posture was now purely southern. His defense of the diffusion of slavery may have fallen short of that of subsequent pro-slavery "fire-eaters," but only by a matter of degree. His unflinching opposition to internal improvements and protective tariffs, like his dogged defense of states' rights, soon became the stock and trade of southern ultras like John C. Calhoun and his fellow nullifiers in South Carolina. Jefferson was, after all, first and foremost a Virginian, and when he saw his region and its interests jeopardized, he did not hesitate to rise to their defense. As in his previous opposition in the 1790s, Jefferson used his pen as his political sword, striking a chord of principled defiance. He wrote to newspaper publishers, suggesting editorial policies and issues for journalistic analysis and exegesis. He even drafted a fresh set of resolves for the Virginia legislature in 1825, protesting consolidation along the same lines he had laid out in his Kentucky Resolutions of 1798. Fortunately, Madison talked him out of submitting it. But this time Jefferson had one more resource at his disposal, one that could help fortify the southern opposition for its coming battles in the ensuing decades, if not generations. That resource was the University of Virginia.[215]

His last great labor of love, the university Jefferson created in Charlottesville not more than four miles from his home served a variety of purposes for the Sage of Monticello. Its physical design gave vent to his artistic genius in a display of grandeur and vision that marked the pinnacle of his architectural achievement. Its ambitious and modern curriculum expressed the broad range of his voracious intellectual appetite, from sciences natural and social to arts linguistic and plastic. But in the final campaign of his closing years, the University of Virginia also served a vital political purpose. Jefferson's institution of higher learning would "expound the principles and structure of government" and inculcate "a sound spirit of legislation" based on personal liberty and states' rights. Equally important, it would "form statesmen, legislators and judges" who would ensure future "prosperity and individual happiness." The University of Virginia would provide a southern education.[216]

Jefferson had long seen the need for southern education. Sending southern youths to Harvard or Princeton filled them with "opinions and principles in discord with those of their own country." This was a "canker" on the body politic "eating on the vitals of our existence, and if not arrested at once, will be beyond remedy." That remedy, of course, was the southern education afforded by the university in Charlottesville. "It is in our Seminary," he wrote to Madison, that the "vestal flame" of true Republican principles "is to be kept alive." From that seminary those principles would "spread anew over our own and the sister states."[217]

The key to the propagation of wholesome Republican doctrines at the University of Virginia was the school of law. The professor of that school was responsible for far more than legal training. He was also required to offer instruction in history, international relations, political theory, and economics. "In the selection of our Law Professor we must be rigorously attentive to his political principles," he insisted to fellow trustee James Madison. Those principles included far more than a commitment to popular or representative government. Any law professor at the university must be committed to a strict construction of the Constitution that clearly proscribed internal improvements and judicial supremacy. Teaching the law also required obeisance to the compact theory of the Constitution and the doctrine of states' rights expressed in the Virginia and Kentucky Resolutions. More than anything, however, the professor of law would have to be a true Virginian and thoroughly orthodox on the Missouri question.[218]

Not content with a test of doctrinal purity for the faculty, Jefferson proposed personally prescribing the political curriculum of the university. Although the Sage of Monticello generally favored allowing each professor to choose his own texts and course of lectures, when it came to the professorship of law he told Madison that "I think we are the best judges." Despite Jefferson's urging, Madison was not willing to actually ban books from an institution of higher learning, but he agreed to a set of suggested texts. The "general principles of liberty" were found in the works of the great seventeenth-century Whigs John Locke and Algernon Sidney. The principles of American union should be limned from the Declaration of Independence, just as those of the Constitution were found in the *The Federalist*. The correct principles of constitutional interpretation were to be extracted from Madison's Virginia Resolutions of 1799, and "political lessons of peculiar value" might be absorbed from Washington's Farewell Address. These were the works that the two Virginia dynasts demanded "shall be used as the texts and documents" of the school of law.[219]

The system of political indoctrination that Jefferson and Madison devised for the University of Virginia would, as they hoped, inform the outlook of generations of southern leaders and statesmen. The system in fact cropped up throughout southern institutions of higher learning in the decades leading up to the Civil War. The Sage of Monticello had created more than a southern education. Remarkable innovator that he was, Thomas Jefferson was the founding father of academic political correctness in America.

There was a bitter quality to Jefferson's last years. Frail, hopelessly in debt, and angry at the folly of his northern foes, whose hypocritical antislavery cant threatened the very existence of the empire of liberty he had labored so hard to establish, Jefferson became increasingly shrill. His great consolation, as he often declared, was that he would not live to see the coming cataclysm. By the very last years, he had become a bitter crank. In his final days and hours, he grimly held on to life until the Fourth of July 1826, fifty years to the day since his Declaration of Independence had signaled a fundamental turning point in modern history. When John Adams died on the same day, the ancient Yankee's final words were "Thomas Jefferson survives." The Virginian, by contrast, in his last delirium, died barking orders.[220]

"TAKE CARE OF ME WHEN DEAD"— THE LEGACY OF THOMAS JEFFERSON

America's founding fathers knew they had played a pivotal role in history. The progenitors of the first successful revolution in modern history, they had ushered in a new political epoch that would transform politics and society in every corner of the world. They also knew that their contributions would ultimately be judged by posterity, and it was that judgment that animated their careers and informed their writings. More than any other generation of American statesmen, the founding fathers were obsessed with their legacies. Thomas Jefferson was no exception. In the last decade of his life, he was consumed with the need to set the historical record straight, perhaps even more than his old friend John Adams.

Jefferson consistently defended his tenure as governor of Virginia and rejected any attempts to question either the centrality or the originality of his Declaration of Independence. In numerous letters he denigrated his rivals such as Patrick Henry and Alexander Hamilton and stressed the critical importance of his own contributions to the early republic. The year before the Missouri controversy erupted, he began composing his *Anas*, a survey of his political battles in the 1790s. Three years later he commenced drafting an autobiography. Both works presented their author as a high-minded man of principle. Both depicted his opponents as dangerous, antirepublican, and self-serving. Ultimately, both were abortive. Like Adams in his essays in the *Boston Patriot*, Jefferson was unable to sustain the effort necessary to complete his justification.

In his final year he turned to his closest friend and associate, James Madison, with one last request. Knowing that death was knocking at his door, he implored his fellow Virginian to "take care of me when dead." He could impose no greater burden.[221]

In the years after his death, Jefferson's imprimatur would be claimed by a broad range of Americans. Northern workers hailed him as the democratic champion of the common man. Southern planters paid homage to his defense of states' rights. Both Jefferson Davis and Abraham Lincoln invoked the mantle of the Sage of Monticello, as have Newt Gingrich and Bill Clinton in our own day. Indeed, no other American statesman's words have been cited so often and for such diametrically opposed purposes.

One legacy, however, is incontestable. Thomas Jefferson created the visionary politics of American Romanticism. His politics of principle transcended the mundane realm of programs and policies and introduced an idealistic, often otherworldly, character into American political discourse. It is this visionary character, far more than the particular principles Jefferson ascribed to, that is his greatest and most enduring contribution to American life.

His soaring rhetoric and Romantic sensibilities transformed the practice of American politics. Since his day, every major political movement has needed some set of transcendent principles to rally the populace, whether New Nationalism or New Freedom, New Deal or New Frontier, Great Society or Morning in America. Republicans and Democrats, Greens and militiamen, all wrap their programs in a rhetoric of glorious ideals and sacred principles. After Jefferson, every successful American politician has had to evoke "the vision thing," and all successful political movements have deployed a visionary rhetoric.

This, Jefferson's greatest legacy, has been decidedly mixed in its results. The visionary character of Jeffersonian political discourse has often served to obscure the real sufferings and injustices in American society under patinas of glittering principles and abstract ideals. In his own day, the dogmas of limited government and states' rights served to occlude any meaningful national discussion about the future of slavery in the early republic, just as his agrarian idyll threw a web of Romantic rhetoric over the underdeveloped and crude character of southern rural society. In the years after his retirement, Manifest Destiny would give divine sanction to a brutal and occasionally genocidal program of conquest and expansion. Woodrow Wilson's rhetorical inflation of the First World War into a struggle for global democracy, human rights, and an end to all future wars was used to justify a draconian suppression of dissent, as was the struggle to defend freedom from the menace of global Communist totalitarianism, albeit on a much smaller scale, in the 1950s. Even when it has not been used to cover malevolent actions, Jefferson's Romantic politics of principle has had a disturbing effect.

Sincere devotion to abstract truths has animated some of the most ferocious and canine partisanship in our nation's history and heightened ideological differences among people whose practical differences might have been easily negotiated. Perhaps most insidious of all, subscribing to some transcendent vision has, for many Americans, served as a proxy for actually redressing the wrongs they purportedly deplore. Maintaining an authentic commitment to a virtuous sentiment has all too often been a means to claim a self-righteous moral superiority that salves the moral sensibilities of concerned citizens without actually helping the objects of their concern. All too often Jefferson's politics of principle has allowed Americans to sin with a good conscience. It was so in his own day as well.

There is, however, a far more positive side to Jefferson's visionary legacy. In times of national crisis, his Romantic rhetoric has proved an irreplaceable resource for rallying the American people. Precisely because of its power to mobilize public opinion, the federal government has rarely had to resort to outright repression and force in moments of national emergency. More than that, the politics of principle has, throughout our history, been a source of inspiration and justification for those who have sought to force the nation to live up to its transcendent ideals. This resource has been especially valuable to those who have been denied full access to the benefits of American life, or who have struggled against its injustices. Since Jefferson's day, it has been impossible to dismiss the dream of any reformer, however utopian or radical, as simply un-American. The gap between Romantic rhetoric and tangible realities has been a constant spur of renewal, forcing all those who deploy it to live up to its ideals.

The visionary politics of principle that Jefferson created has thus exerted an incessant pressure on the nation's public life, one that demands the actualization of lofty goals and the enactment of abstract principles. The visionary character of American political discourse has sustained the hopes of the disadvantaged and maintained the faith of the American people in their government and their future. Thomas Jefferson taught America, as a political entity, to dream. If he had done nothing else in his long and remarkable life, he would still have given us ample reason to take care of him when dead.

NOTES

INTRODUCTION

1. Immanuel Kant, "What is Enlightenment?" in *Kant on History*, ed. Lewis White Beck (Indianapolis, 1963), 3–10. David Hume, "Of Essay Writing," in *Essays Moral, Political, and Literary*, ed. Eugene F. Miller (Indianapolis, 1985), 533–37.

2. For a few examples of differing interpretations of the Enlightenment, see Jürgen Habermas, *The Structural Transformation of the Public Sphere: An Inquiry into a Category of Bourgeois Society*, trans. Thomas Burger (Cambridge, Mass., 1989), Peter Gay, *The Enlightenment: An Interpretation*, vol. 1, *The Rise of Modern Paganism* (New York, 1966) and vol. 2, *The Science of Freedom* (New York, 1969), Roy Porter and Miulas Teich, eds., *The Enlightenment in National Context* (New York, 1981), Jonathan I. Israel, *Radical Enlightenment: Philosophy and the Making of Modernity, 1650–1750* (Oxford, 2001), and Franco Venturi, *Utopia and Reform in the Enlightenment* (Cambridge, 1971).

3. Alexander Pope, "Epitaph Intended for Sir Isaac Newton in Westminster Abbey" (1730), in *The Poems of Alexander Pope*, ed. John Butt (London, 1965), 808.

4. Sir Isaac Newton, "The Method of Natural Philosophy" in *Newton's Philosophy of Nature; Selections from His Writings*, ed. H. S. Thayer (New York, 1953), 5; Newton, "On Creation," ibid., 60; Newton, "On Universal Design," ibid., 65–67.

5. Voltaire, "On Mr. Locke," in *Letters on England*, trans. Leonard Tancock (New York, 1980), 63–64.

6. David Hume, *An Enquiry Concerning Human Understanding*, ed. Eric Steinberg (Indianapolis, 1977), 111.

7. David Hume, *A Treatise of Human Nature*, ed. L. A. Shelby Bigge, 2nd ed. (Oxford, 1978), 415.

8. See, for example, *Spectator* nos. 112, 119, and 126, in *The Works of the Right Honorable Joseph Addison*, ed. Richard Hurd, D.D. (London, 1891–93), 2:446–48, 454–57, and 479–80.

9. *Spectator* nos. 411 and 413, *Works of Addison*, 3:394–96 and 402–403. Also see David Hume, "Of the Standard of Taste," *Essays*, 237.

10. *Spectator* no. 10, *Works of Addison*, 2:253; David Hume, "Of Essay Writing," *Essays*, 535.

11. *Spectator* no. 9, *Works of Addison*, 2:251.

12. *The Autobiography of Benjamin Franklin*, ed. Louis P. Masur (New York, 1993), 72–73, 80.

13. Quoted in Wolfgang Schivelbusch, *Tastes of Paradise: A Social History of Spices, Stimulants, and Intoxicants*, trans. David Jacobson (New York, 1992), 52.

14. Hume, "Of Essay Writing," *Essays*, 536.

15. Voltaire, "On Mr. Locke," *Letters on England*, 67; Hume, "Of Parties in General," *Essays*, 60.

16. Adam Smith, *An Inquiry into the Nature and Causes of the Wealth of Nations*, ed. Edwin Cannan, M.A., LL.D. (Chicago, 1976), 318. Hume, "Of the Coalition of Parties," *Essays*, 494. See "Of the Independency of Parliament," ibid., 42–46, and "Of the Original Contract," ibid., 466.

17. Smith, *Wealth of Nations*, 309. Denis Diderot, "Observations sur le Nakaz," in *Denis Diderot: Political Writings*, trans. and ed. John Hope Mason and Robert Wokler (Cambridge, Eng., 1992), 115–16.

18. Baron de Montesquieu, *The Spirit of the Laws*, trans. Thomas Nugent (New York, 1949), 151. Diderot, "Extracts from the *Histoire des Deux Indes*," *Political Writings*, 188. Voltaire, *Voltaire; Political Writings*, trans. and ed. David Williams (Cambridge, 1994), 60.

19. Voltaire, "On Parliament," *Letters on England*, 45.

20. Montesquieu, *Spirit of the Laws*, 20. Voltaire, *Political Writings*, 60.

21. Diderot, "Extracts from *Deux Indes*," *Political Writings*, 189.

22. Voltaire, *Political Writings*, 59. Ibid., 60.

23. Smith, *Wealth of Nations*, 17. Hume, "Of Commerce," *Essays*, 261.

24. Bernard Mandeville, "The Grumbling Hive: Or, Knaves turn'd Honest," in *The Fable of the Bees, or Private Vices, Publick Benefits*, ed. F. B. Kaye (1924; reprint, Indianapolis, 1988), 1:36.

25. Hume, "Of Refinement in the Arts," *Essays*, 277. Montesquieu, *Spirit of the Laws*, 321.

26. *Spectator* no. 287, *Works of Addison*, 3:298–99.

27. Ibid. Hume, "Of Refinement in the Arts," *Essays*, 270–71.

28. Hume, "Of Commerce," *Essays*, 259. Adam Smith, *The Theory of Moral Sentiments*, ed. D. D. Raphael and A. L. Macfie (Indianapolis, 1984), 23.

29. *Autobiography of Benjamin Franklin*, 89–91. Hume, "Of Refinement in the Arts," *Essays*, 269–71.

30. *Spectator* no. 69, *Works of Addison*, 2:371, 373.

31. John Adams, *Thoughts on Government* in *The Revolutionary Writings of John Adams*, ed. C. Bradley Thompson (Indianapolis, 2000), 293.

CHAPTER ONE. ALEXANDER HAMILTON:
THE ENLIGHTENMENT FULFILLED

1. Talleyrand is quoted in Robert Hendrickson, *Hamilton I (1757–1789)* (New York, 1976), 580.

2. Thomas Jefferson to George Washington, September 9, 1792, in *The Papers of Thomas Jefferson*, ed. Julian P. Boyd et al. (Princeton, N.J., 1950–), 24:358. John Adams to Benjamin Rush, January 25, 1806, in *The Spur of Fame: Dialogues of John Adams and Benjamin Rush, 1805–1813*, ed. John A. Schutz and Douglass Adair (1966; reprint, Indianapolis, 2000), 50. Thomas Jefferson to James Madison, September 21, 1795, in *The Republic of Letters: The Correspondence between Thomas Jefferson and James Madison, 1776–1826*, ed. James Morton Smith (New York, 1995), 2:897. John Adams to Alexander Hamilton, July 21, 1789, in *The Papers of Alexander Hamilton*, ed. Harold C. Syrett (New York, 1961–79), 5:364.

3. James Thomas Flexner, *The Young Hamilton: A Biography* (New York, 1977), 4.

4. George Washington to Alexander Hamilton, April 4, 1784, *Hamilton Papers*, 3:315–16.

5. The totals from *The Federalist* are exclusive of numbers 18–20, which were collaborations between Hamilton and Madison, and numbers 49–58 and 62–63, whose attribution is contested between Madison and Hamilton. Nine months was the period the House had allowed for an annual accounting by the Treasury Department. See *Hamilton Papers*, 13:543n24. The reports Hamilton submitted are listed in ibid., 13:541n20.

6. Quoted in Hendrickson, *Hamilton I*, 165.

7. Thomas Jefferson to James Madison, September 8, 1793, *Republic of Letters*, 2:818–19.

8. La Rochefoucauld-Liancourt quoted in Allan McLane Hamilton, *The Intimate Life of Alexander Hamilton* (New York, 1910), 36–37 and Thomas Jefferson, "The Anas," in *The Life and Selected Writings of Thomas Jefferson*, ed. Adrienne Koch and William Peden (New York, 1993), 117. Morris quoted in Hamilton, *Intimate Life*, 48. Alexander Hamilton to George Clinton, February 13, 1778, *Hamilton Papers*, 1:425–26. Alexander Hamilton to George

Washington, March 25, 1783, *Hamilton Papers*, 3:306. Alexander Hamilton to John Laurens, September 12, 1780, *Hamilton Papers*, 2:427–28.

9. Jefferson, "Anas," *Life and Writings*, 117. The source of Hamilton's defense of influence or "corruption" in British government was David Hume. See his "Of the Independency of Parliament" in *Essays Moral, Political, and Literary*, ed. Eugene F. Miller (Indianapolis, 1985), 42–46. On Hamilton as a Mandevillian statesman, see Paul A. Rahe, *Republics Ancient and Modern*, vol. 3, *Inventions of Prudence: Constituting the American Regime* (Chapel Hill, N.C., 1994), 111. Rahe has claimed that "Alexander Hamilton was arguably the most brilliant of the American Founding Fathers." Ibid.

10. See Karl-Friederich Walling, *Republican Empire: Alexander Hamilton on War and Free Government* (Lawrence, 1999), 247. "Catullus no. 3," *Hamilton Papers*, 12:500–501, 505–506. Alexander Hamilton to Henry Lee, December 1, 1789, in *Hamilton Papers*, 6:1.

11. Jefferson, "Anas," *Life and Writings*, 117.

12. Flexner, *Young Hamilton*, 8–16, Naomi Emery, *Alexander Hamilton: An Intimate Portrait* (New York, 1982), 13–16, and Hendrickson, *Hamilton I*, 1–10.

13. Hamilton, *Intimate Life*, 7–8. Emery, *Intimate Portrait*, 15–17. Flexner, *Young Hamilton*, 16–24. Hendrickson, *Hamilton I*, 10–15.

14. Hendrickson, *Hamilton I*, 15. Flexner, *Young Hamilton*, 24–27.

15. Hendrickson, *Hamilton I*, 16-19. Flexner, *Young Hamilton*, 28–33.

16. Alexander Hamilton to Edward Stevens, November 11, 1769, *Hamilton Papers*, 1:4.

17. Quoted in Richard B. Morris, ed., *Alexander Hamilton and the Founding of the Nation* (1957; reprint, New York, 1969), 602.

18. Flexner claims that Hamilton's choice of King's College was based not on Princeton's refusal to allow him to study at an accelerated pace (which had been granted to James Madison), but on its location in Manhattan: "It was a case of love at first sight." Flexner, *Young Hamilton*, 58–59. The "Corsicans" drilled in St. George's churchyard under the supervision of Major Edward Fleming. Hendrickson, *Hamilton I*, 84. Hamilton was commissioned captain in the New York artillery on March 14, 1776, at the recommendation of Colonel Alexander McDougall, one of the leaders of the Sons of Liberty in New York. Hendrickson, *Hamilton I*, 92–93.

19. On "Hamiltonopolis," see Hendrickson, *Hamilton I*, 43, 515.

20. Thomas Jefferson, *Notes on the State of Virginia*, ed. William Peden (Chapel Hill, N.C., 1982), 146.

21. Hendrickson, *Hamilton I*, 61, and Flexner, *Young Hamilton*, 63–65.

22. Forrest McDonald, *Alexander Hamilton: A Biography* (New York, 1979), 30–31, and Hendrickson, *Hamilton I*, 82. "The Farmer Refuted," February 23, 1775, *Hamilton Papers*, 1:163–65.

23. On republicanism as an ideology, see Caroline Robbins, *The Eighteenth-*

Century Commonwealthman: Studies in the Transmission, Development, and Circumstances of English Liberal Thought from the Restoration of Charles II until the War with the Thirteen Colonies (Cambridge, Mass., 1959), H. Trevor Colburn, *The Lamp of Experience: Whig History and the Intellectual Origins of the American Revolution* (Chapel Hill, N.C., 1965), Bernard Bailyn, *The Ideological Origins of the American Revolution* (Cambridge, Mass., 1967), Gordon Wood, *The Creation of the American Republic, 1776–1787* (Chapel Hill, N.C., 1969), and J.G.A. Pocock, *The Machiavellian Moment: Florentine Political Thought and the Atlantic Republican Tradition* (Princeton, N.J., 1975). On the differences between classical, Renaissance, and modern/enlightened republicanism, see Rahe's brilliant three-volume *Republics Ancient and Modern.* Aristotle, *The Politics,* trans. Carnes Lord (Chicago, 1984), 37, 84. Baron de Montesquieu, *The Spirit of the Laws,* trans. Thomas Nugent (New York, 1949), 20.

24. "A Full Vindication of the Measures of the Congress, from the Calumnies of their Enemies," December 15, 1774, *Hamilton Papers,* 1:47. "Farmer Refuted," ibid., 1:105.

25. "Full Vindication," ibid., 1:50. "Farmer Refuted," ibid., 1:93. "Full Vindication," ibid., 1:64.

26. "Full Vindication," ibid., 1:69. "Remarks on the Quebec Bill: Part II," June 22, 1775, ibid., 1:175.

27. "Farmer Refuted," ibid., 1:156–58.

28. On mixed government, see Bernard Bailyn, *The Origins of American Politics* (New York, 1967).

29. Thomas Jefferson to Edmund Pendleton, August 26, 1776, *Jefferson Papers,* 1:504.

30. Alexander Hamilton to Gouverneur Morris, May 19, 1777, *Hamilton Papers* 1:255.

31. Alexander Hamilton to John Jay, March 14, 1779, ibid., 2:17–18. "Farmer Refuted," ibid., 1:164–65.

32. Rahe, *Republics Ancient and Modern,* 3:118. McDonald, *Hamilton,* 34.

33. Robert Middlekauf, *The Glorious Cause: The American Revolution, 1763–1789* (New York, 1982), 340–41, 346. Hendrickson, *Hamilton I,* 103–104. Middlekauf, *Glorious Cause,* 349.

34. Flexner, *Young Hamilton,* 117. Hendrickson, *Hamilton I,* 105. Middlekauf, *Glorious Cause,* 351. E. Wayne Carp, *To Starve the Army at Pleasure: Continental Army Administration and American Political Culture, 1775–1783* (Chapel Hill, N.C., 1984), 19. Hendrickson, *Hamilton I,* 107. Flexner, *Young Hamilton,* 123. Hendrickson, *Hamilton I,* 107–108. Middlekauf, *Glorious Cause,* 355. Hendrickson, *Hamilton I,* 109–10.

35. George Washington to John Augustine Washington, December 18, 1776, quoted in Carp, *To Starve the Army,* 19.

36. Middlekauf, *Glorious Cause*, 386–89. Hendrickson, *Hamilton I*, 143–48. Flexner, *Young Hamilton*, 183. Middlekauf, *Glorious Cause*, 392–95. Hendrickson, *Hamilton I*, 149–51. Middlekauf, *Glorious Cause*, 370–84.

37. Middlekauf, *Glorious Cause*, 420, 435. Flexner, *Young Hamilton*, 257. Middlekauf, *Glorious Cause*, 449. Don Higgenbotham, "The War for Independence, After Saratoga," in Jack P. Greene and J. R. Pole, eds., *The Blackwell Encyclopedia of the American Revolution* (Cambridge, Mass., 1994), 310. Middlekauf, *Glorious Cause*, 459. E. Wayne Carp, "The Problem of National Defense in the Early Republic," in Jack P. Greene, ed., *The American Revolution: Its Character and Limits* (New York, 1987), 23.

38. Charles Royster, *A Revolutionary People at War: The Continental Army and American Character, 1775–1783* (New York, 1979), 49, 65, 71, 196.

39. Hendrickson, *Hamilton I*, 152–53. Royster, *Revolutionary People*, 183, 46. Alexander Hamilton to George Clinton, February 13, 1778, *Hamilton Papers*, 1:425–26.

40. Quoted in Hendrickson, *Hamilton I*, 110. Walling, *Republican Empire*, 47. Middlekauf, *Glorious Cause*, 511. Hendrickson, *Hamilton I*, 239. Royster, *Revolutionary People*, 299.

41. Washington quoted in Hendrickson, *Hamilton I*, 240.

42. Carp, *To Starve the Army*, 104. Middlekauf, *Glorious Cause*, 516. Carp, *To Starve the Army*, 44.

43. Alexander Hamilton to Isaac Sears, October 12, 1780, *Hamilton Papers*, 2:472.

44. Robert A. Becker, "Currency, Taxation, and Finance, 1778–1787," in Greene and Pole, *Encyclopedia of the American Revolution*, 364. Carp, *To Starve the Army*, 69. Flexner, *Young Hamilton*, 265. Carp, *To Starve the Army*, 171.

45. See Alexander Hamilton to George Clinton, February 13, 1778, *Hamilton Papers*, 1:426–27. Alexander Hamilton to George Clinton, March 12, 1778, quoted in Hendrickson, *Hamilton I*, 184.

46. Flexner, *Young Hamilton*, 239. "Publius no. 1," *Hamilton Papers*, 1:563.

47. Becker, "Currency, Taxation, and Finance," *Encyclopedia*, 366–67. Carp, *To Starve the Army*, 65. Flexner, *Young Hamilton*, 265. Walling, *Republican Empire*, 47. Alexander Hamilton to John Laurens, June 30, 1780, *Hamilton Papers*, 2:347–48.

48. "Farmer Refuted," *Hamilton Papers*, 1:156. Carp, *To Starve the Army*, 65. Royster, *Revolutionary People*, 133.

49. Carp, *To Starve the Army*, 77. Royster, *Revolutionary People*, 265, 295–98. Alexander Hamilton to John Laurens, June 30, 1780, *Hamilton Papers*, 2:347–48.

50. Alexander Hamilton to John Laurens, September 11, 1779, *Hamilton Papers*, 2:166–67. Alexander Hamilton to George Washington, March 25, 1783, ibid., 3:306.

51. Alexander Hamilton to Edward Stevens, November 11, 1769, ibid., 1:4. Hendrickson, *Hamilton I*, 297, 295. Flexner, *Young Hamilton*, 325. Hendrickson, *Hamilton I*, 297–98.

52. The most detailed account of Hamilton's break with Washington can be found in Alexander Hamilton to Philip Schuyler, February 18, 1781, *Hamilton Papers*, 2:563–68. Also see Alexander Hamilton to Major James McHenry, February 18, 1781, ibid., 2:569. Hendrickson, *Hamilton I*, 305–306. Flexner, *Young Hamilton*, 346–47.

53. Hamilton's remarks at the New York ratifying convention (Francis Child's version), June 24, 1788, *Hamilton Papers*, 5:68. "The Continentalist no. 1," July 21, 1781, ibid., 2:650, 649. Hamilton's remarks at the New York ratifying convention (Child's version), ibid., 5:68.

54. "The Continentalist no. 2," July 19, 1781, ibid., 2:654. Hamilton's speech at the Constitutional Convention (Madison's version), June 18, 1787, ibid., 4:189. "The Continentalist no. 3," August 9, 1781, ibid., 2:660.

55. "The Federalist no. 1," ibid., 4:304. "Camillus no. 3," September 29, 1792, ibid., 12:501–502. Alexander Hamilton to George Washington, August 18, 1792, ibid., 12:251–52.

56. "The Federalist no. 31," *Hamilton Papers*, 4:456. Hamilton's speech at the Constitutional Convention (Hamilton's notes), June 18, 1787, ibid., 4:179.

57. Hamilton's speech at the Constitutional Convention (Hamilton's notes), June 18, 1787, ibid., 4:179. Hamilton's speech at the Constitutional Convention (Madison's version), June 18, 1787, ibid., 4:188.

58. Hamilton's speech at the Constitutional Convention (Robert Yates's version), June 18, 1787, ibid., 4:200.

59. Alexander Hamilton to Robert Morris, April 30, 1781, ibid., 2:606. "The Federalist no. 8," ibid., 4:329. "The Federalist no. 30," ibid., 4:450.

60. "The Continentalist no. 6," July 4, 1782, *Hamilton Papers*, 3:103. Hamilton's speech at the Constitutional Convention (Madison's version), June 18, 1787, ibid., 4:188. Continental Congress Remarks on the Collection of Funds by Officers of the United States, January 28, 1783, ibid., 3:246.

61. David Hume, "Of the First Principles of Government," in *Essays*, 32.

62. Hamilton's speech at the Constitutional Convention (Hamilton's notes), June 18, 1787, *Hamilton Papers*, 4:180. Hamilton's first speech of June 21 at the New York Ratifying Convention (Child's version), June 21, 1788, ibid., 5:37.

63. "The Federalist no. 12," ibid., 4:347.

64. "The Federalist no. 30," ibid., 4:450.

65. "The Federalist no. 8," ibid., 4:329. Alexander Hamilton to James Duane, September 3, 1780, ibid., 2:414.

66. Hamilton's remarks at the New York Ratifying Convention (Child's version), June 27, 1788, ibid., 5:101.

67. David Hume, "Of Refinement in the Arts," *Essays*, 270. "The Federalist no. 12," *Hamilton Papers*, 4:347. Final Version of the Report on Manufactures, December 5, 1791, *Hamilton Papers*, 10:249. "The Federalist no. 12," *Hamilton Papers*, 4:347.

68. Hume, "Of Refinement in the Arts," *Essays*, 270–71. Final Version of the Report on Manufactures, December 5, 1791, *Hamilton Papers*, 10:249. First Report on the Further Provision Necessary for Establishing Public Credit, December 13, 1790, *Hamilton Papers*, 7:232.

69. Thomas Jefferson, "Anas," *Life and Works*, 117.

70. David Hume, *A Treatise of Human Nature*, ed. L. A. Shelby Bigge, 2nd ed. (Oxford, 1978), 415.

71. Hamilton's Remarks at the Constitutional Convention (Yates's version), June 22, 1787, *Hamilton Papers*, 4:216–17. Hume, "Of the Independency of Parliament," *Essays*, 42. Remarks at the Constitutional Convention (Yates's version), June 22, 1787, *Hamilton Papers*, 4:216–17.

72. Hamilton's Remarks at the Constitutional Convention (Hamilton's notes), June 18, 1787, *Hamilton Papers*, 4:180. Hamilton's Speech at the Constitutional Convention (Madison's version), June 18, 1787, ibid., 4:189.

73. Alexander Hamilton to James Duane, September 3, 1780, ibid., 2:410. Hamilton's Remarks at the Constitutional Convention (Hamilton's notes), June 18, 1787, ibid., 4:186–87.

74. Hamilton's Remarks at the Constitutional Convention (Hamilton's notes), June 18, 1787, ibid., 4:185. Hamilton's Remarks at the Constitutional Convention (Yates's version), June 18, 1787, ibid., 4:200. Hamilton's Remarks at the Constitutional Convention (Madison's notes), September 8, 1787, ibid., 4:244.

75. Hamilton's Remarks at the Constitutional Convention (Hamilton's notes), June 18, 1787, *Hamilton Papers*, 4:184–87.

76. "The Continentalist no. 5," April 18, 1782, ibid., 3:82.

77. Alexander Hamilton to George Washington, February 13, 1783, ibid., 3:255. Alexander Hamilton to James Duane, September 3, 1780, ibid., 2:414.

78. "The Federalist no. 35," *Hamilton Papers*, 4:480.

79. Ibid., 4:480–82. Also see "The Federalist no. 36," ibid., 4:483.

80. "The Federalist no. 27," ibid., 4:435–36.

81. "The Federalist no. 79," ibid., 4:662.

82. "The Federalist no. 81," ibid., 4:675.

83. On Hamilton's reading of the law of nations, see Alexander Hamilton to George Washington, September 15, 1790, ibid., 7:38–41. "The Federalist no. 35," ibid., 4:482.

84. Alexander Hamilton to Robert Morris, April 30, 1781, ibid., 2:621.

85. Barrington Moore, Jr., *Social Origins of Dictatorship and Democracy: Lord and Peasant in the Making of the Modern World* (Boston, 1966).

86. Emery, *Intimate Portrait*, 143.
87. Stanley Elkins and Eric McKitrick, *The Age of Federalism* (New York, 1993), 115.
88. Debt totals can be found in McDonald, *Hamilton*, 145–48, and Elkins and McKitrick, *Age of Federalism*, 121–23.
89. *Report on Public Credit*, January 14, 1790, *Hamilton Papers*, 6:88–89. Walling, *Republican Empire*, 191. Elkins and McKitrick, *Age of Federalism*, 123. *Report on Public Credit*, *Hamilton Papers*, 6:87–89.
90. *Report on Public Credit*, *Hamilton Papers*, 6:106–107.
91. Ibid., 6:70–71.
92. Ibid., 6:70–72.
93. Richard Brookhiser, *Alexander Hamilton, American* (New York, 1999), 84.
94. Lance Banning, "The Problem of Power: Parties, Aristocracy, and Democracy in Revolutionary Thought," in Greene, ed., *American Revolution*, 118. McDonald, *Hamilton*, 154. *The Defense of the Funding System*, July 1795, *Hamilton Papers*, 19:62.
95. *Report on Public Credit*, *Hamilton Papers*, 6:73–76.
96. Ibid., 6:78–80.
97. On Madison's land speculations, see McDonald, *Hamilton*, 175. Jefferson's account of his and Madison's negotiations with Hamilton can be found in "Anas," *Life and Writings*, 114–15. McDonald, *Hamilton*, 185.
98. *Report on Public Credit*, *Hamilton Papers*, 6:108. McDonald, *Hamilton*, 193. *Report on a National Bank*, *Hamilton Papers*, 7:306–307.
99. McDonald, *Hamilton*, 193–95. *Report on a National Bank*, *Hamilton Papers*, 7:309.
100. Jefferson, "Anas," *Life and Writings*, 114, 116.
101. *Report on Manufactures*, *Hamilton Papers*, 10:236. Drew R. McCoy refers to Jefferson and Madison's anti-industrial policy as expansion across space as opposed to time. See his *The Elusive Republic: Political Economy in Jeffersonian America* (Chapel Hill, N.C., 1980).
102. *Report on Manufactures*, *Hamilton Papers*, 10:236, 241–42, 285–86, 257.
103. Ibid., 10:270, 253, 270.
104. Ibid., 10:267, 296–310, 338–39.
105. Ibid., 10:289, 291.
106. Ibid., 10:293–96.
107. "Farewell Address," in Morris, ed., *Hamilton and the Founding*, 517–18. Alexander Hamilton to Edward Carrington, May 26, 1792, *Hamilton Papers*, 11:439. On Hamilton's Anglophilia, see Elkins and McKitrick, *Age of Federalism*, 128. McDonald, *Hamilton*, 265.
108. Alexander Hamilton to Edward Carrington, May 26, 1792, *Hamilton Papers*, 11:439.

109. Ibid. One study of the Federalist epoch has argued that "the kind of diplomacy Jefferson was engaged in" with Great Britain—consisting exclusively of written charges and countercharges—"virtually guaranteed that there would be no negotiations at all." Elkins and McKitrick, *Age of Federalism*, 254–55. Alexander Hamilton to Edward Carrington, May 26, 1792, *Hamilton Papers*, 11:439.

110. Alexander Hamilton to Marquis de Lafayette, October 6, 1789, *Hamilton Papers*, 5:425.

111. Daniel Roche, *France in the Enlightenment*, trans. Arthur Goldhammer (Cambridge, Mass., 1998), 382. On the breakdown of the French republic of letters, see Dena Goodman, *The Republic of Letters: A Cultural History of the French Enlightenment* (Ithaca, N.Y., 1994) and Simon Schama, *Citizens: A Chronicle of the French Revolution* (New York, 1989), 145–82.

112. "Cabinet Meeting. Opinion on Furnishing Three Million Livres to the Request of the French Minister," February 25, 1793, *Hamilton Papers*, 14:141.

113. "For the Gazette of the United States," March–April 1793, ibid., 14:268. Elkins and McKitrick, *Age of Federalism*, 339.

114. Ibid., 337.

115. McDonald, *Hamilton*, 276. Elkins and McKitrick, *Age of Federalism*, 311, 333–35, 341.

116. McDonald, *Hamilton*, 276–77. Elkins and McKitrick, *Age of Federalism*, 348–51.

117. "Pacificus no. 1," June 22, 1793, *Hamilton Papers*, 15:33–34. "Pacificus no. 2," July 3, 1793, ibid., 15:57–62.

118. "Pacificus no. 4," July 10, 1793, ibid., 15:84–85. "Pacificus no. 5," July 13, 1793, ibid., 15:90–91.

119. "No Jacobin no. 1–4," Morris, ed., *Hamilton and the Founding*, 412–14. "No Jacobin no. 5," August 14, 1793, *Hamilton Papers*, 15:243–44.

120. "No Jacobin no. 5," *Hamilton Papers*, 15:243–44. "No Jacobin no. 7," August 23, 1793, ibid., 15:268. "No Jacobin no. 8," August 26, 1793, ibid., 15:282.

121. Thomas Jefferson to James Madison, July 7, 1793, *Republic of Letters*, 2:792. Thomas Jefferson to James Madison, August 11, 1783, ibid., 2:803.

122. McDonald, *Hamilton*, 289. Elkins and McKitrick, *Age of Federalism*, 389.

123. Alexander Hamilton to George Washington, March 8, 1794, *Hamilton Papers*, 16:134–36. Elkins and McKitrick, *Age of Federalism*, 392–93. Alexander Hamilton to George Washington, April 14, 1794, *Hamilton Papers*, 16:276, 270.

124. McDonald, *Hamilton*, 293. Elkins and McKitrick, *Age of Federalism*, 393–97. Broadus Mitchell, *Alexander Hamilton: A Concise Biography* (New York, 1976), 295.

125. Elkins and McKitrick, *Age of Federalism*, 415–21. James Roger Sharp, *American Politics in the Early Republic: The New Nation in Crisis* (New Haven, Conn., 1993), 119.

126. Remarks on the Treaty of Amity, Commerce, and Navigation Lately Made between the United States and Great Britain, July 9–11, 1795, *Hamilton Papers*, 18:451–53. On American commercial expansion following the Jay Treaty, see Elkins and McKitrick, *Age of Federalism*, 381–83.

127. "The Defense no. 1," July 22, 1795, *Hamilton Papers*, 18:482. "The Defense no. 2," July 25, 1795, ibid., 18:498, 495–96.

128. "The Defense no. 2," July 25, 1795, ibid., 18:500. "The Defense no. 3," July 29, 1795, ibid., 18:517–19. "The Defense no. 5," August 5, 1795, ibid., 19:92–93. "The Defense no. 4," August 1, 1795, ibid., 19:82.

129. "The Defense no. 7," August 12, 1795, ibid., 19:123. "Philo Camillus no. 3," August 12, 1795, ibid., 19:125–26.

130. George Washington to Alexander Hamilton, July 19, 1795, ibid. 18:525. Thomas Jefferson to James Madison, September 21, 1795, *Republic of Letters*, 2:897. Elkins and McKitrick, *Age of Federalism*, 415.

131. Hamilton's Remarks at the Constitutional Convention, June 18, 1787 (Madison's notes), *Hamilton Papers*, 4:194–95. Notes of Objects for Consideration of the President, December 1, 1790, ibid., 7:173. One scholar has analogized Hamilton's view of the legitimacy of the federal government to acceptance of public credit: "Hamilton seems to have believed that the public would accept the powers of the national government in a way comparable to how, in the sphere of economics, people accept the idea of credit . . . Once people came to regard the national government as real, they would cease to pose objections based on extravagant fantasies about its powers." James H. Read, *Power Versus Liberty: Madison, Hamilton, Wilson, and Jefferson* (Charlottesville, Va., 2000), 16.

132. Speech of February 2, 1791, *The Papers of James Madison*, ed. William T. Hutchinson et al. (Chicago, 1926–1977, Charlottesville, Va., 1977–), 13:374–78.

133. "The Federalist no. 44," in *The Federalist: A Commentary on the Constitution of the United States* (New York, 1941), 293.

134. Opinion on the Constitutionality of an Act to Establish a Bank, February 23, 1791, *Hamilton Papers*, 8:97–98.

135. Ibid., 8:100–101, 103.

136. Ibid., 8:104, 120, 119.

137. Ibid., 8:132–33.

138. *Report on Manufactures*, December 5, 1791, ibid., 10:303.

139. Alexander Hamilton to Edward Carrington, May 26, 1792, ibid., 11:443.

140. Thomas P. Slaughter, *The Whiskey Rebellion: Frontier Epilogue to the American Revolution* (New York, 1986), 187.

141. Elkins and McKitrick, *Age of Federalism*, 467. *Report on Public Credit*, January 14, 1790, *Hamilton Papers*, 6:99. Hamilton's estimates are found in his *Report on the Difficulties in the Execution of the Act Laying Duties on*

Distilled Spirits, March 6, 1792, *Hamilton Papers*, 11:98–99. On American alcohol consumption, see table A1.2 in W. J. Rorabaugh, *The Alcoholic Republic: An American Tradition* (New York, 1979), 233. *Report on Public Credit*, *Hamilton Papers*, 6:99.

142. Elkins and McKitrick, *Age of Federalism*, 462.

143. "The federal government paid out four or five times as much to them (for whiskey purchased as army rations) as it collected in taxes from them." McDonald, *Hamilton*, 297. *Report on Distilled Spirits*, *Hamilton Papers*, 11:97, 81.

144. Alexander Hamilton to George Washington, August 5, 1794, *Hamilton Papers*, 17:35–36. Daniel Huger to Alexander Hamilton, June 22–25, 1792, ibid., 11:542. Alexander Hamilton to George Washington, September 1, 1792, ibid., 12:311.

145. McDonald, *Hamilton*, 298.

146. Conference Concerning the Insurrection in Western Pennsylvania, August 2, 1794, *Hamilton Papers*, 17:12–13.

147. McDonald, *Hamilton*, 300. Elkins and McKitrick, *Age of Federalism*, 463. Walling, *Republican Empire*, 138–39. McDonald, *Hamilton*, 301–302.

148. "Tully no. 2," August 26, 1794, *Hamilton Papers*, 17:148–49.

149. "Tully no. 3," August 28, 1794, ibid., 17:159–60.

150. McDonald, *Hamilton*, 302.

151. The best study of Hamilton's reputation is Stephen K. Knott, *Alexander Hamilton and the Persistence of Myth* (Lawrence, Kans., 2002). Dos Passos and Pound are quoted in ibid., 128–29. On Pound's own bizarre predilection for Jefferson, see his *Jefferson and/or Mussolini* (1935; reprint, New York, 1970).

152. Hamilton's Speech at the Constitutional Convention (Yates's version), June 18, 1787, *Hamilton Papers*, 4:200.

153. "The Federalist no. 55," ibid., 4:516.

CHAPTER TWO. JOHN ADAMS:
THE ENLIGHTENMENT TRANSCENDED

1. Jürgen Gebhardt, *Americanism: Revolutionary Order and Societal Self-Interpretation in the American Republic*, trans. Ruth Hein (1976; reprint, Baton Rouge, La., 1993), 6–8.

2. Richard Stockton quoted in *The Works of John Adams, Second President of the United States*, ed. Charles Francis Adams (Boston, 1850–56), 3:56.

3. Quoted in John Ferling, *John Adams: A Life* (New York, 1992), 310.

4. *Diary and Autobiography of John Adams*, ed. L. H. Butterfield (Cambridge, Mass., 1961), 2:362–63.

5. Page Smith, *John Adams* (Garden City, N.Y., 1962), 2:1006.

6. Franklin quoted in Edmund S. Morgan, *Benjamin Franklin* (New Haven, Conn., 2002), 294.

7. James Madison to Thomas Jefferson, February 11, 1783, in *The Republic of Letters: The Correspondence between Thomas Jefferson and James Madison, 1776–1826*, ed. James Morton Smith (New York, 1995), 1:221. Thomas Jefferson to James Madison, January 30 and February 5, 1787, ibid., 1:462. *Diary and Autobiography*, 1:24–25, 37.

8. *Diary and Autobiography*, 1:95. Ibid., 1:22. John Adams to Jonathan Sewall, February 1760, in *The Papers of John Adams*, ed. Robert J. Taylor et al. (Cambridge, Mass., 1977–), 1:42.

9. Smith, *John Adams*, 1:28. C. Bradley Thompson, "Young John Adams and the New Philosophic Rationalism," *William and Mary Quarterly*, 3rd series, 55 (1998), 264–65. C. Bradley Thompson, *John Adams and the Spirit of Liberty* (Lawrence, Kans., 1998), 7–8. *Diary and Autobiography*, 1:6.

10. John Adams to John Wentworth, October–November 1758, in *The Earliest Diary of John Adams*, ed. L. H. Butterfield (Cambridge, Mass., 1966), 65. "On Shakespeare and on Motives to Hard Study" (1758), ibid., 77.

11. Ferling, *Adams*, 170. John Adams to James Warren, August 4, 1778, *Adams Papers*, 6:348.

12. *Diary and Autobiography*, 3:195.

13. Richard D. Brown, "Bulwark of Revolutionary Liberty: Thomas Jefferson's and John Adams's Program for an Informed Citizenry," in James Gilreath, ed., *Thomas Jefferson and the Education of a Citizen* (London, 1999), 93. Robert Zemsky, *Merchants, Farmers, and River Gods: An Essay on Eighteenth-Century American Politics* (Boston, 1971), 34–35. On the learned as a ruling class in Puritan Massachusetts, see Darren M. Staloff, *The Making of an American Thinking Class: Intellectuals and Intelligentsia in Puritan Massachusetts* (New York, 1998).

14. Conrad Edick Wright et al., *Sibley's Harvard Graduates: Biographical Sketches of Those Who Attended Harvard College* (Boston, 1999), 18:xxvi–xxvii.

15. On Adams as a secularized Puritan, see Joseph Ellis, *Passionate Sage: The Character and Legacy of John Adams* (New York, 1993), 52, Paul K. Conkin, *Puritans and Pragmatists: Eight American Thinkers* (London, 1968), 109, Joyce Appleby, *Liberalism and Republicanism in the Historical Imagination* (Cambridge, Mass., 1992), 199, and John Patrick Diggins, *The Lost Soul of American Politics* (New York, 1984), 82.

16. "An Essay on Man's Lust for Power," *Adams Papers*, 1:82–83.

17. John Adams to Benjamin Rush, April 12, 1809, in *The Spur of Fame: Dialogues of John Adams and Benjamin Rush, 1805–1813*, ed. John A. Schutz and Douglass Adair (San Marino, Calif., 1966), 155.

18. John Adams to Benjamin Rush, July 26, 1806, ibid., 65. Ellis, *Passionate Sage*, 26.

19. Ellis, *Passionate Sage*, 173. *Letters to John Taylor of Caroline, Virginia, in Reply to his Strictures on Some Parts of the Defense of the American Constitutions*, no. 3, in *Adams Works*, 6:454.

20. *Diary and Autobiography*, 1:251. Richard D. Brown, *Knowledge Is Power: The Diffusion of Information in Early America, 1700–1865* (New York, 1989), 97. *Diary and Autobiography*, 1:294.

21. To Joseph Hawley, August 25, 1776, *Adams Papers*, 6:495–96. *A Dissertation on the Canon and the Feudal Law*, no. 1, August 12, 1765, *Adams Papers*, 1:111. "Notes for an Oration at Braintree," Spring 1772, *Diary and Autobiography*, 2:58. Also see *The Report of a Constitution, or Form of Government, for the Commonwealth of Massachusetts; Agreed upon by the Committee . . .* , *Adams Papers*, 8:260. *Novanglus; or a History of the Dispute with America, from its origin, in 1754, to the Present Time*, no. 6, 1774, *Adams Works*, 4:94. Also see his entry for August 19, 1760, in *Earliest Diary*, 153.

22. See John Adams to Jonathan Sewall, February 1760, *Adams Papers*, 1:42–43. Also see *Dissertation on the Canon and the Feudal Law*, no. 1, ibid., 1:113–14. "Notes for an Oration at Braintree," *Diary and Autobiography*, 2:56. See his notes to Winthrop's lectures on natural philosophy, April 1, 1754, *Earliest Diary*, 60.

23. "Notes for an Oration at Braintree," *Diary and Autobiography*, 2:56. Also see John R. Howe, Jr., *The Changing Political Thought of John Adams* (Princeton, N.J., 1966), 16. John Adams to James Sullivan, May 26, 1776, *Adams Papers*, 4:210. "Notes for an Oration at Braintree," *Diary and Autobiography*, 2:56.

24. "Notes for an Oration at Braintree," *Diary and Autobiography*, 2:56. *Thoughts on Government: Applicable to the Present State of the American Colonies* (Philadelphia, 1776), *Adams Papers*, 4:86.

25. *Earliest Diary*, 153. *A Dissertation on the Canon and the Feudal Law*, no. 3, *Adams Papers*, 1:121. *A Proclamation by the General Court*, January 19, 1776, *Adams Papers*, 3:385–86. *Thoughts on Government*, *Adams Papers*, 4:91.

26. *A Dissertation on the Canon and the Feudal Law*, no. 3, *Adams Papers*, 1:121. See "Fragmentary Draft of a Dissertation on the Canon and Feudal Law," February 1765, *Diary and Autobiography*, 1:257.

27. *The Report of a Constitution*, *Adams Papers*, 8:260. As Loren Baritz notes, such views were not uncommon at the time, but Adams "was the first to make them a constitutional requirement." Loren Baritz, *City on a Hill: A History of Ideas and Myths in America* (New York, 1964), 124. *The Report of a Constitution*, *Adams Papers*, 8:259.

28. John Adams to James Warren, June 25, 1774, *Adams Papers*, 2:99–100.

29. *A Dissertation on the Canon and the Feudal Law*, no. 4, *Adams Papers*, 1:127.

30. Dugald Stewart, *The Unity of the Sciences*, in Alexander Broadie, ed., *The Scottish Enlightenment: An Anthology* (Edinburgh, 1997), 53.

31. See his entry of January 24, 1765, *Diary and Autobiography*, 1:251. "Frag-

mentary Draft of a Dissertation on the Canon and Feudal Law," ibid., 1:257.
John Adams to Edmund Jennings, April 20, 1780, *Adams Papers*, 9:211.

32. *A Dissertation on the Canon and the Feudal Law*, no. 1, *Adams Papers*, 1:111–12.

33. Ibid., 1:112–14.

34. Ibid., 1:114. *A Dissertation on the Canon and the Feudal Law*, no. 2, *Adams Papers*, 1:116. Ibid., no. 3, *Adams Papers*, 1:120. "Fragmentary Draft of a Dissertation on the Canon and Feudal Law," *Diary and Autobiography*, 1:257. *A Dissertation on the Canon and the Feudal Law*, no. 3, *Adams Papers*, 1:121. "Fragmentary Draft of a Dissertation on the Canon and Feudal Law," *Diary and Autobiography*, 1:257.

35. *A Dissertation on the Canon and the Feudal Law*, no. 4, *Adams Papers*, 1:127. "Notes for an Oration at Braintree," *Diary and Autobiography*, 2:58, 60–61.

36. See Daniel Roche, *France in the Enlightenment*, trans. Arthur Goldhammer (Cambridge, Mass., 1998). *Thoughts on Government*, *Adams Papers*, 4:92.

37. *A Dissertation on the Canon and the Feudal Law*, no. 3, *Adams Papers*, 1:121. Brown, *Knowledge Is Power*, 84.

38. The Earl of Clarendon to William Pym, January 17, 1766, *Adams Papers*, 1:167–68.

39. *Thoughts on Government*, ibid., 4:90–91.

40. *The Report of a Constitution*, ibid., 8:260.

41. *A Dissertation on the Canon and the Feudal Law*, no. 4, ibid., 1:128. Also see *A Dissertation on the Canon and the Feudal Law*, no. 3, ibid., 1:120.

42. "Instructions of Boston to its Representatives in the General Court," June 17, 1768, *Adams Papers*, 1:217.

43. See "Novanglus no. 2," *Adams Works*, 4:21. Adams characterized Hutchinson's junto as "but servile copiers of the Andros, Randolph, Dudley, and other champions of their cause towards the close of the last century." Ibid., 4:18. *Diary and Autobiography*, 3:287–88. "Novanglus no. 4," *Adams Works*, 4:53. "Novanglus no. 5," *Adams Works*, 4:64.

44. "Novanglus no. 5," *Adams Works*, 4:75.

45. "Novanglus no. 3," *Adams Works*, 4:30.

46. See John Adams to Jonathan Dickinson Sergeant, July 21, 1776, *Adams Papers*, 4:397, and John Adams to Joseph Hawley, August 25, 1776, ibid., 4:495–96. John Adams to Jonathan Dickinson Sergeant, ibid., 4:397.

47. Donald H. Meyer, *The Democratic Enlightenment* (New York, 1976), 138. Also see Appleby, *Liberalism and Republicanism*, 190.

48. John Adams, *Discourses on Davila: A Series of Papers on Political History* (Philadelphia, 1790), *Adams Works*, 6:279–80.

49. *Letters to John Taylor*, no. 22, *Adams Works*, 6:495. Voltaire, "On Mr. Locke," in *Letters on England*, trans. Leonard Tancock (New York, 1980), 67. *Letters to John Taylor*, no. 32, *Adams Works*, 6:521.

50. John Adams, *A Defense of the Constitutions of Government of the United States of America, Against the Attack of Mr. Turgot, in his Letter to Dr. Price, dated the Twenty-Second Day of March, 1778*, in *Adams Works*, 4:283–84, 559.

51. *Discourses on Davila, Adams Works*, 6:252, 276.

52. Ibid., 6:239–40. *Defense of the Constitutions, Adams Works*, 4:289–90.

53. *Letters to John Taylor*, no. 31, *Adams Works*, 6:517. No. 32, ibid., 6:521.

54. *Defense of the Constitutions*, ibid., 6:185.

55. *Defense of the Constitutions*, ibid., 6:185–86. *Letters to John Taylor*, no. 22, ibid., 6:495, and no. 10, ibid., 6:467.

56. Mercy Otis Warren, *History of the Rise, Progress and Termination of the American Revolution*, ed. Lester H. Cohen (Indianapolis, 1989), 2:675.

57. John Adams to the President of the Congress, February 27, 1779, *Adams Papers*, 7:430–31.

58. John Adams to James Warren, February 25, 1779, ibid., 7:429. John Adams to Mercy Otis Warren, August 3, 1779, ibid., 8:108. *Defense of the Constitutions, Adams Works*, 6:96.

59. John Adams to Francis Dana, August 16, 1776, *Adams Works*, 9:429.

60. John Adams to Secretary Livingston, July 18, 1783, ibid., 8:108. John Adams to Benjamin Franklin, January 24, 1784, ibid., 8:171.

61. See John Adams to Secretary Jay, October 21, 1785, ibid., 8:332.

62. John Adams to Secretary Jay, November 24, 1785, ibid., 8:347–48.

63. John Adams to James Warren, August 4, 1778, *Adams Papers*, 6:348.

64. John Adams to Samuel Adams, August 7, 1778, ibid., 6:354. John Adams to Samuel Adams, December 7, 1778, ibid., 7:256.

65. See John Adams to Elbridge Gerry, December 5, 1778, ibid, 7:248. John Adams to Roger Sherman, December 6, 1778, ibid., 7:254.

66. John Adams to Secretary Livingston, November 11, 1782, *Adams Works*, 8:11–12.

67. John Adams to Secretary Livingston, July 10, 1783, ibid., 8:89.

68. John Adams to Secretary Livingston, January 23, 1783, ibid., 8:27.

69. Dena Goodman, *The Republic of Letters: A Cultural History of the French Enlightenment* (Ithaca, N.Y., 1994), 3–5, 91–100. David Hume, "Of Essay Writing," in *Essays Moral, Political, and Literary*, ed. Eugene F. Miller (Indianapolis, 1985), 536.

70. Jonathan I. Israel, *Radical Enlightenment: Philosophy and the Making of Modernity, 1650–1750* (New York, 2001), 59–60.

71. Roche, *France in the Enlightenment*, 122.

72. Hume, "Of Essay Writing," *Essays*, 535. Goodman, *Republic of Letters*, 3.

73. See Goodman's treatment of *Lettre à d'Alembert* in *Republic of Letters*, 54–56. Hume, "Of Essay Writing," *Essays*, 536. Rousseau quoted in Goodman, *Republic of Letters*, 55. Simon Schama, *Citizens: A Chronicle of the French Revolution* (New York, 1989), 149–50, 153–54.

74. Ernst Cassirer, *The Philosophy of the Enlightenment*, trans. Fritz C. A. Koelln and James P. Pettegrove (Boston, 1964), 6–7. David Hume, *An Enquiry Concerning Human Understanding*, ed. Eric Steinberg (Indianapolis, 1977), 111. Roche, *France in the Enlightenment*, 154.

75. Anne-Robert Jacques Turgot, "Certainty Attainable in all Sciences," in *The Life and Writings of Turgot, Comptroller General of France, 1774–1776*, ed. W. Walker Stephens (London, 1895), 316. Also see Turgot, "Portrait of a Minister of Commerce," ibid., 244–45.

76. On Adams and "ideology," see Zoltan Haraszti, *John Adams and the Prophets of Progress* (Cambridge, Mass., 1952), 166–67. Ibid., 105.

77. *Diary and Autobiography*, 4:80–81.

78. John Adams to Samuel Perley, June 19, 1809, *Adams Works*, 9:622–23. The quote on Franklin, commonly attributed to Turgot, is in Schama, *Citizens*, 44. Schama, *Citizens*, 43.

79. *Diary and Autobiography*, 4:118–19. John Adams to Cotton Tufts, June 2, 1786, *Adams Works*, 9:550.

80. For an extended discussion of the rejection of balanced constitutionalism in France in the 1770s and 1780s, see Joyce Appleby, "The Jefferson-Adams Rupture and the First French Translation of John Adams' *Defence*," *American Historical Review* 73 (1968), 1084–89, and *Liberalism and Republicanism*, 188–209. Voltaire, "On Parliament," in *Letters on England*, 45. Baron de Montesquieu, *The Spirit of the Laws*, trans. Thomas Nugent (New York, 1949), 151.

81. Jean-Jacques Rousseau, *On the Social Contract*, in *On the Social Contract, Discourse on the Origins of Inequality, Discourse on Political Economy*, trans. and ed. Donald A. Cress (Indianapolis, 1983), 30–31, 74.

82. Baron Anne-Robert Jacques Turgot to Dr. Richard Price, March 22, 1778, in *Life and Writings of Turgot*, 299.

83. John Adams to Thomas Jefferson, July 13, 1813 in *The Adams-Jefferson Letters: The Complete Correspondence Between Thomas Jefferson and Abigail and John Adams*, ed. Lester J. Cappon (1959; reprint, Chapel Hill, N.C., 1987), 355. John Adams to Samuel Perley, June 19, 1809, *Adams Works*, 9:622–23.

84. On Adams's fears of the contagion of French thought in America, see Alfred Iacuzzi, *John Adams Scholar* (New York, 1952), 190–91, Paul A. Rahe, *Republics Ancient and Modern* (Chapel Hill, N.C., 1994), 2:24, and Ferling, *Adams*, 287. Also see John Adams to Richard Price, May 20, 1789, *Adams Works*, 9:558–59. John Adams to Philip Mazzei, June 12, 1787, *Adams Works*, 9:552. John Adams to Thomas Jefferson, March 1, 1787, *Adams-Jefferson Letters*, 176. Thompson, *Spirit of Liberty*, 92–93.

85. From 1812 preface to *Discourses on Davila*, *Adams Works*, 6:227.

86. See John Adams to Count Sarsfield, February 3, 1786, ibid., 9:546, and January 21, 1786, ibid., 8:370.

87. John Adams to Benjamin Rush, April 18, 1790, ibid., 9:565–66. For a compelling argument that Adams's core political convictions did not change, see Thompson, *Spirit of Liberty*.

88. Thompson, *Spirit of Liberty*, 109–11.

89. On Adams's use of Hume, Gibbon, and Robertson, see his *Defense of the Constitutions*, vol. 3, *Adams Works*, 4:298. On his use of Ferguson and Smith, see Iacuzzi, *John Adams Scholar*, 90, 138–39.

90. John Adams to Thomas Jefferson, July 13, 1813, *Adams-Jefferson Letters*, 355.

91. *Defense of the Constitutions*, vol. 3, *Adams Works*, 4: 393, 210. John Adams to John Taylor, no. 3, *Adams Works*, 6:454.

92. *Discourses on Davila, Adams Works*, 6:279.

93. *Discourses on Davila*, ibid., 6:234, 232. See Adam Smith, *The Theory of Moral Sentiments*, ed. D. D. Raphael and A. L. Macfie (Indianapolis, 1984). *Discourses on Davila, Adams Works*, 6:232.

94. *Discourses on Davila, Adams Works*, 6:234. On the role of property in fostering inequality in Adams's thought, see Conkin, *Puritans and Pragmatists*, 141.

95. "Novanglus no. 1," *Adams Works*, 4:14. John Adams to Mercy Otis Warren, August 3, 1779, *Adams Papers*, 8:108. "Novanglus no. 5," *Adams Works*, 4:79.

96. John Adams to Thomas Jefferson, November 25, 1813, *Adams-Jefferson Letters*, 398. John Adams to John Jebb, September 25, 1785, *Adams Works*, 9:544.

97. *Defense of the Constitutions*, vol. 3, *Adams Works*, 6:141, 10. See Samuel Adams to John Adams, November 20, 1790, ibid., 6:421, and John Adams to Samuel Adams, October 18, 1790, ibid., 6:417–18.

98. See, for example, Warren, *History of the American Revolution*, 2:675, and Tunis Wortman, "A Solemn Address to Christians and Patriots" (New York, 1800), in Ellis Sandoz, ed., *Political Sermons of the American Founding Era, 1780–1805* (Indianapolis, 1998), 2:1519. "The belief in the separate and independent existence of an entity called 'the people' struck Adams as a typical act of ideology, the confusion of a romantic sentiment lodged in the minds of theorists and propagandists with a social reality." Ellis, *Passionate Sage*, 130. *Defense of the Constitutions*, vol. 2, *Adams Works*, 5:41.

99. John Adams to Benjamin Rush, March 26, 1806, *Spur of Fame*, 55.

100. John Adams to Count Sarsfield, January 21, 1786, *Adams Works*, 8:370.

101. *Defense of the Constitutions*, vol. 1, ibid., 4:362, 354–55.

102. John Adams to Thomas Jefferson, September 2, 1813, *Adams-Jefferson Letters*, 371. John Adams to Samuel Adams, October 18, 1790, *Adams Works*, 6:417. *Defense of the Constitutions*, vol. 1, *Adams Works*, 4:397.

103. *Defense of the Constitutions*, vol. 1, *Adams Works*, 4:397. John Adams to Thomas Jefferson, November 25, 1813, *Adams-Jefferson Letters*, 400.

104. John Adams to John Taylor, no. 4, *Adams Works*, 6:456. John Adams to John Taylor, no. 7, ibid., 6:461. John Adams to John Taylor, no. 22, ibid., 6:495.

105. John Adams to John Taylor, no. 8, ibid., 6:461. John Adams to Thomas Jefferson, July 9, 1813, *Adams-Jefferson Letters*, 352. John Adams to Samuel Adams, October 18, 1790, *Adams Works*, 6:417.

106. John Adams to Thomas Jefferson, March 1, 1787, *Adams-Jefferson Letters*, 176.

107. John Adams to A. M. Cerisier, February 22, 1784, *Adams Works*, 9:522–23. John Adams to Samuel Adams, September 12, 1790, ibid., 6:411–12.

108. *Defense of the Constitutions*, vol. 3, ibid., 6:185–86. John Adams to John Taylor, no. 27, ibid., 6:506–507.

109. *Discourses on Davila*, ibid., 6:279–80.

110. *Defense of the Constitutions*, vol. 2, ibid., 5:9 10. *Defense of the Constitutions*, vol. 1, ibid., 4:588. On the illegitimacy of parties in contemporary political thought, see Richard Hofstadter, *The Idea of a Party System: The Rise of Legitimate Opposition in the United States, 1780–1840* (Berkeley, Calif., 1969).

111. John Adams to Thomas McKean, September 20, 1779, *Adams Works*, 9:485. *Defense of the Constitutions*, vol. 1, ibid., 4:588. John Adams to Thomas Brand-Hollis, June 11, 1790, ibid., 9:570. *Discourses on Davila*, ibid., 6:279–80.

112. *Defense of the Constitutions*, vol. 1, ibid., 4:398. Ibid., 4:289–90. *Discourses on Davila*, *Adams Works*, 6:280.

113. *Defense of the Constitutions*, vol. 1, ibid., 4:397.

114. Ibid., 4:290. Also see Steven Watts, "Ministers, Misanthropes, and Mandarins: The Federalists and the Culture of Capitalism, 1790–1820," in Doron Ben-Atar and Barbara B. Oberg, eds., *Federalists Reconsidered* (Charlottesville, Va., 1998), 170.

115. *Defense of the Constitutions*, vol. 3, *Adams Works*, 5:473, and ibid., 6:187.

116. *Discourses on Davila*, *Adams Works*, 6:394. John Adams to Alexander Jardine, June 1, 1790, ibid., 9:568.

117. John Adams to Thomas Jefferson, June 25, 1813, *Adams-Jefferson Letters*, 334.

118. John Adams to John Jay, September 22, 1787, *Adams Works*, 8:452.

119. Richard Cranch to John Adams, quoted in Thompson, *Spirit of Liberty*, 252. Smith, *John Adams*, 2:700. Thomas Pinckney to John Adams, July 10, 1787, *Adams Works*, 8:443. John Jay to John Adams, July 25, 1787, *Adams Works*, 8:446. Benjamin Rush to Richard Price, June 2, 1787, in *The Letters*

of Benjamin Rush, ed. L. H. Butterfield (Princeton, N.J., 1951), 1:418. Richard Henry Lee to John Adams, September 3, 1787, *Adams Works*, 9:553. James Madison to Thomas Jefferson, June 6, 1787, *Republic of Letters*, 1:479.

120. Thompson, *Spirit of Liberty*, 260–64.

121. Samuel Bryan, "Centinel no. 1," *Independent Ga{etteer* (Philadelphia, October 5, 1787), in Bernard Bailyn, ed., *The Debate on the Constitution: Federalist and Antifederalist Speeches, Articles, and Letters During the Struggle over Ratification* (New York, 1993), 1:54–55. "John Humble," *Independent Ga{etteer* (Philadelphia, October 29, 1787), in Bailyn, *Debate*, 1:224. "On the New Constitution," *State Ga{ette of South Carolina* (Charleston, January 28, 1788), Bailyn, *Debate*, 2:107.

122. Vanderkemp quoted in Thompson, *Spirit of Liberty*, 254. Richard Henry Lee to John Adams, September 3, 1787, *Adams Works*, 9:554. John Adams to Richard Price, May 20, 1789, *Adams Works*, 9:559.

123. John Adams to Roger Sherman, December 6, 1778, *Adams Papers*, 7:254. John Adams to Elbridge Gerry, December 5, 1778, ibid., 7:249.

124. James Lovell to John Adams, September 27, 1779, ibid., 8:170–72. See his instructions from Congress, ibid., 8:203–204. Smith, *John Adams*, 1:474–75. The exchange between Adams and Vergennes is summarized in an editorial note in *Adams Papers*, 8:516–18.

125. "Autobiography," February 1780, *Diary and Autobiography*, 4:252–53.

126. James H. Hutson, *John Adams and the Diplomacy of the American Revolution* (Lexington, Ky., 1980), 72–73.

127. John Adams to Elbridge Gerry, November 27, 1778, *Adams Papers*, 7:236. John Adams to the President of the Congress, August 4, 1779, ibid., 8:112.

128. Smith, *John Adams*, 1:483. Commonly known as the *Ga{ette de Leyde*, the actual title of Luzac's publication was *Nouvelles de Divers Endroits*. Simon Schama, *Patriots and Liberators: Revolution in the Netherlands, 1780–1813* (New York, 1977), 60. The request for a loan was made in mid-October. John Adams to Hendrick Calkoen, October 17, 1780, *Adams Papers*, 10:232. Schama, *Patriots*, 61. Smith, *John Adams*, 1:286.

129. Jonathan R. Dull, *A Diplomatic History of the American Revolution* (New Haven, Conn., 1985), 126. Hutson, *Adams and the Diplomacy*, 79.

130. Hutson, *Adams and the Diplomacy*, 87–89. Smith, *John Adams*, 1:494.

131. Hutson, *Adams and the Diplomacy*, 92. Adams's "Memorial" quoted in Schama, *Patriots*, 60. Schama, *Patriots*, 61.

132. Smith, *John Adams*, 1:499–500, 502. Ferling, *Adams*, 236–38.

133. Hutson, *Adams and the Diplomacy*, 104. Schama, *Patriots*, 63. Hutson, *Adams and the Diplomacy*, 107–108. Ferling, *Adams*, 240. Smith, *John Adams*, 1:508.

134. Hutson, *Adams and the Diplomacy*, 111. Smith, *John Adams*, 1:509, 533. Smith, *John Adams*, 1:513, 517. Schama, *Patriots*, 59.

135. Ferling, *Adams*, 241. "Diary," November 12, 1782, *Diary and Autobiography*, 3:53.
136. Schama, *Patriots*, 63.
137. Smith, *John Adams*, 2:917.
138. Ralph Adams Brown, *The Presidency of John Adams* (Lawrence, Kans., 1975), 16, and Smith, *John Adams*, 2:895.
139. John Adams to Henry Knox, March 30, 1797, *Adams Works*, 8:535.
140. John Adams to Charles Lee, March 19, 1799, ibid., 8:629.
141. Brown, *Presidency*, 26. Elkins and McKitrick, *Age of Federalism*, 539. Ferling, *Adams*, 411. Elkins and McKitrick, *Age of Federalism*, 631.
142. Brown, *Presidency*, 59.
143. Ibid., 156. Elkins and McKitrick, *Age of Federalism*, 645.
144. Smith, *John Adams*, 2:923–24, and Brown, *Presidency*, 39. Ferling, *Adams*, 342. Smith, *John Adams*, 2:927.
145. Ferling, *Adams*, 340. See John Adams to Henry Knox, March 30, 1797, *Adams Works*, 8:535. Elkins and McKitrick, *Age of Federalism*, 542. Brown, *Presidency*, 28.
146. On March 25 Adams had called for Congress to meet in special session on May 15. Brown, *Presidency*, 39. Smith, *John Adams*, 2:924. "Speech to Both Houses of Congress," May 16, 1797, *Adams Works*, 9:113, 112, 115.
147. Brown, *Presidency*, 43, and *Adams Works*, 9:150. Elkins and McKitrick, *Age of Federalism*, 563. Adams informed Gerry of his nomination on June 20. See John Adams to Elbridge Gerry, June 20, 1797, *Adams Works*, 8:546. See "Speech to Both Houses of Congress," November 23, 1797, *Adams Works*, 9:121–22.
148. Elkins and McKitrick, *Age of Federalism*, 553. John Adams to Timothy Pickering, October 31, 1797, *Adams Works*, 8:560.
149. Elkins and McKitrick, *Age of Federalism*, 555. Brown, *Presidency*, 45. Manning J. Dauer, *The Adams Federalists* (Baltimore, Md., 1953), 149.
150. See "Speech to Both Houses of Congress," November 23, 1797, *Adams Works*, 9:122. Brown, *Presidency*, 45. Smith, *John Adams*, 2:940.
151. Smith, *John Adams*, 2:947. For a good synopsis of the negotiations, see Elkins and McKitrick, *Age of Federalism*, 566–73.
152. John Adams to the Heads of Departments, March 13, 1798, *Adams Works*, 8:568. Smith, *John Adams*, 2:954. James Roger Sharp, *American Politics in the Early Republic: The New Nation in Crisis* (New Haven, Conn., 1993), 173. Elkins and McKitrick, *Age of Federalism*, 588. "Message to Both Houses of Congress," April, 3, 1798, *Adams Works*, 9:158.
153. Theodore Sedgwick quoted in Brown, *Presidency*, 52. Nathanael Emmons, "A Discourse Delivered at the National Fast" (1799), in Charles S. Hyneman and Donald S. Lutz, eds., *American Political Writing During the Founding Era, 1760–1805* (Indianapolis, 1983), 2:1041, and Timothy Dwight, "The

Duty of Americans, at the Present Crisis" (1798), in Sandoz, *Political Sermons*, 2:1391, 1387. Abigail Adams quoted in Brown, *Presidency*, 54.

154. Smith, *John Adams*, 2:962–64. John Adams to the Cincinnati of South Carolina, September 15, 1798, *Adams Works*, 9:223. Brown, *Presidency*, 132–33.

155. Elkins and McKitrick, *Age of Federalism*, 588. Brown, *Presidency*, 53–54. Elkins and McKitrick, *Age of Federalism*, 635. Elkins and McKitrick, *Age of Federalism*, 589. Brown, *Presidency*, 74, 76. Elkins and McKitrick, *Age of Federalism*, 653–54.

156. Brown, *Presidency*, 158–61.

157. See "Proclamation Opening the Trade with Certain Ports of St. Domingo," June 26, 1799, *Adams Works*, 9:176.

158. "Speech to Both Houses of Congress," December 3, 1799, ibid., 9:138. Elkins and McKitrick, *Age of Federalism*, 659. Paul Finkleman, "The Problem of Slavery in the Age of Federalism," in Ben-Atar and Oberg, eds., *Federalists Reconsidered*, 149–52.

159. Elkins and McKitrick, *Age of Federalism*, 591–92.

160. Smith, *John Adams*, 2:975. Ferling, *Adams*, 367. Smith, *John Adams*, 2:976.

161. Elkins and McKitrick, *Age of Federalism*, 595–96.

162. Smith, *John Adams*, 2:1004. Brown, *Presidency*, 127–28. See John Adams to Charles Lee, May 21, 1800, *Adams Works*, 9:60.

163. Smith, *John Adams*, 2:969. "Message to Both Houses of Congress," June 21, 1798, *Adams Works*, 9:159. "Speech to Both Houses of Congress," December 8, 1798, *Adams Works*, 9:130.

164. See "Message to the Senate; Nominating an Envoy to France," February 18, 1799, *Adams Works*, 9:161–62. Ferling, *Adams*, 379. Smith, *John Adams*, 2:1001. Brown, *Presidency*, 95. "Correspondence Originally Published in the *Boston Patriot*," Letter 4, *Adams Works*, 9:248, Smith, *John Adams*, 2:1002–1003, and Dauer, *Adams Federalists*, 238. "Message to the Senate; Nominating Three Envoys to France," February 25, 1799, *Adams Works*, 9:162–63, and Brown, *Presidency*, 100.

165. Brown, *Presidency*, 175. John Ferling has claimed that "perhaps never in United States history has a party turned on its own president as virulently as the High Federalists struck against Adams." Ferling, *Adams*, 379. John Adams to Timothy Pickering, October 20, 1798, *Adams Works*, 8:609, and Brown, *Presidency*, 88. John Adams to Timothy Pickering, January 15, 1799, *Adams Works*, 8:621. Smith, *John Adams*, 2:1003.

166. John Adams to George Washington, February 19, 1799, *Adams Works*, 8:625–26.

167. Smith, *John Adams*, 2:971. Brown, *Presidency*, 61. *Boston Patriot*, Letter 3, *Adams Works*, 9:246. *Boston Patriot*, Letter 3, *Adams Works*, 9:245. William Vans Murray to John Adams, July 17, 1798, *Adams Works*, 8:680.

168. Brown, *Presidency*, 87, 95. The decrees had been revoked the previous July. Smith, *John Adams*, 2:983.

169. John Adams to James McHenry, August 14, 1798, *Adams Works*, 8:580.

170. Smith, *John Adams*, 2:972. John Adams to George Washington, October 9, 1798, *Adams Works*, 8:600–601. Smith, *John Adams*, 2:866. John Adams to John Trumbull, January 23, 1791, *Adams Works*, 9:573.

171. Dauer, *Adams Federalists*, 174. Brown, *Presidency*, 140–42.

172. Brown, *Presidency*, 151. Adams quoted in Elkins and McKitrick, *Age of Federalism*, 616.

173. Ferling, *Adams*, 373. Hamilton to Sedgwick quoted in Brown, *Presidency*, 119, and Richard B. Morris, ed., *Alexander Hamilton and the Founding of the Nation* (1957; New York, reprint, 1969), 282. *Boston Patriot*, Letter 14, *Adams Works*, 9:294.

174. Brown, *Presidency*, 119.

175. Ibid., 102–103. Elkins and McKitrick, *Age of Federalism*, 635, and Smith, *John Adams*, 2:1010. *Boston Patriot*, Letter 6, *Adams Works*, 9:251.

176. Timothy Pickering to John Adams, September 11, 1799, *Adams Works*, 9:25. Timothy Pickering to John Adams, September 16, 1799, ibid., 9:30.

177. Benjamin Stoddert to John Adams, September 13, 1799, ibid., 9:28. Smith, *John Adams*, 2:1013. Brown, *Presidency*, 107, 110.

178. *Boston Patriot*, Letter 6, *Adams Works*, 9:252. Ferling, *Adams*, 385.

179. *Boston Patriot*, Letter 4, *Adams Works*, 9:254–55.

180. Ibid., 9:255. *Boston Patriot*, Letter 12, *Adams Works*, 9:281. Smith, *John Adams*, 2:1016. John Adams to Timothy Pickering, October 16, 1799, *Adams Works*, 9:39.

181. Brown, *Presidency*, 165. Elkins and McKitrick, *Age of Federalism*, 687. Brown, *Presidency*, 164. Ferling, *Adams*, 408. Elkins and McKitrick, *Age of Federalism*, 664.

182. Elkins and McKitrick, *Age of Federalism*, 683. Ferling, *Adams*, 408. The Senate rejected the article deferring the issues of indemnification and prior treaties and limited the terms of the agreement to eight years. Elkins and McKitrick, *Age of Federalism*, 687.

183. Wortman, "Solemn Address to Christians and Patriots," in Sandoz, *Political Sermons*, 2:1519. Michael Durey, *"With the Hammer of Truth": James Thompson Callender and America's Early National Heroes* (Charlottesville, Va., 1990), 123–25. Forrest McDonald, *Alexander Hamilton: A Biography* (New York, 1979), 351, and Elkins and McKitrick, *Age of Federalism*, 737. "The Public Conduct and Character of John Adams, Esq., President of the United States" (New York, 1800), in *The Works of Alexander Hamilton*, ed. John C. Hamilton (New York, 1851), 7:691, 715, 725–26.

184. Elkins and McKitrick, *Age of Federalism*, 739. McDonald, *Hamilton*, 348–49. See John Adams to James McHenry, May 6, 1800, *Adams Works*,

9:51–52; John Adams to Timothy Pickering, May 10, 1800, *Adams Works*, 9:53–54; and John Adams to Timothy Pickering, May 12, 1800, *Adams Works*, 9:55. Ferling, *Adams*, 395. Elkins and McKitrick, *Age of Federalism*, 736–37. See Alexander Hamilton to John Adams, August 1, 1800, in *Works of Hamilton*, 7:726–27.

185. John Adams to Dr. Ogden, December 3, 1800, *Adams Works*, 9:576. Dauer, *Adams Federalists*, 254. See John Adams to John Jay, November 24, 1800, *Adams Works*, 9:91. Brown, *Presidency*, 193.

186. Elkins and McKitrick, *Age of Federalism*, 741, 732. Smith, *John Adams*, 2:1057, and Brown, *Presidency*, 193.

187. *Boston Patriot*, Letter 12, *Adams Works*, 9:281.

188. John Adams to Benjamin Rush, August 31, 1809, *Spur of Fame*, 165.

189. John Adams to Benjamin Rush, June 21, 1811, ibid., 197. John Adams to Thomas Jefferson, July 3, 1813, *Adams-Jefferson Letters*, 349.

190. John Adams to Benjamin Rush, March 23, 1809, *Spur of Fame*, 151.

191. Ferling, *Adams*, 421–22. John Adams to Benjamin Rush, April 12, 1809, *Spur of Fame*, 155. Ferling, *Adams*, 429. John Adams to Benjamin Rush, August 7, 1809, *Spur of Fame*, 162–63. John Adams to Benjamin Rush, April 12, 1809, *Spur of Fame*, 155.

192. John Adams to Benjamin Rush, September 1807, *Spur of Fame*, 101. Benjamin Rush to Thomas Jefferson, February 17, 1812, *Letters of Rush*, 2:1127. Benjamin Rush to John Adams, October 17, 1809, *Letters of Rush*, 2:1021–22. John Adams to Thomas Jefferson, January 1, 1812, *Adams-Jefferson Letters*, 290.

193. Thomas Jefferson to John Adams, August 11, 1815, *Adams-Jefferson Letters*, 453. John Adams to Thomas Jefferson, June 25, 1813, ibid., 333. Thomas Jefferson to John Adams, June 15, 1813, ibid., 331. Thomas Jefferson to John Adams, June 27, 1813, ibid., 337. John Adams to Thomas Jefferson, July 15, 1813, ibid., 358.

194. Benjamin Rush to Thomas Jefferson, March 3, 1712, *Letters of Rush*, 2:1128.

195. Ferling, *Adams*, 433–37.

196. John Adams to Benjamin Rush, February 27, 1805, *Spur of Fame*, 23. Friedrich Nietzsche, *The Gay Science*, trans. Walter Kaufmann (New York, 1974), 76.

197. John Adams to John Jebb, August 21, 1785, *Adams Works*, 9:535.

CHAPTER THREE. THOMAS JEFFERSON:
ROMANTIC AMERICA

1. Kennedy quoted in Merrill D. Peterson, *Thomas Jefferson and the New Nation* (New York, 1970), 724.

2. Thomas Jefferson to James Madison, September 6, 1789, in *The Republic of*

Letters: The Correspondence between Thomas Jefferson and James Madison, 1776–1826, ed. James Morton Smith (New York, 1995), 1:632, and Thomas Jefferson to William S. Smith, November 13, 1787, in *The Papers of Thomas Jefferson*, ed. Julian P. Boyd et al. (Princeton, N.J., 1950–), 12:356–57. Thomas Jefferson to John Adams, October 28, 1813, in *The Adams-Jefferson Letters: The Complete Correspondence Between Thomas Jefferson and Abigail and John Adams*, ed. Lester J. Cappon (1959; reprint, Chapel Hill, N.C., 1987), 388.

3. Peterson, *Jefferson and Nation*, 719. Chastellux quoted in William Sterne Randall, *Thomas Jefferson: A Life* (New York, 1993), 346. Smith quoted in Michael Knox Beran, *Jefferson's Demons: Portrait of a Restless Mind* (New York, 2003), 178.

4. Thomas Jefferson to John Adams, April 8, 1816, *Adams-Jefferson Letters*, 467.

5. Thomas Jefferson, *Notes on the State of Virginia*, ed. William Peden (Chapel Hill, N.C., 1982), 164–65. "The Count de Volney, visiting Monticello, was startled to find that his host, when he went to inspect the fields, carried with him a *fouet*, a small whip." Beran, *Restless Mind*, 90.

6. Randall, *A Life*, 10. Ibid., 2. Chastellux quoted in Alf J. Mapp, Jr., *Thomas Jefferson: A Strange Case of Mistaken Identity* (New York, 1987), 12. *The Autobiography of Thomas Jefferson*, in *The Life and Selected Writings of Thomas Jefferson*, ed. Adrienne Koch and William Peden (New York, 1993), 7, and Mapp, *Strange Case*, 12.

7. On his education, see *Autobiography*, *Life and Writings*, 8, and Randall, *A Life*, 16.

8. Randall, *A Life*, 239–40. Beran, *Restless Mind*, 33–34. Joseph J. Ellis, *American Sphinx: The Character of Thomas Jefferson* (New York, 1997), 196. On Jefferson's problems with debt, see Herbert E. Sloan, *Principle and Interest: Thomas Jefferson and the Problem of Debt* (Charlottesville, Va., 1995).

9. Peterson, *Jefferson and Nation*, 988. John Adams to Benjamin Rush, November 11, 1807, in *The Spur of Fame: Dialogues of John Adams and Benjamin Rush, 1805–1813*, ed. John A. Schutz and Douglass Adair (San Marino, Ca., 1966), 106.

10. John Adams to Benjamin Rush, November 11, 1807, *The Spur of Fame*, 106. Peterson, *Jefferson and Nation*, 37.

11. Thomas Jefferson to John Page, July 15, 1763, *Jefferson Papers*, 1:10. Thomas Jefferson to Thomas Jefferson Randolph, November 24, 1808, in *The Works of Thomas Jefferson*, ed. Paul Leicester Ford (New York, 1905), 11:80–81.

12. On Jefferson's treatment of his slaves, see Lucia C. Stanton, "'Those Who Labor For My Happiness': Thomas Jefferson and His Slaves," in Peter S. Onuf, ed., *Jeffersonian Legacies* (Charlottesville, Va., 1993), 147–80. Thomas Jefferson to Edward Coles, August 25, 1814, *Jefferson Works*, 11:419.

13. Kenneth A. Lockridge, *On the Sources of Patriarchal Rage: The Commonplace Books of William Byrd and Thomas Jefferson and the Gendering of Power in the Eighteenth Century* (New York, 1992). Thomas Jefferson to Anne Willing Bingham, May 11, 1788, *Jefferson Papers*, 8:151. Thomas Jefferson to William Fleming, March 20, 1764, *Jefferson Papers*, 1:16.

14. The statement of John Walker is reproduced in Dumas Malone, *Jefferson the Virginian* (Boston, 1948), 449–50. To his credit, Jefferson never denied his role in the Walker affair.

15. Jefferson, *Notes on Virginia*, 162.

16. The wealth estimates are culled from David Hackett Fischer, *Albion's Seed: Four British Folkways in America* (New York, 1989), 374–75. Kulikoff estimates that the yeomanry was slightly larger, but the planter elite was smaller. Alan Kulikoff, *Tobacco and Slaves: The Development of Southern Cultures in the Chesapeake, 1680–1800* (Chapel Hill, N.C., 1986), 262.

17. Quoted in Stanton, "Those Who Labor," *Jeffersonian Legacies*, 150.

18. Samuel Johnson, "Taxation no Tyranny," in *Samuel Johnson: Political Writings*, ed. Donald J. Greene (Indianapolis, 1977), 454. Thomas Jefferson to John Holmes, April 22, 1820, *Jefferson Works*, 12:158–59.

19. Thomas Jefferson to Robert Skipwith, August 3, 1771, *Jefferson Papers*, 1:78–80. Mapp, *Strange Case*, 5.

20. Thomas Jefferson, *A Summary View of the Rights of British America*, in *Thomas Jefferson: An Anthology*, ed. Peter Onuf (New York, 1999), 27.

21. Ibid., 36, 37. "A Declaration by the Representatives of the United States of America, in General Congress Assembled, 4 July, 1776," in ibid., 42, 45. Jay Fliegelman, *Declaring Independence: Jefferson, Natural Language, and the Culture of Performance* (Stanford, Calif., 1993).

22. Andrew Burstein, *The Inner Jefferson: Portrait of a Grieving Optimist* (Charlottesville, Va., 1995), 288.

23. *Autobiography*, *Life and Writings*, 8. Randall, *A Life*, 21–22.

24. Randall, *A Life*, 38.

25. Peterson, *Jefferson and Nation*, 12. *Autobiography*, *Life and Writings*, 8.

26. *Autobiography*, *Life and Writings*, 8.

27. Peterson, *Jefferson and Nation*, 14. Randall, *A Life*, 47–48, 56. Quoted in Randall, *A Life*, 57.

28. See Thomas Jefferson to Robert Skipwith, August 3, 1771, *Jefferson Papers*, 1:78–80.

29. Randall, *A Life*, 53, Peterson, *Jefferson and Nation*, 15, and *Autobiography*, *Life and Writings*, 8. Malone, *Virginian*, xv.

30. "A Bill for the More General Diffusion of Knowledge," *Jefferson Papers*, 2:526–27.

31. "Bill for Diffusion," ibid., 2:528. *Notes on Virginia*, 146–47. "Bill for Diffusion," *Jefferson Papers*, 2:526–27, 531–33. *Notes on Virginia*, 146.

32. "Bill for Diffusion," *Jefferson Papers*, 2:526–27.

33. "A Bill for Amending the Constitution of the college of William and Mary and substituting more certain revenues for its support," *Jefferson Papers*, 2:541–42, and *Notes on Virginia*, 150–51.

34. See "A Bill for Establishing a Public Library," number 81, listed in "Catalogue of Bills," *Jefferson Papers*, 2:331. Thomas Jefferson to Edward Carrington, January 16, 1789, ibid., 11:49. "Draft Constitution for Virginia," ibid., 1:353.

35. Rhys Isaac, "Evangelical Revolt: The Nature of the Baptists' Challenge to the Traditional Order in Virginia, 1765 to 1775," *William and Mary Quarterly*, 3rd series, 31 (1974), 345–68. "A Bill for Establishing Religious Freedom," *Jefferson Papers*, 2:545–46. *Notes on Virginia*, 121.

36. "Draft Constitution for Virginia," *Jefferson Papers*, 1:347–52.

37. Ellis, *Sphinx*, 67. See "Catalogue of Bills Prepared by the Committee of Revisors," *Jefferson Papers*, 2:329–33. "A Bill for Proportioning Crimes and Punishments," *Jefferson Papers*, 2:494–504.

38. Quoted in Doron S. Ben-Atar, *The Origins of Jeffersonian Commercial Policy and Diplomacy* (New York, 1993), 27. Peterson, *Jefferson and Nation*, 23. *Summary View, Jefferson: An Anthology*, 28. Ben-Atar, *Commercial Policy*, 33. Malone, *Virginian*, 318.

39. *Summary View, Jefferson: An Anthology*, 33. "A Declaration," *Jefferson: An Anthology*, 44. Thomas Jefferson to Edward Coles, August 25, 1814, *Jefferson Works*, 11:416–17, and Malone, *Virginian*, 141. "A Bill to Prevent the Importation of Slaves," *Jefferson Papers*, 2:24. "A Bill concerning Slaves," ibid., 2:470. *Notes on Virginia*, 137.

40. Denis Diderot, "Observations sur le Nakaz," in *Denis Diderot: Political Writings*, trans. and ed. John Hope Mason and Robert Wokler (Cambridge, Eng., 1992), 115–16. David Hume, "Of the Coalition of Parties," in *Essays Moral, Political, and Literary*, ed. Eugene F. Miller (Indianapolis, 1985), 494.

41. *Notes on Virginia*, 147. Thomas Jefferson to Peter Carr, September 7, 1814, in *Thomas Jefferson, Writings*, ed. Merrill D. Peterson (New York, 1984), 1348–49.

42. "Draft Constitution for Virginia," *Jefferson Papers*, 1:340–41. Thomas Jefferson to Edmund Pendleton, August 26, 1776, ibid., 1:503–504. "Draft Constitution for Virginia," ibid., 1:350–51.

43. "A Bill for Proportioning Crimes and Punishments," ibid., 2:497–98. Thomas Jefferson to George Wythe, November 1, 1778, ibid., 2:230.

44. "A Bill Concerning Slaves," ibid., 2:471.

45. *Notes on Virginia*, 138.

46. David Hume, "Of Superstition and Enthusiasm," *Essays*, 75.

47. Baruch Spinoza, *The Ethics and Selected Letters*, trans. Samuel Shirley and ed. Seymour Feldman (Indianapolis, 1982), 59. Voltaire, *Candide*, trans. Daniel Gordon (New York, 1995), 42.

48. David Hume, "Of Refinement in the Arts," *Essays*, 269, 277.

49. Adam Smith, *The Theory of Moral Sentiments*, ed. D. D. Raphael and A. L. Macfie (Indianapolis, 1984), 23.

50. Bernard Mandeville, "An Enquiry into the Origins of Moral Virtue," in *The Fable of the Bees, or Private Vices, Publick Benefits*, ed. F. B. Kaye (1924; reprint, Indianapolis, 1988), 1:42–43.

51. David Hume, *An Enquiry Concerning the Principles of Morals*, ed. J. B. Schneewind (Indianapolis, 1983), 43. Francis Hutcheson, "An Inquiry Concerning the Original of our Ideas of Virtue or Moral Good," in *Francis Hutcheson: Philosophical Writings*, ed. R. S. Downie (London, 1994), 90.

52. *Spectator* nos. 411 and 413, in *The Works of the Right Honorable Joseph Addison*, ed. Richard Hurd, D.D. (London, 1893), 3:394–96, 402–403. David Hume, "Of the Standard of Taste," *Essays*, 237.

53. Hutcheson, "An Inquiry Concerning Beauty, Order, Harmony, Design," *Philosophical Writings*, 15, 19–20.

54. Edmund Burke, *A Philosophical Enquiry into the Origins of our Ideas of the Sublime and Beautiful*, ed. Adam Phillips (New York, 1990), 47, 119.

55. Ibid., 122–23.

56. Thomas Jefferson to John Trumbull, February 15, 1788, *Jefferson Papers*, 14:561.

57. J. H. Bumfritt, *The French Enlightenment* (London, 1972), 111. Burstein, *Inner Jefferson*, 39. John Patrick Diggins, *The Lost Soul of American Politics: Virtue, Self-Interest, and the Foundations of Liberalism* (New York, 1984), 45.

58. *Notes on Virginia*, 165. Also see Thomas Jefferson to James Madison, January 30, 1787, *Jefferson Papers*, 11:92–93, and Thomas Jefferson to Edward Carrington, January 16, 1787, *Jefferson Papers*, 11:49.

59. Burstein, *Inner Jefferson*, 33. Thomas Jefferson to Charles Macpherson, February 25, 1773, *Jefferson Papers*, 1:96. See Robert Darnton, "Readers Respond to Rousseau: The Fabrication of Romantic Sensitivity," in *The Great Cat Massacre and Other Episodes in French Cultural History* (New York, 1984), 215–56. Burstein, *Inner Jefferson*, 43. Thomas Jefferson to Peter Carr, August 10, 1787, *Jefferson Papers*, 12:15.

60. See Roy Porter, *The Creation of the Modern World: The Untold Story of the British Enlightenment* (New York, 2000), 283. Thomas Jefferson to Maria Cosway, October 12, 1786, *Jefferson Papers*, 10:450. Thomas Jefferson to Martha Jefferson, December 11, 1783, *Jefferson Papers*, 6:380.

61. Burstein, *Inner Jefferson*, 158.

62. "Both the expectations that Jefferson harbored for his private life in his mansion on the mountain, as well as his way of trying to design and construct it, suggested a level of indulged sentimentality that one normally associates with an adolescent." Ellis, *Sphinx*, 35. Peterson, *Jefferson and Nation*, 26. *Notes on Virginia*, 24–25.

63. Burstein, *Inner Jefferson*, 287. Simon Schama, *Citizens: A Chronicle of the French Revolution* (New York, 1989), 149. Also see Schama, *Citizens*, 145–62.

64. Thomas Jefferson to James Monroe, May 20, 1782, *Jefferson Papers*, 6:184–85.

65. *Notes on Virginia*, 118. Malone, *Virginian*, 253.

66. Malone, *Virginian*, 315. Ibid., 319.

67. Peterson, *Jefferson and Nation*, 169.

68. Ibid., 197. Horatio Gates to Thomas Jefferson, October 6, 1780, *Jefferson Papers*, 4:16.

69. Horatio Gates to Thomas Jefferson, August 3, 1780, *Jefferson Papers*, 3:524–25.

70. Peterson, *Jefferson and Nation*, 198–99. Mapp, *Strange Case*, 143.

71. See George Washington to Thomas Jefferson, December 11, 1779, *Jefferson Papers*, 3:217. William Tatham to William Armistead Burwell, June 13, 1805, ibid., 4:273–74.

72. Mapp, *Strange Case*, 153. John Beckley to Thomas Jefferson, enclosing a Resolution of the House of Delegates, June 12, 1781, *Jefferson Papers*, 6:88.

73. "Diary of Arnold's Invasion of 1781," *Jefferson Papers*, 4:260. Thomas Jefferson to James Monroe, May 20, 1782, ibid., 6:184–85.

74. Peterson, *Jefferson and Nation*, 171. John Taylor to Thomas Jefferson, December 5, 1780, *Jefferson Papers*, 4:181.

75. Mapp, *Strange Case*, 139. Peterson, *Jefferson and Nation*, 233.

76. Mapp, *Strange Case*, 148–49. Baron Steuben to Thomas Jefferson, February 11, 1781, *Jefferson Papers*, 4:584. Thomas Jefferson to Baron Steuben, February 12, 1781, *Jefferson Papers*, 4:592–93.

77. Thomas Jefferson to the County Lieutenants of Hampshire and Berkeley, December 24, 1780, *Jefferson Papers*, 4:229. The other directives are in ibid., 4:230–32. Thomas Jefferson to George Rogers Clark, April 19, 1780, ibid., 3:356. Mapp, *Strange Case*, 147. Ellis, *Sphinx*, 66. Greene quoted in Peterson, *Jefferson and Nation*, 219.

78. "Diary of Arnold's Invasion," *Jefferson Papers*, 4:264. "Resolution of Thanks to Jefferson by the Virginia General Assembly," ibid., 6:135–36.

79. Peterson, *Jefferson and Nation*, 202. See "Marbois's Queries concerning Virginia," *Jefferson Papers*, 4:166–67.

80. Richard Price to Thomas Jefferson, July 2, 1785, *Jefferson Papers*, 8:258–59.

81. Ibid.

82. David Hume, "Of Refinement in the Arts," *Essays*, 271. Adam Smith, *An Inquiry into the Nature and Causes of the Wealth of Nations*, ed. Edwin Cannan (Chicago, 1976), 426. Smith further argued that good government and liberty were brought to the countryside by the cities, thus destroying baronial power; Smith, *Wealth of Nations*, 432–45.

83. *Spectator* no. 69, *Works of Addison*, 2:373. Voltaire, "Of Commerce," in *Letters on England*, trans. Leonard Tancock (New York, 1980), 52. Hume, "Of Commerce," *Essays*, 262.

84. *Notes on Virginia*, 108–109.
85. Ibid., 164–65.
86. Edmund S. Morgan, *Inventing the People: The Rise of Popular Sovereignty in England and America* (New York, 1988), 169.
87. *Notes on Virginia*, 174.
88. Ibid., 93. Also see Thomas Jefferson to Edward Carrington, January 16, 1787, *Jefferson Papers*, 11:49.
89. John Adams to Thomas Jefferson, May 22, 1785, *Adams-Jefferson Letters*, 21. *Notes on Virginia*, 138, 143.
90. Winthrop D. Jordan, *White Over Black: American Attitudes Toward the Negro, 1550–1812* (New York, 1968), 455. According to John C. Miller, "Jefferson helped to inaugurate the historical tendency in America to invest racial prejudice with the gloss of pseudo-scientific verification it occupied in the nineteenth century." John Chester Miller, *The Wolf by the Ears: Thomas Jefferson and Slavery* (Charlottesville, Va., 1977), 58.
91. *Notes on Virginia*, 138–39.
92. Ibid., 139–41.
93. Ibid., 140.
94. Ibid., 139–42.
95. Ibid., 139–40.
96. Ibid., 142. Gary Wills, *Inventing America: Jefferson's Declaration of Independence* (New York, 1978), 211–28. Also see Richard K. Matthews, *The Radical Politics of Thomas Jefferson: A Revisionist View* (Lawrence, Kans., 1984), 53–71.
97. For Hutcheson, the moral sense presupposes the sense of beauty, for it is only in the latter that, pace Mandeville (which was the point after all), we can find clear evidence of disinterested human judgment. Hutcheson not only frequently analogized the moral sense to the aesthetic imagination, he often treated the former as a species of the latter. Thus the origins of our notions of good and virtue are traced to "a distinct perception of *beauty or excellence* in the kind affections of rational agents," a perception that is later shown to be rooted in our "sense of *goodness* and *moral beauty* in actions." Like all aesthetic judgments, Hutcheson insists that these moral perceptions are thoroughly "distinct from advantage" or the selfish calculus of interest found in egoists and Epicureans like Mandeville. Frances Hutcheson, "An Inquiry Concerning the Original of Our Ideas of Virtue or Moral Good," *Philosophical Writings*, 70, 95. For evidence that Jefferson also saw the aesthetic sense as critical to the moral sense, see Charles A. Miller, *Jefferson and Nature: An Interpretation* (Baltimore, 1988), 103. Francis Hutcheson, "A Short Introduction to Moral Philosophy," *Philosophical Writings*, 161. "For 'tis plainly for the common good, that no mortal endowed with reason and forethought should be . . . subjected to the will of his fellow," Hutcheson claimed, adding pointedly, "except

in some rare cases, that the interest of a society may make it necessary."
Philosophical Writings, 168.

98. *Notes on Virginia*, 87. In a letter to Thomas Cooper written in 1814,
Jefferson compared the plight of slaves favorably to that of English work-
ers. Slaves were "better fed in the States, warmer clothed, and labor less . . .
They have the comfort, too, of numerous families." Quoted in Garrett
Ward Sheldon, *The Political Philosophy of Thomas Jefferson* (Baltimore,
1991), 128. *Notes on Virginia*, 139.

99. *Notes on Virginia*, 162.

100. Ibid., 163.

101. Ibid. See, for example, Miller's observation that "from his student days until the end of his life he doubted the existence of an immaterial soul or
spirit." Miller, *Jefferson and Nature*, 25.

102. *Notes on Virginia*, 143, 138.

103. Ibid., 137–38.

104. La Rochefoucauld quoted in Jordan, *White Over Black*, 553. Thomas
Jefferson to John Holmes, April 22, 1820, *Jefferson Works*, 12:158–59. The
same argument can be found in Thomas Jefferson to Albert Gallatin,
December 26, 1820, *Jefferson Works*, 12:186–89.

105. Thomas Jefferson to John Holmes, April 22, 1820, *Jefferson Works*,
12:158–60.

106. Ellis, *Sphinx*, 35.

107. *Notes on Virginia*, 175.

108. Thomas Jefferson to Philip Mazzei, April 24, 1796, *Jefferson Papers*, 29:82.

109. Thomas Jefferson to Edmund Pendleton, August 26, 1776, ibid., 1:503.
Thomas Jefferson to Edmund Randolph, August 18, 1799, *Jefferson Works*,
9:74, "Opinion on the Treaties with France," April 28, 1793, *Jefferson
Papers*, 25:608–609.

110. Jean-Jacques Rousseau, *On the Social Contract*, in *On the Social Contract,
Discourse on the Origin of Inequality, Discourse on Political Economy*, trans.
and ed. Donald A. Cress (Indianapolis, 1983), 31–32, James Madison to
Thomas Jefferson, October 24 and November 1, 1787, *Republic of Letters*,
1:500–501. "Response to the Citizens of Albermarle," February 12, 1790,
Jefferson Papers, 16:179.

111. Matthews, *Radical Politics*, 126. Thomas Jefferson to John Taylor, May 28,
1816, *Jefferson Works*, 11:529. Thomas Jefferson to Joseph C. Cabell,
February 2, 1816, *Jefferson Writings*, 1380.

112. Thomas Jefferson to John Taylor, May 28, 1816, *Jefferson Works*, 11:529.
Thomas Jefferson to Joseph C. Cabell, February 2, 1816, *Jefferson Writings*,
1380.

113. Thomas Jefferson to Samuel Kercheval, July 12, 1816, *Jefferson Works*,
12:8–9. Thomas Jefferson to John Tyler, May 26, 1810, *Jefferson Writings*,

1226–27. Thomas Jefferson to Samuel Kercheval, July 12, 1816, *Jefferson Works*, 12:8–9. Thomas Jefferson to John Taylor, May 28, 1816, *Jefferson Works*, 11:530–31. Thomas Jefferson to John Tyler, May 26, 1810, *Jefferson Writings*, 1226–27.

114. Thomas Jefferson to Samuel Kercheval, July 12, 1816, *Jefferson Works*, 12:7. Thomas Jefferson to Edward Carrington, January 16, 1787, *Jefferson Papers*, 11:49.

115. Thomas Jefferson to James Madison, December 16, 1787, *Republic of Letters*, 1:458. Thomas Jefferson to John Adams, November 13, 1787, *Adams-Jefferson Letters*, 212. See Thomas Jefferson to Edward Carrington, August 4, 1787, *Jefferson Papers*, 11:678, and Thomas Jefferson to George Washington, August 14, 1787, ibid., 12:36.

116. James Madison to Thomas Jefferson, March 19, 1787, *Republic of Letters*, 1:470. Thomas Jefferson to James Madison, June 20, 1787, ibid., 1:480.

117. James Madison to Thomas Jefferson, October 24 and November 1, 1787, ibid., 1:496.

118. James Madison to Thomas Jefferson, October 17, 1788, *Republic of Letters*, 1:564.

119. Alexander Hamilton to James A. Bayard, January 16, 1801, in Richard B. Morris, ed., *Alexander Hamilton and the Founding of the Nation* (1957; reprint, New York, 1969), 540.

120. Thomas Jefferson to John C. Colvin, September 20, 1810, *Jefferson Works*, 11:146–50.

121. Thomas Jefferson to James Madison, October 28, 1785, *Jefferson Papers*, 7:682. See John Locke, *Second Treatise of Government*, ed. C. B. Macpherson (Indianapolis, 1980), 18–30. Matthews, *Radical Politics*, 50. Thomas Jefferson to James Madison, October 28, 1785, *Jefferson Papers*, 7:682.

122. Thomas Jefferson to James Madison, September 6, 1789, *Republic of Letters*, 1:631–32.

123. Sloan, *Principle and Interest*, 55. Thomas Jefferson to James Madison, September 6, 1789, *Republic of Letters*, 1:633–34.

124. Sloan, *Principle and Interest*, 53. Thomas Jefferson to James Madison, September 6, 1789, *Republic of Letters*, 1:634. Jefferson made the same argument in 1816. See Thomas Jefferson to Samuel Kercheval, July 12, 1816, *Jefferson Works*, 12:12–13.

125. James Madison to Thomas Jefferson, June 19, 1786, *Republic of Letters*, 1:424. James Madison to Thomas Jefferson, February 4, 1790, ibid., 1:650–51.

126. Thomas Jefferson to James Madison, October 28, 1785, *Jefferson Papers*, 7:682. Thomas Jefferson to Marquis de Chastellux, June 7, 1785, ibid., 8:184.

127. Thomas Jefferson to James Madison, January 30, 1787, ibid., 11:92–93. Thomas Jefferson to William S. Smith, November 13, 1787, ibid., 12:356–57. Matthews, *Radical Politics*, 22, 125.

128. Washington quoted in Richard B. Morris, *The Forging of the Union, 1781–1789* (New York, 1987), 266.

129. Thomas Jefferson to David Hartley, July 2, 1787, *Jefferson Papers*, 11:526. Thomas Jefferson to William S. Smith, November 13, 1787, ibid., 12:356–57. Thomas Jefferson to James Madison, January 30, 1787, ibid., 11:92–93.

130. Thomas Jefferson to James Monroe, August 9, 1788, ibid., 13:489. See Thomas Jefferson to Diodati, August 3, 1789, ibid., 15:325. Conor Cruise O'Brien, *The Long Affair: Thomas Jefferson and the French Revolution, 1785–1800* (Chicago, 1996). Thomas Jefferson to George Washington, December 4, 1788, *Jefferson Papers*, 14:330.

131. Thomas Jefferson to George Washington, December 4, 1788, *Jefferson Papers*, 14:330. Thomas Jefferson to James Madison, August 28, 1789, *Republic of Letters*, 1:629.

132. Thomas Jefferson to George Mason, February 4, 1791, *Jefferson Papers*, 19:241.

133. Thomas Jefferson to William Short, January 3, 1793, ibid., 25:14–15.

134. Ibid. See O'Brien, *Long Affair*, 150.

135. Thomas Jefferson to Thomas Lomax, March 12, 1799, *Jefferson Works*, 9:64.

136. Ellis, *Sphinx*, 90.

137. Patrick Henry quoted in O'Brien, *Long Affair*, 71–72.

138. Fisher Ames, "The Dangers of American Liberty" (Boston, 1805), in Charles S. Hyneman and Donald Lutz, eds., *American Political Writing During the Founding Era, 1760–1805* (Indianapolis, 1983), 2:1307.

139. Peterson, *Jefferson and Nation*, 402. Thomas Jefferson, "The Anas," *Life and Writings*, 114–15.

140. Forrest McDonald, *Alexander Hamilton: A Biography* (New York, 1979), 185.

141. "Opinion on the Constitutionality of the Bill for Establishing a National Bank," February 15, 1791, *Jefferson Papers*, 19:276.

142. See Thomas Jefferson to James Madison, June 21, 1792, *Republic of Letters*, 2:731–32. Andrew Shankman, "'A New Thing on Earth': Alexander Hamilton, Pro-Manufacturing Republicans, and the Democratization of American Political Economy," in *Journal of the Early Republic* 23 (Fall 2003), 323–52.

143. Jefferson quoted in Dumas Malone, *Jefferson and the Rights of Man* (Boston, 1951), 424.

144. Thomas Jefferson to James Madison, May 9, 1791, *Republic of Letters*, 2:687–88. Thomas Jefferson to George Washington, May 8, 1791, *Jefferson*

Papers, 20:292. See Thomas Jefferson to John Adams, July 17, 1791, and August 30, 1791, *Adams-Jefferson Letters*, 245–46, 250–51.

145. *Adams-Jefferson Letters*, 251. John Adams to Thomas Jefferson, July 29, 1791, *Adams-Jefferson Letters*, 248–49.

146. "An American no. 1," August 4, 1792, in *The Papers of Alexander Hamilton*, ed. Harold C. Syrett (New York, 1961–79), 12:158–59. "T. L.," July 25, 1792, ibid., 12:107. "An American no. 2," August 11, 1792, ibid., 12:193, and "An American no. 1," ibid., 12:160–61. "An American no. 1," ibid., 12:163–64. "An American no. 2," ibid., 12:193.

147. Thomas Jefferson to George Washington, September 9, 1792, *Jefferson Papers*, 24:353, 354.

148. Ibid., 24:358.

149. McDonald, *Hamilton*, 260–61. Thomas Jefferson to James Madison, February 21–27, 1793, *Republic of Letters*, 2:763–64

150. Thomas Jefferson to James Madison, May 13, 1793, *Republic of Letters*, 2:774.

151. Thomas Jefferson to James Madison, April 28, 1793, ibid., 2:770. Thomas Jefferson to James Madison, June 19, 1793, ibid., 2:786. Peterson, *Jefferson and Nation*, 490. Thomas Jefferson to James Madison, May 19, 1793, *Republic of Letters*, 2:775.

152. Thomas Jefferson to James Madison, July 7, 1793, *Republic of Letters*, 2:792.

153. Thomas Jefferson to James Madison, August 11, 1793, ibid., 2:803.

154. "Final State of the Report on Commerce," December 16, 1793, *Jefferson Papers*, 27:575–76.

155. Peterson, *Jefferson and Nation*, 511.

156. George Washington to Thomas Jefferson, July 6, 1796, *Jefferson Papers*, 29:142–43. James Monroe to Thomas Jefferson, September 3, 1793, ibid., 27:27. Thomas Jefferson to James Madison, August 3, 1793, *Republic of Letters*, 2:798.

157. Thomas Jefferson to Edward Rutledge, November 30, 1795, *Jefferson Papers*, 28:542. Thomas Jefferson to William Branch Giles, December 31, 1795, ibid., 28:565. Thomas Jefferson to James Monroe, March 21, 1796, ibid., 29:42.

158. James Madison to Thomas Jefferson, May 22, 1796, *Republic of Letters*, 2:938. Thomas Jefferson to James Monroe, July 10, 1796, *Jefferson Papers*, 29:147.

159. "Notes on the Letter to Christoph Daniel Ebeling," after October 15, 1795, *Jefferson Papers*, 28:508–509. Thomas Jefferson to Philip Mazzei, April 24, 1796, ibid., 29:82.

160. Thomas Jefferson to James Madison, April 25, 1795, *Republic of Letters*, 2:877–78. Thomas Jefferson to Thomas Mann Randolph, November 28, 1796, *Jefferson Papers*, 29:211.

161. "Jefferson's Letter to Adams," December 28, 1796, *Jefferson Papers*, 29:235. Thomas Jefferson to James Madison, January 1, 1797, *Republic of Letters*, 2:953. James Madison to Thomas Jefferson, January 15, 1797, *Republic of*

Letters, 2:957. See Michael Durey, *"With the Hammer of Truth": James Thompson Callender and America's Early National Heroes* (Charlottesville, Va., 1990), 96–97.

162. Thomas Jefferson to Edward Rutledge, June 24, 1797, *Jefferson Papers*, 29:456–57.

163. See Thomas Jefferson to James Monroe, December 17, 1797, ibid., 29:594. Thomas Jefferson to James Monroe, March 21, 1798, ibid., 30:191.

164. Thomas Jefferson to John Taylor, April 6, 1798, ibid., 30:252. John Taylor to Thomas Jefferson, before May 13, 1798, ibid., 30:191.

165. Thomas Jefferson to John Taylor, June 4, 1798, ibid., 30:388–89.

166. "Jefferson's Fair Copy," before October 4, 1798, *Jefferson Papers*, 30:545–46, 544–45, 546, 548.

167. Ibid., 30:543–44, 547.

168. See "Resolutions Adopted by the Kentucky General Assembly," November 10, 1798, ibid., 30:550–55.

169. Thomas Jefferson to James Madison, January 30, 1799, *Republic of Letters*, 2:1091.

170. See "Congressional Report Defending the Alien and Sedition Laws," February 21, 1799, *Republic of Letters*, 2:1100–1107. Thomas Jefferson to James Monroe, February 11, 1799, *Jefferson Works*, 9:38. Thomas Jefferson to James Madison, February 12, 1799, *Republic of Letters*, 2:1095.

171. Thomas Jefferson to James Madison, August 23, 1799, *Republic of Letters*, 2:1119.

172. Thomas Jefferson to James Madison, November 26, 1799, ibid., 2:1122.

173. Thomas Jefferson to James Monroe, January 12, 1800, *Jefferson Works*, 9:91.

174. McDonald, *Hamilton*, 352–53. Alexander Hamilton to John Rutledge, December 1800, in Morris, ed., *Hamilton and the Founding*, 536. Alexander Hamilton to James Bayard, August 6, 1800, December 27, 1800, and January 16, 1801, Morris, ed., *Hamilton and the Founding*, 536, 539, and 540.

175. "Inaugural Address," March 4, 1801, *Jefferson Works*, 9:194, 200.

176. For an example of Jefferson's use of patronage in the military, see Theodore J. Crackel, "Jefferson, Politics, and the Army: An Examination of the Military Peace Establishment Act of 1802," *Journal of the Early Republic* 2 (1982), 21–38. Randall, *A Life*, 552.

177. "First Inaugural Address," March 4, 1801, *Jefferson Works*, 9:198, 197.

178. Ibid., 197–98. Ellis, *Sphinx*, 171.

179. "First Annual Message," December 8, 1801, *Jefferson Works*, 9:333–34. "Second Inaugural Address," March 4, 1805, *Jefferson Works*, 10:129.

180. See Dumas Malone, *Jefferson the President: 1801–1805, First Term* (Boston, 1970), 104–106, and Peterson, *Jefferson and Nation*, 687–88. Sloan, *Principle and Interest*, 199. "Sixth Annual Message," December 2, 1806, *Jefferson Works*, 10:317.

181. Peterson, *Jefferson and Nation*, 687–88. Jefferson quoted in Malone, *First Term*, 101. Peterson, *Jefferson and Nation*, 665, 688. "Eighth Annual Message," November 8, 1808, *Jefferson Works*, 11:68–69. "First Annual Message," *Jefferson Works*, 9:338.

182. "First Annual Message," *Jefferson Works*, 9:339. Ben-Atar, *Commercial Policy*, 152.

183. Ames, "The Dangers of American Liberty," *American Political Writing*, 2:1317–18, 1331.

184. Randall, *A Life*, 560. Ben-Atar, *Commercial Policy*, 160. Randall, *A Life*, 564.

185. See John Murrin, "The Great Inversion, or Court Versus Country: A Comparison of the Revolution Settlements in England (1688–1721) and America (1776–1816)," in J.G.A. Pocock, ed., *Three British Revolutions: 1641, 1688, 1776* (Princeton, N.J., 1980), 368–453. "Sixth Annual Message," December 2, 1806, *Jefferson Works*, 10:317–18. Also see Joseph H. Harrison, *"Sic et Non*: Thomas Jefferson and Internal Improvments," *Journal of the Early Republic* 8 (1987), 335–49.

186. Thomas Jefferson to James Madison, December 20, 1787, *Jefferson Papers*, 7:442.

187. See Walter LeFeber, "Jefferson and an American Foreign Policy," *Jeffersonian Legacies*, 379.

188. Bernard W. Sheehan, "The Indian Problem in the Northwest: From Conquest to Philanthropy," in Ronald Hoffman and Peter J. Albert, eds., *Launching the "Extended Republic": The Federalist Era* (Charlottesville, Va., 1996), 190–222. Thomas Jefferson to Benjamin Hawkins, February 18, 1803, *Jefferson Works*, 9:446–47. Quoted in Anthony F. C. Wallace, *Jefferson and the Indians: The Tragic Fate of the First Americans* (Cambridge, Mass., 1999), 238. Also see Thomas Jefferson to Governor William H. Harrison, February 27, 1803, *Jefferson Writings*, 1118. Wallace, *Tragic Fate*, 239. Jefferson to Harrison, February 27, 1803, *Jefferson Writings*, 1118.

189. Malone, *First Term*, 273.

190. Thomas Jefferson to Archibald Stuart, January 25, 1786, *Jefferson Papers*, 9:218. Thomas Jefferson to Gov. William C. Claiborne, July 13, 1801, *Jefferson Works*, 9:275.

191. Thomas Jefferson to James Monroe, May 26, 1801, *Jefferson Works*, 9:260. Thomas Jefferson to James Monroe, January 13, 1803, ibid., 9:418. Peterson, *Jefferson and Nation*, 759.

192. Merrill Peterson notes that "the trade of New Orleans, in fact, never effectively closed, regaining its old footing in April" 1803. Peterson, *Jefferson and Nation*, 757. Thomas Jefferson to John Bacon, April 30, 1803, *Jefferson Works*, 9:464.

193. Malone, *First Term*, 348, 352. See Thomas Jefferson to John Dickinson, August 9, 1803, *Jefferson Works*, 10:29, and Thomas Jefferson to John C.

Breckenridge, August 12, 1803, *Jefferson Writings*, 1138–39. See Thomas Jefferson to James Madison, July 1803, and James Madison to Thomas Jefferson, July 1, 1803, *Republic of Letters*, 2:1269–70. Malone, *First Term*, 315–16. Thomas Jefferson to James Madison, August 18, 1803, *Republic of Letters*, 2:1278.

194. "Second Inaugural Address," March 4, 1805, *Jefferson Works*, 10:131. Peterson, *Jefferson and Nation*, 772.

195. Andrew Siegel, "'Steady Habits' Under Siege: The Defense of Federalism in Jeffersonian Connecticut," in Doron Ben-Atar and Barbara B. Oberg, eds., *Federalists Reconsidered* (Charlottesville, Va., 1998), 217. Ira Berlin, *Many Thousands Gone: The First Two Centuries of Slavery in North America* (Cambridge, Mass., 1998), 325–57. John Craig Hammond, "'They Are Very Much Interested in Obtaining an Unlimited Slavery': Rethinking the Expansion of Slavery in the Louisiana Purchase Territories, 1803–1805," *Journal of the Early Republic* 23 (2003), 353–80. See his two drafts of "A Proposed Constitutional Amendment on Louisiana," *Republic of Letters*, 2:1269–71, as well as Thomas Jefferson to Horatio Gates, July 11, 1803, *Jefferson Works*, 10:12–13. Quoted in Siegel, "Defense of Federalism," *Federalists Reconsidered*, 218.

196. "First Inaugural Address," March 4, 1801, *Jefferson Works*, 9:197. Peterson, *Jefferson and Nation*, 800.

197. *Republic of Letters*, 3:1360, and Peterson, *Jefferson and Nation*, 806. The actual number Madison arrived at was 2,273. *Republic of Letters*, 3:1409.

198. "Special Message on Great Britain," December 3, 1806, *Jefferson Works*, 10:320–21. "'Chesapeake' Proclamation," July 2, 1807, ibid., 10:445. Noble E. Cunningham, *In Pursuit of Reason: The Life of Thomas Jefferson* (New York, 1987), 311. Thomas Jefferson to James Madison, December 17, 1807, *Republic of Letters*, 3:1513. "Special Message on Commercial Depredations," December 18, 1807, *Jefferson Works*, 10:530–31.

199. Peterson, *Jefferson and Nation*, 828. J. R. Pole, *Foundations of American Independence, 1763–1815* (New York, 1972), 226, and *Republic of Letters*, 3:1446.

200. Thomas Jefferson to James Madison, February 1, 1807, *Republic of Letters*, 3:1464. Thomas Jefferson to James Monroe, March 21, 1807, *Jefferson Works*, 10:380–81. Peterson, *Jefferson and Nation*, 827.

201. Peterson, *Jefferson and Nation*, 885. Thomas Jefferson to United States Minister to France, John Armstrong, May 2, 1808, *Jefferson Works*, 11:30. Thomas Jefferson to United States Minister to France, Robert R. Livingston, September 9, 1801, *Jefferson Works*, 9:300.

202. Douglass C. North, *The Economic Growth of the United States, 1790–1860* (New York, 1966), 55. Peterson, *Jefferson and Nation*, 893. Pole, *Foundations*, 227.

203. Thomas Jefferson to Albert Gallatin, August 11, 1808, *Jefferson Works*, 11:41. The best treatment of Jefferson's handling of the embargo is Leonard W. Levy, *Jefferson and Civil Liberties: The Darker Side* (Chicago, 1963), 93–141.

204. *Republic of Letters*, 3:1507. Thomas Jefferson to James Madison, March 11, 1808, ibid., 3:1515. Ibid., 3:1509.

205. Peterson, *Jefferson and Nation*, 910. James Madison and Albert Gallatin to Thomas Jefferson, November 15, 1808, *Republic of Letters*, 3:1557–58.

206. Thomas Jefferson to James Monroe, January 28, 1809, *Jefferson Works*, 11:95. Thomas Jefferson to Thomas Mann Randolph, February 7, 1809, ibid., 11:96–97.

207. Thomas Jefferson to Henry Dearborn, July 16, 1810, ibid., 11:142–43.

208. John Adams to Benjamin Rush, April 18, 1808, *Spur of Fame*, 117.

209. Thomas Jefferson to John Holmes, April 22, 1820, *Jefferson Works*, 12:158. Thomas Jefferson to Hugh Nelson, February 7, 1820, ibid., 12:157, and Thomas Jefferson to John Adams, December 10, 1819, *Adams-Jefferson Letters*, 549. Ellis, *Sphinx*, 270.

210. Thomas Jefferson to John Holmes, April 22, 1820, *Jefferson Works*, 12:158–59. Thomas Jefferson to the Marquis de Lafayette, December 26, 1820, ibid., 12:191. Thomas Jefferson to John Dickinson, January 13, 1807, ibid., 10:130. Thomas Jefferson to Albert Gallatin, December 26, 1820, ibid., 12:187. Thomas Jefferson to the Marquis de Lafayette, December 26, 1820, ibid., 12:191, and Thomas Jefferson to John Holmes, April 22, 1820, ibid., 12:159. Thomas Jefferson to Albert Gallatin, December 26, 1820, ibid., 12:187.

211. Thomas Jefferson to David Bailey Warden, December 26, 1820, *Jefferson Works*, 12:180. Also see Thomas Jefferson to Charles Pinckney, September 30, 1820, ibid., 12:165. Thomas Jefferson to Albert Gallatin, December 26, 1820, ibid., 12:187. Thomas Jefferson to the Marquis de Lafayette, November 4, 1823, ibid., 12:323. Thomas Jefferson to John Holmes, April 22, 1820, ibid., 12:158, 159–60.

212. Thomas Jefferson to Albert Gallatin, December 26, 1820, ibid., 12:187. Thomas Jefferson to John Adams, January 22, 1821, *Adams-Jefferson Letters*, 570. Ellis, *Sphinx*, 265.

213. Thomas Jefferson to Marquis de Lafayette, November 4, 1823, *Jefferson Works*, 12:324. Thomas Jefferson to Thomas Ritchie, December 25, 1820, ibid., 12:177. Thomas Jefferson to Archibald Thweat, January 19, 1821, ibid., 12:196. Thomas Jefferson to Nathaniel Macon, August 19, 1821, ibid., 12:207. Thomas Jefferson to James Pleasants, December 26, 1821, ibid., 12:214. Thomas Jefferson to Judge Spencer Roane, September 6, 1819, ibid., 12:137.

214. Thomas Jefferson to Richard Rush, October 13, 1824, ibid., 12:381. Thomas Jefferson to William Branch Giles, December 26, 1825, ibid., 12:425, 426–27. Thomas Jefferson to Justice William Johnson, October 27, 1822, ibid., 12:250–51. Thomas Jefferson to William Branch Giles, December 26, 1825, ibid., 12:426.

215. See the enclosure in Thomas Jefferson to James Madison, December 24, 1825, *Republic of Letters*, 3:1944–46. James Madison to Thomas Jefferson, February 24, 1826, ibid., 3:1968. Also see James Madison to Thomas Jefferson, December 28, 1825, ibid., 3:1947.

216. "Report of the Commissioners of the University of Virginia," August 4, 1818, *Jefferson Writings*, 459–60.

217. See Thomas Jefferson to Colonel Charles Yancey, January 6, 1816, *Jefferson Works*, 11:497. Thomas Jefferson to General James Breckenridge, February 15, 1821, *Jefferson Writings*, 1452. Thomas Jefferson to James Madison, February 17, 1826, *Republic of Letters*, 3:1965.

218. "Report of the Commissioners," August 4, 1818, *Jefferson Writings*, 463. Thomas Jefferson to James Madison, February 17, 1826, *Republic of Letters*, 3:1965.

219. Thomas Jefferson to James Madison, February 1, 1825, *Republic of Letters*, 3:1923. James Madison to Thomas Jefferson, February 8, 1825, ibid., 3:1925. "From the Minutes of the Board of Visitors, University of Virginia," March 4, 1825, *Jefferson Writings*, 479–80.

220. Page Smith, *John Adams* (Garden City, N.Y., 1962), 2:1137. Ellis, *Sphinx*, 235.

221. Thomas Jefferson to James Madison, February 17, 1826, *Republic of Letters*, 3:1967.

ACKNOWLEDGMENTS

This book has been a long time coming, and in that time I have run up no small number of intellectual and scholarly debts. To list them all would be impossible, but some loom especially large and need to be acknowledged. Throughout this process my family has supported and encouraged me, and for that I am inordinately grateful. My parents and siblings took a polite interest in the subject matter of my work (which is to say they patiently put up with my long-winded discourses on the subject), and my nephews took an even keener interest, actually asking me additional questions and putting up with additional blather. By far my greatest debt, however, is to my wife. Tatiana not only read every page of every draft with her demanding eye, she endured my absent-minded immersion in research and my incessant ruminations and rantings on the politics of Enlightenment and things even marginally related. Throughout she was encouraging, supportive, and patient. It is a debt I can never hope to repay.

Friends and colleagues also offered support and sage advice. Robert Twombly indulged me in interminable conversations about my work, as did Cliff Rosenberg. My good friend Peter Field read early and painfully rough drafts of the first two chapters, and much of what is sensible in them now is a result of his suggestions and comments. Judith Stein read much of the semifinished product, and thanks to her counsel, it is a much shorter book than it was before. Finally, I have a particularly large debt to my good friend and colleague Lou Masur, who not only read and commented on the manuscript but also helped me formulate the entire project and the approach I took to telling the story. His support and encouragement have been a great source of pleasure and satisfaction throughout the writing of this book.

The completion of this book was greatly facilitated by a Rifkind fellowship and sabbatical I received from the City College of New York. For this I am truly grateful, especially towards the Dean of Humanities, James Watts, who has always supported my scholarship and professional development. Finally, I need to thank two of the people who saw this book through the publishing process. Kristina McGowan was cheerful, helpful, and professional, and made the production process as smooth and anxiety-free as possible. My editor, Thomas Lebien, was a godsend. Not only were his editorial suggestions trenchant and right on target, his belief and confidence in the project inspired me to try to fulfill his great expectations. To the extent that I have succeeded, much of the credit must go to him.

Darren Staloff

February 2, 2005

INDEX